The Structure of English
for Readers, Writers, and Teachers

Mary M. Clark

College Publishing books are printed on acid-free paper.

ISBN 978-1-932780-05-5
Library of Congress Control Number 2010902763

College Publishing
12309 Lynwood Drive, Glen Allen, Virginia 23059
T (804) 364-8410 F (804) 364-8408
Email collegepub@mindspring.com
Internet www.collegepublishing.us

The Structure of English for Readers, Writers, and Teachers

Second Edition

Mary M. Clark

College Publishing
Glen Allen, Virginia

Contents

Acknowledgments

I gratefully acknowledge the helpful comments of the following reviewers who read various versions of this manuscipt: Jeanette K. Grundel, University of Minnesota; Susan Smith, University of Oregon; Madelyn J. Kissock, Oakland University; Gregory K. Iverson, University of Wisconsin-Milwaukee; Gabriella Hermon, University of Delaware; Ellen Barton, Wayne State University; Michael Dukes, University of California, Los Angeles; Francis Peters, Bloomsburg University. Thanks, also, to the students in my English grammar class at the University of New Hampshire, who tested every part of this text and gave me their honest opinions as I constructed it, gradually, over the years. My gratitude and affection to Susannah Clark and Joshua Wilson, who helped create the exercises, and to Julia and Wesley Curl, who provided some of the data on children's speech and writing. And finally, thanks to Bernie, who keeps me sailing smoothly however rough the seas.

Preface

The Structure of English for Readers, Writers, and Teachers offers an up-to-date survey of the grammar of English (our pronunciation, our spelling system, our vocabulary, and the structure of our words, phrases, and sentences) with applications for writers, teachers of language arts, and students of literature. The analysis is presented within a simplified generative-transformational framework based on the Chomskian insight that every phrase consists of a head word (a noun, verb, adjective, etc.) together with its specifier, complement(s), and modifiers, and that a sentence can be "transformed" by placing one or more elements outside its normal position, as in the question **Which book** *is she reading?,* where the direct-object *which book* appears at the beginning of the sentence rather than in the usual direct-object position after the verb (*She is reading* **this book**).

Throughout the text, applications are made, as immediately as possible, to real-life questions: Where did our words come from? How systematic is English spelling? How does written language differ from spoken language? What steps do children go through in acquiring spoken, and then written, language? What features distinguish the regional and class-based dialects of English, and how do writers represent those features in the speech of their characters? Attention is given, at appropriate points, to some of the questions that trouble writers: how to use the passive voice, when to allow a preposition at the end of a clause, when to use *who* and *whom*, and so forth. The Appendix, at the end of the book, provides authentic samples of English – literary passages, pieces of student writing, and examples of children's early speech – which serve as the focus of exercises throughout the text.

This second edition of the text has been expanded to include applications for teachers of English as a Second Language. To accommodate this expanded focus, a new chapter has been added on pronunciation, a topic that requires considerably more attention for English learners than for native-speaking students. In addition, most chapters have been re-organized by moving the application sections, which were formally interspersed with the theoretical sections, to the end of the chapter, and dividing them into "Applications for Teachers of Literature," "Applications for Writers," "Applications for Teachers of English as a Second Language," and so forth.

I should, perhaps, say something about terminology. The field of TESOL (Teaching English to Speakers of Other Languages) is filled with overlapping acronyms such as ESOL (English for Speakers of Other Languages), ESL (English as a Second Language), EFL (English as a Foreign Language), ELL (English Language Learner), and EL (English Learners), which move in and out of political favor. For this text, I have chosen the term *ESL* (English as a Second Language) over other currently more fashionable terms, for two reasons: (1) In the modern world, most students of English, even those outside Kachru's inner- and outer-circle English-speaking countries, are learning English as a "second", rather than a "foreign" language, in that they expect to use English in their professional or educational lives, as a medium for conducting business or for accessing other academic subjects. (2) Research on second language acquisition shows that students have greater success both in English and in their academic studies if they maintain and strenghthen their first language at the same time that they are learning English. The term "English as a Second Language," more than its alternatives, clarifies our goal of *adding* English as a second (or third or fourth) language, rather than *replacing* our students' first language with English.

The present text contains sixteen chapters, which is more than can be covered easily in a single semester; instructors who are using this text for a semester-long course will need to select the chapters and chapter sections that are most appropriate for their own students. For example, Chapter 6 ("The Dictionary") and Sections 12.5–12.8 of Chapter 12 ("Variation in English") will be of interest primarily to students of language arts and literature, while the second half of Chapter 4 ("Pronunciation: Applications for ESL teachers") is directed at teachers of English as a Second Language.

CHAPTER 1

Introduction

The teaching of formal grammar has a negligible or, because it usually displaces some instruction and practice in actual composition, even a harmful effect on the improvement of writing.
—Richard Braddock, Richard Lloyd-Jones,
and Lowell Schoer, 1963

[A] schoolchild should be taught grammar—for the same reason that a medical student should study anatomy. Having learned about the exciting mysteries of an English sentence, the child can then go forth and speak and write any damn way he pleases.
—E. B. White, 1947

. . . what was stopped [in the schools] was not just bad *teaching of grammar, but* all *teaching of grammar. In retrospect this is a clear case of an important baby being thrown out with some rather dirty bathwater.*
—Richard Hudson, 1992

The best reason for studying grammar is that grammar is interesting.
—Paul Roberts, 1958

1.1 What Is Grammar?

Since this is a book about English grammar, we should begin by establishing what we mean by that term. In this text, the term *grammar* will be used to refer to the system we follow, whether consciously or unconsciously, in creating well-formed phrases and sentences. By *well-formed*, I mean well-formed within a particular language variety; for example, sentences that are well-formed in British English may not be well-formed in American English; sentences that are well-formed in conversational English may not be well-formed in formal writing; sentences that are well-formed in African-American Vernacular may not be well-formed in Standard American English (and vice versa). The goal of this text is not to pare English down to a single approved variety (formal written English), but to look at the various forms that English takes, with some attention to the question of which forms are appropriate under which circumstances.

1.2 Why Study Grammar?

As you can see from the quotations at the beginning of this chapter, people have very different opinions about the study of grammar. (Some of these differences probably derive from a

1

difference in how the term is defined.) Those who believe in the study of grammar usually base that belief on one or more of the following arguments:

1. A knowledge of grammar can help with some aspects of writing. For example, the following sentences contain constructions that are unacceptable in formal speech or writing. Try to identify the problem in each sentence:

> *Industries now tend to use more machines and less people.*
> *Jane looked awfully well in her dress.*
> *You are the person whom I think would do the best job.*

A writer who understands grammar will be less likely to stumble into questionable constructions like these. A strong sense of grammatical structure is also helpful at the editing stage of composition when we are considering how to eliminate redundancies, reorder information within a sentence, break up long, awkward sentences, or combine short, choppy sentences into longer, smoother ones.

2. Teachers who work with student writers need a conscious awareness of sentence structure in order to monitor their students' progress. For example, the writers below are starting to use structures that are normally found only in written English, not in conversation:

> *The sounds, <u>although totally disconnected</u>, seemed to form a weird symphony which*
> *was going somewhere.* (Twelve-year-old, cited in Perera 1984, 236)
> *He is just a ghost <u>to whom I pay no attention at all</u>.* (Thirteen-year-old, cited in Perera,*
> 237)
> *One [of them] was getting very intelligent, like plucking at moving things. <u>This one</u> we*
> *called Charlie.* (Thirteen-year-old, cited in Perera, 250)

These students are acquiring written English structures in the same way they acquired their spoken language—by assimilating, intuitively, the forms they hear and see. They do not need a formal grammatical analysis of these structures. However, the parents and teachers of these students will be able to provide more intelligent assistance if they have a conscious understanding of the structures the children are using and of the stages the children typically go through on their way to becoming proficient adult writers.

3. A third reason for studying grammar is to develop the vocabulary and concepts to talk about language. One student told me that her literature professor had asked the class to watch for changes of tense in a short story by James Baldwin, but because she had never taken a course in grammar, she did not understand the assignment. A course in the structure of English would have helped her to address this assignment with confidence, and to talk about other topics such as the following:

> the language of a two-year-old who is just learning to talk
> the spelling of a first-grader who is just learning to read
> the sentence structure of a fourth-grader who is beginning to write more fluently
> the written English of a college freshman who is acquiring the register of academic
> discourse

the language of a poem or story

the language of another era (that of Shakespeare, for example, or of Jane Austen), and how it differs from our own

the language of another dialect (the speech of a presidential candidate from Texas, for example, or of African Americans in the inner city)

the varieties of English that are used by one individual speaker in different places and circumstances

the shared language of a sports team or a group of friends

the differences between English and other languages such as French, Spanish, or Japanese

the problems of students who are learning English as a second language

the differences between male and female language

the language we use to handle awkward social situations such as making excuses or ending conversations

the language of the characters in a story

4. Finally, as stated by Paul Roberts (1958) in the quote that appears at the beginning of this chapter, grammar is worth studying because it is interesting. The system we use to create phrases and sentences in English and other languages is astonishingly complex. For example, consider the construction called the "tag question," which is illustrated in the examples below. Native speakers of English have no difficulty in creating these tags; you were able to form them by the time you were about four years old. But if you look at this construction carefully, you will see that it is a great deal more intricate than you may have realized. First, ascertain that you know how to form tag questions by filling in the missing tags below. Then, try to figure out the system you follow in creating these tags. (*Hint:* Each set of four sentences requires a further elaboration of the rule.)

You can go, can't you?
He should know, _____?
They are leaving, _____?
We've done a good job, _____?

Sue can go, _____?
Bill should know, _____?
Bill and Sue are leaving, _____?
You and I have done a good job, _____?

Sue can't go, _____?
Bill shouldn't know, _____?
Bill and Sue aren't leaving, _____?
You and I haven't done a very good job, _____?

She knows, _____?
They always finish on time, _____?
We enjoy ourselves, _____?
They left, _____?

Figuring out the rules for tag questions will not help you speak or write better English, but it should give you a new appreciation of the linguistic system you use every day, even when you think you are following no rules at all. As observed by Noam Chomsky, the MIT linguist who founded transformational generative grammar,

> *Few students are aware of the fact that in their normal, everyday life they are constantly creating new linguistic structures that are immediately understood, despite their novelty, by those to whom they speak or write. They are never brought to the realization of how amazing an accomplishment this is, and of how limited is our comprehension of what makes it possible. Nor do they acquire any insight into the remarkable intricacy of the grammar that they use unconsciously, even insofar as this system is understood and can be explicitly presented. . . . [S]ome way [should] be found to introduce students to the tantalizing problems that language has always posed for those who are puzzled and intrigued by the mysteries of human intelligence (Noam Chomsky, 1969, 12).*

1.3 The Purpose of This Text

This text is designed for students who want to learn something about the English language as preparation for teaching, or for studying literature or foreign languages, or because they are trying to become better writers. Linguists traditionally distinguish between *prescriptive* grammars, which tell people how they should speak or write, and *descriptive* grammars, which describe the language we actually use. Insofar as it deals with the improvement of writing, the present text will contain some prescriptive elements, with an emphasis on improving the overall structure of sentences rather than avoiding grammatical "errors." However, the primary approach of this text will be descriptive, with a focus on the third goal discussed earlier: learning to observe and talk about language. Topics such as dialect variation, the historical development of our vocabulary, and the acquisition of language by children are worth studying for their own sake and should be especially interesting to those who want to read, write, or teach English.

1.4 The Organization of Language

Human languages have a particular organization, which is set out in Figure 1.1. All human languages are based on meaningful units called words, which we learn over the course of a lifetime by hearing or reading them in context. Complex words such as *disapproval* can be broken into parts called *morphemes*—in this case, a prefix (*dis-*), a root (*approve*), and a suffix (*-al*); we use our knowledge of morphemes to invent and interpret new words.

At a more basic level, words and morphemes are made up of consonant and vowel sounds (in spoken language) or of letters (in written language). The sounds and letters have no meanings of their own—meanings are attached only to the words and morphemes that the sounds or letters represent. The expressive power of human language derives from this hierarchical structure. If all we had were the *sounds* of English, then we would be able to make only about forty-four different utterances (depending on the number of consonant and vowel sounds in our particular dialect). Similarly, if all we had were the words, then we could express some 75,000 notions, which is the approximate number of words that an average speaker commands. However, because words are made up of *sequences* of sounds or letters, we can create as many words as we like, and because we have a system for combining words into meaningful phrases and sentences, the number of ideas we can express is unlimited. Speakers of human languages can, in principle, produce an infinite number of words and phrases, each with its own unique meaning.

1.5 The Organization of This Text

This text will begin at the midpoint of the linguistic hierarchy, with the structure of words, in Chapter 2. Chapter 3 will set out the grammatical categories ("parts of speech"); the grammatical category of a word determines where it can be placed in a sentence. Chapter 4 will consider the sound system of English, and Chapter 5 will review our spelling system and how it works (or does not work). Chapter 6 is concerned with the dictionary and the information that is given there.

Chapters 7 and 8 begin the grammar "proper," with an overview of the structure of statements and the basic types of phrases: noun phrases, verb phrases, adjective phrases, adverb phrases, and prepositional phrases. Chapter 9, on semantics, is concerned with the *meaning* of a statement and how that meaning is determined from the words the sentence contains and the way they are put together. Chapters 10 and 11 discuss the English tense system and the formation of interrogative, exclamative, and imperative sentences.

Discourse

Sentences: *A murmur of disapproval filled the classroom. Why did you open the window?*

Phrases: *a murmur of disapproval, of disapproval, filled the classroom, the classroom*

Words: *a, murmur, of, disapproval, filled, the, classroom*

Morphemes (=prefixes, suffixes, and roots): *a, murmur, of, dis-, approve (ad + prove), -al, fill, -ed, the, class, room*

Phonemes (Sounds): [ă], [ā], [ô], [o͞o], [ə], [h], [hw], [sh], [th], [*th*], [k], etc.
or
Letters: <a>, <d>, <i>, <s>, <p>, <r>, <o>, <v>, <e>, <n>, etc.

Figure 1.1 Chart of the hierarchical structure of a human language.

Chapter 12 provides a short respite from the grammatical analysis, by applying the concepts that have been developed so far to the study of variation—variation in the language of individual speakers, as well as variation in dialect across geographical regions and social groups. Chapters 13 and 14 describe the grammar of sentences that contain more than one clause. Finally, Chapters 15 and 16 are "application" chapters which apply the grammatical analysis to questions regarding punctuation, especially commas (Chapter 16), and the presentation of information in connected discourse (Chapter 15).

Most chapters begin with a presentation of the important facts and concepts on the topic at hand, followed by a section of "applications" for teachers of writing, for students and teachers of literature, and for teachers of English as a Second Language. The application sections are identified, so that readers can ignore the sections that are not relevant to them. Chapter 4, on the *pronunciation* of English, has a different organization, in that it begins with concepts that are relevant to all teachers, such as the representation of pronunciation in American dictionaries, followed by an "applications" section that talks about meter and other sound effects in poetry. A long final section, called "Applications for Teachers of English as a Second Language," then sets out both concepts and applications that are relevant particularly to ESL. Chapter 15 ("Presenting Information") and Chapter 16 ("Colons, Semi-colons, and Commas") have a more "applied" focus than other chapters; the applications sections in these chapters are interspersed with the conceptual material.

No one can learn grammar simply from reading about it; you will have to make use of what you have learned. Thus, this book is filled with exercises, and the exercises are interspersed with the text. I urge you to at least try the exercises in each section before going on. Each concept builds on previous ones, and you will need a reasonably solid understanding of one concept in order to understand the next one.

1.6   Some Things to Do

Please turn now to the Appendix and skim over the samples of written and spoken English that are presented there. You will be asked to observe and think about these selections as you read. Some of the samples are excerpts from short stories, and you may want to read the entire story if you have not done so already. You are also asked to provide some samples of your own—a sample of your writing, and a short conversation that you have recorded and transcribed.

1.7   Dictionaries

As you work through this text, you will need a good, up-to-date college dictionary (not an abridged paperback version). Any of the following would be a good choice:

> *Merriam Webster's Collegiate Dictionary,* 11th ed. Springfield, MA: Merriam-Webster, 2003.
> *Random House Webster's College Dictionary,* 2nd ed. New York: Random House, 2000.
> *The American Heritage College Dictionary,* 4th ed. Boston: Houghton Mifflin, 2002.
> *The Concise Oxford Dictionary,* 11th ed. Oxford: Oxford University Press, 2004.
> *Webster's New World College Dictionary,* 4th ed. Cleveland, OH: Wiley Publishing, Inc., 2008.

CHAPTER 2

The Vocabulary of English: Where Do Our Words Come From?

If you think about the construction of [an anthill] by a colony of a million ants, each one working ceaselessly and compulsively [on] his region of the structure without having the faintest notion of what is being constructed elsewhere . . . there is only one human activity that is like this, and it is language. . . . We can never let up; we scramble our way through one civilization after another, metamorphosing, sprouting tools and cities everywhere, and all the time new words keep tumbling out . . . each one perfectly designed for its use.

—Lewis Thomas, 1978

2.1   Introduction

Part of what characterizes a particular piece of discourse in English is the words that are used—whether they are formal (*catharsis*), informal (*chow*), or neutral (*table*); whether they are nouns (*clarity*) or adjectives (*clear*); whether they have subjective meanings (*dismal*) or (at least potentially) objective meanings (*dark*).

English has a very large number of words to choose from—unabridged dictionaries contain some 500,000–600,000 lexical entries, each with a number of subentries. Of course, no individual speaker knows all of these words (you probably know fifteen to twenty percent of them), but each word in the dictionary is known and used by English speakers somewhere—otherwise it wouldn't be listed in the dictionary. In this chapter, we will talk about where all these words come from and how the historical origin of a word affects its use in modern English.

EXERCISE 1.   Estimate the size of your own vocabulary, using the following technique:

(1) Choose ten pages at random from a good college dictionary.

(2) On each page, make a tick beside every word you know. If there are additional words at the end of an entry (for example, *anarchistic* at the end of the entry for *anarchist*; *catch on*, *catch up,* and *catch it* at the end of the entry for *catch*), then count those as well, if you know them.

(3) Count the total number of ticks and divide by ten. This gives you the number of words that you know, on average, on each page of the dictionary.

(4) Multiply this number by the total number of pages in the dictionary; this gives you an estimated number for the size of your vocabulary.

Caution: The Merriam Webster's Collegiate Dictionary lists each part of speech as a separate word; for example, the word *measure* is listed twice—first as a noun and then as a verb. Other dictionaries list *measure* only once, with the noun and verb meanings included under one large entry. Thus, your vocabulary will appear larger if you use *Merriam Webster* for this exercise than if you use another dictionary. Do you see any other problems with this method of estimating vocabulary size?

EXERCISE 2. This exercise will ask you to talk about the content of your vocabulary, and how it resembles or differs from that of other English speakers.

There is a core vocabulary that is known by all English speakers: If you don't know the words *house, car, water,* and *foot,* then you don't know how to speak English! However, many of the words you know depend on who you are, where you live, and what you are interested in: If you call a refrigerator an *icebox,* then you are probably a member of the older generation; if you call a milk shake a *frappe,* then you are probably from eastern New England; if you know the word *morpheme,* then you have probably taken a course in linguistics; if you are not interested in cooking, then you probably don't know the word *parboil.*

Write a 500 word essay describing your vocabulary and explaining how it derives from who and what you are. Be sure to give examples. Include some of the vocabulary that you share with all English speakers, as well as the special words that you know because of your age, geographical location, education, job, hobbies, or other interests. If you can, find one or two words that are in your vocabulary but which are not listed in the dictionary; these might be "family" words that you use at home or slang words that you use with a group of friends.

Caution: When a word is used as a word, it must be italicized, underlined, or surrounded with quotation marks; for example,

I never heard the expression *wicked good* until I moved to New England.

or

I never heard the expression <u>wicked good</u> until I moved to New England.

or

I never heard the expression "wicked good" until I moved to New England.

2.2 Where Do Our Words Come From?

In order to understand the vocabulary of English, you will need to know something about its historical development.

English is a European language, brought to America by settlers from England, Scotland, and Ireland. Like most European languages, it is a member of the Indo-European language family. Languages in this family are descended from an ancient language called Proto-Indo-European, which is believed to have been spoken near the border of Europe and Asia somewhere around 4500 B.C. (the exact date is controversial). The linguistic descendants of the Proto-Indo-Europeans spread out in two directions: northwest into Europe, and southeast into Iran, Pakistan, and northern India, as shown in Figure 2.1. Since writing had not yet been invented in 4500 B.C., there are no written records of Proto-Indo-European; everything we know about this ancient language is obtained by studying the languages that are descended from it and then reasoning backwards to determine what the parent language must have been like.

EXERCISE 3. Many descendants of Proto-Indo-European (PIE) words can be recognized in Modern English. Use the sound and meaning of the PIE roots below to find their Modern English offspring:

ad-	'at'	*dheu-*	'to flow'	*er-*	'earth'
agro-	'field'	*dhreg-*	'drink'	*gel-*	'to freeze'
angh-	'painful'	*dhughəter*	'daughter'	*gembh-*	'to comb'
ant-	'front'	*dō-*	'give'	*genu-*	'knee'
ayer-	'day'	*dwo-*	'two'	*ghabh-*	'to give'
bhardh-	'beard'	*ed-*	'to eat'	*kan-*	'to sing'
bher-	'carry'	*eg*	'I'	*kand-*	'to shine'
bhergh-	'high'	*eghs*	'out'	*kwetwer-*	'four'
bhrāter	'brother'	*el-*	'elbow'	*man-*	'hand'
dekm	'ten'	*en*	'in'	*me-*	'me'
deru-	'steadfast'	*epi*	'also'	*medhyo-*	'middle'

As Indo-European spread over a larger and larger geographical area, the speakers of the language became isolated from one another, and subfamilies developed, as shown in the "family tree" in Figure 2.2. English belongs to the Western branch of the Germanic subfamily of Indo-European; our closest linguistic relatives are the four other West Germanic languages: Dutch, German, Frisian, and Yiddish.

2.3 The History of English

English originated as a dialect of Proto-Germanic, spoken by three Germanic tribes—the Angles, the Saxons, and the Jutes—who lived in northern Europe, in what is now part of Germany and Denmark. Britain, at that time, was inhabited by the Celts (the ancestors of the modern Irish, Scots, and Welsh), under the rule of the Romans. When the Romans withdrew in 410 A.D., the Angles, Saxons, and Jutes invaded England and pushed the Celts back into what is now Scotland and Wales. The name "English" comes from the name "Angles"; the language they spoke was called *Angl-isc*. In its basic structure—its grammar, its core vocabulary, and its pronunciation— English still shows its Germanic origins. However, as we will see later in this section, English, more than most languages, has borrowed vocabulary from foreign sources.

The history of English is divided into three periods: the Anglo-Saxon or Old English period (449–1100), the Middle English period (1100–1500), and the Modern English period (1500–present).

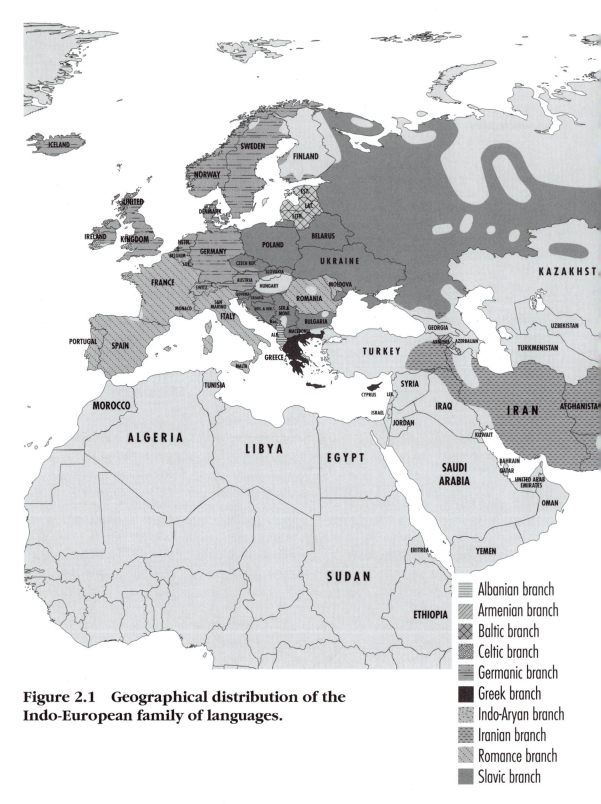

Figure 2.1 Geographical distribution of the Indo-European family of languages.

Legend:
- Albanian branch
- Armenian branch
- Baltic branch
- Celtic branch
- Germanic branch
- Greek branch
- Indo-Aryan branch
- Iranian branch
- Romance branch
- Slavic branch

Table 2.1   Some Other Language Families

Uralic:	Finnish, Hungarian, . . .
Altaic:	Turkish, Mongolian, Korean, Japanese, . . .
Sino-Tibetan:	Chinese, Tibetan, . . .
Niger-Congo:	Swahili, Zulu, Igbo, . . .
Khoisan:	!Kung, Nama, Sandawe, . . .
Austronesian:	Hawaiian, Maori, Samoan, Tagalog, . . .
Semitic:	Arabic, Hebrew, . . .
Na-Dene:	Navaho, Apache, Salish, . . .
Amerind:	Algonquian, Mayan, Aztec (Nahuatl), Quechua, . . .
Eskimo-Aleut:	Inuit, Yupik, . . .
Australian:	Tiwi, Warlpiri, . . .

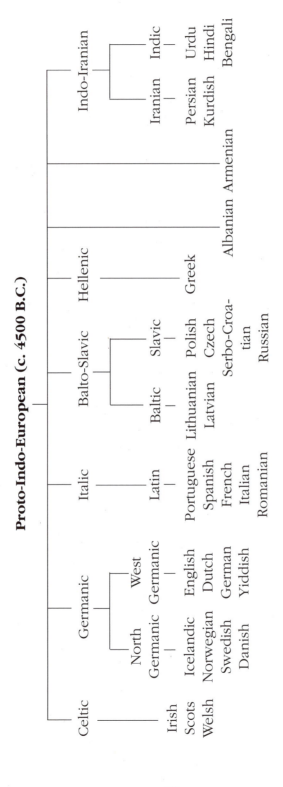

Figure 2.2   Indo-European family tree.

Old English (449–1100)

Students are often surprised to learn that the language of Shakespeare and the *King James Bible* is not Old English, but Early Modern English. Old English was spoken long before Shakespeare's time and is so different from Modern English that it seems like a foreign language. Here is a sample of Old English; see if you can figure out what it says:

1 Fæder ure þu ðe eart on heofonum si þin nama gehalgod. Tobecume
2 þin rice. Gewurðe þin willa on eorðan swa swa on heofonum. Urne
3 gedæghwamlican hlaf syle us to dæg. And forgyf us ure gyltas swa swa
4 we forgyfaþ urum gyltendum. and ne gelæd þu us on costnunge ac alys
5 us of yfele. Soðlice.

—From Paul Roberts (1958, 37)

The grammar of Old English was like that of Modern German, with an elaborate system of suffixes to indicate tense, person (first, second, third), number, gender, and case (which indicates the grammatical function of a noun within a sentence). Suffixes that provide this sort of information are called "inflectional suffixes." For example, in the Lord's Prayer, just above, the word "our" appears in three different forms:

ur-e	*Fæder ure*	'our Father'
ur-e	*ure gyltas*	(forgive us) 'our sins'
ur-ne	*urne gedæghwamlican hlaf*	(give us) 'our daily bread'
ur-um	*urum gyltendum*	(to) 'our debtors'

The inflectional suffixes *-e*, *-ne*, and *-um* which appear at the end of this possessive pronoun indicate whether the noun phrase is the addressee (*Fæder ure*), the direct object of the verb (*urne gedæghwamlican hlaf*), or the object of an (understood) preposition (*urum gyltendum*). The *number* of the head noun (singular or plural) and its *gender* (masculine, feminine, or neuter) are also relevant. Thus, with masculine singular nouns like *Fæder ure*, the form *ure* indicates that this is the person who is being addressed, but with feminine plural nouns (ure gyltas), *ure* indicates that this is the object of a verb. In other words, there are several different *-e* suffixes, each indicating some combination of number, gender, and syntactic function for the noun phrase. The order of the words within an Old English sentence was also different from Modern English, and less rigid.

The vocabulary of Old English was almost entirely Germanic as well, and much of our conversational vocabulary still derives from this source; words like *man, child, house, strong, eat, drink*, and *fight* are all Germanic in origin. However, Old English also contained a small number of words that had been borrowed from Latin, as a result of contact with the Romans either in England or while the Angles, Saxons, and Jutes were still living on the continent of Europe. Some Latin words that entered English in this way are *cheese, wine, butter, angel, school*, and *street*.

A more important source of borrowing into Old English was Old Norse. During the eighth century, the Vikings, who spoke Old Norse, began a series of raids against the English coast, and in the ninth and tenth centuries they established permanent settlements in the northeastern part of England. These invaders eventually intermarried with the English, and many words from Old

Norse entered the English language. A few examples are *sky, skirt, egg, fellow, freckle, sister, dirt, die, rake, scowl,* and *take*—plus our third person plural pronouns *they, their,* and *them.* Because Old Norse and Old English were closely related languages, and because the Old Norse borrowings entered our ordinary conversational vocabulary, it is difficult for a speaker of Modern English to determine, by ear, which words came from which source. To determine the origin of an individual word that was already present in Old English, you will have to consult a dictionary.

Middle English (1100–1500)

Middle English originated with the Norman Conquest of 1066—the invasion of England by the Normans, who came from France, under William the Conqueror. The Norman invaders took control of the great estates of England, as well as assuming important positions in the government and in the church, and for several generations—until they became thoroughly assimilated to British society—they continued to speak French. Thus, for the next three hundred years, French (or Old French, as the French of that time is called) was the predominant language of the English aristocracy. By the fourteenth century, when English reemerged as the dominant language, thousands of French words had been borrowed into English—words having to do with government (*parliament, treaty, tax*), with the church (*religion, baptism, faith*), with the law (*sentence, fine, prison*), with food (*salmon, oyster, pork, bacon, beef*), and with fashionable life (*curtain, chair, music, dalliance,* and *conversation*).

Perhaps the best known example of Middle English is Chaucer's *Prologue to the Canterbury Tales,* the first few lines of which are quoted below:

Whan that Aprill with his shoures soote	1
The droghte of March hath perced to the roote,	2
And bathed every veyne in swich licour	3
Of which vertu engendred is the flour;	4
Whan Zephirus eek with his sweete breeth	5
Inspired hath in every holt and heeth	6
The tendre croppes, and the yonge sonne	7
Hath in the Ram his halve cours yronne	8
And smale foweles maken melodye,	9
That slepen all the nyght with open ye	10
(So priketh hem nature in his corages);	11
Thanne longen folk to goon on pilgrimages . . .	12

This selection, though still strange to our ears, is far more accessible than the Old English passage of the previous section. First, the grammar of Middle English had become more like that of Modern English. Most of the inflectional suffixes that we saw in Old English had been lost; Middle English, like Modern English, relied primarily on word order and structural words (auxiliaries, prepositions, and so forth) to establish grammatical relationships within the sentence. However, the chief characteristic that makes this passage more accessible to us is its lexicon; Chaucer was using the French words that make up so much of our vocabulary today. Words like *perced* 'pierced', *veyne* 'vine', *licour* 'liquor' (='liquid'), *vertu* 'virtue', *engendred* 'engendered', *flour* 'flower', *inspired* 'inspired', *tendre* 'tender', *cours* 'course', *melodie* 'melody', *corages* 'courage' (='emotions'), and *pilgrimages* 'pilgrimages' were borrowed from French during Middle

English times and are still in use today, though sometimes with a slightly different spelling and meaning.

Modern English (1500–present)

The Modern English period was ushered in by the invention of the printing press, which was introduced to England by William Caxton in 1475. Books suddenly became more common, and many people learned to read and write. To satisfy the public demand for learning, classical works were translated into English from Latin, Greek, and French, and this brought a further augmentation to our vocabulary. When a translator came across a Latin or Greek word that could not easily be rendered into English, he often simply appropriated the original term, sometimes with a slight change in spelling. It was in this way that English acquired such words as *pedestrian, bonus, insurgent, palliate, paradox, philanthropy, cosmos,* and *amphibious.* Note that these words were borrowed from written texts rather than from spoken conversation, and even today they retain their character as primarily *written,* rather than spoken, words.

Early Modern English (1500–1700)

The most familiar example of Early Modern English (aside from the *King James Bible*) is Shakespeare. Here is a brief excerpt from the first act of *Hamlet,* immediately following the appearance of the ghost:

Marcellus. 'Tis gone!	1
We do it wrong being so majestical	2
To offer it the show of violence,	3
For it is as the air, invulnerable,	4
And our vain blows malicious mockery.	5
Bernardo. It was about to speak when the cock crew.	6
Horatio. And then it started like a guilty thing,	7
Upon a fearful summons; I have heard	8
The cock that is the trumpet to the morn	9
Doth with his lofty and shrill-sounding throat	10
Awake the god of day, and at his warning	11
Whether in sea or fire, in earth or air,	12
Th'extravagant and erring spirit hies	13
To his confine, and of the truth herein	14
This present object made probation.	15

Shakespeare is not easy to read. (It helps if you read along with a recorded performance of the play, so that you have the benefit of both the spoken and the written word.) His grammar is sometimes different from ours—for example, he uses some inflectional forms that we no longer use (the third person singular form *doth* 'does' and the past tense form *crew* 'crowed'). And some words have different meanings (for example, *erring* in line 13 is used to mean 'wandering'). However, the words themselves are, for the most part, familiar to us; Shakespeare's vocabulary, like ours, contains native English words (*wrong, god, fearful*), Norman French words (*guilty, vain, violence*), and also words like *invulnerable* and *object,* which were borrowed into English from Latin texts.

Late Modern English (1700–present)

In Late Modern times, English has become a world language. It is the national language not just of England, but also of the United States, Canada, Australia, and New Zealand. In dozens of other countries—India, Nigeria, Ghana, and Singapore, to name just a few—English is an official "second" language, used for official business and for education.

In this global environment, English has taken in words from many different languages; the examples below are a very small sampling:

> French: *chic, savoir faire, hors d'oevres, mousse, fatigue, fiancé*
> Italian: *pizza, opera, piazza, fortissimo, spaghetti, ciao*
> Spanish: *adobe, lasso, hombre, marijuana, tomato, coyote, cafeteria, bonanza, peon, patio, tornado, savvy, pronto*
> Dutch: *Santa Claus, cookie, caboose, sloop, cole slaw, waffle, boss, sleigh, poppycock*
> Native American languages: *wigwam, moccasin, teepee, toboggan, moose, raccoon, skunk, powwow, totem,* and many American place names
> African languages: *okra, gumbo, voodoo, chimpanzee, tsetse fly, banana, jazz,* and possibly *o.k.*
> Hindi: *bangle, Brahman, bungalow, dinghy, jungle, nirvana, pariah, thug, toddy, verandah*
> Japanese: *futon, hibachi, sushi, honcho, kimono, daikon*
> Chinese: *chop suey, kowtow, chow*
> Yiddish: *mensch, schnozz, chutzpah, glitch, schlep, schlemiel, schmuck*

2.4   Using a Dictionary to Find the Origin of a Word

The words of Modern English have entered the language in three ways: Some are *native* (i.e., present in the language from the time of the Anglo-Saxons), some were *borrowed* from other languages, and some were *invented* by English speakers. If we ignore, for a moment, the category of invented words, then the vocabulary of English can be classified, historically, as follows:

1. **Native vocabulary**
2. **Borrowed vocabulary**
   a.   From (spoken) Latin into Old English
   b.   From Old Norse into Old English and Middle English
   c.   From Old French into Middle English in the aftermath of the Norman invasion
   d.   From classical writings in Old French, Latin, and Greek into Middle English and Modern English
   e.   From modern spoken languages into Modern English

In some cases, you will be able to guess the historical origin of an English word from its internal structure and its level of formality. For example, words that are borrowed from Latin often have prefixes and/or suffixes and seem formal in register. In other cases, you will have to look in the dictionary. The origin or *etymology* of the word is given in square brackets either at the beginning or, in some dictionaries, at the end of the entry.

Illustrations are given below for the six major historical sources of English words. These etymologies follow the format of the *American Heritage Dictionary*; other college dictionaries may use *fr.* 'from' instead of "<". The *Merriam Webster's Collegiate Dictionary* lists, in addition to the etymology, the earliest date at which the word is known to have occurred in English. Dictionaries may also list related words from other languages (*akin to ...*); for example, if a word has been borrowed into English from French, then there will probably be kindred words in other Romance languages, such as Spanish, Portuguese, and Italian.

1. Native vocabulary

child [ME < OE *cild*]

This etymology indicates that the word *child* was present in Middle English (ME) and that it was derived from the Old English (OE) word *cild*. Since no further information is given, we can conclude that the word was not borrowed from any other language, but has been present in English as far back as can be traced. Thus it is part of our native vocabulary.

2. Borrowed vocabulary

a. <u>From Latin into Old English</u>

aloe [ME < OE *aluwe* < Lat. *aloe* < Gk.]

According to this etymology, the word *aloe* was present in Middle English (ME) and Old English (OE), where it was spelled *aluwe*. OE borrowed it from Latin, (Lat.); thus, *aloe* is not a *native* English word, but a borrowing from Latin into OE (while Latin was still a spoken language). The entry also tells us that Latin borrowed the word from Greek (Gk.), but that is outside our sphere of interest; we are not asking where the word came from *originally,* but how it came into English.

b. <u>Borrowings from Old Norse into OE and ME</u>

skin [ME < ON *skinn*]

The etymologys tell us that this word was borrowed from Old Norse (ON) during the ME period.

c. <u>From Old French into Middle English in the aftermath of the Norman invasion</u>

chair [ME *chaiere* < OFr. < Lat. *cathedra,* chair < Gk. *kathedra*]

The etymology tells us that *chair* was borrowed from Old French (OFr.) during the Middle English (ME) period.

d. <u>From classical writings in Latin, Greek, and Old French into Middle English and Modern English</u>

anatomy [ME *anatomie* < LLat. *anatomia* < Gk. *anatome,* dissection]

The etymology tells us that the word *anatomy* was borrowed into Middle English (ME) from Late Latin (LLat.). By that time, Latin was no longer a spoken language; thus *anatomy* must have been borrowed into English from a written Latin text.

pedestrian [Lat. *pedester,* going on foot]

The etymology tells us that the word *pedestrian* was not present in Middle English. (If the word were present in Middle English, the etymology would say so.) Therefore, it must have been borrowed in Modern English times from (written) Latin.

archaic [Gk. *arkhaikos,* old-fashioned < *arkhaios,* ancient]

The etymology tells us that the word *archaic* was borrowed into Modern English from Greek. We put this word in the 2d (classical borrowings) category rather than 2e (borrowings from modern spoken languages) on the grounds that it is a formal, written word rather than a conversational word.

In the etymologies above, we are also told that Latin borrowed the word *anatomia* from Greek and that the Greek word *arkhaikos* was derived from an earlier word, *arkhaios*; however, this information is irrelevant to the question we are concerned with here, which is how these words came into English.

> e. <u>From modern spoken languages into Modern English</u>
>
> *naive* [Fr. *naive,* fem. of *naif* < OFr, natural, native < Lat. *nativus,* rustic]

The etymology tells us that the word *naive* was borrowed into Modern English (it was not present in Middle English) from French.

> *nabob* [Hindi *nawab, nabab* < Ar. *nuwwab,* pl. of *na'ib,* deputy]

The etymology tells us that the word *nabob* was borrowed into Modern English from Hindi.

> *nip* 'a small amount of liquor' [Prob. short for *nipperkin,* of LGer. origin]

The etymology tells us that the word *nip* 'a small amount of liquor' was probably borrowed into Modern English from Low German (LGer.).

> *kangaroo* [Guugu Yimidhirr (an Aboriginal language of NE Australia)]

The etymology tells us that the word *kangaroo* was borrowed from Guugu Yimidhirr, an Aboriginal language of northeast Australia.

EXERCISE 4.   Use the pages from the *American Heritage Dictionary, 2nd College Edition* (Figures 2.3 and 2.4) to determine the origins of the following words: *guru, gush, gust[1], gustation, gusto, gut, gutter, gutteral, guy[1], guzzle, gymnasium, gymnast, gymnosophist, gymnosperm, -gyne, gyneco-, skulk, skunk, sky, slab[1], slack[1], slag, slake, slalom, slander.* Try to place each word in one of the categories we discussed above:
(1) Native or
(2) Borrowed
>   (a) from spoken Latin into OE,
>   (b) from ON into OE or ME,
>   (c) from Old French into ME in the aftermath of the Norman invasion,
>   (d) from classical writings in Old French, Latin, and Greek into ME and NE,
>   (e) from modern spoken languages into NE.

Caution: In some cases, you will have to say that the answer is uncertain or unknown. If the dictionary editors don't know where a word came from, then you won't know, either.

2.5   The Register of a Word and Its Relation to Historical Origin

A *register* is a variety of language that is associated with a particular social context. Speaking in general terms, we can identify a word as formal, informal, or neutral in register. For example, *desultory* is a formal word usually found in writing rather than in speech; in fact, some of you may recognize this word but not know how to pronounce it. Other words, such as *veggies,* are informal; they are found in conversation and in informal writing, such as a letter to a friend. Words like *understand* are neutral in register, meaning that they can be used in either a formal or an informal setting.

We can also identify more specific registers. For example, the expressions *fly ball* and *pop up* belong to the register of baseball, and the phrase *privileges pertaining thereunto* belongs to

powders used to propel projectiles from guns, esp. a black explosive mixture of potassium nitrate, charcoal, and sulfur.
gun·pow·der tea *n.* A green tea whose leaves are rolled into pellets.
gun·room (gŭn′rōom′, -rŏom′) *n.* The quarters of midshipmen and junior officers on a British warship.
gun·run·ner (gŭn′rŭn′ər) *n.* One that smuggles firearms and ammunition. —**gun′run′ning** *n.*
gun·shot (gŭn′shŏt′) *n.* **1.** Shot fired from a gun. **2.** The range of a gun.
gun-shy (gŭn′shī′) *adj.* **1.** Afraid of loud noise, as that made by gunfire. **2.** Extremely distrustful or wary.
gun·sling·er (gŭn′slĭng′ər) *n.* A gunman. —**gun′sling′ing** *n.*
gun·smith (gŭn′smĭth′) *n.* One who makes or repairs firearms.
gun·stock (gŭn′stŏk′) *n.* A handle on a gun; stock.
Gun·ter's chain (gŭn′tərz) *n.* A chain (sense 9). [After Edmund *Gunter* (1581–1626).]
Gun·ther (gōon′tər) *n.* In the *Nibelungenlied,* a king of Burgundy and husband of Brunhild. [G.]
gun·wale also **gun·nel** (gŭn′əl) *n.* The upper edge of a ship's side.
Guo·yu (kwō′yōo′) *n.* Mandarin (sense 3). [Chin. : *guo²,* nation + *yu³,* language.]
gup·py (gŭp′ē) *n., pl.* **-pies.** A small, brightly colored freshwater fish, *Poecilia reticulata* or *Lebistes reticulatus,* of northern South America and adjacent islands of the West Indies, that is popular in home aquariums. [After R.J.L. *Guppy* (1836–1916).]
gur·gi·ta·tion (gûr′jĭ-tā′shən) *n.* A whirling motion; ebullition. [< LLat. *gurgitare,* to engulf < *gurges,* whirlpool.]
gur·gle (gûr′gəl) *v.* **-gled, -gling, -gles.** —*intr.* **1.** To flow in a broken, uneven current making intermittent low sounds. **2.** To make a gurgling sound. —*tr.* To express or pronounce with a gurgling sound. —*n.* The act or sound of gurgling. [Prob. imit.] —**gur′gling·ly** *adv.*
Gur·kha (gōor′kə) *n.* **1.** A member of a Rajput ethnic group predominant in Nepal. **2.** A soldier from Nepal serving in the British or Indian armies.
gur·nard (gûr′nərd) *n., pl.* **-nards** or **gurnard. 1.** Any of various marine fishes of the family Triglidae, and esp. of the Old World genus *Trigla,* having large, fanlike pectoral fins. **2.** The flying gurnard. [ME < OFr. *gornart.*]
gur·ney (gûr′nē) *n., pl.* **-neys.** A wheeled stretcher or litter.
gu·ru (gōor′ōo, gōo-rōo′) *n., pl.* **-rus. 1.** *Hinduism.* A personal spiritual teacher. **2. a.** A recognized leader or guide. **b.** An acknowledged advocate, as of a movement or idea. [Hindi *gurū* < Skt. *guru-,* venerable.]
gush (gŭsh) *v.* **gushed, gush·ing, gush·es.** —*intr.* **1.** To flow forth suddenly and violently. **2.** To issue or emit an abundant flow. **3.** To make an excessive display of sentiment or enthusiasm. —*tr.* To emit abundantly. —*n.* **1.** A sudden, violent, or copious outflow: *a gush of tears.* **2.** Something emitted by gushing. **3.** An excessive display of sentiment. [ME *gushen,* prob. of Scand. orig.]
gush·er (gŭsh′ər) *n.* **1.** One that gushes. **2.** A gas or oil well with an abundant natural flow.
gush·y (gŭsh′ē) *adj.* **-i·er, -i·est.** Characterized by excessive displays of sentiment or enthusiasm. —**gush′i·ly** *adv.* —**gush′i·ness** *n.*
gus·set (gŭs′ĭt) *n.* A triangular insert, as in a garment, for strengthening or enlarging. [ME < OFr. *gosset.*]
gus·sy (gŭs′ē) *tr.v.* **-sied, -sy·ing, -sies.** To dress up; decorate: *all gussied up in sequins and feathers.* [Orig. unknown.]
gust¹ (gŭst) *n.* **1.** A violent, abrupt rush of wind. **2.** An abrupt or sudden outburst. —*intr.v.* **gust·ed, gust·ing, gusts.** To blow in gusts. [Prob. < ON *gustr.*] —**gust′i·ly** *adv.* —**gust′i·ness** *n.* —**gust′y** *adj.*
gust² (gŭst) *n.* **1.** *Archaic.* Relish; gusto. **2.** *Obs.* Personal taste or inclination; liking. [ME *guste,* taste < Lat. *gustus.*]
gus·ta·tion (gŭ-stā′shən) *n.* The act or faculty of tasting. [Lat. *gustatio,* a tasting < *gustare,* to taste < *gustus,* taste.]
gus·ta·tive (gŭs′tə-tĭv) *adj.* Gustatory.
gus·ta·to·ry (gŭs′tə-tôr′ē, -tōr′ē) *adj.* Of or pertaining to the sense of taste. —**gus′ta·to′ri·ly** *adv.*
gus·to (gŭs′tō) *n., pl.* **-toes. 1.** A special or individual taste. **2.** Vigorous enjoyment; zest. **3.** *Archaic.* Artistic style. [Ital. < Lat. *gustus,* taste.]
gut (gŭt) *n.* **1.** The alimentary canal or a portion thereof, esp. the intestine or stomach. **2. guts.** The bowels; entrails. **3. guts.** The essential contents of something: *the guts of an old television set.* **4.** The intestines of some animals used as strings for musical instruments or as surgical sutures. **5. guts.** *Slang.* Courage; fortitude. **6.** A narrow passage or channel. **7.** Fibrous material taken from the silk gland of a silkworm before it spins a cocoon, used for fishing tackle. —*tr.v.* **gut·ted, gut·ting, guts. 1.** To remove the entrails of; eviscerate. **2.** To destroy the interior of: *gut a house.* —*adj. Slang.* **1.** Arousing or involving basic emotions; visceral: *a gut issue; a gut response.* **2.** Easy: *gut courses.* [< ME *guttes,* entrails < OE *guttas.*] —**gut′ty** *adj.*
Guth·run (gōoth′rōon′) *n.* Variant of **Gudrun.**
gut·less (gŭt′lĭs) *adj.* Lacking courage. —**gut′less·ness** *n.*
guts·y (gŭt′sē) *adj.* **-i·er, -i·est.** *Slang.* Full of courage; plucky. —**guts′i·ly** *adv.* —**guts′i·ness** *n.*
gut·ta (gŭt′ə) *n., pl.* **gut·tae** (gŭt′ē′). **1.** *Archit.* One of a group

of small, droplike ornaments on a Doric entablature. **2.** *Med.* A drop. [Lat., drop.]
gut·ta-per·cha (gŭt′ə-pûr′chə) *n.* A rubbery substance derived from the latex of any of several tropical trees of the genera *Palaquium* and *Payena* and used as electrical insulation and for waterproofing. [Malay *gětah percha* : *gětah,* sap + *percha,* strip of cloth.]
gut·tate (gŭt′āt′) also **gut·tat·ed** (-ā′tĭd) *adj.* **1. a.** In the form of drops. **b.** Having drops. **2.** Spotted as if by drops. [Lat. *guttatus,* speckled < *gutta,* drop.]
gut·ter (gŭt′ər) *n.* **1.** A channel for draining off water at the edge of a street or road. **2.** A pipe or trough for draining off water under the border of a roof. **3.** A furrow or groove formed by running water. **4.** The trough on either side of a bowling alley. **5.** *Printing.* The white space between the facing pages of a book. **6.** The lowest class or state of human existence. —*v.* **-tered, -ter·ing, -ters.** —*tr.* To form gutters or furrows in. —*intr.* **1.** To flow in channels or rivulets. **2.** To melt away through the channel in the side of the hollow formed by a burning wick. Used of a candle. **3.** To burn with a low flame; flicker. [ME *goter* < OFr. *gotier* < VLat. *guttarie* < Lat. *gutta,* drop.]
gut·ter·snipe (gŭt′ər-snīp′) *n.* **1.** A street urchin. **2.** A person of the lowest class.
gut·tur·al (gŭt′ər-əl) *adj.* **1.** Of or pertaining to the throat. **2.** Produced in the throat. **3.** Velar. [OFr. < Lat. *guttur,* throat.] —**gut′tur·al** *n.* —**gut′tur·al·ism** *n.* —**gut·tur·al′i·ty** (-ə-răl′ĭ-tē) *n.* —**gut′tur·al·ly** *adv.* —**gut′tur·al·ness** *n.*
gut·tur·al·ize (gŭt′ər-ə-līz′) *tr.v.* **-ized, -iz·ing, -iz·es. 1.** To pronounce gutturally. **2.** To velarize. —**gut′tur·al·i·za′tion** *n.*
guy¹ (gī) *n.* A rope, cord, or cable used for steadying, guiding, or holding something. —*tr.v.* **guyed, guy·ing, guys.** To steady, guide, or hold with a guy. [Prob. of LG orig.]
guy² (gī) *n.* **1.** *Informal.* A man; fellow. **2.** *Informal.* **guys.** Persons of either sex: *What are you guys doing?* **3.** *Chiefly Brit.* A person of odd or grotesque appearance or dress. **4.** Often *Guy.* An effigy of Guy Fawkes paraded through the streets of English towns and burned on Guy Fawkes Day. —*tr.v.* **guyed, guy·ing, guys.** To make fun of; mock. [After *Guy Fawkes* (1570–1606).]
Guy Fawkes Day (gī′ fôks′) *n.* November 5 celebrated in commemoration of the 1605 attempt led by Guy Fawkes to assassinate the king and assembled parliament in retaliation for increasing repression of Roman Catholics in England.
guy·ot (gē′ō) *n.* A flat-topped seamount. [After Arnold H. *Guyot* (1807–1884).]
guz·zle (gŭz′əl) *v.* **-zled, -zling, -zles.** —*tr.* To drink greedily or habitually: *guzzle whisky.* —*intr.* To drink esp. alcoholic beverages greedily or habitually. [Orig. unknown.] —**guz′zler** *n.*
gybe (jīb) *v. & n.* Variant of **jibe¹.**
gym (jĭm) *n. Informal.* **1.** A gymnasium. **2.** Physical education. **3.** A frame supporting structures used in outdoor play.
gym·kha·na (jĭm-kä′nə) *n. Chiefly Brit.* A display of athletic or equestrian contests. [Prob. alteration of Hindi *gendkhānā,* racket court.]
gym·na·si·um (jĭm-nā′zē-əm) *n., pl.* **-si·ums** or **-si·a** (-zē-ə). **1.** A room or building equipped for gymnastics and sports. **2.** (gĭm-nä′zē-ōom′). An academic high school in various European countries, esp. Germany, that prepares students for studies at a university. [Lat., school < Gk. *gumnasion* < *gumnazein,* to exercise naked < *gumnos,* naked.]
gym·nast (jĭm′năst′) *n.* One skilled in gymnastic exercises. [Gk. *gumnastēs* < *gumnazein,* to exercise naked < *gumnos,* naked.]
gym·nas·tic (jĭm-năs′tĭk) *adj.* Of or pertaining to gymnastics. —**gym·nas′ti·cal·ly** *adv.*
gym·nas·tics (jĭm-năs′tĭks) *n. (used with a sing. or pl. verb).* Body-building exercises, esp. those performed with special apparatus in a gymnasium.
gym·nos·o·phist (jĭm-nŏs′ə-fĭst) *n.* One of an ancient sect of naked Hindu ascetics, as reported in classical antiquity. [Lat. *gymnosophista* < Gk. *gumnosophistēs* : *gumnos,* naked + *sophistēs,* expert. —see SOPHIST.]
gym·no·sperm (jĭm′nə-spûrm′) *n.* A plant of the class Gymnospermae, which includes the coniferous trees and other plants having seeds not enclosed within an ovary. [NLat. *Gymnòspermae,* class name : Gk. *gumnos,* naked + Gk. *sperma,* seed.] —**gym′no·sper′mous** *adj.* —**gym′no·sper′my** *n.*
gyn- *pref.* Variant of **gyno-.**
gynaeco- or **gynaeco-** *pref.* Variants of **gyneco-.**
gy·nan·dro·morph (jī-năn′drə-môrf′, gī-) *n.* An individual having male and female characteristics. —**gy·nan′dro·mor′phic, gy·nan′dro·mor′phous** *adj.* —**gy·nan′dro·mor′phism, gy·nan′dro·mor′phy** *n.*
gy·nan·drous (jī-năn′drəs, gī-) *n.* **1.** Having the stamens and pistil united to form a column. **2.** Hermaphroditic.
gyn·ar·chy (jĭn′är′kē, jī′när′-, gī′-) *n., pl.* **-chies.** Government by women. —**gyn·ar′chic** *adj.*
-gyne *suff.* Female reproductive organ: *trichogyne.* [< Gk. *gunē,* woman.]
gyneco- or **gynec-** or **gynaeco-** or **gynaec-** *pref.* Woman: *gynecology.* [Gk. *gunaiko-* < *gunē,* woman.]
gyn·e·coc·ra·cy (jĭn′ĭ-kŏk′rə-sē, gī′nĭ-) *n., pl.* **-cies.** Political

p pop / r roar / s sauce / sh ship, dish / t tight / th thin, path / *th* this, bathe / ŭ cut / ûr urge / v valve / w with / y yes / z zebra, size / zh vision / ə about, item, edible, gallop, circus / œ Fr. feu, Ger. schön / ü Fr. tu, Ger. über / кн Ger. ich, Scot. loch / N Fr. bon.

Figure 2.3   *The American Heritage Dictionary, Second College Edition,* **583.** Copyright © 1991 by Houghton Mifflin Company. Reproduced by permission from *The American Heritage Dictionary, Second College Edition.*

The Structure of English for Readers, Writers, and Teachers

of sheepskin and used for bookbinding. **2.** One that skives. **3.** A knife or other cutting device used in skiving.

Skiv·vies (skĭv′ēz). A trademark for underwear.

ski·wear (skē′wâr′) *n.* Clothing that is appropriate to wear for skiing.

skoal (skōl) *interj.* Used as a drinking toast. [Dan. and Norw. *skaal,* cup.]

sku·a (skyo͞o′ə) *n.* **1.** A predatory gull-like sea bird, *Catharacta skua,* of northern regions, having brownish plumage. **2.** *Chiefly Brit.* A jaeger. [NLat. < Faroese *skúvur* < ON *skúfr.*]

skul·dug·ger·y (skŭl-dŭg′ə-rē) *n.* Variant of **skullduggery.**

skulk (skŭlk) *intr.v.* **skulked, skulk·ing, skulks. 1.** To lie in hiding; lurk. **2.** To move about stealthily. **3.** To evade work or obligation; malinger. —*n.* **1.** One who skulks. **2.** A group of foxes. [ME *skulken,* of Scand. orig.] —**skulk′er** *n.*

skull (skŭl) *n.* **1.** The framework of the head of vertebrates, made up of the bones of the brain case and face. **2.** The head, esp. regarded as the seat of thought or intelligence. **3.** A death's-head. [ME *skulle.*]

skull and crossbones *n.* A representation of a human skull above two long crossed bones, a symbol of death once used by pirates and now used as a warning label on poisons.

skull·cap (skŭl′kăp′) *n.* **1. a.** A light, close-fitting, brimless cap sometimes worn indoors. **b.** A yarmulke. **2.** Any of various plants of the genus *Scutellaria,* having clusters of two-lipped flowers.

skull·dug·ger·y also **skul·dug·ger·y** (skŭl-dŭg′ə-rē) *n., pl.* **-ger·ies.** Crafty deception or trickery. [Orig. unknown.]

skunk (skŭngk) *n.* **1.** Any of several small, carnivorous New World mammals of the genus *Mephitis* and related genera, having a bushy tail and black fur with white markings and ejecting a malodorous secretion from glands near the anus. **2.** The glossy black and white fur of the skunk. **3.** *Slang.* A mean or despicable person. —*tr.v.* **skunked, skunk·ing, skunks.** *Slang.* **1.** To defeat overwhelmingly, esp. by keeping from scoring. **2. a.** To cheat. **b.** To fail to pay. [Massachuset *squnck.*]

skunk cabbage *n.* **1.** An ill-smelling swamp plant, *Symplocarpus foetidus,* of eastern North America, having minute flowers enclosed in a mottled greenish or purplish spathe. **2.** A plant, *Lysichitum americanum,* of western North America similar to skunk cabbage.

skunkweed (skŭngk′wēd) *n.* Skunk cabbage.

sky (skī) *n., pl.* **skies. 1.** The upper atmosphere, appearing as a hemisphere above the earth. **2.** The highest level or degree: *reaching for the sky.* **3.** The celestial or heavenly regions. **4.** Often **skies.** The appearance of the upper atmosphere, esp. with respect to weather: *threatening skies.* —*tr.v.* **skied, sky·ing, skies. 1.** To hit or throw (a ball, for example) high in the air. **2.** To hang (a painting, for example) high up on the wall, above the line of vision, esp. in an exhibition. [ME < ON *sky,* cloud.]

sky blue *n.* A light to pale blue, from a light greenish to light purplish blue.

sky·borne (skī′bôrn′, -bōrn′) *adj.* Airborne.

sky·cap (skī′kăp′) *n.* An airport employee who carries luggage. [SKY + (RED)CAP.]

sky·dive (skī′dīv′) *intr.v.* **-dived, -div·ing, -dives.** *Sports.* To jump from an airplane, performing various maneuvers before pulling the ripcord of a parachute. —**sky′div′er** *n.* —**sky′div′ing** *n.*

Skye terrier (skī) *n.* A small terrier of a breed native to the Isle of Skye, having a long, low body, short legs, and shaggy hair.

sky·ey (skī′ē) *adj.* Of or resembling the sky.

sky·high (skī′hī′) *adv.* **1.** To a very high level: *garbage piled sky-high.* **2.** In a lavish or enthusiastic manner. **3.** In pieces or to pieces; apart: *blew the bridge sky-high.* —*adj.* **1.** High up in the air. **2.** Exorbitantly high: *sky-high prices.*

sky·jack (skī′jăk′) *tr.v.* **-jacked, -jack·ing, -jacks.** To hijack (an airplane, esp. one in flight) through the use or threat of force. [SKY + (HI)JACK.] —**sky′jack′er** *n.* —**sky′jack′ing** *n.*

sky·lark (skī′lärk′) *n.* An Old World bird, *Alauda arvensis,* having brownish plumage and noted for its singing while in flight. —*intr.v.* **-larked, -lark·ing, -larks.** To indulge in frolic.

sky·light (skī′līt′) *n.* An overhead window admitting daylight.

sky·line (skī′līn′) *n.* **1.** The line along which the surface of the earth and sky appear to meet; horizon. **2.** The outline of a group of buildings or a mountain range seen against the sky.

sky·lounge (skī′lounj′) *n.* A vehicle that collects passengers and then is carried by a helicopter between a downtown terminal and an airport.

sky marshal *n.* An armed federal law-enforcement officer assigned to prevent skyjackings.

sky pilot *n. Slang.* A clergyman; chaplain.

sky·rock·et (skī′rŏk′ĭt) *n.* A firework that ascends high into the air where it explodes in a brilliant cascade of flares and starlike sparks. —*intr. & tr.v.* **-et·ed, -et·ing, -ets.** To rise or cause to rise rapidly and suddenly, as in amount, position, or reputation.

sky·sail (skī′sāl, -săl′) *n.* A small square sail above the royal in a square-rigged vessel.

sky·scrap·er (skī′skrā′pər) *n.* A very tall building.

sky·walk (skī′wôk′) *n.* An elevated usually enclosed walkway between two buildings.

sky·ward (skī′wərd) *adj. & adv.* At or toward the sky. —**sky′-wards** *adv.*

sky wave *n.* A radio wave.

sky·way (skī′wā′) *n.* **1.** An airline route; air lane. **2.** An elevated highway.

sky·writ·ing (skī′rī′tĭng) *n.* **1.** The process of writing in the sky by releasing a visible vapor from an airplane. **2.** The letters or words formed in skywriting. —**sky′writ′er** *n.*

slab¹ (slăb) *n.* **1.** A broad, flat, somewhat thick piece, as of cake, stone, or cheese. **2.** An outside piece cut from a log when squaring it for lumber. **3.** *Baseball.* The pitcher's rubber. —*tr.v.* **slabbed, slab·bing, slabs. 1.** To make or shape into a slab. **2.** To cover or pave with slabs. **3.** To dress (a log) by cutting slabs. [ME *slabbe.*]

slab² (slăb) *adj. Archaic.* Viscid. Used in the phrase *thick and slab.* [Prob. of Scand. orig.]

slab-sid·ed (slăb′sī′dĭd) *adj. Informal.* **1.** Having flat sides. **2.** Tall and slim; lanky.

slack¹ (slăk) *adj.* **1.** Not lively or moving; sluggish. **2.** Not busy; lacking in work: *a slack business season.* **3.** Not tense or taut; loose: *a slack rope.* **4.** Lacking firmness: *a slack grip.* **5.** Lacking in diligence; negligent: *a slack worker.* **6.** Flowing or blowing with little speed. Used of the wind or tide. —*v.* **slacked, slack·ing, slacks.** —*tr.* **1.** To slacken. **2.** To be remiss about. **3.** To slake (lime). —*intr.* **1.** To be or become slack. —*phrasal verb.* **slack off.** To decrease in activity or intensity; abate. —*n.* **1. a.** A loose or slack part or portion of something, such as a rope or sail. **2.** A lack of tension; looseness. **3.** A period of little activity; lull. **4. a.** A cessation of movement in a current of air or water. **b.** An area of still water. **5. slacks.** Separate trousers not part of a suit. —*adv.* In a slack manner; slackly. [ME *slak* < OE *slæc.*] —**slack′ly** *adv.* —**slack′ness** *n.*

slack² (slăk) *n.* A mixture of coal fragments, coal dust, and dirt that remains after screening coal. [ME *sleck.*]

slack³ (slăk) *n. Chiefly Brit.* **1.** A small dell or hollow. **2.** A bog; morass. [ME *slak* < ON *slakki.*]

slack-baked (slăk′bākt′) *adj.* **1.** Not perfectly baked; underdone; half-baked. Used chiefly of bread. **2.** Imperfectly made.

slack·en (slăk′ən) *v.* **-ened, -en·ing, -ens.** —*tr.* **1.** To make slower; slow down: *The runners slackened their pace.* **2.** To make less vigorous, intense, firm, or severe. **3.** To reduce the tension or tautness of; loosen. —*intr.* **1.** To slow down. **2.** To become less energetic, active, firm, or strict. **3.** To become less tense or taut; loosen.

slack·er (slăk′ər) *n.* A person who shirks work or responsibility, esp. one who tries to evade military service in wartime.

slack water *n.* **1.** The period at high or low tide when there is no visible flow of water. **2.** An area in a sea or river unaffected by currents; still water.

slag (slăg) *n.* **1.** The vitreous mass left as a residue by the smelting of metallic ore. **2.** Scoria (sense 1). —*v.* **slagged, slag·ging, slags.** —*tr.* To change into slag. —*intr.* To form slag; become slaglike. [MLG *slagge.*] —**slag′gy** *adj.*

slain (slān) *v.* Past participle of **slay.**

slake (slāk) *v.* **slaked, slak·ing, slakes.** —*tr.* **1.** To quench or satisfy: *slaked her thirst.* **2.** To lessen the force or activity of; moderate: *slaking his anger.* **3.** To cool or refresh by wetting or moistening. **4.** To combine (lime) chemically with water or moist air. —*intr.* To undergo a slaking process; crumble or disintegrate, as lime. [ME *slaken,* to abate < OE *slacian* < *slæc,* slack, sluggish.]

sla·lom (slä′ləm) *n.* **1.** Skiing in a zigzag course. **2.** A race along such a course, laid out with flag-marked poles. [Norw. : *slad,* sloping + *lom,* path.] —**sla′lom** *v.* (**-lomed, -lom·ing, -loms**)

slam¹ (slăm) *v.* **slammed, slam·ming, slams.** —*tr.* **1.** To shut with force and loud noise: *slammed the door.* **2.** To put, throw, or otherwise forcefully move so as to produce a loud noise: *slammed the book on the desk.* **3.** To hit or strike with great force. **4.** *Slang.* To criticize harshly; attack verbally. —*intr.* **1.** To close or swing into place with force so as to produce a loud noise. **2.** To hit something with force; crash. —*n.* **1. a.** A forceful movement that produces a loud noise. **b.** The noise so produced. **2.** *Slang.* A harsh or devastating criticism. [Perh. of Scand. orig.]

slam² (slăm) *n.* In bridge and other whist-derived card games, the winning of all the tricks or all but one during the play of one hand. [Orig. unknown.]

slam-bang (slăm′băng′) *adv.* **1.** Swiftly and noisily. **2.** Recklessly.

slam·mer (slăm′ər) *n. Slang.* A jail: *"If he doesn't wind up in the slammer, he's likely to get a job teaching journalism"* (Nat Hentoff). [< SLAM¹.]

slan·der (slăn′dər) *n.* **1.** *Law.* The utterance of defamatory statements injurious to the reputation or well-being of a person. **2.** A malicious statement or report. —*v.* **-dered, -der·ing, -ders.** —*tr.* To utter damaging reports about. —*intr.* To utter or spread slander. [ME *slaundre* < OFr. *esclandre* < Lat. *scandalum,* scandal < Gk. *skandalon,* trap.] —**slan′der·er** *n.* —**slan′der·ous** *adj.* —**slan′der·ous·ly** *adv.*

ă pat / ā pay / âr care / ä father / b bib / ch church / d deed / ĕ pet / ē be / f fife / g gag / h hat / hw which / ĭ pit / ī pie / îr pier / j judge / k kick / l lid, needle / m mum / n no, sudden / ng thing / ŏ pot / ō toe / ô paw, for / oi noise / ou out / o͝o took / o͞o boot /

Figure 2.4 **_The American Heritage Dictionary, Second College Edition,_** **1148.** Copyright © 1991 by Houghton Mifflin Company. Reproduced by permission from *The American Heritage Dictionary, Second College Edition.*

the legal register. The word *gigabyte* is technical in register; *bogie* is from the language of golf; *seminar* is from the academic register. The word *cute* is used by female speakers more than by males, while *take it easy* as a parting remark is more common among males. These are all observations about the register of words.

The register of a word is often related to its historical origin—how it came into English. The words we learn at home as children are, for the most part, words that were already present in Old English (categories 1, 2a, and 2b above). Throughout our lives, these are the words we use in ordinary conversation and which have the strongest meaning for us; thus, they are used even in formal contexts by speakers and writers who want an emotional connection with their audience. In contrast, classical borrowings like *anatomy* and *pedestrian* (category 2d) were taken originally from written texts, and they are found, even today, primarily in written language. These are the words that appear on vocabulary lists and on the college board exams. We learn them in school rather than at home, and we use them to display our educational level or technical expertise. They tend to be intellectual in tone rather than emotional. Words borrowed from Norman French (category 2c) have an intermediate status: some of them, such as *lesion,* are formal in register; others, like *curtain,* are neutral. Words borrowed into Modern English from modern spoken languages (category 2e) often retain a foreign flavor: *kimono* (from Japanese), *bidet* (from French), *teepee* (from Sioux), *lox* (from Yiddish).

EXERCISE 5.   The words below are all native English words and, like most native words, are neutral in register. Find Old French or classical borrowings (categories 2c and 2d) whose meanings are similar to these words. For example, corresponding to the native English word *big*, we have the Latin and Greek derivatives *enormous* and *gigantic*; corresponding to the native English word *drink,* we have the Latin borrowing *imbibe.* In looking for classical correlates of these native English words, begin by making the best guess you can, relying on meaning and on your sense of the formality level of the words. Then check your answer with your college dictionary. The point of the exercise is for you to see that you already have a pretty good sense of the distinction between native vocabulary and Old French or classical borrowings.

big	*brotherly*	*buy*	*childish*	*die*
drink	*eat*	*farming*	*on foot*	*give*
give up	*hate*	*look at*	*lucky*	*shorten*

EXERCISE 6.   The following is a selection from a speech that Winston Churchill gave at the beginning of World War II, when Britain declared war against Germany. Almost all the vocabulary of this passage is native English and Old Norse; however, there are six words that were borrowed from Old French or Latin during Middle English times. Find them, by first making the best guess you can, and then checking with your dictionary:

> *We shall go on to the end, we shall fight in France, we shall fight on the seas and oceans, we shall fight with growing confidence and growing strength in the air, we shall defend our Island, whatever the cost may be, we shall fight on the beaches, we shall fight on the landing grounds, we*

shall fight in the fields and in the streets, we shall fight in the hills; we shall never surrender.

—Winston Churchill, 1940

Why did Churchill choose mostly native and Old Norse vocabulary for this speech?

EXERCISE 7.   In order to do this exercise, you will need to know the difference between **content** words [nouns, verbs (except *is*), adjectives, and adverbs] and **structural** or **function** words (words like *a, the, and, of, to, with, some, other, it,* etc.) The content words, as their name implies, provide the semantic content of the sentence; the function words are there primarily to set up the grammatical structure. Except for the third person plural pronouns *they, them,* and *their,* our function words are all native to English; when we borrow words, we borrow into the content (or "open") categories: nouns (*sauerkraut*), verbs (*denote*), adjectives (*primary*), and adverbs (*occasionally*).

a. First, pick out the content words in the following passage from the *University of New Hampshire Catalog.*

b. Except for eleven native English words and one word from Old Norse, all the content words in this passage are classical borrowings (category 2d). Your assignment is to find the content words that are *not* classical borrowings. (Of course, even in this academic register, the *function* words [the words that you have *not* picked out] are native English and Old Norse.) Then say why you think this passage contains so much classical vocabulary.

> *The general education program is designed to emphasize the acquisition and improvement of those fundamental skills essential to advanced college work, especially the abilities to think critically, to read with discernment, to write effectively, and to understand quantitative data. It aims to acquaint the student with some of the major modes of thought necessary to understanding oneself, others, and the environment. It seeks to develop a critical appreciation of both the value and the limitations of significant methods of inquiry and analysis. Its goal, moreover, is the student's achievement of at least the minimal level of literacy in mathematics, in science and technology, in historical perspectives and the comprehension of our own and other cultures, in aesthetic sensibility, and in the diverse approaches of the humanities. . . .*

EXERCISE 8.   The following words are borrowed from modern spoken languages. First try to *guess* their origins; then check your intuitions with your college dictionary:

gesundheit	*ciao*	*ginseng*	*guru*	*hummus*
chimpanzee	*karate*	*kayak*	*klutz*	*kvetch*
macho	*maestro*	*rouge*	*sauté*	*tortilla*

The purpose of this exercise is for you to notice that these words still have a foreign flavor and that, in many cases, you can identify the language of origin.

2.6 Invented Vocabulary

In addition to our native vocabulary and the words that we borrow from other languages, English (like other languages) contains many words that we have simply invented. Words are usually not invented arbitrarily, but are created by one of the following methods:

1. Imitation or "Onomatopoeia." Words like *slurp* and *ding* are imitative words; that is, they designate a sound that is similar to the sound of the word itself. Words for animal noises are also onomatopoetic: *baa, moo, neigh, woof, cock-a-doodle-doo,* and so forth.

EXERCISE 9. Find onomatopoetic words in another language and compare them with the corresponding English words.

2. Reduplication. Reduplicated words are formed by repeating a word, usually with a change in one sound: *hodgepodge, hurly-burly, nitty-gritty, flimflam, harum-skarum, seesaw, teeter-totter, knickknack.*[1]

EXERCISE 10.
   a. List ten additional reduplicated words in English.
   b. Some reduplicated words are written as one word, and some are written with a hyphen. What is the rule? (*Hint:* It has to do with the number of syllables in the word.)

3. Formation of Compounds and Idiomatic Phrases. Compounds are created by combining two or more words to make a new word, as in the slang word *airhead* 'a silly, unintelligent person,' which is created by combining the words *air* and *head.* Compounds are written sometimes as a single word (a *slingshot*), sometimes as two words (a *fork lift*), and sometimes with a hyphen between the two parts (a *slip-on*). There is no general rule; you will have to consult a dictionary if you are uncertain, and even dictionaries are sometimes inconsistent.

What identifies a word as a compound is its pronunciation, with heaviest stress on the first element; this differs from phrasal stress, with emphasis on the *final* element. Pronounce the examples below, and notice the difference in stress:

Compound		Phrase	
a blackboard	'a chalk board'	*a black board*	'a board that is black'
the White House	'the house of the President'	*a white house*	'a house that is white'
a bigmouth	'a loud-mouthed person'	*a big mouth*	'a mouth that is big'
a roundhouse	'a building for repairing trains'	*a round house*	'a house that is round'

Compounds often have *idiomatic* (unpredictable) meanings (a *blackboard* is not necessarily black, a *clotheshorse* is not a horse, a *nest egg* is not an egg), but some compounds have *compositional* (predictable) meanings (a *grocery store, a nerve cell, a frying pan*). Phrases usually have compositional meanings (a *black board, a big mouth*), but some phrases are *idiomatic* (a *green*

---

1. From the National Public Radio program *Says You!* of 6/3/01: Give a double reduplication to describe a really fine train. (Answer: *a lulu choochoo*)

thumb, a swelled head, hot air, meaning 'boastful talk'). Phrases with idiomatic meanings are called *idiomatic phrases* or *lexicalized phrases,* and they are listed in the dictionary.

EXERCISE 11.

a. Pronounce each expression below, and use the stress pattern to identify it as a compound or a phrase.

animal crackers	*(a) bargain basement*	*French fries*
animal husbandry	*bargain hunting*	*French toast*
mashed potatoes	*(an) iron hand*	*(a) free throw*
(a) couch potato	*(the) Iron Age*	*free enterprise*

b. Say whether each expression is compositional or idiomatic in meaning. (For example, *bargain hunting* is a compound with a compositional meaning, in that it means 'hunting for bargains'; *iron hand* is a phrase with an idiomatic meaning—its compositional meaning would be 'a hand made out of iron.') After you have finished the exercise, check to see if the compound or phrase is listed in the dictionary; if it is, then the editors of the dictionary have judged it to be idiomatic.

4. Affixation (Sometimes Called "Derivation").   Once a word has entered our lexicon, new words can be created from it by adding *affixes* (prefixes or suffixes). For example, to the word *plane* (created by the shortening of *airplane*), flight attendants have added the prefixes *em-* and *de-* to create *emplane* 'get on a plane' and *deplane* 'get off a plane.' Similarly, to the slang word *nerd,* which was invented by Dr. Seuss, slang users have added the suffix *-y* to create the adjective *nerdy* and then the suffix *-ness* to create the abstract noun *nerdiness.* In a TV interview about women students' reluctance to enter scientific fields, the astronaut Sally Ride spoke of the *nerdification* of the field of computer science.

EXERCISE 12.   Prefixes and suffixes make up the class of *affixes.* Prefixes, suffixes, and roots are called *morphemes.* Find the morphemes in the following words, and identify each morpheme as an affix or a root.

a. *happy, happily, unhappily*
b. *soft, softer, soften, softened*
c. *sand, sandy, sandbox*
d. *work, worker, worker's, workers'*
e. *oyster, oysters*
f. *true, truth, untrue*

The structure of words formed by affixation depends on their historical origin. If a word was formed in English, its root will be a complete word (a "free" root). For example, the root of the word *sandy* (Exercise 12 above) is the word *sand.*

Affixes that are still being used to create new words in English are called "productive affixes." For example, the suffix *-ness* is a productive suffix because we still use it to create new words such as *dorkiness* 'the state of being dorky.' The English suffix *-th* of *stealth* and *warmth* is, by contrast, no longer productive. A list of productive affixes is given in Figure 2.5. Note that these suffixes attach to complete words, as is characteristic of English, and have specific requirements about the grammatical category of the word to which they attach. For example, the suffix *-ness* attaches to adjectives to create nouns with the meaning 'quality or state of being . . ..' Thus *dorkiness* means 'the quality or state of being dorky.'

a. Affixation in Words Borrowed from Latin.

As we have seen, English has a large number of words that were borrowed from Latin (sometimes by way of French). Latin words were built from *bound roots;* that is, the root of the word was not itself a word. For example, the word *reject* consists of the prefix *re-* plus the bound root *ject,* meaning 'throw.' This root appears in many English words which were borrowed from Latin: *in-ject, e-ject, de-ject-ed, con-ject-ture,* and so forth. That is why words borrowed from Latin almost always have two or more syllables: every word must have a prefix or suffix in addition to the root.

EXERCISE 13. Because formal vocabulary in English is often borrowed from Latin, a study of Latin roots and affixes is a good way to build vocabulary. Create as many English words as you can in ten minutes, using Latin prefixes, roots, and suffixes from the following table.

Prefixes		Roots		Suffixes
ad-,ac-,ag-,al-,ar-,as-	'to'	*ag, act*	'do, move'	*-al*
ab-	'from'	*cede, ceed, cess*	'go'	*-able/-ible*
ambi-	'two'	*ceive, cept*	'take'	*-ance/-ence*
con-,col-,com-,cor-	'with, together'	*dict*	'speak'	*-ant/-ent*
contra-	'against'	*duce, duct*	'lead'	*-(at)ion*
de-	'down, away from'	*fend, fens(e)*	'act against'	*-ile*
di-,dis-[2]	'away, apart'	*fer*	'carry'	*-ity*
e-,ex-	'out from'	*flect, flex*	'bend'	*-ive*
inter-	'between'	*ject*	'throw'	*-ment*
in-,il-,im-,ir-	'not'	*port*	'carry'	*-or*
in-,il-,im-,ir-	'in, into'	*pos(e)*	'put'	
inter-	'between'	*riv(e)*	'flow'	
ob-	'against'	*scend, scent*	'climb'	
pre-	'before'	*scrib(e), script*	'write'	
post-	'after'	*spic, spect*	'look'	
pro-	'for, forward'	*tain, ten(t)*	'hold'	
re-	'back'	*tend, tens(e)*	'stretch'	
sub-,suf-,sup-	'under'	*tract*	'pull'	
trans-	'across'	*vert*	'turn'	
		voc	'call'	

---

2. Note that some English affixes do double duty. For example, the prefix *dis-* 'apart' that appears in words like *disperse* and *disturb* is a Latin prefix which attaches to bound roots. This *dis-* is not productive in English. However, there is another *dis-* that is productive—the *dis-* meaning 'not', that appears in words like *dishonest* and *disloyal.*

PREFIX	MEANING	EXAMPLES	FROM	TO
ex-	'former . . .'	ex-president, ex-con	noun	noun
dis-	'not . . .'	dishonest, disloyal, dissatisfied	adj	adj
fore-	'. . . before'	foresee, foreshorten, foreshadow	verb	verb
in-	'not . . .'	incompetent, incomplete, intolerable	adj	adj
mid-	'in the middle of . . .'	midseason, midweek, midair	noun	noun
mis-	'. . . in a wrong manner'	mistake, misunderstand, misspell	verb	verb
re-	'. . . again'	rework, rethink, reevaluate, redo	verb	verb
un-	'not . . .'	unhappy, untrue, unsure, unconscious	adj	adj
un-	'do the opposite of . . .'	untie, unwrap, uncover, undo, unfold	verb	verb

SUFFIX	MEANING	EXAMPLES	FROM	TO
-able	'able to be . . .ed'	lovable, fixable, breakable, washable	verb	adj
-(i)al	'pertaining to . . .'	national, musical, presidential	noun	adj
-ation	'act of . . .ing'	relaxation, meditation, realization	verb	noun
-dom	'state of being . . .'	wisdom, freedom, boredom	adj	noun
-en	'make . . .'	gladden, widen, soften, roughen, redden	adj	verb
-er	'one who . . .s'	baker, teacher, owner, wanderer	verb	noun
-ful	'full of . . .'	graceful, joyful, playful, hopeful	noun	adj
-hood	'state of being a . . .'	sisterhood, childhood, neighborhood	noun	noun
-ic	'pertaining to . . .'	organic, atmospheric	noun	adj
-ify	'make (into a) . . .'	classify, objectify, solidify	noun/adj	verb
-ion	'act or result of . . .ing'	protection, compensation, reflection	verb	noun
-ish	'like a . . .'	boyish, childish, foolish, sheepish	noun	adj
-ity	'the quality of being . . .'	sanity, activity, passivity, masculinity	adj	noun
-ive	'tending to . . .'	assertive, comprehensive, reflective	verb	adj
-ize	'make . . .'	visualize, unionize, crystallize	noun/adj	verb
-less	'without . . .'	penniless, priceless, hopeless	noun	adj
-ly	'like a . . .'	friendly, womanly, manly, cowardly	noun	adj
-ly	'in a . . . manner'	slowly, happily, hurriedly, foolishly,	adj	adv
-ment	'act or result of . . .ing'	adjournment, government, movement	verb	noun
-ness	'quality of being . . .'	happiness, firmness, kindness	adj	noun
-ous	'characterized by . . .'	famous, poisonous, rancorous	noun	adj
-ship	'state of being (a) . . .'	championship, kinship, governorship	noun	noun
-some	'characterized by . . .'	troublesome, burdensome, worrisome	noun	adj
-y	'-like . . .'	mealy, pulpy, mousy, icy, fruity, fiery	noun	adj

Figure 2.5 Productive Affixes. (My thanks to my student Linda Thiel for her assistance in putting together this chart.)

b. Affixation (and Compounding) in Words Derived from Greek

Greek roots, like Latin roots, are "bound," meaning that the root by itself is not a word. Some Greek words, such as *chron-ic,* consist of a root plus a suffix. However, Greek words often have a compound root with a vowel (usually *-o-*) between the two parts, and followed by prefixes or suffixes, if any:

> *anthrop - o - log - y*   *gram - o - phone*   *phon - o - graph*
> *matr - i - arch - y*   *patr - i - arch - y*

EXERCISE 14. A knowledge of Greek roots and affixes is useful for vocabulary building and for spelling; words borrowed from Greek follow a spelling system of their own which differs in some ways from the usual spelling system of English. Create as many words as you can in ten minutes, using Greek prefixes, suffixes, and roots from the following table:

Prefixes		Roots		Suffixes
a-/an-	'without'	*andr*	'male'	*-ia*
amphi-	'two'	*anthrop*	'human'	*-ic(al)*
anti-	'against'	*arche*	'rule'	*-ism*
auto-	'self'	*audi*	'sound'	*-ist*
di-	'two'	*bibli*	'book'	*-ize*
dia-	'across'	*bi*	'life'	*-oid*
dys-	'faulty'	*chron*	'time'	*-ous*
eu-	good'	*ge*	'earth'	*-y*
ex-	'out'	*gene*	'birth'	
homo-	'same'	*gon*	'angle'	
hyper-	'beyond'	*gram/graph*	'writing'	
hypo-	'under'	*gyn(ec)*	'female'	
mega-	'big'	*log*	'study'	
micro-	'small'	*met(e)r*	'measurement'	
penta-	'five'	*mat(e)r*	'mother'	
poly-	'many'	*nom/nym*	'name'	
pro-	'for, forward'	*pat(e)r*	'father'	
pseudo-	'false'	*phil(e)*	'love'	
syn- or *sym-*	'together'	*phob(e)*	'fear'	
tele-	'far'	*phon(e)*	'sound'	
		phot	'light'	
		psych(e)	'mind, soul'	
		soph	'wisdom'	
		therm	'heat'	
		zo	'animal'	

EXERCISE 15. In Exercise 14, you were asked to find real English words constructed from Greek morphemes. However, English speakers also often *invent* words using these morphemes. The following words were invented by a previous class that used this text; give definitions of their words and see if you can come up with some yourself:

a. *We have such enormous <u>sympsychia</u> that we've decided to get married.*

b. *She's a real <u>phobophile</u>—always reading Stephen King novels.*

c. *College is full of <u>pseudosophs</u>.*

d. *Many couples are now choosing <u>polynyms</u> for their children to acknowledge their full family lineage.*

(Thanks to my colleague Cinthia Gannett, who suggested this exercise.)

5. Acronymy.   Acronyms (words formed by combining the first letter or first part of each word of a phrase) are very common, especially in institutional settings. Acronyms may be pronounced in either of two ways: as a series of letter names, as in UNH (<u>U</u>niversity of <u>N</u>ew <u>H</u>ampshire), or as a word, as in Wasp (<u>w</u>hite <u>A</u>nglo-<u>S</u>axon <u>P</u>rotestant).

EXERCISE 16.

a. Identify the origin of the following acronyms. Indicate whether each acronym is pronounced as a word or as a sequence of letters. (Note that some of these acronyms have more than one possible interpretation.)

OD	*NCTE*	*op-ed (page)*	*PBS*	*RBI*
NATO	*GI*	*snafu*	*CPR*	*ROTC*
UNICEF	*FBI*	*NBA*	*scuba*	*dink*
ERA	*CIA*	*NYPD*	*laser*	*NCAA*

b. Acronyms are commonly found in *institutional* language. List ten acronyms that are used in an organization or institution with which you are associated.

c. Acronyms like LOL and TTYL are now common in text messaging. List as many text-messaging acronyms as you can, with their meanings.

6. Shortening or "Clipping."   Words are often shortened in conversation, as when *information* is called *info*. Sometimes the original long form of the word is lost; most people do not know that *bus* is short for *omnibus*, or that *piano* is short for pianoforte.

EXERCISE 17.   Give the long versions of the following shortened forms: *diss, gym, phone, math, fridge, mike, Sis, Mom, perp, perm, perk, nuke, lit, bio, psych, narc, disco, rev* (as in *"Rev up the engines"*), *blog, zine.*

Back-formation is a type of shortening in which a portion of a word which appears to be an affix is removed. Examples are *emote* (from *emotion*), *enthuse* (from *enthusiasm*), *liaise* (from *liaison*), *lase* (from *laser*), *couth* (from *uncouth*), and *typewrite* (from *typewriter*). The word *pea* was derived by back-formation from Middle English *pease*, which sounded like a plural. Young children can sometimes be heard making a back-formation from the plural noun *clothes*, pronounced [klōz]: The child creates a corresponding singular form [klō] ("I can't find my clo!")

7. Blending. In blending, the beginning of one word is joined with the end of another to create a single word. An example is the word *smog*, from *smoke* + *fog*.

EXERCISE 18. Determine the origins of the following blends: *motel, brunch, electrocute, stagflation, dancercise, Spanglish, New Yorican, emoticon, spork, frenemy.*

---

8. Category Shift. Category shift is the movement of a word from one syntactic category to another, as when the noun *floor* comes to be used as a verb ("You really floored me with that announcement."). English makes very frequent use of category shift, especially the use of nouns as verbs. In fact, most common nouns can also be used as verbs, as when we *book* a flight, *table* a motion, *wall* up an opening, or *paper* something over. Verbs can also often be used as nouns, as in *a run, a jump, a laugh,* or *a cry.*

EXERCISE 19.
  a. The names of body parts are basically nouns, but many of them can also be used as verbs. Which of the following body-part names can be used as verbs? Support your answer by using the word in a sentence: *head, hair, eye, nose, mouth, ear, neck, shoulder, back, stomach, arm, hand, finger, thumb, hip, leg, elbow, knee, foot, ankle, toe.*
  b. Try the same with the names of animals. For example, *dog* is a noun that can also be used as a verb.

One special type of category shift is the use of a proper name as a common noun or verb, as when we use the trademark *Xerox* to mean "make a copy," or the word *watt* (from the name of the inventor James Watt) to refer to a unit of electricity, or create the verb *tantalize* from the name of the mythological character Tantalus. When a person's name is used in this way (as in *watt*), then the word is called an *eponym,* and the word-formation process is called *eponymy.*

9. Semantic Extension. Perhaps the most common method of word formation is the addition of a new meaning to an already existing word. Thus, for example, when new words were needed to support the invention of photography, the words that were employed generally already existed in the language, with other meanings: *shutter, lens, film, negative, develop.* Or consider the sport of basketball: words like *basket, dribble,* and *travel* already existed in English, but were given special meanings within this sport.

EXERCISE 20. First decide on a basic meaning for each of the following words, and then find several extended meanings for each word: *heart, graft, cold, bright, sink.*

2.7 Exercises on Invented Words

The following exercises will serve as a review of the word-formation processes that have been introduced in this section.

EXERCISE 21. Identify the word-formation processes by which the words in the left-hand column were converted into those on the right. Your choices are *imitation (onomatopoeia), compounding, formation of an idiomatic phrase, affixation, acronymy, shortening (including back-formation), blending, category shift,* and *semantic extension.*

a. television	→	televise
b. environment	→	environmentalist
c. happening, circumstance	→	happenstance
d. hook, shot	→	hook shot
e. market	→	to market (a product)
f. a psychopath	→	(a) psycho
g. slave	→	antislavery
h. dance, marathon	→	danceathon
i. day, break	→	daybreak
j. stroll	→	stroller
k. binary, digit	→	bit
l. biology	→	bio
m. short, fuse	→	(She has a) short fuse
n. National Education Association	→	NEA
o. (a) demonstration model	→	(a) demo

EXERCISE 22. *(Patterned after an exercise in O'Grady, Dobrovolsky, and Aronoff, 1993)* Create new words with the specified meanings, using the suggested word-formation processes:

a. Use onomatopoeia to create a word that means 'the sound of leaves blowing in the wind.'
   Outside the window, we would hear a gentle _____.

b. Use reduplication to create a name for the mud that gets tracked into the house during a rainstorm.
   After you've taken out the trash, please clean up the _____ from the hallway.

c. Use compounding to create a name for the artificial smile people use when they're not really happy.
Sharon _____ed when George said she didn't look half as bad as she did yesterday.

d. Use affixation to create a word for the process of knocking the outside mirror off your car:
When I drove too close to the wall, I accidentally _____ed my car.

e. Use acronymy for the gum left overnight on the bedpost. (Note: Function words need not be included in acronyms.)
The first thing I did when I woke up was reclaim my _____.

f. Use backformation to create a verb from the adjective *breathtaking*.
Mom's going to _____ when she sees how clean the kitchen is.

g. Use blending to name a child after his parents.
Samantha and Emmanuel named their son _____.

h. Use shortening to create a slang word for *adjective*.
My writing instructor said I should use more _____.

i. Use category shift for the act of playing tennis.
We golfed all morning and _____ed during the afternoon.

j. Use acronymy to create a name for the anxiety students feel during final exams.
She did yoga exercises to control her _____.

EXERCISE 23. Discuss the register of words that are formed by each of the word-formation processes described in this section: *imitation, reduplication, compounding, affixation, acronymy, shortening, blending, category shift,* and *semantic extension*. Do the words that are formed by each method tend to belong to a particular register? Are they formal or informal? Can you make any other observations about the circumstances in which each type of word is used?

EXERCISE 24. The *Barnhart Dictionary of New English* lists words that have come into use during the past thirty years or so. A page from the *Barnhart Dictionary* is reproduced in Figure 2.6. Identify the source of each word that is listed on this page. Your choices are the same as in Exercise 21, with two additions: *borrowing* and *the formation of a lexicalized phrase*. (Note: Because these are real-life examples, they will not always fall neatly into a single category; some words may have been formed by a combination of processes.)

2.8   Applications for Students and Teachers of Literature

Every sample of English, whether written or spoken, belongs to a particular "register"—that is, it is appropriate for a particular social context or range of contexts; the words you would use to tell your friend about your recent accident are not the same as those you would use with a

leopard, clouded leopard, La Plata otter and giant otter. Times (London) 1/26/72, p16 [**1971**]

gigabit ('dʒɪgəˌbit), *n.* a unit of information equivalent to one billion bits of binary digits. Compare KILOBIT, MEGABIT, TERABIT. *The four-minute-mile for electronics engineers has been the gigabit computer, a computer that can process a billion bits of information per second.* Science News 4/4/70, p345 [**1970**, from *giga-* one billion (from Greek *gigas* giant) + *bit*]

giggle-smoke, *n. U.S. Slang.* marijuana. . . . *the young soldier was saying that here in Vietnam cannabis, pot, the weed, giggle-smoke, grass, Mary Jane, call it what you will, is readily available and freely used.* Manchester Guardian Weekly 6/20/70, p6 [**1970**]

GIGO ('gaɪˌgou *or* 'giːˌgou), *n.* acronym for *garbage in, garbage out* (in reference to unreliable data fed into a computer that produces worthless output). *Most of us are familiar with GIGO—garbage in, garbage out—and we try in our systems to eliminate the vast printouts from the computer.* New Scientist and Science Journal 3/11/71, p575 *New technology and curriculum changes, he says, can be beneficial, but "it's a matter of GIGO—Garbage In, Garbage Out. You put garbage into a computer, you get garbage out." Simply investing money into new ideas isn't enough.* Science News 3/24/73, p186 [**1966**]

gimme cap ('gimi:), *U.S.* a visored cap with a clasp for adjusting it to any head size. . . . *Jay Dusard has photographed many modern cowboys with seeming realism . . . you will not see his cowboys fixing a baler or wearing the increasingly common "gimme" caps. They wear broadrimmed hats, chaps and kerchiefs. They ride horses, not pickups. They look just like cowboys should look.* Newsweek 12/12/83, p98 [**1978**, from *gimme* representing an informal pronunciation of *give me;* apparently so called from their being given out freely upon request ("gimme one") as a promotion item by various companies whose names often appear on the caps]

Ginnie Mae, *U.S.* **1** nickname for the Government National Mortgage Association. Compare FREDDIE MAC. *"Ginnie Mae" has been more active than ever before, particularly in the area of "pass-through" securities where "Ginnie" guarantees securities issued by lenders that represent loans in which the net principal and interest on the mortgage loan are passed through to investors each month.* Americana Annual 1975, p285 **2** a stock certificate issued by this agency. *Ginnie Maes—which normally come in minimum amounts of $25,000—provide both high interest yields and also return part of your investment to you each month. Any brokerage firm can provide you with complete details.* New York Post 12/1/78, p65 [**1975**, from pronunciation of the abbreviation *GNMA,* patterned after earlier (1953) *Fannie Mae,* nickname for the Federal National Mortgage Association (from its abbreviation, *FNMA*)]

girlcott, *v.t.* (said of women, in humorous analogy to *boycott*) to join in a boycott against someone or something prejudicial to women. *The Y.W.C.A., Feminists in the Arts, Radicalesbians, National Organization for Women—and anyone of taste—will find much to girlcott in Quiet Days in Clichy* [a motion picture]. Time 10/12/70, pJ9 [**1959**]

giveback, *n. U.S.* the surrendering of fringe benefits or other advantages gained previously by a labor union, usually in return for an increase in wages or other concessions by management. *New York City and its Transit Authority are both demanding givebacks to compensate for pay increases sought by their unions.* NY Times 3/26/78, p1 *Murdoch got most of the rest of the staff cut he was looking for by laying off eighteen people at the bottom of the seniority roll. That left an imposing list of givebacks still on Murdoch's "must" list.* New Yorker 1/22/79, p61 [**1978**, from the verb phrase *give back*]

given, *n.* something taken for granted; a fact. *Loneliness is a human given, and commitment and the public aspects of a relationship are probably things we'll always want.* New Yorker 11/28/70, p76 *The access of moneys to power is simply one of the givens in Washington.* Atlantic 3/71, p22 [**1965**, noun use of the adjective] ►The noun has been formerly restricted in use to technical contexts in logic and mathematics.

give-up, *n. U.S. Stock Market.* a practice in which financial institutions, such as mutual funds, instruct brokers executing transactions for them to yield part of their commissions to other brokers, usually ones who have been performing services for the institution. *At issue was Fidelity's use of what are known as "give-ups." This is the cushion of the sales commissions on stock transactions that the broker actually handling the trade frequently gives to another broker on the instructions of his customer, generally a mutual fund.* NY Times 7/24/68, p53 [**1968**]

glam, *n. Informal.* short for *glamour. A champagne reception before the awards had the glitz and glam the Genies need, and the stars turned out in relative force—Jack Lemmon, Donald Sutherland, Helen Shaver, Margot Kidder, Lee Majors, Céline Lomez.* Maclean's 3/31/80, p49 [**1961**]

glasnost, *n.* an official policy of open and public discussion of problems and issues in the Soviet Union. *Furthermore, in this period of glasnost and uneasy détente, there are people in both governments who perceive the joint exploration of Mars as contributing to world peace.* New Yorker 6/8/87, p81 [**1985**, from Russian *glasnost'* a being public, public knowledge; also found in earlier references in English from 1972]

glasphalt, *n.* a material made from glass for paving roads. . . . *an experimental product called "glasphalt" . . . uses finely ground glass granules to replace the rock aggregates now used as a construction material for highways.* Time 3/16/70, p62 [**1970**, blend of *glass* and *asphalt*]

glass arm, an injured or sore arm resulting from tendons weakened or damaged by throwing or pitching balls. *Countless more suffered chronic maladies ranging from the annoying, like athlete's foot and jock itch, to the exotic and painful, like glass arm (loss of throwing ability from damaged tendons, common in baseball players), hollow foot (a strained instep found in ballet dancers) and web split (splitting of skin between the fingers).* Newsweek 4/2/73, p65 [**1966**, patterned after *glass jaw* (of a boxer)]

glass cord, cord made of fiberglass. *Another material that may make possible cheaper radials in glass cord. Glass cord can save tiremakers as much as $1 per tire, and some companies have already started to make glass-belted radials.* Encyclopedia Science Supplement (Grolier) 1972, p397 [**1968**]

glasshouse effect, British name for GREENHOUSE EFFECT. *According to Dr Sawyer the direct effect of carbon dioxide on mankind is negligible, with atmospheric content now being 319 parts per million to be compared with about 290 parts per million at the end of the nineteenth century. The indirect effect—the trapping of heat within the atmosphere, the so-called glasshouse effect—is however not so easily evaluated.* Nature 5/5/72, p5 [**1972**]

glassteel, *adj.* made of glass and steel. *The only trouble is that the Sondheim score does not have any integrity. It flirts with various styles, and is as neutral and eclectic as the glassteel skyscraper projections used as a backdrop.* Harper's 7/70, p108 [**1970**]

glass tissue, *British.* a fabric made of fiberglass. *Glass tissue, of which the initial annual production will be about 60 square metres, can be used as a base for roofing materials, wall covering, and other building purposes.* Times (London) 4/2/76, p20 [**1976**]

GLCM, abbreviation or acronym of *ground-launched cruise missile.* See CRUISE MISSILE. *The GLCM (or "glickum," in Pentagon jargon), to be deployed in Britain, West Germany and Italy, and later, perhaps, in Belgium and The Netherlands, is a dry-land version of the U.S. Navy's Tomahawk sea-launched cruise missile. It is designed to be a subsonic weapon with a range of about 1,500 miles and a lot of maneuverability. . . .* Time 12/24/79, p30 [**1979**]

gleamer, *n.* a cosmetic for making the skin of the face gleam. *Some* [candidates for Miss Teenage America Pageant in Texas] *wore pancake or foundation and blotches spread, islands of*

Figure 2.6   The *Third Barnhart Dictionary of New English*, 206.
Reprinted by permission of the H. W. Wilson Company.

police officer or with your father. Literary passages, also, have a register. For example, the passage from Hemingway's "Hills Like White Elephants" (Appendix Section I) is neutral in register, with mostly "core" vocabulary such as *hills, sun, long, white, made, hung.* As we observed earlier in this chapter, words in this register usually date back at least to Middle English times: they are native English words or borrowings from spoken Latin, Old Norse, or Old French. Contrast this passage with the passage from D.H. Lawrence, also in Appendix Section I. The Lawrence passage is written in a formal register, with formal, Latinate vocabulary such as *desolate, attempting, desultory,* and *consultation.*

EXERCISE 25.   In this exercise, you will be asked to comment on the register of several of the literary passages in Appendix Section I.

a. List ten content words from the Hemingway passage that were already present in Old English. Are there any words in this list that do not belong to the core vocabulary of English?

b. The Hemingway passage also contains a number of words that were borrowed into English in Middle English times. List ten of them. Do these words belong to the core vocabulary of English, or are some of them formal or technical in register? What did Hemingway accomplish by choosing mostly core vocabulary for this passage?

c. Find five Latin or French borrowings in the D.H. Lawrence passage. What is the register of this passage? What is the literary effect of this choice of register?

d. The James Joyce passage uses vocabulary that was already present in English by Middle English times. (Can you find any exceptions to this statement?) However, rather than being conversational in register, this passage has a rather "poetic" register, in that some of its words are found more typically in poetry than in fiction. List five words from this passage that seem to you to be poetic.

e. The Toni Morrison passage has a mixed register, in that some sections are conversational in register, while other sections use formal, Latinate vocabulary. Give examples of both registers. What does Morrison achieve by switching back and forth in this way from one register to another?

f. Consider the expository passages from Carson, Thomas, (Samuel Eliot) Morison, and Hawking. Judging from the samples in Appendix Section I, do expository writers use more or less Latinate vocabulary than fiction writers? Give a few examples. Some of the expository passages can be said to exemplify a "technical" register. Which passage is the most technical? Identify some words that give that passage a technical register.

Writers also make use of invented vocabulary; for example, J. K. Rowling's Harry Potter novels are full of invented words like *quidditch, muggle,* and *patronus.*

EXERCISE 26.   Find five invented words in the following poem by Quincy Troupe, and say how each word was formed. What is the effect of invented vocabulary in this poem?

take it to the hoop, magic johnson
by Quincy Troupe

take it to the hoop, "magic" johnson	1
take the ball dazzling down the open lane	2
herk & jerk & raise your six-foot, nine-inch frame	3
into air sweating screams of your neon name	4
"magic" johnson, nicknamed "Windex" way back in high school	5
'cause you wiped glass backboards so clean,	6
where you first juked & shook,	7
wiled your way to glory	8
a new-style fusion of Shake 'n Bake	9
energy, using everything possible,	10
you created your own space to fly through—	11
any moment now	12
we expect your wings to spread	13
feathers for that spooky take off of yours	14
then, shake & glide & ride up in space	15
till you hammer home a clothes-lining deuce off glass now,	16
come back down with a reverse hoodoo gem	17
off the spin & stick it in sweet, popping	18
nets clean from twenty feet, right side	19
so put the ball on the floor again, "magic"	20
slide the dribble behind your back,	21
ease it deftly between your bony stork legs, head bobbing everwhichaway	22
up & down, you see everything on the court	23
off the high yo-yo patter	24
stop & go dribble	25
you thread a needle-rope pass sweet home	26
to kareem cutting through the lane	27
his skyhook pops the cords	28
now, lead the fastbreak, hit worthy on the fly	29
now, blindside a pinpoint behind-the-back pass	30
for two more off the fake,	31
looking the other way,	32
you raise off balance into electric space	33
sweating chants of your name	34
turn, 180 degrees off the move, your legs scissoring space	35
like a swimmer's yo-yoing motion in deep water	36
stretching out now toward free flight	37
you double-pump through human trees	38
hang in place	39
slip the ball into your left hand	40
then deal it like a las vegas card dealer off squared glass	41

into nets, living up to your singular nickname	42
so "bad" you cartwheel the crowd	43
towards frenzy, wearing now your	44
electric smile, neon as your name	45
in victory, we suddenly sense your	46
glorious uplift your urgent need to be	47
champion	48
& so we cheer with you,	49
rejoice with you, for this	50
quicksilver, quicksilver,	51
quicksilver moment of fame,	52
so put the ball on the floor again, "magic"	53
juke & dazzle, Shake 'n Bake down the lane	54
take the sucker to the hoop, "magic" johnson	55
recreate reverse hoodoo gems off the spin	56
deal alley-oop dunkathon magician passes	57
now, double-pump, scissor, vamp through space	58
hang in place	59
& put it all up in the sucker's face, "magic" johnson,	60
& deal the roundball, like the juju man that you am	61
like the sho-nuff shaman that you am, "magic,"	62
like the sho-nuff spaceman you am	63

2.9 Applications for Students and Teachers of Writing

Children learn how to *speak* English before they learn to write it. In fact, some scholars speculate that the custom of starting school at age 5 or 6 is based on our informal observation that children of this age seem to have mastered conversational English; now that they can speak almost as well as adults, we reason, it's time for them to begin learning to read and write.

Children's early writing closely parallels their speech; at this stage the children are learning how to write down the words that they would use in telling a story orally. However, because the children have heard written stories read aloud, they also have some familiarity with written registers. Thus, in the writing samples from first-, second-, and third-graders in Appendix Section II, two of the children begin their stories with the expression *Once upon a time*, which is the traditional beginning in children's storybooks.

EXERCISE 27.

a. Look over the samples of first-, second-, and third-grade writing in Appendix Sections II and III. Find three words or expressions that, in your view, belong to the written register of English and three that belong, properly, to a conversational register. The point of this exercise is for you to see that the children are starting to develop an understanding of the differences between the spoken and written English, but they still have a long way to go.

b. High school and college writers sometimes use conversational vocabulary in contexts that call for a more formal register. Look through the secondary-school essays in Appendix Section IV and your own writing sample in Appendix Section V to see if you can find any problems of this sort.

When children begin to read fluently and copiously, usually in fifth or sixth grade, they go through a stage of rapid vocabulary development in which they acquire hundreds of words from Latin and Greek—words that are found in written stories and textbooks but only rarely in speech. If you are around children of this age, you may be amused to hear them mispronouncing words like *subtle* or *innocuous* which they have learned from their reading. Some of this elevated vocabulary shows up in the children's writing; for example, the fourth-grade story "Billy's Unusual Frog" contains several Latinate words (*unique, customer, purchase*) and one Greek borrowing (*aerobics*).

EXERCISE 28.

a. First look over the samples of first-, second-, and third-grade writing in the Appendix Sections II and III and satisfy yourself that there is very little Latinate vocabulary in the children's writing at this level. Then look at the older writers (grade 5 and beyond) in Appendix Sections II and III and make a list of Latinate words that you find.

b. Look over your own writing sample(s) in Appendix Section IV. How much Latinate vocabulary do you use? (Give examples.) Does your choice of vocabulary depend on the type of writing you are doing? For example, if you write both academic papers and fictional narratives, do you use Latinate vocabulary with equal frequency in the two genres?

2.10 Applications for ESL Teachers

As we observed earlier in this chapter, native speakers of English generally learn first the Germanic portion of our vocabulary and then the borrowings from Latin and Greek. (Words that were borrowed from Old French in Middle English times have an intermediate status; some of them, such as *family* and *table*, belong to the core vocabulary that we learn as children; others, such as *disperse* and *induce*, are part of the academic vocabulary that we learn in school.)

ESL students approach the vocabulary of English in a different way. Speakers of German may follow a pattern that resembles that of native English speakers, since core vocabulary like *house* (*Haus*), *cool* (*kühl*), and *thanks* (*Danke*) will carry over from their first language with very little change. However, students who come from Romance languages may find our Latinate vocabulary to be easier and more familiar than our Germanic vocabulary. A Spanish-speaking student may find it more natural to say "Extinguish the lights" than "Turn off the lights" (cf. Spanish *extinguir* 'extinguish, switch off'); these students will need extra help with the vocabulary of everyday conversation. Speakers from both language backgrounds have to be careful of false cognates; for example, Spanish speakers learning English are sometimes confused by *sympathy* cards, which sound too much like friendship cards (*simpatía* 'affection') and German speakers have to be careful with *dame*, which is related to the German word *Dame* 'woman,' but has a very different connotation in English.

Despite these difficulties, students whose first-language vocabularies overlap with that of English have an enormous advantage over those from languages like Japanese, Chinese, Hungarian, and Turkish, which share little, if any, of our vocabulary. Students from these language backgrounds are in almost the same situation as a child learning English as a first language, in that they have to learn the entire vocabulary of English from scratch. You may find, however, that these ESL students have a stronger grasp of our academic Latinate vocabulary than of the words we use in ordinary conversation; students who have studied English in their own countries have almost always had more exposure to written language, in books, than to the English that we speak in our daily lives.

2.11 Summary of the Chapter

In this chapter, we have traced the history of English and observed that our words come from three sources:

1. Native vocabulary
2. Borrowed vocabulary
3. Invented vocabulary

English has borrowed words from five main sources:

a. From (spoken) Latin into Old English
b. From Old Norse into Old English and Middle English
c. From Old French into Middle English in the aftermath of the Norman invasion
d. From the classical languages Latin and Greek into Middle English and Modern English
e. From modern spoken languages into Modern English

We also constantly invent new words, by the following methods:

a. Imitation or "Onomatopoeia"
b. Reduplication
c. Formation of Compounds and Idiomatic Phrases
d. Affixation or "Derivation"
e. Acronymy
f. Shortening or "Clipping"
g. Blending
h. Category Shift
i. Semantic Extension

The register of a word in Modern English is often related to its historical origin. For example, most native English words are neutral in register (meaning that they can be used in any context), while words that were borrowed from the classical languages are usually formal or technical in register. The same is true for invented vocabulary: reduplicated words (*flimflam, harum-scarum*) have a playful feel in English, shortened words are common in slang, and acronyms are characteristic of institutional language. Because of this connection between origin and register, speakers of English can often guess the origin of a word without looking it up. However, information about historical origin can also be found in college dictionaries, which provide etymologies for both native and borrowed words. Dictionaries usually do not provide etymologies for invented words, since, in most cases, the origin of the word is obvious from its form.

English-speaking children have a good mastery of the core vocabulary of English by the time they begin school. As they learn to read fluently and have more exposure to written English, they gradually develop a larger, more formal vocabulary, including many words that were borrowed into English from classical languages. Writers of all ages must take care to choose the appropriate register for a particular piece of writing and to stay consistently in that register throughout the piece. The choice of register is an important part of a writer's "style." Some writers prefer formal, Latinate vocabulary, while others deliberately adopt a neutral or even informal register.

ESL students follow a more complicated path into the vocabulary of English. Which words seem easier and most natural to them often depends on the overlap (if any) between English and their previous language(s). The nature of these students' vocabularies also depends on the circumstances in which they have studied English.

CHAPTER 3

The Grammatical Properties of Words: Morphology and "Parts of Speech"

A part of speech . . . is not a kind of meaning; it is a kind of token that obeys certain formal rules, like a chess piece or a poker chip.

—Steven Pinker, 1994

3.1 Introduction

The way words combine to form new words, phrases, and sentences is determined by their membership in grammatical categories such as *noun, verb, adjective,* or *adverb*. Traditional grammarians identified eight "parts of speech," based on a classification that was developed, originally, by the ancient Greeks:

> *nouns*
> *pronouns*
> *verbs*
> *adjectives*
> *adverbs*
> *prepositions*
> *conjunctions*
> *interjections*

EXERCISE 1. Assign the following words to the categories in the list above: *her, thin, tall, and, honesty, ouch, under.*

Some of the traditional categories are very diverse. For example, the traditional category **adjectives** includes words like *some* and *this* as well as those like *small* and *noisy*, and the traditional category **verbs** includes words like *will* and *may* as well as those like *sing* and *sleep*. The category **adverb** is the most diverse, including words like *too, very, however,* and *nevertheless,* as well as those like *sweetly* and *quietly*.

Modern grammarians find it useful to set up a longer list of categories, as shown in Table 3.1, with a more precise definition of each category. With this longer list, each category can be given a more uniform membership. For example, if the words *some* and *this* are called "determiners" rather than "adjectives," then the label "adjective" can be reserved for words like *small* and *noisy*, which modify nouns (*a small house, a noisy motor*) and which can be compared (*smaller, noisier*).

The syntactic categories can be divided into two sets, as shown in Table 3.1 on the following page. The *content* categories (noun, verb, adjective, and adverb) provide most of the meaning

Table 3.1   Modern Grammatical Categories

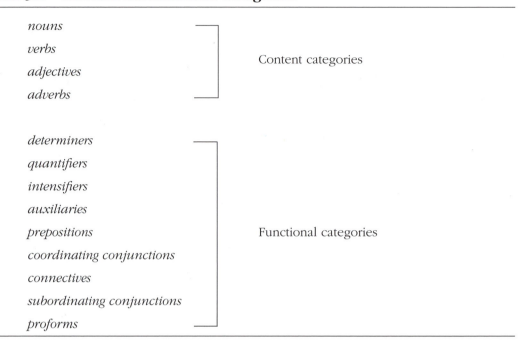

nouns	
verbs	
adjectives	Content categories
adverbs	
determiners	
quantifiers	
intensifiers	
auxiliaries	
prepositions	Functional categories
coordinating conjunctions	
connectives	
subordinating conjunctions	
proforms	

of a sentence; the *functional* (or *structural*) categories set up the grammatical structure of the sentence—for example, they help to indicate whether a particular word is a noun or a verb. The functional categories are also sometimes called "closed" categories, because they seldom add new members; words are invented or borrowed into the "open" categories—noun, verb, adjective, and adverb. In this chapter, we will consider first the functional categories, one by one, and then the content categories. The content categories have the same names as their traditional counterparts but will be defined in a slightly different way. As you work through this chapter, you may find it useful to refer to the charts in Figures 3.1 and 3.2 at the end of this chapter. Figure 3.1 shows the correspondence between the traditional and modern systems. Figure 3.2 provides a summary of the inflectional forms for each content category.

3.2   The Functional Categories

Determiners appear before a noun and indicate how the referent of the noun is to be chosen. In other words, in noun phrases like *the book, a house, this garbage, my dog, every assignment,* etc., the determiner helps the reader or listener to determine which book, house, garbage, or dog the speaker has in mind. There are two subclasses of determiners. **Definite determiners** such as *the, this, that, my, your,* and so on pick out entities whose identity is clear to both speaker and hearer. **Indefinite determiners** such as *a, every, some,* and *any* pick out referents whose identity has not yet been fully specified. A noun has at most one determiner: **the a book; *this my house.* [The asterisk (*) indicates that a sentence or phrase is ungrammatical.]

Quantifiers are noun modifiers that indicate quantity: *one* world, *two* trees, *many* moons, *all people,* and so on. Quantifiers can co-occur with determiners: *these two trees, her many friends, all the members,* and so forth.

Intensifiers modify adjectives and adverbs. They indicate degree: <u>*very*</u> *tall,* <u>*too*</u> *tall,* <u>*this*</u> *tall,* <u>*very*</u> *slowly,* <u>*too*</u> *slowly,* <u>*this*</u> *slowly.* The intensifier *enough* is irregular in that it *follows* the adjective or adverb it modifies: *tall <u>enough</u>; slowly <u>enough</u>.*

Auxiliaries appear before the verb in statements (<u>*can*</u> *swim,* <u>*will*</u> *understand,* <u>*may*</u> *leave,* and so on), but move to the left in questions. There are two classes of auxiliaries: (1) the modal auxiliaries *can, could, may, might, will, would, shall, should,* and *must:*

Statement	Question
She *can* swim.	*Can* she swim?
They *will* understand.	*Will* they understand?
We *may* leave.	*May* we leave?

and (2) the auxiliary verbs (*have*$_{perfect}$, *be*$_{progressive}$, *be*$_{passive}$, and *do*):

	Statement	Question
have$_{perf}$	George *has* left.	*Has* George left?
be$_{prog}$	They *are* eating.	*Are* they eating?
be$_{pass}$	The desserts *are* made on the premises.	*Are* the desserts made on the premises?
do	You *do* understand.	*Do* you understand?

Both types of auxiliaries move to the left in questions, but auxiliary verbs have the additional property that they must agree with the subject: *she <u>has</u> spoken, they <u>have</u> spoken* vs. *she <u>can</u> swim, they <u>can</u> swim.* Auxiliaries are very important in the grammar of English, and you will be hearing a lot about them as you work through this text.

EXERCISE 2.

a. In the following examples, which *is* is the main verb *be* and which is the auxiliary *be: She is here* vs. *She is studying*? How do you know?

b. In the following examples, which *was* is an instance of *be*$_{prog}$ and which is an instance of *be*$_{pass}$: *He was leaving* vs. *He was left*? How do you know?

Prepositions join with noun phrases to form prepositional phrases: <u>*in*</u> *the house,* <u>*at*</u> *the zoo,* <u>*around*</u> *the block,* <u>*before*</u> *lunch,* and so forth. Here is a list of common prepositions:

about	*above*	*across*	*after*	*against*
among	*around*	*ago*	*as*	*at*
before	*behind*	*below*	*beside*	*between*
but	*by*	*despite*	*down*	*during*
for	*from*	*in*	*inside*	*into*
off	*on*	*out*	*over*	*past*
since	*than*	*through*	*to*	*toward*
under	*until*	*up*	*with*	*without*

The preposition *ago* is irregular in that it *follows* its object: *three years <u>ago</u>.*

The **coordinating conjunctions** *and, or, but, yet,* and *so* join two or more constituents of the same type, as in *The exercise was easy, <u>but</u> it was very long* (where the conjunction *but* joins two sentences), or *Jack <u>and</u> Jill went up the hill* (where the conjunction *and* joins two nouns). Coordinating conjunctions sometimes have two parts—e.g., <u>both</u> *Jack <u>and</u> Jill,* with one part at the beginning and one in the middle, as shown. Conjunctions of this type are called *correlative conjunctions.* Other correlative conjunctions are *either . . . or, neither . . . nor,* and *not only . . . but.*

Connectives like *however, furthermore,* and *nevertheless* (traditionally called *conjunctive adverbs*) indicate a logical relationship between two ideas:

> *The exercise was easy; <u>however</u>, it was very long.*
> *The exercise was difficult; <u>furthermore</u>, it was very long.*

Connectives differ from coordinating conjunctions in that they do not create a *grammatical* link between constituents—only a logical one. Thus the component sentences in the examples above (*the exercise was easy/difficult* and *it was very long*) must be joined by a semicolon (;). If the semicolon is replaced by a comma, the result is a fused sentence of the type called a "comma-splice":

> **The exercise was easy, however it was very long.*
> (cf.   *The exercise was easy; however, it was very long,*
>   *The exercise was very easy, but it was very long.*)

We will come back to this point in Chapter 13.

Subordinating conjunctions such as *that, because, if,* and *although* convert a sentence into a subordinate or "dependent" clause—that is, the sentence can no longer stand on its own but becomes part of a larger sentence:

> *[<u>Because</u> the wind was behind us], we made better time.*
> *[<u>Although</u> I told the truth], no one believed me.*
> *[<u>That</u> he lost the election] was hardly surprising.*
> *I didn't ask [<u>if</u> he would be here].*

Proforms are words that substitute for other expressions. They take their reference from the context in which they appear—either from an "antecedent" that occurred previously in the utterance or from the situation in which utterance is used. The underlined proforms in the following examples all take their reference from an antecedent:

> *When the people heard his words, <u>they</u> were astonished.* The antecedent of the proform *they* is *the people.*
> *If I see you on Sunday, we'll discuss it <u>then</u>.* The antecedent of the proform *then* is *on Sunday.*
> *If I see you at the meeting, we'll discuss it <u>there</u>.* The antecedent of the proform *there* is *at the meeting.*
> *I've never eaten snails and I hope never to <u>do so</u>.* The antecedent of the proform *do so* is *eaten snails.*

However, the following proforms take their reference from outside the sentence:

> *They* did it (pointing to a group of students).
> Put it *there* (pointing to a position on the floor).

The reference of proforms like *I* and *you* always depends on the situational context—we don't know who "I" is unless we know who is speaking.

The class of proforms can be divided into several subclasses. The most familiar of these is the class of ***personal pronouns***, which substitute for noun phrases: *When the dog heard a noise, he* [= the dog] *began to bark.* Personal pronouns are "inflected" for person (1st, 2nd, or 3rd), number (singular or plural), case (subject, object, or possessive), and gender (masculine, feminine, or neuter), as shown in Table 3.2. Notice the generic pronouns *you* (informal) and *one* (formal), as in the examples below:

> **You** *never know what will happen next.*
> **One** *never knows what will happen next.*

Until the 17th century, English had an additional personal pronoun—the 2nd person singular pronoun *thou* (subject), *thee* (object), *thy/thine* (possessive). This was a "familiar" *you*, like the *tu* of French or Spanish or the *du* of German. As time went on, customs changed so that fewer and fewer people could be addressed with the familiar form; now, in modern English, it is used only in religious contexts, as a term of address for God. That leaves us with just one 2nd person pronoun, *you,* which is used for both singular and plural. (But notice that some spoken dialects have introduced 2nd-person plural pronouns, like the Southern American pronoun *y'all* or the Pennsylvania pronouns *youse* and *y'un*).

Table 3.2   Personal Pronouns

Number	Person	Subject or Nominative Case	Object or Accusative Case	Possessive Case Determiner	Possessive Case Independent Pronoun
Singular	First person	*I*	*me*	*my*	*mine*
	Second person				
	personal	*you*	*you*	*your*	*yours*
	generic	*you*	*you*	*your*	*yours*
	Third person				
	masculine	*he*	*him*	*his*	*his*
	feminine	*she*	*her*	*her*	*hers*
	neuter	*it*	*it*	*its*	—
	generic	*one*	*one*	*one's*	—
Plural	First person	*we*	*us*	*our*	*ours*
	Second person	*you*	*you*	*your*	*yours*
	Third person	*they*	*them*	*their*	*theirs*

EXERCISE 3.   Find personal pronouns in the Lawrence, Thomas, and Morrison passages in Appendix Section I, and say whether each pronoun takes its reference from the situational context or from an antecedent. What antecendent? Are there any pronouns whose reference is difficult to determine?

The ***reflexive pronouns*** of English are listed in Table 3.3. Reflexive pronouns are inflected for person (1st, 2nd, 3rd), number (singular or plural), and gender (masculine, feminine, neuter). A reflexive pronoun is required when the antecedent is inside the same clause as the pronoun, as shown below:

> *We played with the toys, and* [***the children*** *painted* ***themselves*** *with magic markers*].
> (The reflexive pronoun *themselves* and its antecedent *the children* are in the same clause.)

EXERCISE 4.
a. Sometimes a reflexive pronoun is used to emphasize an existing noun phrase, as in the example *George* ***himself*** *would never hurt you*. A reflexive pronoun that is used in this way is called an "intensive" pronoun. Find an intensive pronoun in the Lawrence passage in Appendix Section I.
b. Some speakers use the forms *hisself* and *theirselves* in place of the standard 3rd-person reflexive pronouns *himself* and *themselves*. What is the logic behind these non-standard forms? (*Hint:* Try to state a "rule" for the formation of reflexive pronouns in Standard English and then in this non-Standard dialect, beginning with the 1st- and 2nd-person pronouns, and then moving to the 3rd person.)

Table 3.3   Reflexive Pronouns

Reflexive pronouns		Singular	Plural
First person		*myself*	*ourselves*
Second person		*yourself*	*yourselves*
Third person	masculine	*himself*	*themselves*
	feminine	*herself*	
	neuter	*itself*	

English also has two **reciprocal pronouns**—*each other* and *one another*. Reciprocal pronouns are like reflexive pronouns, in that the pronoun and its antecedent are in the same clause:

> *Bill and Susan know* [*that **we** met **each other/one another** on the Internet*]. (The reciprocal pronoun *each other/one another* and its antecedent *we* are in the same clause.)

Some determiners and quantifiers, including *this, that, some,* and *all,* may also act as pronouns. We will call these **determiner pronouns**:

> **This** *is my mother.*
> **All** *of us are worried.*

A word of this class is considered a determiner or quantifier if it is followed by a noun, but if it stands alone, without a noun after it, then it is considered a pronoun.[1]

EXERCISE 5.   Identify each underlined word as a determiner, quantifier, or pronoun:
a. *I certainly didn't expect her to say <u>that</u>.*
b. *<u>This</u> puzzle is too hard for me.*
c. *<u>All</u> men are mortal.*
d. *We'll give it our <u>all</u>.*

Finally, pronouns like *one,*[2] *everybody, everyone, somebody, someone, nobody, no one, something,* etc. are called **indefinite pronouns**. These pronouns differ from the personal pronouns that we looked at above in that they substitute for *part* of a noun phrase rather than the entire phrase. For example, in the sentence *I'd like* [*the green **one***], the indefinite pronoun *one* substitutes just for the head noun (*the green <u>pencil</u>*, perhaps). Indefinite pronouns such as *somebody* and *something* are exceptional, in that a modifying adjective must come after the pronoun rather than before it:

> *Let me introduce you to **somebody nice**.* (**a nice somebody*)
> **Something awful** *had happened.* (**an awful something*)

---

1. This may lead you to wonder whether there is really a distinction between determiners and pronouns. Some linguists have argued that they are, in fact, two manifestations of a single category.
2. This is the *one* of *a green one.* It has the same spelling and pronunciation as the generic personal pronoun *one* (**one** *never knows who may show up for class*), but it has a different meaning and different grammatical behavior.

Other minor categories. This discussion does not exhaust the grammatical categories of English. English, like other languages, contains additional small sets of words that should, ideally, be treated as separate categories. For example, the infinitive particle *to* (as in ***To** know her is **to** love her*) does not fit neatly into any category; it is in a category by itself. And what about *ever* and *never*? What category do they belong to? To avoid loose ends, words like these are sometimes squeezed into other categories; for example, *ever* and *never* are sometimes classified as adverbs. But they really constitute separate categories, too small to be given names of their own.

EXERCISE 6.   Read through the transcription of the child "Eve" in Appendix Section VIII and answer the following questions:

a. When children first begin to speak, they use a "telegraphic" syntax in which most function words are omitted. Notice this phenomenon in Eve's speech at 18 months. Does she use any function words at all? What content categories (nouns, verbs, adjectives, adverbs) does she use?

b. By the age of 27 months, Eve has added many of the functional categories that were missing earlier. Which functional categories are now included, and which are still missing? Please consider the following functional categories: *determiners, quantifiers, auxiliaries, intensifiers, prepositions, connectives, coordinating conjunctions, subordinating conjunctions, proforms.* (Notice that Eve also sometimes omits the main verb *be,* which has some characteristics of a function word. Omission of the verb *be* (the "copula") is common in children's speech at this stage.)

c. Which of the *content* categories (nouns, verbs, adjectives, adverbs) does Eve use/not use at 27 months? Obviously she would not be able to tell us the *names* of these categories, but does she know which category each word belongs to? How can you tell?

3.3 The Content (Open) Categories

The categories noun, verb, adjective, and adverb are called *content* categories because they carry the meaning (the semantic content) of the sentence. These categories are also called *open* categories, because they willingly accept new members; words that have been borrowed into English from other languages belong almost exclusively to the content categories.

You are probably familiar with the traditional definitions of these categories:

Noun	The name of a person, place, or thing.
Verb	A word that expresses action or being.
Adjective	A word that modifies a noun.
Adverb	A word that modifies a verb, an adjective, or another adverb.

Modern grammarians find several problems in these definitions. First, they are inconsistent, in that two of them (noun and verb) are based on *meaning*, while the other two (adjective and adverb) are based on the function of the word in a sentence. To be consistent, we should define the categories *adjective* and *adverb* in semantic terms:

Adjective   A word that describes a person, place, or thing.

Adverb   A word that describes the manner, frequency, or degree of an action or condition.

Secondly, the application of the definitions is unclear in some cases. For example, the words *appetite* and *impossibility* are nouns, yet neither of them is the name of a person, place, or thing. Exceptions of this sort are usually dealt with by extending the definition of a noun to include qualities and ideas as well as persons, places, and things, but it is not clear, then, when the definition is complete. Similarly, the word *seem* is a verb even though it does not express action or being, and the word *action,* which does express action, is a noun rather than a verb.

The third and most serious problem with the traditional definitions is that we can usually identify the syntactic category of a word in context even when we *do not know* its meaning, as in Lewis Carroll's (1897) poem "Jabberwocky," excerpted below from *Through the Looking Glass*:

> *'Twas brillig, and the slithy toves*
> *Did gyre and gimble in the wabe;*
> *All mimsy were the borogoves,*
> *And the mome raths outgrabe.*

Most people agree that *slithy, mimsy,* and *mome* are adjectives, that *toves, wabe, borogoves,* and *raths* are nouns, and that *gyre* and *gimble* are verbs. *Brillig* is either an adjective or a noun (on the pattern of *'Twas cloudy* or *'Twas evening*) and *outgrabe* is probably a verb. The fact that we can identify the categories of these words without knowing their meaning shows that, contrary to the traditional definitions, we do not rely entirely on meaning when we assign words to categories; our judgement is also based on formal characteristics such as the morphological composition of the word and its position in the sentence. For example, *slithy* can be identified as an adjective by its position between the determiner *the* and the noun *toves,* and this identification is further supported by the final *-y,* which appears to be the adjective-forming suffix of *sand-y, slim-y,* and *water-y.*

EXERCISE 7.   Give evidence for the syntactic category of each open-class word in the "Jabberwocky" stanza, as in the discussion of the word *slithy,* just above. *Caution:* Since you do not know the meanings of these words, you will have to rely on observations about the words' position or morphological composition.

The characteristic semantic, morphological, and syntactic properties of nouns, verbs, adjectives, and adverbs are set out in Tables 3.4 through 3.7. Note that individual members of these categories do not necessarily satisfy *all* these criteria; rather, a word is assigned to a category on the grounds that it satisfies *some* of the criteria for that category and none of the criteria for the other open-class categories.

Table 3.4   Noun

Meaning: Names an entity such as a person, place, thing, or idea.

Affixation: May end with a noun-forming suffix such as

-er/-or	*owner, actor*
-ity	*brevity*
-ment	*government*
-ness	*happiness*
-th	*strength*
-(t)ion	*vision, rendition*
-ure	*creature*

Inflection: Takes one or more of the inflectional forms that are typical of nouns:

singular	*John*	*chair*	*appetite*
plural	—	*chairs*	*appetites*
singular possessive	*John's*	*chair's*	*appetite's*
plural possessive	—	*chairs'*	*appetites'*

Some nouns—including *man, child,* and *deer*—make their plural irregularly.

Syntactic position: Occupies positions such as the following:

a. After a determiner plus optional adjective within a noun phrase: *an (ornate)* <u>*bannister*</u>
b. After a verb such as *enjoy: enjoy* <u>*movies*</u>
c. After a preposition such as *about: about* <u>*money*</u>

Nouns are divided into two subclasses: *proper* vs. *common.* Proper nouns such as *George Bush* name individual persons, places, or things and (in the singular) they do not accept a determiner (**the George Bush*). Common nouns, such as *city* or *person,* name categories of things rather than individual things.

The class of common nouns is, in turn, divided into two subclasses: *Count nouns* and *non-count or "mass" nouns.* Count nouns have a singular and plural form (*chair ~ chairs*), and the singular form requires a determiner such as *a(n): I'd like a chair,* not **I'd like chair."* Noncount nouns like *homework, happiness,* and *honesty* appear to be singular, in that they take a singular verb (*is* rather than *are*), but they do not accept the determiner *a(n)* (**Please don't give us **a** homework*) and they have no plural (*honesty ~ *honesties*).

Table 3.5   Verb

Meaning: Indicates the occurrence of an action, event, process, or situation.

Affixation: May carry a verb-forming affix such as

-ate	*designate*
-ify	*terrify*
-ize	*unionize*
-en	*darken*
en-	*enroll, ennoble*

Inflection: Takes the inflectional forms that are typical of verbs in English:

base form:	*go*	*put*	*play*
general present tense:	*go*	*put*	*play*
present tense third person singular:	*goes*	*puts*	*plays*
past tense:	*went*	*put*	*played*
present participle (after *be$_{prog}$*):	*going*	*putting*	*playing*
perfect participle (after *have$_{perf}$*):	*gone*	*put*	*played*
passive participle (after *be$_{pass}$*):	—	*put*	*played*

Verbs like *play,* which make their past tense, perfect participle, and passive participle with the suffix *-ed*, are called "regular" verbs. *Go* and *put* are "irregular" verbs.

Syntactic position: Occupies positions such as the following:

a. after the infinitive particle *to* in an infinitive: *to jump, to seem*
b. after an auxiliary: *should go, may be, is going, has gone, was decided*

In Standard English, a verb is modified by an adverb rather than an adjective:

Drive *carefully*.   (*Drive *careful*.)

(The asterisk, remember, indicates that the sentence is ungrammatical.)

Note that English verbs have two present-tense forms—the "general" form which has no suffix, and the 3rd-person singular form, which carries the inflectional suffix *-s*:

I think	*we think*
you think	*you (pl) think*
*he/she/it think**s***	*they think*

The use of an affix to make the verb agree with the subject is called "subject-verb agreement."

Table 3.6   Adjective

Meaning: Attributes a quality or condition to some entity.

Affixation: May end with an adjective-forming suffix such as

-able	*readable*
-ed	*frightened*
-ful	*hopeful*
-(i)al	*controversial*
-ic(al)	*historic(al)*
-ing	*frightening*
-ish	*childish*
-ive	*defective*
-less	*hopeless*
-ous	*pompous*
-y	*sandy*

Inflection: Has positive, comparative, and superlative forms:

positive:	*tall*	*intelligent*	*good*	*bad*
comparative:	*taller*	*more intelligent*	*better*	*worse*
superlative:	*tallest*	*most intelligent*	*best*	*worst*

Regular adjectives form their comparative with *-er* or *more* and their superlative with *-est* or *most*. Adjectives like *good* and *bad* are irregular (**gooder, *baddest*).

Syntactic position: Occupies syntactic positions such as the following:

a. Following an intensifier such as *very* or *too*: *very* <u>*tall*</u>, *too* <u>*rainy*</u>.
b. Between the determiner and the noun of a noun phrase: *a* <u>*tall*</u> *tree, a* <u>*rainy*</u> *day*. Adjectives that occupy this position are called "attributive" or "pre-nominal" adjectives.
c. After the linking verb *seem,* which, in American English, requires an adjective phrase as its complement: *The paper seemed* <u>*satisfactory*</u>. Adjectives that occupy this position are called "predicate adjectives."

Some adjectives, such as *atomic, hydrochloric,* and *wooden* (with the meaning 'made of wood'), do not allow comparison or modification with intensifiers (**This bomb is very atomic*). Adjectives of this type are called *nongradable adjectives*. The adjectives *unique* and *perfect* should, logically, be nongradable, but they are sometimes treated as gradable, as in the opening lines of the Constitution:

> *We the people of the United States of America, in order to form a* <u>*more perfect*</u> *union . . .*

Table 3.7   Adverb

Meaning: Indicates the manner, frequency, or degree of an action or condition.

Affixation: Is normally formed by adding the suffix *-ly* to an adjective:[3]

slow	→	*slowly*
occasional	→	*occasionally*
terrible	→	*terribly*

Inflection: Has positive, comparative, and superlative forms, usually created by adding the intensifiers *more* and *most*:

positive	*slowly*
comparative	*more slowly*
superlative	*most slowly*

Syntactic position: Occupies positions such as the following:

a. Following an intensifier, as in *very <u>slowly</u>; too <u>slowly</u>.*
b. As the modifier of a verb, as in *He did it <u>carefully</u>,* or of an entire sentence, as in *<u>Obviously</u>, he did it.*

EXERCISE 8.

a. List the inflectional forms (singular, plural, singular possessive, plural possessive) of the following nouns: *sheep, house, loyalty, foot.* Which of these nouns are irregular?

b. List the inflectional forms (base form, general present tense, 3rd person singular present tense, past tense, present participle, perfect participle, passive participle) of the following verbs: *think, enjoy, bring, swim, dive, lie down, wake up.* Identify each verb as regular or irregular. If you are like most people, you will be uncertain about some of the inflectional forms for these verbs; in that case, look up the verb in the dictionary and say whether the inflectional paradigm that the dictionary provides is the same as the one you use in ordinary conversation.

c. List the inflectional forms (positive, comparative, superlative) of the following adjectives: *young, good, bad, fast, happy, narrow, handsome, beautiful, flexible.* Which are irregular? For regular adjectives, what determines whether the adjective is inflected with *-er/-est* or with *more/most?*

d. The following nouns lack one or more of the inflectional forms that are typical for nouns: *homework, trousers, news.* For each noun, determine which inflectional forms are present/absent.

---

3. Some adjectives can be converted to adverbs without adding *-ly*. For example,

    This car is <u>fast</u> (Adj).   *She spoke <u>very fast</u>* (Adv).

EXERCISE 9. Name the category and inflectional form of the following words; for example, you would say that *toys* is a noun in the plural form and *tiny* is an adjective in the positive form. Some examples have more than one possible answer. A summary of the inflectional forms is provided in Figure 3.2 at the end of this chapter.

toys	*tiny*	*children's*	*unremarkable*
calculating	*bookshops*	*listened*	*kitten's*
improbability	*happiest*	*disarms*	*untidiness*
fatherly	*repayment*	*realignments*	*stolen*

EXERCISE 10.

a. Words ending in *-ed* or *-en* may be adjectives or verbs. In the sentences below, say whether the underlined words are adjectives or verbs. *Hint:* Consider whether the word can be modified with an intensifier like *very*, and whether the verb *be* could be replaced with *seem*.

    i.   *The students will be <u>exhausted</u>.*

    ii. *Their supplies will be <u>exhausted</u>.*

    iii. *Their parents will be <u>worried</u>.*

    iv. *Their money will be <u>stolen</u>.*

b. (*Advanced*) Verbs in the present participle (*-ing*) form may, over time, be converted to the category noun or adjective. Determine the category of the *-ing* words in the following sentences and give evidence to support your answer. *Hint:* Consider whether the word is or could be preceded by a determiner, auxiliary, or intensifier and whether it is or could be modified by an adjective or an adverb. Some examples have more than one possible answer.

    i.   *The movie was <u>boring</u>.*

    ii.   *The children had been <u>playing</u> in the alley.*

    iii.   *We were startled by the sudden <u>opening</u> of the door.*

    iv.   *<u>Playing</u> tennis is good exercise.*

    v.   *<u>Swimming</u> is good exercise.*

    vi.   *The children <u>playing</u> in the yard belong to my next door neighbor.*

    vii.   *Did you hear the <u>crying</u> of the loons?*

    viii. *We could hear a <u>crying</u> baby.*

    ix.   *We heard an <u>annoying</u> sound.*

EXERCISE 11. When space is at a premium, as in headlines and telegrams, we sometimes try to manage with content words alone (or *almost* alone), as in *Museum receives collection of books*, *Parking seen as last hurdle*, or *Arriving noon Sunday*. Sentences like these are called "telegraphic."

Because function words play an important role in identifying the categories of content words, telegraphic sentences are often ambiguous. Each of the following headlines[4] is ambiguous because it contains one or more words that can be understood either as a noun or as a verb. Find the ambiguous word(s) in each headline, and eliminate the ambiguity, if possible, by inserting appropriate function words. For example, the first headline is ambiguous because it is not clear whether *burn* is a verb (the silly meaning) or part of a compound noun (*burn victims*, the intended meaning). If we insert the infinitive particle *to* before *burn*, we identify this word as a verb: *Neighbors help [to] <u>burn</u> victims*; if, instead, we insert the determiner *the* before *burn,* we identify this word as (part of) a compound noun: *Neighbors help [the] <u>burn victims</u>*.

> *Neighbors help burn victims.*
> *Yellow perch decline to be studied.*
> *Canada seals deal with creditors.*
> *Spot searches dog bus riders.*
> *Hershey bars protest.*

3.4   The Internal Structure of Words

We have already observed (Chapter 2, Section 2.5), that words are made up of smaller parts called "morphemes." (If this doesn't sound familiar, go back to Chapter 2 and review Exercise 12.)

Morphemes can be classified as affixes or roots; English affixes are either prefixes (*un-, dis-, ex-,* etc.) or suffixes (*-ness, -ment, -y,* etc.). Affixes such as *-s* and *-ed,* which are used to create different grammatical forms of a single word, are called "inflectional affixes." Affixes such as *un-, dis-, -ity, -ize,* and *-ous,* which change the meaning or grammatical category of a word, are called "derivational" affixes.

EXERCISE 12.

a. English has ten inflectional suffixes. List the inflectional suffixes that create the following grammatical forms in regular nouns, verbs, and adjectives. For example, for noun plurals, the inflectional suffix is *-s*.

For nouns: plural, singular possessive,[5] plural possessive

For verbs: 3rd-person singular present tense, past tense, present participle, perfect participle, passive participle

For adjectives: comparative, superlative

---

4. These examples are taken from various issues of the *Columbia Review of Journalism,* which regularly publishes erroneous or ambiguous headlines.
5. Students sometimes ask how to spell the possessive suffixes for singular nouns that end in *s*, and plural nouns that don't end in *s*. For plural nouns that do not end in *s*, the possessive is spelled *'s*, as in *the children's toys*. For singular nouns that end in *s*, the answer depends on how the possessive suffix is pronounced. If it is pronounced as a separate syllable, then it is spelled in the normal way, as *'s*: the *Jones's house, Amos's house*. If the suffix is not pronounced as a separate syllable, then it is represented simply with an apostrophe: *Moses' brother*.

b. Affixes that change the meaning or grammatical category of the word to which they attach are called "derivational" affixes.

    i. Use derivational suffixes to convert the following words to nouns. For example, the adjective *active* can be converted to a noun by adding the suffix *-ity*.

active	*stupid*
please	*foolish*
invest	*teach*
follow	*warm*

    ii. Use derivational prefixes or suffixes to convert the following words to verbs. For example, the adjective *light* can be converted to a verb by adding the suffix *-en*.

light	*magnet*
code	*legal*
crystal	*sign*
hyphen	*weak*

c. Some verbs can be converted to nouns without adding an affix. This conversion, called "category shift" (Chapter 2), may be accompanied by a change in the position of stress; for example, the verb *record* has its stress on the second syllable, but the noun *record* is stressed on the *first* syllable. Decide, for each word, whether there is a change in the position of the stress when the word changes from a verb to a noun:

record	*remark*
convict	*surprise*
report	*progress*
protest	

EXERCISE 13. Fill in the following word-family chart; for example, for the adjective *final*, you should fill in the related words *finality*, *finalize*, and *finally*. In some cases, you will have to add and/or subtract a derivational affix; in others, a single form can be used in more than one category (by category shift). There are also cases in which the root of the word changes with a move from one category to another. *Caution:* Some blanks cannot be filled; don't force it!

Noun	Verb	Adjective	Adverb
		final	
	enjoy		
		eager	
fright			
	construct		
	think		
planet			
	compute		

Noun	Verb	Adjective	Adverb
		corrupt	
	reflect		
		perpetual	
		apparent	
	destroy		
sympathy			
colony			
		strong	
	describe		
mathematics			

The internal structure of a word can be displayed in the form of a "tree diagram" like the ones below, which show the structure of the compound words *blackboard* and *skydive,* the derived words *foolishness* and *unreliable,* and the inflected words *children's* and *unlocked*:

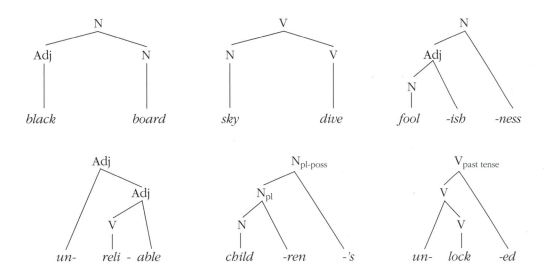

EXERCISE 14. Draw word trees like the ones above for the following words: *horseshoe, babysit, unproductive, dishonesty, reported, boys'*.

Words that are created in English, by English speakers, have "free" roots—meaning that the root of the word is already a word. For example, the word *blissful* was formed by attaching the suffix *-ful* to the root word *bliss*, and the word *unhappy* was formed by attaching the prefix *un-* to the root word *happy*. Words like *stult-ify, re-sist,* or *log-ic,* which have "bound" roots, were formed in Latin or Greek, not in English (see Chapter 2, Section 2.6). Some affixes are "mixed," appearing sometimes in Latin or Greek words, where they attach to bound roots, and sometimes in words that were created in English, where they attach to free roots. For example, our English prefix *dis-* (*dishonest, disloyal, dissatisfied*) is descended from the Latin prefix *dis-,* which appears in words like *discord, disturb*, and *disburse*. When *dis-* is used productively in English, it attaches to adjectives and carries the meaning 'not' (*dishonest = not honest*). But in words that we borrowed from Latin or French, *dis-* is attached to bound roots and carries the meaning 'apart'.

Affixes that are used productively in English follow a strict pattern with regard to the category or categories of the words they attach to, and the changes they effect in the category and meaning of that word. For example, as we saw in the previous paragraph, the productive prefix *dis-* attaches to adjectives and forms adjectives with the meaning 'not [adjective]'. Similarly, the productive suffix *-able* attaches to verbs (*washable, doable, readable, understandable,* etc.) and changes them to adjectives with the meaning 'able to be [verb]ed' These examples illustrate another property of English morphology—namely, that derivational *suffixes* usually change both the category and the meaning of the word, while derivational *prefixes* change only the meaning. The prefix *en-* of *encamp, entangle, enthrone,* etc. is an exception to this generalization, in that it changes nouns to verbs with the meaning 'put into/onto a [noun].'

EXERCISE 15. When a prefix or suffix is used to form a new word in English, it attaches to a complete word which belongs to a particular syntactic category. (Words like *stult-ify, re-sist,* or *log-ic,* in which affixes are attached to bound roots, were formed in Latin or Greek, not in English.) Consider the prefixes and suffixes below. From the examples given, determine a. what part of speech each affix combines with when it is used to form new words in English, b. what part of speech it forms, and c. the approximate meaning of the suffix. The first one is done for you, as an example:

i. *-able:* washable, doable, readable, understandable
    The suffix *-able* attaches to verbs and changes them to adjectives. The resultant word, *X-able,* means 'able to be X'd.'

ii. *-ful:* helpful, thankful, hopeful, sorrowful, harmful, peaceful

iii. *-ly₁-:* motherly, sisterly, friendly, homely, orderly

iv. *-ly₂ -:* quickly, happily, conscientiously, notoriously, unpleasantly

v. *-ity:* sanity, rigidity, hostility, intensity, responsibility

vi. *-ize:* unionize, crystallize, magnetize, hospitalize

vii. *-ion:* invention, injection, narration, expression, pollution

viii. *-en:* cheapen, worsen, shorten, weaken, redden, harden

ix. *dis-:* dishonest, dissatisfied, disloyal, disinterested, disinherit, disintegrate, disinfect

x. *en-:* encamp, encapsule, entangle, encrust, endanger, empanel, embody

xi. *in-:* inadequate, immeasurable, improper, insufferable, incorrigible, irreverent

xii. *re:* rethink, redo, rework, reconsider, replay, rewrap

3.5 Applications for Students and Teachers of Literature

Parts of Speech. Writers sometimes rely heavily on one or two parts of speech to do the descriptive work of a passage. For example, in the Hemingway passage in Appendix Section I, the verbs provide very little information (*were, was, sat, come, stopped, went on, etc.*); the description is carried by the nouns (*hills, valley, trees, station, rails, sun, shadow,* etc.) and the adjectives (*long, white, warm, open, hot*). Other writers may favor other parts of speech.

EXERCISE 16. Look over the Joyce passage and the passages from Carson and Thomas in Appendix Section I. What syntactic categories do the most descriptive work in these passages? Give examples to illustrate. (*Caution*: We are not concerned here with *how many* nouns, verbs, or adjectives the writer uses, but with which categories carry the most interesting and powerful meanings.)

Person. A narrative is said to be written in 1st, 2nd, or 3rd person, depending on whether the narrator is a character in the story or is looking on from the outside. In a 1st-person narrative, the story is told from one character's point of view, which may or may not be entirely reliable. A 3rd-person narrative provides a more objective "outside" viewpoint, but may not show us the inner feelings and thoughts of the characters. In some cases, however, a 3rd-person narrator is allowed to see into the minds of the characters; such a narrator is said to be "omniscient." In some 3rd-person narratives, the narrator identifies with one character more than others, and shows us what is passing through the mind of *that* character, while the thoughts and feelings of other characters remain hidden. Sometimes, less commonly, a narrative is written in *2nd* person, with the hearer or reader inserted as a participant into the events of the story. (This is different from a direct address to the reader, as in some traditional novels, in which the author breaks into the narrative to discuss the events of the story with the reader.)

EXERCISE 17. Discuss the use of person in the passages of Appendix Section I, including some observations about the *effect* of these choices. For example, the passage from Rachel Carson is partly in 2nd person, in that it places the reader in the scene, as a participant, and describes the scene from the reader's point of view. Why do you think Carson made this choice?

3.6 Applications for Students and Teachers of English as a Second Language

There are three skills in this chapter which are important for teachers and students of ESL: (1) Learning to recognize the categories of the content words so that they can be placed appropriately in sentences, (2) learning to form and use the proper inflectional forms for content words, and (3) learning to use function words such as prepositions and determiners.

3.6.1   Recognizing the Categories of the Content Words

Because ESL students may lack clear intuitions about the grammatical categories of words (or can't come up with the appropriate form when they need it), they sometimes use a noun where the corresponding verb or adjective is required, or vice-versa: *You have to make a decide*, with the verb *decide* in place of the noun *decision*, or *When you vote it makes you self-reliance*, with the noun *self-reliance* in place of the adjective *self-reliant*, or *Dr. Costa will departure from Lisbon on July 10*, with the noun *departure* in place of the verb *depart*.

EXERCISE 18. Find examples of parts-of-speech confusions in "A Review of the Film 'Baraka'" and "A Memory in America," Appendix Section V.

3.6.2   Learning the Inflectional Forms

Even when they find the right category for a word, ESL students sometimes mix up the inflectional form, using the singular form of a noun instead of the plural (*They spent more than a million dollar*), or the base form of a verb where the past tense is required (*I departed from Lisbon at 19:00 and arrive in Boston at 21:15*), or an active-voice verb instead of the passive (*If someone commits an offence, s/he will punish* (instead of *be punished*).

Subject-verb agreement is often lacking as well, as in *That kind of exercise never improve conversation ability*. In Old English times, the grammar of English was like that of modern Spanish or French or German, with a suffix at the end of every tensed verb to make it agree with its subject. Over the centuries, most of these suffixes were lost, so that Modern English is left with only one agreement suffix—the *-s* that attaches to a present-tense verb when the subject is 3rd-person singular:

Present tense		Past tense (no agreement)	
I know	*We know*	*I knew*	*We knew*
You know	*You (all) know*	*You knew*	*You (all) knew*
He/she/it knows	*They know*	*He/she/it knew*	*They knew*

One might expect that this paucity of subject-verb agreement would make things easy for the learner, but, instead, the fact that agreement is usually unimportant in English seems to make it difficult for students of English to remember that tiny little *-s* suffix when it is required.[6]

---

6. ESOL students sometimes omit inflectional suffixes in spoken English for reasons having to do with pronunciation rather than grammar. Many languages do not allow sequences of consonant sounds at the end of a word. Students who come from languages of this sort may leave off the final consonant sound in words like *dogs* [gz] and *walked* [kt] and *laughs* [fs] in order to make these words easier to pronounce. See Chapter 4, Section 4.7.3.

EXERCISE 19.

a. One verb, the verb *be,* still retains some of the agreement inflection that has been lost from other verbs. Write out the present and past tense forms of the verb *be,* as in the paradigm above for the verb *know,* and identify the "extra" inflectional forms for *be.*

b. Find examples of confusion with tense, number, and agreement in the ESOL writing passages of Appendix Section V.

3.6.3   Learning to Use Function Words

For ESL students, just as for children learning English as their first language, it is the function words (determiners, prepositions, auxiliaries) that cause the most difficulty. Determiners (*a(n),* *these, much,* etc.) are a particular problem. One source of confusion is the rule that requires a singular count noun to have a determiner. Students whose first languages do not require determiners may be inclined to leave out what seems like an unnecessary word in English: **Bring me chair* instead of *Bring me a/the/one chair.*)

Another source of difficulty is the requirement that a determiner or quantifier must agree with the noun that it combines with. As we observed above, English nouns are divided into two categories, proper (*Bill Clinton*) or common (*man*), and common nouns are further classified as count (*chair ~ chairs*) or mass (*money*). "Count" nouns normally have a singular and a plural form, which take the determiners *a(n)* and *some,* respectively. "Mass" nouns, also called "non-count" nouns, have no plural form (**moneys, *happinesses, *rices,* etc.), and they use the determiner *some,* rather than *a(n),* in the singular:

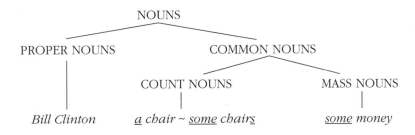

ESL students often have difficulty adhering to this complex pattern, and, to make matters worse, they may not be sure which nouns are "count" and which are "mass." Meaning is not always helpful, as can be seen from the fact the nouns with very similar meanings sometimes belong to different categories:[7]

an assignment: a count noun
some homework: a mass noun

---

7. Because native speakers of English already know which nouns are count nouns and which nouns are mass nouns, this information is not included in dictionaries that are written for native speakers. However, "learners'" dictionaries such as *The Longman Dictionary of Contemporary English* do contain this information, and ESL students should be taught to use such dictionaries.

EXERCISE 20.

a. Proper names generally do not require a determiner: *Hillary Clinton, Amsterdam, Guatemala, America, Lake Michigan, Mount Washington*. However, the following proper names require the determiner *the*: *the Clintons, the United States, the Netherlands, the Great Lakes, the Alps, the Americas*. What is the rule?[8]

b. As we noted in the text, a determiner or quantifier must "agree" with the noun it combines with (*this question, these questions*). A list of determiners and quantifiers is given below. Make a chart showing which class(es) of nouns each one combines with: singular count, plural count, mass, or some combination of these. (Reminder: *Chair* is a singular count noun, *chairs* is a plural count noun, and *money* is a mass noun.)

Articles: *the, a*

Demonstrative determiners: *this, that, these, those*

Possessive determiners: *his, her, their*

Indefinite determiners: *some, any, each, every, either, neither, another, several, a few, a little, no, more, less*

Quantifiers: *all, both, one, two, much, many*

c. Classify the following nouns as count or mass, and give evidence, by showing what determiners/quantifiers the noun combines with and what sort of verb it takes (general present or 3rd-singular present): *milk, table, news, alphabet, cash, dollar, progress*.

d. Some nouns function either as count nouns or as mass nouns, depending on their meaning. Give definitions for the following nouns as count nouns and as mass nouns: *beer, oil, pie, activity*.

"Generic" noun phrases (i.e., noun phrases that refer to a *class* of entities) also have special rules in English, which may be different from those of other languages. In English, a generic noun phrase usually consists of a plural or mass noun with no determiner:[9]

> *Money is the root of all evil.*
> *Horses were domesticated by nomadic herdsmen around 4000 B.C.*

Things work differently in Romance languages; here generics are formed with the definite determiner plus a plural noun:

> *Los caballos tienen cuatro piernas.*   '(The) horses have four legs.' (Spanish)
> *Les chevaux ont quatre jambes.*   '(The) horses have four legs.' (French)

Students who come from a Romance language background will tend to transfer their pattern into English.

---

8. There are other classes of proper names that idiosyncratically require *the*: names of rivers (*the Mississippi River*), names of oceans (*the Indian Ocean*), and names of newspapers (*the Miami Herald*), among others.

9. Generic noun phrases can also be formed with singular count nouns, with either *a* or *the*:

  a. A singular noun with *a*:   *A horse has four legs.*

  b. A singular noun with *the*:   *The horse has four legs.* (for whole species, only)

EXERCISE 21. Find errors with determiners in the examples of ESL writing in Appendix Section V. Give a brief statement of the rule that is violated by each error. (For example, "A singular count noun must have a determiner," "Plural generic nouns do not use the determiner *the*.")

ESL students often make errors with other functional categories as well, not just with determiners. For example, a student may say or write *We been swimming*, leaving out the auxiliary *have*, or *He translated <u>to</u> me*, using the preposition *to* instead of the preposition *for*. Omission of the copula (the verb *be*) is also common, as in this sentence from a Turkish student: *This my first lobster and I don't know which part edible.*

EXERCISE 22. Look through the examples of ESL writing in Appendix Section V, and find examples of (i) errors with the choice of preposition, and (ii) omission of an auxiliary or the copula.

3.7 Summary of the Chapter

In this chapter, we have argued for an expanded list of grammatical categories, including the following:

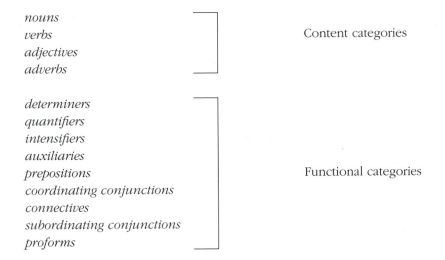

nouns	
verbs	Content categories
adjectives	
adverbs	
determiners	
quantifiers	
intensifiers	
auxiliaries	
prepositions	Functional categories
coordinating conjunctions	
connectives	
subordinating conjunctions	
proforms	

We have identified the content categories—noun, verb, adjective, and adverb—not just by their meaning, as in traditional grammar, but also by their morphology (what affixes they contain or will accept), their inflection (for person, number, tense, degree, etc.), and their syntactic position, especially what functional categories they combine with. We have also looked at the internal structure of words and noted that English prefixes and suffixes are attached to complete words—not to bound roots, as was the case in Latin and Greek, and that they impose specific requirements about the category of the word to which they attach.

For students and teachers of literature, we have pointed out the importance of the person in which a narrative is presented (1st, 2nd, or 3rd) and have observed that writers sometimes favor certain parts of speech in that, for example, one piece of writing may contain very powerful adjectives while another uses nouns and verbs to carry the description.

For students and teachers of English as a Second Language, we have observed that ESL students sometimes mix up the categories of the words, using the verb *decide*, for example, where the noun *decision* is needed. The categorization of nouns as count or mass is a further difficulty. ESL students also struggle with inflection, particularly for irregular verbs, and with the use of function words such as determiners, auxiliaries, and prepositions.

Traditional Category	Modern Category	Examples
NOUN	noun (N)	proper nouns: *Chicago, George Bush, the Mississippi River*
		common nouns
		count nouns: *dish, tree, president, assignment, accident*
		noncount (mass) nouns: *soup, water, honesty, pie (the substance), life (the state)*
PRONOUN	pronoun (PRO)	personal pronouns: *I, me, you, they, one*
		reflexive pronouns: *myself, yourselves*
		reciprocal pronouns: *each other, one another*
		pronouns formed from determiners and quantifiers: *this, some, another, one, several*
		indefinite pronouns: *everybody, no one, one, some one*
		"WH" pronouns: *who, whose, what, which*
VERB	verb (V)	*sing, go, think, undergo, seem*
	auxiliary (AUX)	modal auxiliaries: *shall, should, can, could, may, might, must, will, would*
		auxiliary verbs: *have$_{perf}$, be$_{prog}$, be$_{pass}$, do*
ADVERB	adverb (ADV)	*slowly, happily, well, entirely*
	intensifier (INT)	*very, so, as, too, enough, this, that*
	connective (CONN)	*however, nevertheless, therefore, furthermore, thus, consequently*
ADJECTIVE	adjective (ADJ)	gradable: *polite, handsome, intelligent, unworthy, safe*
		nongradable: *entire, atomic, hydrochloric, wooden (=made of wood)*
	determiner (D)	possessive: *his, her, your, my*
		demonstrative: *this, that, these, those*
		articles: *a, the*
		definite: *the, this, that*
		indefinite: *a, any, some, either, a few*
	quantifier (Q)	numerals: *one, two, first, second*
		other quantifiers: *both, all, many, few*
PREPOSITION	preposition (P)	*in, at, under, beyond, around, near*
CONJUNCTION	coordinating conjunction (CONJ)	simple: *and, or, but, yet*
		correlative: *either . . . or; both . . . and, not only . . . but*
	subordinating conjunction (C)	*that, than, if, although, because, when, after*

Figure 3.1   Syntactic categories: A summary.

NOUNS

singular	plural	singular possessive	plural possessive
boy	*boys*	*boy's*	*boys'*
child	*children*	*child's*	*children's*
sheep	*sheep*	*sheep's*	*sheep's*
happiness	—	—	—
news	—	—	—
—	*trousers*	—	*trousers'*
Mount Washington	—	*Mount Washington's*	—
Susan	—	*Susan's*	—

VERBS

base	present tense		past tense	present participle	perfect participle	passive participle
	general	**3rd pers. sg.**				
go	*go*	*goes*	*went*	*going*	*gone*	—
think	*think*	*thinks*	*thought*	*thinking*	*thought*	*thought*
see	*see*	*sees*	*saw*	*seeing*	*seen*	*seen*
put	*put*	*puts*	*put*	*putting*	*put*	*put*
seem	*seem*	*seems*	*seemed*	*seeming*	*seemed*	—
have	*have*	*has*	*had*	*having*	*had*	*had*
be	*are* (am)	*is*	*were* (was)	*being*	*been*	—

ADJECTIVES AND ADVERBS

Positive	Comparative	Superlative
tall	*taller*	*tallest*
narrow	*narrower*	*narrowest*
pretty	*prettier*	*prettiest*
wonderful	*more wonderful*	*most wonderful*
bad	*worse*	*worst*
tired	*(?) tireder/more tired*	*(?) tiredest/most tired*
unique	*(?) more unique*	*(?) most unique*
dead	*deader*	*deadest*
slowly	*more slowly*	*most slowly*

Figure 3.2   Summary of inflection.

CHAPTER 4

The Pronunciation of English

4.1 Introduction

Students and teachers of English need an understanding of the sound system of English in order to understand the representations of pronunciation that are given in dictionaries, to identify and appreciate the sound effects in poetic language, and to understand the process that children go through in learning to read and write. The first part of this chapter provides background relevant to these issues. Students and teachers of English as a *Second* Language need to know a great many other things about the pronunciation of English; the latter part of the chapter will provide information that is useful for them.

4.2 Consonant and Vowel Sounds

Dictionaries give representations of spelling and pronunciation for each entry. (The *Oxford English Dictionary* saves space by listing pronunciations only for words that may be difficult for native speakers of English.) To represent pronunciation, European dictionaries, including those published in Britain, use the International Phonetic Alphabet, or IPA, which provides a symbol for every consonant and vowel sound that is known to occur in a human language. IPA symbols for the sounds of English are listed in Table 4.1.

The IPA can be difficult for English speakers, for two reasons: First, it has special symbols for some sounds, such as [ð] for the first sound of *this*, [ʃ] for the first sound of *ship*, and so forth. Secondly, the symbols for the vowel sounds are based on the orthography of European languages rather than that of English; for example, the vowel of *see* is represented as [i] and the vowel of *say* as [e]. (This will make sense to you if you have studied French, Spanish, or Italian.)

American dictionaries try to make things easier for their readers by using symbols that are based on the spelling system of English. The symbols from *The American Heritage Dictionary* are shown in Figure 4.1. Be sure to notice the [ə] (called "schwa") and its partner [ər] ("schwar"). These symbols represent the *a* of ***about*** and the *er* of *butt**er***, respectively. [ə] (***about***) and [ər] (*butt**er***) are similar to [ŭ] (***bu**t*) and [ûr] (***bird***), but the symbols [ŭ] and [ûr] are used when the vowel is stressed, while the symbols [ə] and [ər] are used when the vowel is unstressed.

In the first four sections of this chapter, which are intended for the general reader, the sounds of English will be represented by dictionary symbols. In Section 4.7, which is intended for ESL teachers, we will switch to IPA.

Table 4.1 International Phonetic Alphabet Symbols for English

Vowels

IPA Symbol	Examples	IPA Symbol	Examples
[i:][a]	*bead*	[aɪ]	*lied*
[ɪ]	*bid*	[aʊ]	*loud*
[e:]	*fade*	[ɔɪ]	*boy*
[ɛ]	*fed*	[ɪɚ] or [ɪə]	*here*
[æ]	*fad*	[ɛɚ] or [ɛə]	*wear*
[ʌ]	*suds*	[ʊɚ] or [ʊə]	*tour*
[ɝ:]	*bird*	[ɔɚ] or [ɔ:]	*more*
[ɑ:]	*calm*	[aɚ] or [a:]	*car*
[ɑ]	*cod*		
[u:]	*cooed*	[ə]	*sofa, Rosa's*
[ʊ]	*could*	[ɚ]	*over*
[o:]	*code*	[i]	*roses*
[ɔ:]	*cawed*		

Consonants

IPA Symbol	Examples	IPA Symbol	Examples
[p]	*pot, top*	[ʃ]	*ship, machine, wish*
[b]	*big, bib*	[ʒ]	*measure, beige*
[t]	*tip, pat*	[h]	*help*
[d]	*dim, mad*	[tʃ]	*choose, match*
[k]	*cat, tack*	[dʒ]	*judge, cage*
[g]	*gun, tag*	[m]	*man, dim*
[f]	*fill, phone, rough, off*	[n]	*nap, hen*
[v]	*vine, love*	[ŋ]	*sing, think*
[θ]	*think, bath*	[l]	*live, fill*
[ð]	*this, loathe*	[r]	*ring, wrong*
[s]	*sink, bus, kiss*	[w]	*wish*
[z]	*zoo, lose*	[ʍ]	*which*
		[j]	*yellow*

a The ":" indicates that the vowel sound is long.

PRONUNCIATION KEY

The system of indicating pronunciations in the Dictionary is explained in the section headed ''Pronunciation'' in the ''Guide to the Dictionary.'' The column below headed AHD represents the pronunciation key used in the Dictionary. The right-hand column, labeled IPA, contains symbols from the International Phonetic Alphabet, widely used by scholars. The two systems do not precisely correspond, because they were differently conceived for somewhat different purposes.

spellings	AHD	IPA	spellings	AHD	IPA
pat	ă	æ	ship, dish	sh	ʃ
pay	ā	e	tight, stopp**ed**	t	t
care	âr	ɛr, er	thin	th	θ
father	ä	ɑ:, ɑ	this	*th*	ð
bib	b	b	cut	ŭ	ʌ
church	ch	tʃ	urge, term, firm,	ûr	ɝ, ɝr
deed, milled	d	d	word, heard		
pet	ě	ɛ	valve	v	v
bee	ē	i	with	w	w
fife, phase, rough	f	f	yes	y	j
gag	g	g	zebra, xylem	z	z
hat	h	h	vision, pleasure,	zh	ʒ
which	hw	hw (also ʍ)	garage		
pit	ĭ	ɪ	about, item, edible,	ə	ə
pie, by	ī	aɪ	gallop, circus		
pier	îr	ɪr, ir	butter	ər	ɚ
judge	j	dʒ			
kick, cat, pique	k	k			
lid, needle	l (nēd'l)	l, ḷ ['nidḷ]			

FOREIGN

spellings	AHD	IPA		AHD	IPA
mum	m	m			
no, sudden	n (sŭd'n)	n, ņ ['sʌdņ]	*French* **feu,**	œ	œ
thing	ng	ŋ	*German* **schön**		
pot, horrid	ŏ	ɑ	*French* **tu,**	ü	y
toe, hoarse	ō	o	*German* **über**		
caught, paw, for	ô	ɔ	*German* **ich,**	KH	x
noise	oi	ɔɪ	*Scottish* **loch**		
took	ŏŏ	ʊ	*French* **bon**	N	õ, æ̃, ã, œ̃
boot	ōō	u			
out	ou	aʊ			

STRESS

pop	p	p	Primary stress	' **bi·ol'o·gy** (bī-ŏl'ə-jē)
roar	r	r	Secondary stress	' **bi'o·log'i·cal**
sauce	s	s		(bī'ə-lŏj'ĭ-kəl)

Figure 4.1   American Heritage Dictionary Pronunciation Key. Copyright © 2002 by Houghton Mifflin. Reproduced by permission from *The American Heritage Dictionary of the English Language*, Fourth Edition.

EXERCISE 1.

a. There may be more symbols in Figure 4.1 than are needed for your speech. For example, it is possible that you do not distinguish between the sounds [w] 'witch' and [hw] 'which', and, if you are an American, you probably do not make a three-way distinction among the vowel sounds [ä] 'f<u>a</u>ther', [ŏ] 'p<u>o</u>p', and [ô] 'l<u>aw</u>.'

    i.   How many distinctions do you make among these vowel sounds?

    ii.   If you make a two-way distinction, which two symbols represent the same sound for you?

b. The pronunciation symbols in other American dictionaries are similar to those of the *American Heritage Dictionary*, with a few minor variations. Look at another dictionary and make note of the differences you find.

EXERCISE 2.

Identify the following words, written in dictionary pronunciation symbols:

[brē*th*]	[ĭg.zăkt´]	[nô]	[rē´bāt´]
[bĕr´ē]	[fə.tēg´]	[lā´sē]	[rōch]
[kwīr]	[flī]	[lŭv]	[säm´bə]
[kyo͞o]	[flŭngk]	[myo͞o´zĭk]	[sĭks]
[sĭ.mĕnt´]	[frē´kwənt]	[prē´tĕkst´]	[wûrm]
[kən.sûrn´]	[jĕn´tl]	[po͞ol]	[rĭst]
[dĭ.zŏlv´]	[gônt]	[po͞ol]	[mĕ´nē]
[ē´zē]	[gōt]	[kwôrt]	[mŭ´nē]

EXERCISE 3.

Transcribe the following words into dictionary pronunciation symbols. An answer key is provided in Figure 4.2 for the author's pronunciation. (Your pronunciation may be different from the author's for some words.)

ghost	*who*	*balanced*	*faith*	*ink*
tough	*gym*	*winked*	*finger*	*tango*
Thomas	*vision*	*taxis*	*xerox*	*hangs*
bath	*sword*	*taxes*	*long*	*skunk*
bathe	*fishing*	*high*	*longer*	*these*
scent	*elves*	*though*	*razor*	*shoes*
face	*composure*	*choke*	*racer*	*buy*
hose	*composer*	*batch*	*when*	*bury*
sure	*this*	*singer*	*thistle*	*watches*
garage	*the*	*thing*	*circle*	*while*

[gōst]	[hoo͞]	[bă′lənst]	[fāth]	[ĭngk]
[tŭf]	[jĭm]	[wĭngkt]	[fĭng′gər]	[tăng′gō]
[tŏm′əs]	[vĭ′zhən]	[tăk′sēz]	[zîr′ŏks′]	[hăngz]
[băth]	[sôrd]	[tăk′sĭz]	[lông]	[skŭngk]
[bā*th*]	[fĭsh′ĭng]	[hī]	[lông′gər]	[*th*ēz]
[sĕnt]	[ĕlvz]	[*th*ō]	[rā′zər]	[shoo͞z]
[fās]	[kəm.pō′zhər]	[chōk]	[rā′sər]	[bī]
[hōz]	[kəm.pō′zər]	[băch]	[hwĕn]	[bĕr′ē]
[shoo͞r]	[*th*ĭs]	[sĭng′ər]	[thĭs′əl]	[wŏch′ĭz]
[gə.räzh′] or [gə.räj′]	[*th*ə]	[thĭng]	[sûr′kəl]	[hwīl]

Figure 4.2   Answers to Exercise 3.

EXERCISE 4.

a. The following words have two or more standard pronunciations. Give a representation for each pronunciation that you are aware of:

aunt	*vase*	*creek*	*roof*
harassment	*abdomen*	*Uranus*	*dour*
envelope (n.)	*route*	*pecan*	*apricot*

Students are sometimes told that the only correct pronunciation is the one that the dictionary lists first. In fact, *all* the pronunciations that are listed in dictionaries are standard pronunciations. Pronunciations that are considered nonstandard (such as [noo͞′kyələr] for *nuclear*) are not listed at all.

b. Because we learn many words (especially Latinate words) from written texts rather than from speech, we sometimes find to our embarrassment that we have been pronouncing a word in a way that differs from its standard pronunciation. English spelling can be very misleading! The following words are sometimes mispronounced; look them up in your dictionary to see whether you have been using the standard pronunciation:

desultory	*gibbet*	*azure*	*plethora*	*mauve*	*archipelago*
automata	*vehemently*	*crevasse*	*discomfiture*	*ensemble*	*podiatry*

Name at least one other word whose pronunciation you have been confused about because you learned it from reading, without hearing it pronounced.

4.3   Classes of Speech Sounds

You are, of course, already familiar with the distinction between vowels and consonants.[1] The class of consonants can be further subdivided according to their acoustic properties and their

---

1. But note that we are talking about *sounds*, not letters. Students sometimes learn in school that the vowels are *a, e, i, o, u* and sometimes *y* and *w*. This means that the letters *a, e, i, o, u* are used to spell vowel sounds, and that the letters *y* and *w* are sometimes used to represent vowel sounds. In the word *happy*, the letter <y> represents the vowel sound [e·], but in the word *yes* it represents the consonant sound [y]; in the word *shallow*, the letter <w> is part of the representation of the vowel sound [ō], but in the word *wide*, it represents the consonant sound [w].)

manner of production. The consonant sounds [p], [b], [t], [d], [ch], [j], [k], and [g] are called "oral stops" or "plosives," because in the production of these sounds the air is stopped momentarily from passing through the mouth and then allowed to burst out, suddenly. (Please try this now!) The sounds [f], [v], [th], [*th*], [s], [z], [sh], and [zh] are called "fricatives," because air is pushed through a narrow space in the vocal tract, creating friction. (Now try these sounds and listen for the "friction.") These two classes of consonants—oral stops and fricatives, together—are called "obstruents," because both classes of sounds are formed by creating an *obstruction* in the vocal tract which interrupts the free flow of air. The noisiest of the obstruents—the stops [ch] and [j] and the fricatives [s], [z], [sh], and [zh]—are called "sibilants" or "stridents."

At the other end of the spectrum, we have the "sonorant" consonants [m], [n], [ng], [l], [r], [w], [hw], [y], and [h], which allow the air to flow freely through the vocal tract, with a resonant quality. For the *oral* sonorants [l], [r], [w], [hw], [y], and [h], the air flows out through the oral cavity (the mouth). For the *nasal* sonorants, [m], [n], and [ng], the oral cavity is closed off, just as for the oral stops [b], [d], and [g], but the air is allowed to pass out through the nose. (You can test this by trying to say one of these consonants while holding your nose.) Because the airflow is blocked in the oral cavity, [m], [n], and [ng] are classified as *stops*, but they are *sonorants* rather than *obstruents*, because the air still flows out freely (through the nose).

A classification that cuts across the other categories is that of "voiced" vs."voiceless" sounds. "Voiced" sounds are accompanied by vibration of the vocal folds in the larynx or "voice box" at the front of your throat. Voicing is easiest to hear in the fricative consonants. If you pronounce the consonants [s] and [z] with your fingers pressed against your Adam's apple, you should be able to feel a vibration during the voiced fricative [z], but not during the voiceless fricative [s]. Also try pronouncing these sounds with your fingers in your ears; you will hear a loud buzz when you say [z], but not when you say [s]. The voiced fricatives are [v], [*th*], [z], and [zh]; their voiceless counterparts are [f], [th], [s], and [sh], respectively. Voicing is harder to hear with the oral stops, because it is difficult to hold their articulation long enough to tell whether the vocal folds are vibrating. But if you listen carefully just to the consonant and not to the vowel sound that follows it, you should be able to hear that [b], [d], [j], and [g] are voiced, while [p], [t], [ch], and [k] are not.

The vowels and sonorant consonants are all voiced, with two exceptions, [h] and [hw], which are voiceless. (But many English speakers don't use [hw], so [h] may be your only voiceless sonorant.)

EXERCISE 5.

   a. Without looking at the text, assign the following consonants to the categories oral stop, fricative, or sonorant: [f], [t], [m], [b], [ch], [l], [sh]. Two of these consonants are strident; which ones?

   b. Go back through the list of (a) and say whether each consonant is voiced or voiceless.

4.4 Syllables

Consonant and vowel sounds are organized into syllables, with the following structure:

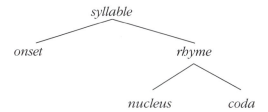

Vowels are found in the *center* of the syllable (the nucleus), while consonants normally occupy the periphery (the onset and the coda).[2] Every syllable contains a nucleus; the onset and coda are optional. Some representative English syllables are set out below. (Remember that the digraph [sh] represents one sound in English and therefore takes up just one space in the syllable structure):

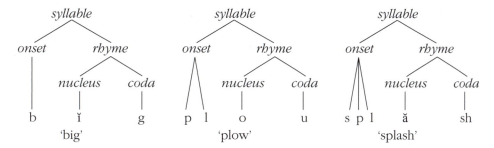

The *rhyme* of the syllable is the part that is repeated in rhyming words like *splash ~ dash*.[3]

4.5 Stress

A word spoken in isolation must have at least one stressed syllable. You can identify the stressed syllable by pronouncing the word with statement intonation and noticing where the pitch of your voice goes *down*: the pitch goes down immediately after the stressed syllable (or *during* the stressed syllable, if it is the last syllable of the word):

fin | al ist   (The word has three syllables, with stress on the first.)

per | miss | ion   (The word has three syllables, with stress on the second.)

re | port   (The word has two syllables, with stress on the second.)

---

2. The nucleus is sometimes occupied by a sonorant consonant rather than a vowel. For example, the second syllable of the word *kitten* consists only of the nasal consonant [n], which is, in this case, the nucleus of its syllable.

3. A rhyme like *splash ~ dash*, which repeats just the rhyme part of a stressed syllable, is called a "masculine" rhyme; "feminine" rhymes like *splashing ~ dashing* repeat the rhyme part of the stressed syllable plus the unstressed syllable that follows it.

Dictionaries mark primary stress in either of two ways: One is to place a heavy accent mark after the stressed syllable; the other is to place a raised tick *before* the stressed syllable. These two systems are illustrated below with the word *permission*, which is stressed on the second syllable:

[pər.mĭsh´ən]   or   [pər´mĭsh.ən]   'permission'

American dictionaries usually use the first notation, while British dictionaries use the second.

In addition to their primary or "main" stress, many words also have one or more *secondary* stresses. Dictionaries mark secondary stress in either of two ways. One system, used by most American dictionaries, is to place a light accent mark after the stressed syllable; the other, used by most British dictionaries, is to place a subscripted tick right *before* the stressed syllable:

[ă´pə.lă´chə.kō´lə]   or   [ˌă.pəˌlă.chəˈkō.lə]   'Apalachicola' (a river in Florida)

The most reliable way to hear a secondary stress is to listen for the quality of the vowel: stressed syllables in English maintain the full quality of the vowel, while unstressed syllables "reduce" their vowel sound to [ə] or [ĭ].[4] For example, the word *Apalachicola* has six syllables, with secondary stress on the first and third syllables and primary stress on the fifth syllable. The three stressed syllables are the only syllables in which the vowel is fully pronounced; in the unstressed syllables the vowel is reduced to [ə] or [ĭ]. (Say this word slowly, out loud, and listen for the reduced vowels.)

EXERCISE 6.

a. Count the number of syllables in each of the following words and decide which syllable is stressed. (Each of these words has just one stressed syllable.)
   banana   calendar   loveable   custom   sabbatical   contain
   Look to see how stress is represented in your dictionary and use that notation to mark the stress in each word above.

b. The following words have more than one stressed syllable. Count the number of syllables in each word and decide which syllables are stressed:
   alphabetize   understandable   plagiarism   California   Ticonderoga
   Mark the primary and secondary stresses in each word, following the system that is used in your dictionary.

4.6 Applications for Students and Teachers of Literature

In poetic language, the *sound* of the words is as important as their meaning. Poems contain patterns of sound that are pleasurable in themselves, but which also serve to emphasize certain words, link words together, or support the poem's imagery.

---

4. **Exception:** The vowel sounds [ē] and [ō] keep their full value at the end of a word, even if they are unstressed: ˈprĭtē 'pretty', ˈwin.dō 'window.'

4.6.1   Sound Effects in Poetry

Poets sometimes use sound to emphasize certain words; for example, in Shakespeare's sonnet 73, the word *cold* (ln. 3) is highlighted by the fact that it rhymes with *behold* (ln. 1):

1	*That time of year thou mayst in me behold*
2	*When yellow leaves, or none, or few, do hang*
3	*Upon those boughs which shake against the cold,*
4	*Bare ruined choirs where late the sweet birds sang.*
5	*In me thou see'st the twilight of such day*
6	*As after sunset fadeth in the West,*
7	*Which by-and-by black night doth take away,*
8	*Death's second self, that seals up all in rest.*
9	*In me thou see'st the glowing of such fire*
10	*That on the ashes of his youth doth lie,*
11	*As the deathbed whereon it must expire,*
12	*Consumed with that which it was nourished by.*
13	*This thou perceiv'st, which makes thy love more strong,*
14	*To love that well which thou must leave ere long.*

—William Shakespeare

In addition, sounds may be used to link words, lines, or phrases together. For example, the Shakespeare sonnet consists of six sentences—four sentences of four lines each, and one (final) sentence of two lines. These sentences are delineated by the rhyme scheme—the four "quatrains" (lns. 1–4; 5–8; 9–12; 13–14) by the rhyme scheme *abab*, and the "couplet" (lns. 13–14) by the rhyme scheme *aa*.

Within the lines, words may be linked by repeated consonant or vowel sounds; for example, the phrase *mayst in me* (ln. 1 of the sonnet) is held together by the consonant sound [m], the phrase *yellow leaves* (ln. 2) by the consonant sound [l], and the phrase *In me thou see'st* (ln. 4) by the vowel sound [ē]. Repetition of this type is called *consonance* (for consonant sounds), or *assonance* (for vowel sounds); consonance that repeats the onset of a stressed syllable, as in *mayst in me* (ln. 1), is called *alliteration*.

Assonance, consonance, and alliteration may also be used to link words from *different* lines or phrases in order to make a connection between the words' meanings. For example, the words *me* and *leaves* (lns. 1 and 2 in the sonnet) are linked by the vowel sound [ē]—a phonological pointer to the analogy the poet is making between himself (*me*) and the *leaves* that are about to fall. Other examples include *boughs ~ bare* (lns. 3 and 4), which are linked phonetically by the consonant sound [b], and *cold ~ choir* (lns. 3 and 4), which are linked phonetically by the consonant sound [k]. These phonetic echoes suggest semantic associations between words and help to create multiple layers of meaning within the poem.

Finally, sound patterns in poetry may be onomatopoetic, in that the *sound* of the words may reflect their meaning. This technique can be seen in line 4 of the sonnet; the first part of the line, which describes a ruined choir, *sounds* like an out-of-tune choir, and the final words, about the singing of birds, sounds like birdsong. Some of the sounds that contribute to these effects are indicated below:

> *Bare ruined choirs where late the sweet birds sang*
> [r][r]   [r]   [r]   [s] [ē]   [dz][s][ă]

73

Sound repetitions are not always total; sometimes what is repeated is a phonetic property rather than a whole sound. For example, the following lines from Longfellow's poem "A Psalm of Life" are full of sonorant consonants ([l], [m], [n], [r]), which reinforce the poem's imagery of "mourning" and "dreams":

> *Tell me not in mournful numbers*
> *Life is but an empty dream*

EXERCISE 7.

a. Find other instances of consonance and assonance in the Shakespeare sonnet and discuss their effect. Do they emphasize certain words, create links between words, or echo, onomatopoetically, the meaning of the phrase?

b. Identify repetitions of sounds and phonetic features in the passages below:

> *A sweet disorder in the dress*
> *Kindles in clothes a wantonness*
> > —from a poem by Robert Herrick

> *Death be not proud, though some have called thee*
> *Mighty and dreadful, for thou art not so*
> > —from a poem by John Donne

> *Nothing so sensual was ever so innocent.*
> > —from a Revlon ad

> *Lovely luxurious leather*
> > —from an ad for Amity wallets

c. The following poem by Emily Dickinson uses an intricate pattern of consonance and alliteration. Find repetitions of vowel and consonant sounds in the first stanza and say what words or phrases are linked by these repetitions.

   Now look at the second stanza. List words that begin with the consonant sound [d] or that contain the consonant sounds [k] and [s]. What semantic concept is contained in the words you have listed, and how does that concept relate to the theme of the poem?

> *Safe in their Alabaster Chambers —*
> *Untouched by Morning —*
> *And untouched by Noon —*
> *Lie the meek members of the Resurrection —*
> *Rafter of Satin — and Roof of Stone!*

> *Grand go the Years — in the Crescent — above them —*
> *Worlds scoop their Arcs —*
> *And Firmaments — row —*
> *Diadems — drop — and Doges — surrender —*
> *Soundless as dots — on a Disc of Snow —*
> > —Emily Dickinson (version of 1861)

d. Prose passages are sometimes written in a poetic register that contains sound effects like those of poetry. We have already pointed out the poetic register of the James Joyce passage in Appendix Section I (Chapter 2, Exercise 25d). Find sound repetitions or other phonetic phenomena in this passage and comment on their literary effect. (For example, do they bind the words of a phrase? Link words that share a common meaning? Create an onomatopoetic effect?)

e. Advertising slogans use some of the same phonetic devices as poetry, though for a less noble purpose. Find sound effects in the following advertising slogans and comment on their purpose:

Guts, not glitz (for Adidas sneakers)

Skin feels best when it's caressed (for Caress soap)

Toothpaste proven to get to the root of cavities (for Crest toothpaste)

Bacardi Breezer. Bright. Light. Refreshing. (for Bacardi rum).

Peachtree jazzes ginger ale. It's deliciously DeKuyper. (for a DeKuyper liqueur).[5]

4.6.2 Meter

Traditional poetry is composed with a regular rhythm called "meter." Metrical rhythm is pleasurable in itself, like the rhythm of music; before the advent of writing, when poems were recited orally, the meter also served as an aid to memory.

In a poem with a regular meter, the lines can be divided into "feet," where a foot consists of a stressed syllable along with one or more unstressed syllables. The *name* of the foot depends on (1) the number of syllables and (2) the position of the stressed syllable. The following are the most important kinds of feet in English poetry:

Iambic (/ ˘ ´/)	two beats with the strong beat at the end: *on tíme*
Trochaic (/ ´ ˘/)	two beats with the strong beat at the beginning: *síng.ing*
Anapestic (/ ˘ ˘ ´/)	three beats with the strong beat at the end: *un.der.stánd*
Dactylic (/ ´ ˘ ˘ /)	three beats with the strong beat at the beginning: *háp.pil.y*

The meter of a poem is identified by stating (1) what kind of feet it has (predominantly) and (2) how many feet there are in a line (*monometer* = one foot per line, *dimeter* = two feet per line, *trimeter* = three feet per line, *tetrameter* = four feet per line, *pentameter* = five feet per line, *hexameter* = six feet per line, and so forth). Longfellow's poem "Excelsior," whose first stanza is set out below, is written in iambic tetrameter—"iambic" because the feet are predominantly of the form / ˘ ´/, and "tetrameter" because there are four feet in each line:

> *The shades of night were falling fast,*
> *As through an Alpine village passed*
> *A youth, who bore, 'mid snow and ice,*
> *A banner with the strange device,*
> > *Excelsior!*

—Henry Wadsworth Longfellow

---

5. Thanks to my student Colleen Murphy, who provided these examples.

Meter can be displayed overtly by means of a "scansion," which shows the boundaries of the feet and the position of the weak and strong syllables within each foot:

/ Thĕ shádes / ŏf níght / wĕre fál / lĭng fást /

EXERCISE 8.

a. Write out scansions for the next three lines of "Excelsior" to show that the entire stanza is in iambic tetrameter.

b. Write out scansions for the following three stanzas and identify the meter of each. (*Hint*: One is trochaic tetrameter, one is dactylic tetrameter, and one is anapestic trimeter/ dimeter. Be aware, also, that the weak beat of a foot is not necessarily filled with a syllable.)

> *When the hours of Day are numbered,*
> *And the voices of the Night*
> *Wake the better soul, that slumbered,*
> *To a holy, calm delight;*
>   —Henry Wadsworth Longfellow

> *A flee and a fly in a flue*
> *Were imprisoned, so what could they do?*
> *Said the fly, "Let us flee!"*
> *Said the flea, "Let us fly!"*
> *So they flew through a flaw in the flue.*
>   —a popular jingle

> *Hush-a-bye, baby, on the tree top!*
> *When the wind blows the cradle will rock;*
> *When the bough breaks the cradle will fall;*
> *Down will come baby, cradle and all.*
>   —Traditional lullaby

Metrical patterns are not followed perfectly, as you may have noticed in doing Exercise 8. For example, lines written in trochaic or dactylic meter often have a "short" foot at the end of the line, so as to avoid "feminine" rhymes like *splashing ~ dashing* or *Tennyson ~ venison*, which are disfavored in English. The first line of "Hush-a-bye Baby" also has a short foot in the middle of the line; because of the generally regular rhythm, the reader tends to compensate by making a brief pause, called a "caesura," in place of the missing syllable:

/ Húsh-ă-byĕ / bábў˘ / ón thĕ trĕe / tóp ˘ ˘ /

This line has a further irregularity in that the syllables *bye* and *tree*, which occupy weak positions within the foot, are not entirely unstressed; both these syllables carry some stress, though not the primary stress.

Popular verse tends to have a very regular, even singsong, rhythm, but serious poetry is less rigidly metrical; literary poetry often contains feet with a missing syllable, feet with two stressed syllables (called "spondees"), or "inverted" feet, with the stressed and unstressed positions reversed. These departures from regular rhythm serve to emphasize certain words or may relate onomatopoetically to the meaning of the poem. For example, Robert Herrick's poem "Delight in Disorder" is written in iambic tetrameter, but the second line is somewhat ametrical, in keeping with the notion of "disorder" which was introduced in the previous line:

> *ă swéet / dĭsór / dĕr ĭn / thĕ dréss*   (Metrical except for the third foot, which has no stress.)
>
> *Kíndlĕs / ĭn clóthes / ă wán / tŏnnĕss*   (First foot is inverted, fourth foot has no stress.)

For another example, consider Shakespeare's sonnet 73 (Section 4.6.1 above), which is written in iambic pentameter. In our previous discussion of this sonnet, we observed that the fourth line is onomatopoetic, in that the sound of the words mimics, first, an out-of-tune choir and then a bird call. We can now observe that this effect comes from the *rhythm* of the line as well as its consonant and vowel sounds: the first phrase (*Bare ruined choirs*) is ametrical, as the scansion shows, like a choir with bad timing, and the final foot is inverted, giving it the rhythm (as well as the sound) of a bird call:

> *Báre rúined / chóirs ˘ / whĕre láte / thĕ swéet // bírds săng /.*
>
> (The first foot has two stresses, the second foot is missing a syllable, and the fifth foot is inverted, with a / ´ ˘ / pattern rather than the expected / ˘ ´ /.)

EXERCISE 9. Do a complete scansion of Shakespeare's sonnet 73 (at the beginning of Section 4.6.1). Note any departures from strict iambic pentameter, and, if appropriate, say how those departures enhance the content of the lines by creating onomatopoetic effects or calling attention to particular words.

4.7 Applications for Students and Teachers of English as a Second Language

ESL teachers need a strong background in the phonetics and phonology. While young ESL students (under the age of 14 or so) will probably "pick up" the pronunciation they hear around them, older students will require special training in the pronunciation of English, as will younger students who are studying English in a non-English-speaking environment.[6] This section will provide some of the information that ESL teachers need in order to teach pronunciation effectively. At this point we abandon the pronunciation symbols that are used by American dictionaries and

---

6. Jenkins (2000) points out that students who learn English outside an English-speaking environment will adjust their pronunciation toward a common norm that will be intelligible to their classmates. This works well if the students come from different language backgrounds, but not so well when everyone speaks the same first language. What seems intelligible in such a classroom may not be intelligible to native English speakers or to speakers of English as an international language.

move to the International Phonetic Alphabet, which is used in ESL pronunciation textbooks and in learners' dictionaries.

EXERCISE 10. If you used American dictionary symbols in doing Exercise 3 above, go back now and re-do that exercise using the IPA symbols that are provided in Table 4.1.

4.7.1   Distinguishing the Phonemes

The consonant and vowel sounds that make up the words of a language are called "phonemes." Some phonemes, including the consonant sounds /p/, /t/, /n/ and the vowel sounds /i/ and /a/, are found in nearly every language, but others are less common and may cause difficulty for language learners. You may have encountered such problems yourself in studying a foreign language. If you have studied Spanish, then you probably struggled with its two "r" phonemes (*pero* 'but' vs. *perro* 'dog'). In French, you may have had difficulty with the vowel sounds of *tu* 'you' and *un peu* 'a little'. If you studied German, you will have encountered these same challenging vowel phonemes (in *kühl* 'cool' and *Höhle* 'cave') and may have struggled, also, with the final consonant sound of *Buch* 'book'.

English, also, has consonant and vowel sounds that are difficult for speakers of other languages. For example, our /θ/ 'thing' and /ð/ 'this' are notoriously difficult; you may have heard *this thing* (/ðɪs θɪŋ/) pronounced as /dɪs tɪŋ/ or /zɪs sɪŋ/. The distinction between /v/ and /w/ is tricky for speakers of German, and speakers of many east Asian languages have difficulty distinguishing /l/ from /r/. Nearly everybody struggles with the American English /r/, which differs from the /r/ sounds in most other languages, and with our vowels—especially the /æ/ of 'bat', the /ʌ/ of 'but', and the distinction we make between long and short vowel sounds (/i:/ 'beat' vs. /ɪ/ 'bit'; /e:/ 'bait' vs. /ɛ/ 'bet', /u:/ 'suit' vs. /ʊ/ 'soot', and /o:/ 'hope' vs. /ɑ/ 'hop') are almost always a problem.

Nilsen and Nilsen's *Pronunciation Contrasts in English* is a good resource for identifying potential pronunciation problems. It lists consonant and vowel sounds that are likely to be difficult for speakers of particular languages, and also provides "minimal pairs" for use in pronunciation exercises. A minimal pair is a set of words that differ only in the target sound; for example, for the contrast /th/ ~ /t/, Nilsen and Nilsen provide such pairs as *thank ~ tank, pithy ~ pity*, and *forth ~ fort*.[7] The teacher begins by pronouncing pairs of words from the list (for example, *thank ~ thank*, or *thank ~ tank*) and asking the students to say whether she has pronounced one word twice ("same") or two different words ("different"). Once the students can handle this task, the teacher pronounces one word at a time and asks the students to identify it—for example, by saying whether it comes from list #1 or list #2. As a final step, the students pronounce the words themselves, with the teacher or a student partner giving them feedback about what sound they heard. Once the students can handle words in isolation, they can try words in sentences; Nilsen and Nilsen provide the minimal sentences *He **thought/taught** about her* and *It's the new **math/mat***. I suggest that you teach your students the IPA symbols for the sounds they are practicing

---

7. Notice that the contrast is illustrated in several contexts—at the beginning, middle, and end of a word; this is important because a sound's pronunciation may change somewhat, depending on its position in the word and what sounds surround it.

Table 4.2 Places of Articulation for English Consonants[a]

		lips	lower lip against upper teeth	tongue blade against upper teeth	tongue tip or blade against tooth ridge	tongue blade and body spread across tooth ridge and roof of mouth	tongue body against roof of mouth	back of tongue against soft palate	vocal folds
oral stops	voiced	*p*			*t*	*tʃ*		*k*	
	voiceless	*b*			*d*	*dʒ*		*g*	
fricatives	voiced		*f*	*θ*	*s*[b]	*ʃ*			
	voiceless		*v*	*ð*	*z*	*ʒ*			
nasal sonorants[c]		*m*			*n*			*ŋ*	
oral sonorants					*l*	*j*	*r*	*w*[d]	*h*

a. For students who want to know the technical terms for the places of articulation for consonants, they are as follows: made with the two lips = *bilabial*; made with the lower lip and upper teeth = *labiodental*; made with the tongue blade and upper teeth = *interdental*; made with the blade of the tongue near the tooth ridge = *alveolar*; made with the tongue body near the tooth ridge and roof of mouth = *palato-alveolar*; made with the tongue body near the roof of the mouth = *palatal*; made with the back of the tongue near the soft palate = *velar*; made with the vocal folds = *glottal*.

b. Most alveolar consonants are made by pressing the tip of the tongue against the alveolar ridge. For [s] and [z], however, the tip of the tongue may be placed behind the lower teeth, so that the front of the tongue (the tongue "blade") approaches the alveolar ridge. This level of detail is ignored in Table 4.2, but you will want to be aware of exactly how you pronounce each sound, in case it is an issue for your students.

c. Except for [h], the sonorant consonants are all voiced. (Some speakers also have a voiceless *velar* sonorant, [hw].)

d. Because [w] is pronounced with rounding of the lips, it has a labial articulation as well as velar.

so that you can refer to these symbols (and the illustrative words that go with them) when the problem crops up again.[8]

Students may also appreciate some instruction about how to *produce* the sounds of English. English uses eight points of articulation for consonants, as shown in Table 4.2.

---

8. Even dictionaries that use IPA may differ somewhat in the exact representations they use; the teacher should use the symbols that the students will find in their dictionaries. Having a way to represent pronunciation visually is especially useful when teaching vocabulary words like *leopard* or *sword*, whose spelling is misleading. No matter how many times they practice these words in class, students are likely to come back the next day pronouncing them as [ˈli ə ˌpard] and [swɔrd]. (In fact, a native speaker of English tried to persuade me that the correct pronunciation *is* [swɔrd].)

EXERCISE 11. Pronounce the consonant sounds of Table 4.2 one by one to be sure you understand what is stated there about their articulation. Then, without looking at the table, give the place of articulation, manner of articulation (stop, fricative, nasal sonorant, or oral sonorant) and voicing (voiced or voiceless) for each of the following consonant sounds:

[t][9]

[dʒ]

[ŋ]

[l]

[j]

[ʃ]

ESL students may want to see pictures illustrating the articulation of sounds that are difficult for them. Figure 4.3a (from Nilsen and Nilsen, 1971) shows the articulation of the "th" sounds [θ] and [ð], with the tongue blade positioned just below the upper teeth so that the air can flow out, with friction. (Note that [θ] and [ð] are made with the same mouth position; they differ in that [ð] is voiced, while [θ] is voiceless.) Figure 4.3b illustrates the articulation of [w] and [v]; Figure 4.3c illustrates the articulation of [l] vs. [r].

Note that for [l], the tip of the tongue is pressed against the alveolar ridge, while the body and sides of the tongue are pulled down to allow the air to pass. [r] is just the opposite: the body of the tongue is bunched up near the roof of the mouth (the hard palate), but the tip and sides of the tongue are pulled down. If you can't tell where your tongue *is* when you make [r], then pronounce the words *ring* and *here* with your finger in your mouth. (You may want to wait until you are in private!)

4.7.2 The Vowel Phonemes of English

English, like most other languages, has both "simple" vowels and diphthongs. (A diphthong is *two* vowel sounds in such close proximity that they form just one syllable.) English has up to thirteen "simple" vowels: /iː/ 'beet', /ɪ/ 'bit', /eː/ 'bait',[10] /ɛ/ 'bet', /æ/ 'bat', /ʌ/ 'but', /ɜː/ 'Burt', /ɑː/ 'balm', /ɒ/ 'bomb', /uː/ 'boot', /ʊ/ 'put', /oː/ 'boat', and /ɔː/ 'bought'.[11] However, speakers of American English do not usually use all these vowels. Many speakers make no distinction between the /ɑː/ of *balm* and the /ɒ/ of *bomb*, or between the /ɒ/ of *bomb* and the /ɔː/ of *bought*; some speakers use just one same vowel sound in all these words.

Vowel sounds differ in the *vertical* position of the jaw (high, mid, or low) and the *horizontal* position of the tongue body (front, central, or back), as shown in Table 4.3. Before

---

9. When we are talking about the repertoire of consonant and vowel sounds for a particular language (the "phonemes" of the language), the symbol is enclosed in angle brackets (//). When we are describing how the sound is made, the symbol is enclosed in square brackets ([]). See Section 4.7.4 below for discussion of the fact that a single phoneme such as /t/ (note the angle brackets) may be pronounced in several different ways: [t], [tʰ], [tˀ], or [ɾ] (note the square brackets).

10. The long mid vowels /eː/ and /oː/ are often pronounced as diphthongs—as [eɪ] and [oʊ].

11. These are the "full" (unreduced) vowels. The "reduced" vowels ([ə], [ɨ], and [ɚ]) will be discussed later in this section.

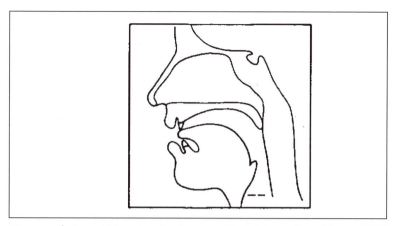

Figure 4.3a   The Articulatory Position for [θ] and [ð].

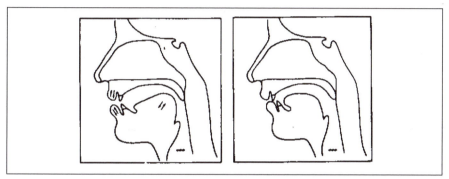

Figure 4.3b   The Articulatory Positions for [w] and [v].

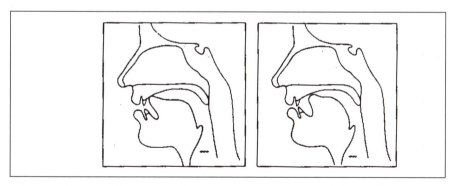

Figure 4.3c   The Articulatory Positions for [l] and [r].
Figures 4.3a–c reprinted by permission of Waveland Press, Inc. from Don L. F. Nilsen and Alleen Pace Nilsen, *Pronunciation Contrasts in English*. (Long Grove, IL: Waveland Press, Inc., 1973 [reissued 2002]) All rights reserved.

Table 4.3 Tongue and Jaw Position for Vowel Sounds

horizontal position of tongue body

		Front	Central	Back
vertical position of jaw	**High**	i: 'beet' I 'bit'		u: 'boot' ʊ 'put'
	Mid	e: 'bait' ɛ 'bet'	ɝ: 'Burt' ʌ 'but'	o: 'boat' ɔ: 'bought
	Low	æ 'bat'		ɑ: 'balm' ɒ 'bomb'

reading any further, pronounce these vowel sounds in order—first going horizontally across the rows and then vertically up and down the columns—and observe the change in your tongue and jaw position as you move from one vowel to another. The changes in tongue position will be easier to observe if you put something in your mouth (in my introductory linguistics class, I pass out lollipops for this purpose); or you may find it helpful to watch yourself in a mirror.[12]

English vowels are difficult for ESL students because we have so many. (The most typical number of vowel sounds in the languages of the world is *five*.) Students have difficulty not only in *producing* these vowel sounds, but also in *hearing the difference* between them, however obvious that may seem to our ears. The distinction between long and short vowels, shown in Table 4.4,[13] is particularly difficult. This distinction is unusual in human languages, and many students find it difficult to hear or make the difference between vowel pairs such as /i:/ ~ /ɪ/, or /e:/ ~ /ɛ/, which differ only in this feature.

The diphthongs of English are listed in Table 4.5; this table also includes the "r-colored vowels," which move from the position of the primary vowel to the position for [ɚ].[14]

---

12. Notice that vowels with similar articulation, such as [e:] and [ɛ], often have different *spellings* in English (as <a> and <e>). This is because our spelling system was established before the occurrence of a pronunciation change called The Great Vowel Shift, which took place around Shakespeare's time and which shifted the positions of our long vowel sounds. Our spelling system reflects the way the long and short vowels were paired before the Great Vowel Shift.

13. Short vowels are called "short" because they take up less space in the syllable rhyme. Long vowels can stand alone in the rhyme of a syllable, as in /bi:/ 'bee', /be:/ 'bay', /bɝ:/ 'burr', etc., but short vowels need a following consonant: */mɪ/, */mɛ/, or */mæ/. Furthermore, only short vowels can appear before a two-consonant sequence such as [sk] or [lp]. Thus we can have /dɪsk/ 'disk' and /dɛsk/ 'desk', with short vowels, but not */di:sk/ or */de:sk/, where the vowel is long. Long and short vowels also differ in their articulation: for long vowels, the tongue is tenser and is pushed toward the edges of the vocal tract; short vowels (also called "lax" vowels) have less tension in the tongue and are articulated in a more central position.

14. Speakers who are "r-droppers" move, instead, to the position of [ə]. In the Boston area, for /aɚ/, speakers simply lengthen the [a].

Table 4.4   Long vs. Short Vowel Sounds

Simple vowels	
Long vowel	**Corresponding short vowel**
/iː/ 'bead', 'be'	/ɪ/ 'bit', 'disk'
/eː/ 'bait', 'bay'	/ɛ/ 'bet', 'desk'
	/æ/ 'bat', 'ask'
/ɝː/ 'Burt', 'burr'	/ʌ/ 'but', 'bust'
/ɑː/ 'balm', 'Pa'	/ɒ/ 'bomb', 'mosque'
/uː/ 'boot', 'boo'	/ʊ/ 'put'
/oː/ 'boat', 'bow'	
/ɔː/ 'bought', 'law'	

Table 4.5   The Diphthongs of English[a]

/aɪ/	'wry', 'write'[b]
/aʊ/	'now', 'loud'
/ɔɪ/	'boy', 'coin'
/ɪɚ/[c]	'beer', 'beard'[d]
/ɛɚ/	'air', 'paired'
/ʊɚ/[e]	'poor', 'toured'
/ɔɚ/	'shore'. 'corn'
/aɚ/	'car', 'part'

a. As we noted above, the long vowels [eː] and [oː] may also be pronounced as diphthongs ([eɪ], [oʊ]).

b. In the southern and midwestern U.S., this diphthong is sometimes pronounced as a long, low, central vowel: [aː].

c. You may feel that these diphthongs should be represented as [iɚ] and [eɚ] rather than [ɪɚ] and [ɛɚ]. It doesn't actually matter much which representation we choose: The important thing is that whichever representation we use, we should use it consistently, because speakers of American English do not distinguish between [ɪ] and [i] or between [e] and [ɛ] before *r*. If you sometimes write [ɪɚ] and sometimes [iɚ], you are suggesting that you make a *difference* between these two sounds, which is unlikely.

d. In "r-dropping" dialects the "r-colored" vowels end with [ə] rather than [ɚ].

e. Many English speakers don't use this diphthong, but pronounce *poor* and *tour* with the same vowel as *shore*.

EXERCISE 12.

a. Pronounce the vowel sounds of *boot, put, boat,* and *bought* in front of a mirror, and notice the position of your lips. Do you pronounce these vowels with rounded lips? (Watch yourself in the mirror, if necessary.) If you are from the Northeast or from outside the U.S., check to see whether you have a rounded vowel for *bomb* and *mosque*. Write the IPA symbols for the vowels that you use for these words.

b. Without looking at the text, say whether the vowel sound of each word is long or short:

ship	*tell*	*lame*	*socks*	*learn*
sheep	*tale*	*good*	*pool*	*mud*
lap	*boat*	*thought*	*pull*	

Identify the vowel sound of each word, using IPA symbols.

c. Make a list of the vowel sounds you use in your own speech, using the appropriate IPA symbol along with a key word for each sound. Include both diphthongs and simple vowels. (*Caution*: Your list may differ slightly from the lists of Tables 4.3, 4.4, and 4.5.)

ESL students can practice vowel sounds using "minimal pairs" like those that were described earlier for consonants; for example, for the contrast /i:/ vs. /ɪ/, Nilsen and Nilsen list minimal pairs such as *leave ~ live* and *team ~ Tim*, and minimal sentences such as *Feel/Fill this bag* and *Don't sleep/slip on the deck*. Don't be too fussy, however! As we noted above, there are some vowel contrasts such as *cot* (/ɒ/) vs. *caught* (/ɔ:/) that are not always observed by native speakers of English. If many native speakers don't care about this contrast, then ESL students shouldn't have to worry about it, either.

4.7.3 Consonant Clusters

In addition to problems with individual phonemes, ESL students may find it difficult to fit the sounds (especially the consonants) into syllables. English, more than most languages, allows consonants to pile up at the beginnings and ends of syllables to form "consonant clusters":

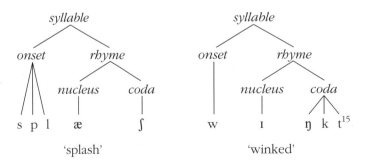

---

15. English normally allows two consonant sounds at the end of a syllable, as in [mɪlk] 'milk' or [æsk] 'ask.' However, a sequence of three or even four consonants is possible if the "extra" consonants are front-of-the-tongue obstruents (/t/, /d/, /s/, /z/, /θ/). Examples are [θɪŋks] 'thinks' and [sɪksθs] 'sixths.'

Students whose first languages do not allow clusters like these may leave out some consonants (for example, saying [wɪŋ] or [wɪŋk] instead of [wɪŋkt] 'winked') or may break up the cluster by inserting *extra* vowels, pronouncing *winked* as [wɪŋkɪd] or *splash* as [ɛsˈplæʃ] or [sə.pəˈlæ.ʃə]). Even native speakers of English find some consonant clusters impossible to pronounce; do you pronounce all the consonant sounds in *sixths* [sɪksθs], or do you, like the author of this text, leave out the [θ]?[16]

Even a single consonant can be hard to pronounce at the end of a syllable. Because Spanish does not allow final [p], [t], or [k], Spanish speakers sometimes drop these sounds at the end of an English word. Japanese speakers, whose own language excludes almost all coda consonants, may pronounce the word *baseball* as a four-syllable word ([ˈbesəɪbɔɾu]), inserting a vowel after the [s] and after the final [l], which may be replaced with an r-like sound. This allows them to pronounce the [s] and [l]/[r] as syllable onsets rather than syllable codas.

EXERCISE 13. Transcribe the following passage from Steven Pinker's *The Language Instinct* (1994, 161), using IPA symbols. Circle all consonant clusters, and indicate which clusters you might simplify in casual speech:

> *[T]he sequence of sounds we think we hear within a word are an illusion. If you were to cut up a tape of someone saying* cat, *you would not get pieces that sounded like* k, æ, *and* t . . . And if you spliced the pieces together in the reverse order, they would be unintelligible, not* tack.

Now think about the sound that *follows* each cluster. Does it matter whether it is a consonant or a vowel? If you listen carefully, you will see that consonants are more likely to be retained when the following sound is a vowel. Why should that be?

4.7.4 Phonological Rules

So far we have been speaking as if each phoneme were a uniform entity, always pronounced the same way, but we must now take note of the fact that a phoneme may be pronounced in several different ways, depending on its position in the utterance. Variations in the pronunciation of a phoneme are called the "allophones" of that phoneme. In American English there are at least four allophones of the phoneme /t/:

a.	Plain /t/	[t]	(as in [stɑp] 'stop')
b.	Aspirated /t/	[tʰ]	(as in [tʰɑp] 'top')[17]
c.	Unreleased /t/	[t˺]	(as in [gɛt˺ ðæt˺] 'get that')
d.	Flapped /t/	[ɾ]	(as in [ˈweːɾɪd] 'waited')[18]

---

16. The pronunciation of a consonant cluster sometimes depends on the sound that *follows*. For example, in the phrase *the weakest element*, where the consonant cluster [st] is followed by a vowel sound, a careful speaker may pronounce the entire cluster, but in the phrase *my weakest subject*, most speakers drop the [t] of *weakest*, and many speakers, including the author of this text, also drop the [t] of *subject*: [ˌmaɪ ˈwiːkɪs ˈsʌb.dʒɪk].

17. If you hold your hand in front of your mouth while saying *stop* and *top*, you should be able to feel a stronger puff of air with the [tʰ] of *top*. That's what we mean by "aspiration."

18. The phoneme /d/ can also be pronounced as [ɾ], so that in American English there is no distinction between *waited* and *waded*.

For English speakers, these four kinds of /t/'s are experienced as a single sound; because the choice between "allophones" is completely automatic, most speakers do not realize that they are making a change.[19] In fact, however, when /t/ is at the beginning of a word or the beginning of a stressed syllable, as in *top*, we automatically "aspirate" it ([tʰ]); when /t/ is at the end of the utterance or before a consonant, as in both /t/'s of *get that,* we often leave it unreleased ([t̚]); when /t/ appears between vowels, as in *waited*, but not in the onset of a stressed syllable, Americans pronounce it as a "flap" ([ɾ]); and when none of these conditions apply, we use a plain *t* ([t]), as in *stop*. However, although these alternations are automatic for us, they do not come automatically to ESL students. These variations in the pronunciation of /t/ are specific to English, and ESL students must *learn* to hear and produce them.

The processes that create the various allophones of a phoneme are called "phonological rules." Some phonological rules that ESL teachers should be aware of are listed below:

Vowel Reduction. An unstressed vowel is "reduced" to [ə], [ɨ], or [ɚ], as in [ˌæ.pəˌlæ.t͡ʃɨˌkō.lə ˈrɪ.vɚ] 'Appalachicola River', with reduced, centralized vowels ([ə], [ɨ], or [ɚ]) in the unstressed syllables.[20] The effects of Vowel Reduction can be seen most clearly when the position of stress is *changed* in a word, usually as a result of suffixation.[21] For example, consider the word *parental* [pʰəˈrɛn.təl], which is built from the root word *parent* [ˈpʰæ.rɨnt]. Notice that the addition of the suffix *-al* causes the stress to shift to the right. If we assume that the underlying root (/pærent/) has the vowels /æ/ and /ɛ/, as the spelling suggests, then the [ɨ] of [ˈpʰæ.rɨnt] and the [ə] of [pʰəˈrɛn.təl] are both a consequence of Vowel Reduction; when the syllable is not stressed, its vowel "reduces" to [ɨ] or [ə].[22]

There is an exception to Vowel Reduction that you should be aware of: In Standard American English the vowels /iː/, /uː/, and /oː/ do not reduce at the end of a word or immediately before another vowel. Examples include [ˈlaɪˌbrɛ.ri] 'library', [laɪˈbrɛ.ri.ən] 'librarian', [ˈbɪ.lo] 'billow', [ˈbɪ.lo.ɪŋ] 'billowing', [ˈɑr.gju] 'argue', and [ˈɑr.gju.ɪŋ] 'arguing.'[23]

---

19. But young children, who are more aware of these differences, are sometimes reluctant to use a single spelling for the /t/ sound in all these words. Spellings like *bedy* 'Betty' and *sdop* 'stop' are common among beginning writers.

20. It is not always easy to distinguish between the vowels [ə] and [ɨ], and speakers may differ in their choice of vowel in any particular instance. To hear the difference between the two, try the minimal pair *roses* vs. *Rosa's*. *Roses* has [ɨ] in the second syllable, while *Rosa's* has [ə].

21. Where the English stress system works regularly (and there are many, many irregularities), the primary stress is placed on one of the last three syllables of the word, depending on the shape of the next-to-last syllable, and whether the word is a noun, verb, or adjective. Because the stress position is counted from the end of the word, it may be affected by the addition of a suffix: ˈphotoˌgraph ~ phoˈtography, ˈmagnet ~ ˌmagˈnetic, ˈfinal ~ ˌfiˈnality, etc. For historical reasons, it is only a small set of Latin and Greek suffixes (*-y*, *-ic*, *-ity*, etc.) that have this effect; native English suffixes such as *-ness*, *-er*, and *-able* leave the position of stress unchanged (ˈcomfort ~ ˈcomfortable ~ ˈcomfortableness).

22. Students ask why the /ɛ/ gets reduced to [ɨ], while the /æ/ gets reduced to [ə]. It depends partly on the nature of the underlying vowel, and partly on the consonants that surround it. There are also differences between speakers: You may feel that you reduce the /ɛ/ to [ə], rather than to [ɨ]. If so, that's fine. Except for a few contrasts like *Rosa's* vs. *roses*, nobody cares about the difference between [ə] and [ɨ].

23. Some speakers, including the author of this text, make an exception only for /iː/ and not for /uː/ and /oː/, pronouncing *window* and *argue* as [ˈwɪn.də] and [ˈɑr.gjə].

Because of the great difference between stressed and unstressed syllables in English, an incorrect placement of stress may interfere with intelligibility, as when a French speaker of my acquaintance pronounced the word *adolescent* as [əˈdɑləsənt] instead of [ˌædəˈlɛsənt]. Vowel Reduction is also important in the pronunciation of small "function" words such as *the, is, or,* and *of* (see Chapter 3, Section 3.2), as in [ˈaɪ kʰɨn ˈgoː] 'I can go' (not [ˈaɪ ˈkʰæn ˈgoː]), [ə ˈpʰiːs əv ˈkʰeːk] 'a piece of cake' (not [ˈeː ˈpʰiːs ˈɑv ˈkʰeːk]), [ˈdʒæk ɨn ˈdʒɪl] 'Jack and Jill' (not [ˈdʒæk ˈænd ˈdʒɪl]). ESL speakers must learn to reduce the vowels in these small function words; otherwise they may not be understood.[24]

Some function words undergo still further reduction, as in [ˈwɔ.nə] 'wanna' (for 'want to') and [ˈgɪ.mi] 'gimme' (for 'give me'). ESL students must learn to *understand* these reductions, but should not necessarily use them in their own speech. Exercises on the reduction of vowels in unstressed syllables can be found in standard pronunciation textbooks such as *Sound Advantage, Well Said,* and *Targeting Pronunciation.* Nina Weinstein's *Whaddaya Say?* is a good source of exercises on the reduction of function words.

Aspiration (discussed previously in this section). A voiceless stop consonant (/p/, /t/, /tʃ/, or /k/) is aspirated when it comes at the beginning of a word or the beginning of a stressed syllable, as in [pʰəˈtʰeːro] 'potato', where the /p/ is aspirated because it is at the beginning of the word, and the first /t/ is aspirated because it is at the beginning of a stressed syllable. Aspiration is important in English, because we tend to interpret an unaspirated voiceless stop as if it were voiced; for example, the name "Patsy," if pronounced with an unaspirated [p], may be heard as "Batsy." ESL students sometimes practice aspiration by holding a piece of paper in front of their mouth: the aspiration should be strong enough to move the paper.

Flapping (discussed previously in this section). In American English, a /t/ or /d/ that comes between vowels may be pronounced as a "flap" ([ɾ]); for example, *waited* and *waded* are both pronounced [ˈwe.ɾɨd]. However, Flapping takes a back seat to Aspiration; for example, in the word [pʰəˈtʰeːro] 'potato', where both /t/'s are between vowels, only the second /t/ is pronounced as a flap ([ɾ])—the first /t/ is aspirated ([tʰ]) rather than Flapped, because it is at the beginning of a stressed syllable.

The Flap rule is not universal among English speakers, and ESL students do not necessarily have to learn to produce it; however, they must be able to interpret it when they hear it.

Non-release of stops. An oral stop (/p/, /b/, /t/, /d/, /k/, or /g/) which is not followed by a vowel may be left "unreleased."[25] Pronounce the words *hip, hit,* and *hick,* and notice that you may, optionally, cut off the air stream before the final consonant, without releasing it. Non-release of a consonant is indicated by a small, raised corner immediately after the consonant: [hɪp˺], [hɪt˺], [hɪk˺]. ESL students sometimes fail to hear the unreleased consonant as a distinct sound, and may

---

24. Because we don't like to have too many unstressed syllables in a row, *some* function words may be preserved when they are next to other, reduced words. For example, the phrase *Give it to her* may be pronounced either as [ˈgɪv ɨt ˈtu ɚ], with reduction of *her,* or as [ˈgɪv ɨt tə ˈhɝ], with reduction of *to,* but we can't reduce *to* and *her* at the same time.

25. The "affricated" stops [tʃ] and [dʒ] cannot be left unreleased, because the consonant ends as a fricative, which is inherently "released."

pronounce *hip*, *hit*, and *hick* all as [hɪʔ].[26] In fact, however, the difference between *hip*, *hit*, and *hick* is perfectly audible even when the final consonant is not released, because the consonant affects the sound of the vowel that comes before it; the important thing is to move to the position for the consonant before cutting off the airflow. Most ESL pronunciation texts provide exercises on the pronunciation of words with final stop consonants.

Notice that a final stop can be left unreleased only when the preceding sound is a vowel or a sonorant consonant (such as /l/ or /n/); try pronouncing *ask* and *asp* without releasing the final consonant; the two words are indistinguishable. To preserve the distinction in words of this type, a stop consonant that is preceded by a non-sonorant consonant must be released.

Voicing Assimilation. Non-sonorant consonants ("obstruents") come in two versions—voiced and voiceless. Thus we have the voiced oral stop /b/ and its voiceless counterpart /p/, the voiced fricative /z/ and its voiceless counterpart /s/, and so forth, as shown in Table 4.6.

English, like other languages, prefers that adjacent obstruents should agree in voicing. Our rule of Voicing Assimilation helps to create this situation by changing a voiced obstruent to voiceless when it follows a voiceless obstruent within the same syllable. Thus, in syllable onsets that begin with /s/, we find /sp/, /st/, and /sk/, but never */sb/, */sd/, or */sg/; because the /s/ is voiceless, the obstruent that comes after it must be voiceless also.[27] Similarly, in the syllable rhyme, we can have /æsk/ or /æft/, but not */æsg/ or */æfd/. For the same reason, the *z* of *waltz* must be pronounced as [s].

The rule of Voicing Assimilation affects the pronunciation of the plural and past-tense suffixes (spelled -*s* and -*ed*, respectively).[28] Since the <e> in the past tense suffix is pronounced only after /t/ or /d/ (see the discussion of [ɨ]-Insertion, just below), let us assume that the "basic" pronunciation of the past-tense suffix is simply [d], as in [kʰɪld] 'killed', [hʌmd] 'hummed', [bu:d] 'booed', etc. However, when the suffix comes after a voiceless obstruent, the rule of Voicing Assimilation changes its pronunciation to (voiceless) [t], so that, for example, /kɪs/ + /d/ ⟹ [kʰɪst] 'kissed', and /hɑp/ + /d/ ⟹ [hɑpʾt] 'hopped.'

The plural (and possessive and 3rd singular present tense) suffixes, all spelled -*s*, work the same way: the "basic" pronunciation of these suffixes is /z/, as in [bʌgz] 'bugs', [rɪbz] 'ribs', [sɔŋz] 'songs', and [gluz] 'glues' (the fact that they are spelled -*s* is not relevant; the /z/ sound is often spelled *s* in English). When a /z/ suffix is placed after a voiceless obstruent, the rule of Voicing Assimilation changes its pronunciation to [s], so that, for example, /bæt/ + /z/ ⟹ [bæts] 'bats').

[ɨ]-Insertion.[29] This rule comes into play when a consonant cannot be syllabified; we "rescue" the stranded consonant by inserting a reduced vowel. For example, since English does not allow

---

26. The symbol [ʔ] represents a "glottal stop"—the sound that is heard in the middle of the expression 'uh-oh.'

27. /sn/, /sl/, /spr/, etc. are OK, because /n/, /l/, and /r/ are sonorants, not obstruents; thus they are not affected by the rule of Voicing Assimilation.

28. The discussion that follows applies to the possessive suffix (-'s) and the 3rd-person singular present-tense suffix (-*s*), as well as the plural suffix (-*s*), and to the perfect participle and passive participle suffixes (-*ed*) as well as to the past tense.

29. The inserted vowel may be [ə] rather than [ɨ].

Table 4.6 Voiced and Voiceless Obstruents

Oral stops		Fricatives	
voiced	**voiceless**	**voiced**	**voiceless**
/b/	/p/	/v/	/f/
/d/	/t/	/ð/	/θ/
/dʒ/	/tʃ/	/d/	/t/
/g/	/k/	/z/	/s/
		/ʒ/	/ʃ/

consonant sequences of the form [dv], [dn], or [nk] in the onset of a syllable, English speakers may pronounce the names *Dvořak* (a Czech composer) and Dnieper (a Russian River) and Nkrumah (former president of Ghana) as [dɨˈvɔɚʒɑk], [dɨˈniːpɚ], and [nɨˈkruːmə] or [ɨnˈkruːmə], respectively, inserting an [ɨ] to support the stranded consonant.

The rule of [ɨ]-Insertion applies, also, when a consonantal suffix cannot fit into the syllable structure. For the /d/ suffixes, this problem arises when the base word ends in /d/ or /t/, as in /niːd/ 'need' or /weːt/ 'wait'; if we simply added the suffix to make *[weːdd] and *[weːtd], the result would not be pronounceable. [ɨ]-Insertion allows the suffix to be pronounced: /weːd/ + /d/ ⇒ [ˈweːr.ɨd] 'waded'[30] and /weːt/ + /d/ ⇒ [ˈweːr.ɨd] 'waited.'[31] The same situation arises for the /z/ suffixes when the base word ends in a strident consonant (/tʃ/, /dʒ/, /s/, /z/, /ʃ/, and /ʒ/), as in *bus*, *bush*, *watch*, or *judge*. If we simply added /z/, the result would not be pronounceable in English: *[bʌsz], *[buʃz], *[wɑtʃz], *[dʒʌdʒz]. Again, the rule of [ɨ]-Insertion comes to the rescue: /bʌs/ + /z/ ⇒ [ˈbʌs.ɨz] 'busses', /wɑtʃ/ + /z/ ⇒ [ˈwɑtʃ.ɨz] 'watches', and so forth.

ESL students often struggle with the pronunciation of the /d/ and /z/ suffixes—partly because of the difficult consonant clusters that these suffixes sometimes create (cf. [rʌbˀd] 'rubbed') and partly because of spelling: the *e* in the spelling may trick the student into pronouncing *rubbed*, for example, as *[ˈrʌbɨd].[32] Similarly, the silent *e* in the spelling of plural nouns like *robes* [roːbˀz], *miles* [mɑɪlz], *clues* [kʰluːz] may cause students to mispronounce them as *[ˈroːbɨz], *[ˈmɑɪlɨz], and *[kʰluɨz].

Velarization of /l/. The consonant /l/ has two allophones, called "clear /l/" and "dark /l/." Both /l/'s are made with the tip of the tongue touching the alveolar ridge (the ridge behind the teeth), but for clear /l/ ([l]) the body of the tongue is flat, while for dark /l/ ([ɫ]) the back of the tongue is bunched up near the soft palate (the "velum")—hence the term "velarization." We use clear /l/ in the onset of a syllable, as in [lɪpˀ] 'lip', [slʌm] 'slum', or [lɔgˀ] 'log.' In the *coda* of a syllable, we use dark [ɫ], as in [fɪɫ] 'fill', [hɔɫ] 'hall', or [pʰʊɫ] 'pull.'[33] (Pronounce these words now and notice the

---

30. Note that Flapping applies, also, once the [ɨ] is inserted.

31. Note that *waded* and *waited* are indistinguishable once Flapping has applied to change the /t/ and /d/ to [r].

32. The *-ed* spelling is a holdover from an earlier time when this suffix was pronounced as a full syllable.

33. When /l/ is between vowels, as in *dollar*, *hilly*, or *sailing*, its syllabification is ambiguous: Is it the coda of the first syllable or the onset of the second? It is not surprising, then, that speakers differ in their choice of allophone for this position; some speakers use a dark /l/ while others use a clear /l/.

difference between the two allophones of /l/.) ESL students must learn to velarize /l/ in the coda of the syllable, because the position of the tongue affects the sound of the preceding vowel. As an ESL teacher, you may think, at first, that your students are mispronouncing the vowel, but if you can teach them to make the [ɫ] correctly, then the sound of the vowel will improve automatically.

EXERCISE 14.

a. Transcribe the following place names into IPA, taking care to show reduced vowels in the unstressed syllables (if any): *Bermuda, Canada, Jamaica, Germany, Ukraine, Ethiopia, Ghana, Mexico, Denmark, Italy.*

b. Give an IPA transcription of the following movie titles, paying particular attention to small function words that would be reduced in ordinary conversation:

The Wizard of Oz
Charlie and the Chocolate Factory
Gone with the Wind
Two for the Road
To Kill a Mockingbird
A Place in the Sun
A Funny Thing Happened on the Way to the Forum

c. (*Advanced*) Transcribe the following words into IPA, paying particular attention to the pronunciation of the /d/ or /z/ suffix. Mark the words in which Voicing Assimilation or [ɨ]-Insertion have played a role.

waited	*rubbed*	*rings*	*raises*	*helps*
tilted	*waltzed*	*passes*	*paws*	*bathes*
filled	*sighed*	*bakes*	*hatches*	*froths*
waded	*planned*	*cares*	*judges*	*sloshes*
thanked	*chimed*	*laughs*	*boos*	*plows*

d. Give an IPA transcription of the following passage from Steven Pinker's *The Language Instinct* (1994, p. 182), paying particular attention to Vowel Reduction, both inside words and in the small function words that would be reduced in normal speech. (Don't concern yourself, in this transcription, with the aspiration of stop consonants, the non-release of stop consonants, the flapping of /t/'s and /d/'s, and the velarization of /l/'s.)

> *The reason that speech recognition is so hard is that there's many a slip 'twixt brain and lip. No two people's voices are alike, either in the shape of the vocal tract that sculpts the sounds, or in the person's precise habits of articulation. Phonemes also sound very different depending on how much they are stressed and how quickly they are spoken; in rapid speech, many are swallowed outright.*

e. (*Advanced*) Transcribe the following passage from Steven Pinker's *The Language Instinct* (1994, p. 180), indicating the reduction of function words, the aspiration of stop consonants, the non-release of stop consonants, the flapping of /t/'s and /d/'s, and the velarization of /l/'s:

> *In 1992 an ordinance was proposed that would have banned the hiring of any immigrant teacher who "speaks with an accent" in—I am not making this up—Westfield, Massachusetts. An incredulous woman wrote to the* Boston Globe *recalling how her native New England teacher defined "homonym" using the example* orphan *and* often. *Another amused reader remembered incurring the teacher's wrath when he spelled [kə'ri.ə] k-o-r-e-a and [kə'ri.ɚ] c-a-r-e-e-r, rather than vice-versa.*

4.7.5   Intonational Melodies

Words are not usually pronounced singly, in isolation, but are joined together into *phrases*. Within a phrase, the words blend together to some extent, so that they sound almost like one word. For example, word-final stops are always released when they are followed by a vowel sound within the same phrase, as in [ˈkʰiːp ˈaut] 'Keep out!' (not *[ˈkʰiːp˺ ˈaut]), and word-final /t/'s and /d/'s are "flapped" between vowels: [ˈɡɛɾ ˈaut] 'Get out!'; [ˈhɛɾ ˈaut] 'Head out!' This blending of words within a phrase is called "linking."

Each phrase is marked by an intonational melody such as the following, where M = mid pitch, H = high, H* = extra-high, and LM = a low rising pitch:

The statement melody:	M H̲ L
The *yes-no* question melody:	M H̲ H*
The unfinished melody:	M H̲ LM

The "nuclear tone" of the melody (the tone that is underlined in the formulas above) is realized on the "nuclear stress"—the most heavily stressed syllable of the phrase. In a neutral statement like that of Figure 4.4,[34] the nuclear stress is the main stressed syllable of the last important word—in this case, *Tuesday.*

In a short statement like *Today's Tuesday* (Figure 4.4), the entire statement will probably be pronounced as a single phrase. But a long utterance like *George Washington, who was our first president, wore ill-fitting false teeth* will be broken into several phrases, as shown in Figure 4.5.[35] Because this is a statement, the final phrase of the sentence carries the MH̲L melody that is characteristic of statements, but the two internal phrases carry the "unfinished" melody (MH̲LM), as shown, which

---

34. The intonation contours in this chapter were created by means of a wonderful phonetic-analysis program called Praat, which was developed by Paul Boersma and David Weenink, of the Institute of Phonetics Sciences at the University of Amsterdam. To do phonetic analyses of your own speech, download their free program from their web site: www.praat.org.

35. Normally, each new piece of information within the utterance will have its own phrase. For example, if we have just been talking about Friday (*What's happening on Friday?*), then the statement *Friday is a holiday* can be pronounced as one intonation phrase. But if we are going through the days of the week (*What's happening on Wednesday, Thursday, and Friday?*), then the statement will be divided into two phrases (*And Friday // is a holiday*), with the unfinished melody on the first phrase and the statement melody on the second.

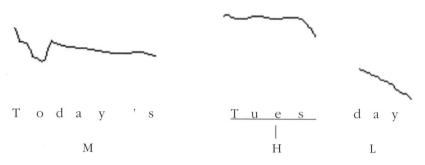

Figure 4.4   The Statement Melody (M<u>H</u>L).

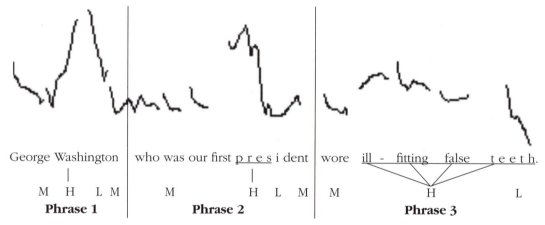

Figure 4.5   A Statement that is Broken into Three Intonation Phrases.

indicates that the utterance is not yet finished.[36] Note that each phrase has its own nuclear stress, and that the nuclear tone is attached to the syllable that carries the nuclear stress.

Yes/no questions like *Is today Tuesday?* carry a different melody—the "question" melody (MHH*), as shown in Figure 4.6, with (<u>H</u>) as the nuclear tone. The question melody is used only for *yes/no* questions like *Is today Tuesday?* "Information" questions such as *What day is it?* carry the statement melody, as shown in Figure 4.7.

Figure 4.8 shows the intonation of the "alternative" (*either/or*) question like *Is it Tuesday or Thursday?* Notice that alternative questions are broken into *two* intonational phrases, each with its own nuclear stress. The first phrase carries the question melody (M<u>H</u>H*) and the second phrase carries the statement melody (M<u>H</u>L).

There are other intonation melodies in English (for example, the "list" melody that is found in lists like *January, February, March, April, and May*).[37] Standard pronunciation textbooks such as *Sound Advantage, Well Said*, and *Targeting Pronunciation* present a basic repertoire of English intonation melodies, with exercises for practice. Intonation is particularly important for social

---

36. The unfinished melody can also be used as the final melody of an utterance, to indicate that something still remains to be said on the matter. (*Today's Tuesday* . . . [so why isn't the office open?])

37. In a list like this one, each item of the list is treated as a separate intonation phrase. Each phrase except the last one carries the melody M<u>H</u>. The last phrase carries the statement melody.

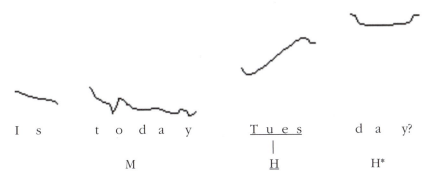

Figure 4.6   The *Yes/No* Question Melody (MH̲H*).

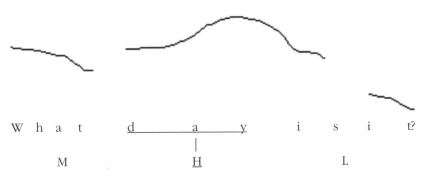

Figure 4.7   Information Question with Statement Melody.

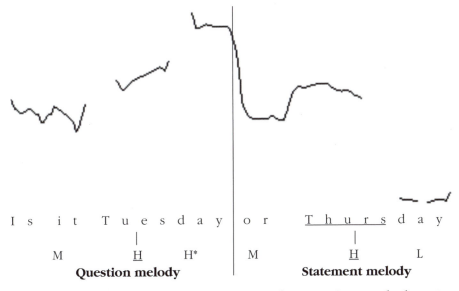

Figure 4.8   Alternative Question with Question Melody + Statement Melody.

functions such as apologizing, giving instructions, and making requests, where an inappropriate intonation can seem rude. Give your students (or let them create) short dialogs of this type and have them practice them over and over until the intonation is acceptable.

EXERCISE 15.

a. Choose an appropriate intonation melody (MHL or MHH*) for each sentence and write it under the sentence, with the nuclear tone attached to the nuclear syllable.
  i.   *What would you like to drink?*
  ii.   *Would you like coffee?*
  iii. *I'd like some orange juice.*[38]

b. The following sentences each contain two or more intonation phrases. Copy each sentence and divide it into phrases. Choose an appropriate intonation melody (MHL, MHH*, or MHLM) for each phrase, write the melody under the phrase, and link the nuclear tone to the nuclear stress.
  i.   *Would you like coffee, tea, or juice?*
  ii.   *Is this the north gate or the south gate?*
  iii. *In Chinese, a syllable contains at most one final consonant sound.*
  iv.   *People who live in glass houses shouldn't throw stones.*
  v.   *Idle hands are the devil's workshop.*
  vi.   *A penny saved is a penny earned.*
  vii. *A rolling stone gathers no moss.*

4.7.6 Using Intonation to Mark Contrast and Focus

As we saw in the previous section, the nuclear stress and the nuclear tone normally fall on the last important word of the phrase, as in *Today is Tuesday*, or *What day is it?* However, the nuclear stress can be moved to another position to indicate emphasis or contrast. If I am simply informing you what day it is, I will use the "neutral" pronunciation in Figure 4.4, with nuclear stress on *Tuesday*. But if you ask me, "Which day is Tuesday?" I will probably answer as shown in Figure 4.9, with the nuclear stress/tone on *today* (the information that I want to focus). Or if you say, "I wish *today* were Tuesday!", then I may answer as shown in Figure 4.10, with the nuclear stress/tone on the word *is*, to emphasize the affirmative polarity of this sentence. In other words, the nuclear stress can be placed on any word of the phrase, depending on which part of the utterance we want to focus. The nuclear tone of the intonation melody (in this case, the H) attaches to the nuclear stress, wherever it may be, and the other tones of the melody distribute themselves over the remainder of the utterance.

This same system applies to other melodies such as the question melody, as illustrated in Figures 4.11 and 4.12. In other words, no matter what melody is chosen, its nuclear tone will be placed on the word or phrase that the speaker wants to focus. This is an important feature of the pronunciation of English, and one that requires a lot of practice for ESL students.

---

38. *Orange juice* is a compound noun which, like other compound nouns, places its main stress on its first word (*orange*). (See Chapter 2, Exercise 11.)

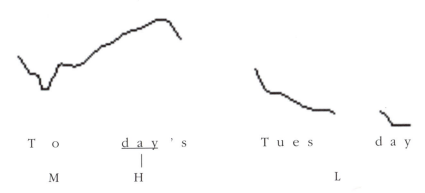

T o   d a y ' s   T u e s   d a y

M   H   L

Figure 4.9   Statement melody with nuclear stress on *to<u>day</u>*.

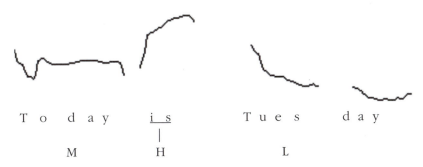

T o   d a y   i s   T u e s   d a y

M   H   L

Figure 4.10   Statement melody with nuclear stress on *is*.

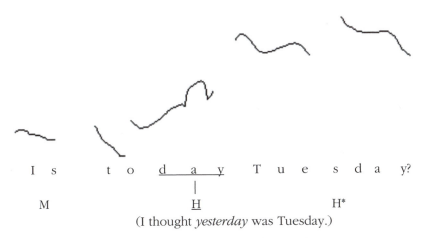

I s   t o <u>d a y</u>   T u e s   d a y?

M   <u>H</u>   H*

(I thought *yesterday* was Tuesday.)

Figure 4.11   Question melody with nuclear stress on *to<u>day</u>*.

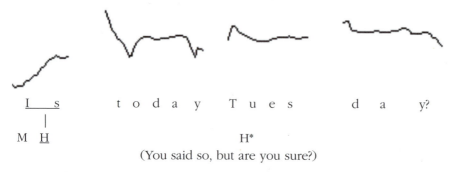

(You said so, but are you sure?)

Figure 4.12   Question melody with nuclear stress on *is*.

EXERCISE 16.   Treat each of the following utterances as a single intonation phrase, and draw intonation melodies for each one, with the nuclear stress/pitch placed, in turn, on each underlined word. Then provide a context in which that pronunciation of the sentence would be appropriate. For example, with the nuclear stress/pitch in position (i), sentence (a) below would be an appropriate answer to the question *Who was the first president of the United States?* With the nuclear stress in position (ii), this sentence would be an appropriate response to the statement *I thought George Washington was the first president of the United States. Caution*: Be sure to pronounce the sentence as just one intonation phrase, with one nuclear stress and one intonation melody.

a. *George <u>Washington</u> <u>was</u> the first <u>president</u> of the United <u>States</u>.*
    i   ii   iii   iv

b. *There are <u>four</u> <u>cups</u> in a <u>quart</u>.*
        i   ii   iii

c. *The <u>Normans</u> invaded <u>England</u> in <u>ten</u>-<u>sixty</u>-<u>six</u>.*
        i   ii   iii iv   v

4.7.7   More Intonation Phrases ~ More Elements in Focus

Since each intonation phrase has only one nuclear stress/tone, we can focus additional elements only by breaking the sentence into more than one intonation phrase. For example, if the sentence *Nobody said good morning to <u>George</u>* is treated as one phrase, with nuclear stress/pitch on *George*, then *George* is the only focused element in the sentence.[39] But the sentence can also be pronounced as two phrases, with two focused elements: *<u>Nobody</u> // said good morning to*

---

39. As we observed in the previous section, it is possible to place the nuclear stress/tone in different positions in the phrase; for example, *<u>Nobody</u> said good morning to George*. This would be an appropriate pronunciation if we were already discussing who said good morning to George, so that *good morning* and *George* had already been introduced into the conversation. The only new information is *nobody*, and it therefore carries the nuclear stress.

George. Or it can be pronounced as three phrases, with three focused elements: *Nobody // said good morning // to George*.

Making intonation breaks in the right places is an important part of the pronunciation of English. A good exercise for ESL students is to have them mark appropriate intonation boundaries in a short written text, and then read the text out loud, observing the intonation boundaries that they have marked.

EXERCISE 17. Pronounce the sentence *Nobody said good morning to George* as one intonation phrase, then as two, and then as three. Draw an intonation diagram for each version of the sentence, showing the intonation melody for each phrase with the nuclear tone assigned to the focused element. Then pronounce each of the following sentences in three different ways by breaking the sentence into one, two, or three intonation phrases. Draw an intonation diagram for each pronunciation:

a. *English was brought to America by British immigrants.*

b. *Johnson published his dictionary of English in 1755.*

4.8 Summary of Chapter

We began this chapter by listing the consonant and vowel sounds of English, using, first, the **International Phonetic Alphabet (IPA)** and then the symbols that are used in most American dictionaries. The dictionary symbols are usually sufficient for native speakers of English, but ESL teachers and others who want a more detailed understanding of the sound system of English will have to learn IPA. The consonant and vowel sounds that are used to create words in a given language are called **phonemes**. Each language has its own repertoire of phonemes which differs somewhat from that of other languages.

Consonant sounds can be divided into several subcategories. In Section 4.3 we discussed the **obstruent consonants** (the **oral stops** and **fricatives**) and the **sonorant consonants** (**nasal** and **oral sonorants**). Obstruents may be **voiced** or **voiceless**. Sonorant consonants are usually voiced, though English has two voiceless sonorants—[h] and (for some speakers) [hw]. Obstruent consonants with a very noisy sound are called **stridents**. Students of literature need an awareness of the phonemes of English in order to identify sound effects in poetry—repetition of consonant and vowel sounds (**consonance** and **assonance**) and rhyme (**masculine** and **feminine rhyme**). A knowledge of the subclasses of consonant sounds allows us to identify *partial* consonance or assonance—a string of sonorant consonants, for example, or of consonants that are strident.

When we speak, we organize our consonant and vowel sounds into units called **syllables**, with a vowel at the center (the **nucleus**).[40] The nucleus and **coda**, together, make up the **rhyme** of the syllable. Consonants that appear before the nucleus are called the **onset**. English allows a greater number of consonants in the onset and coda than most other languages.

---

40. Sonorant consonants can sometimes occupy the center of a syllable, as in the word *mitten*, where the second syllable consists only of the "syllabic" consonant [n̩]. (The line under the [n] indicates that it forms a syllable by itself, without a supporting vowel.)

Syllables may be **stressed** or **unstressed**. Stressed syllables carry a full vowel sound, such as [ē] or [ô], while unstressed syllables have the "reduced" vowel sounds [ə], [ɚ], or [ɨ]. The **main** stressed syllable of the word is the syllable that carries the "nuclear" tone (H) when the word is pronounced in isolation with the statement melody. A metrical pattern such as **iambic pentameter** or **trochaic tetrameter** establishes a regular alternation of stress and unstressed syllables. Deliberate departures from the regular metrical pattern may be used to create special literary effects.

Teachers of English as a second language—especially those who work with adult students or in a non-English-speaking environment—need a sophisticated understanding of the sound system of English in order to help their students achieve acceptable pronunciation. Dictionaries for ESL students use IPA symbols to represent the pronunciation of words. ESL teachers should be familiar with these symbols and should know which sound contrasts are especially difficult for their students. They should be able to explain how each phoneme is produced and how its pronunciation is affected by phonological rules such as **Vowel Reduction**, **Aspiration of Voiceless Stops**, **Flapping**, **Non-release of Stops**, **Voicing Assimilation**, **[ɨ]-Insertion**, and **Velarization of /l/**. They should also be aware of the difficulty presented by consonant clusters and by the reduction of small function words in connected speech.

ESL teachers should also be aware of the **intonation melodies** of English, including the **Statement Melody**, the *yes/no* **Question Melody**, and the **Unfinished Melody**. They must be able to teach students how to divide long utterances into **intonation phrases**, each with its own melody, and how to create **contrast** and **focus** by shifting the position of the **nuclear stress and tone** within the intonation phrase.

CHAPTER 5

Spelling

School superintendent stands on principal in Michigan
—Newspaper headline, quoted in the *Columbia Journalism Review*

5.1 Introduction

English is famous for its difficult spelling. The written word is often a poor guide to pronunciation (*would, know, leopard,* and *sword,* for example), and pronunciation is sometimes very little help with spelling (*Chanukkah,* for example, or *hors d'oeuvres*). How did we get into such a mess?

Some problems stem from the fact that, from the very beginning, our alphabet was not entirely suited for English; the Irish monks who first wrote English in the 7th and 8th centuries simply adapted the Roman alphabet, which was designed for Latin. This worked well where Latin and English had corresponding sounds—for example, since both languages had the consonant sounds [p] and [t], the letters <p> and <t> could be applied to English in a very straightforward way. However, the Roman alphabet had no letters for our consonant sounds [ch], [sh], [th] and [*th*], because these sounds did not occur in classical Latin. The situation was even worse for the vowels. The Roman alphabet had five vowel letters (*a, e, i, o,* and *u*), making it ill-suited for a language like English, which has thirteen "simple" vowel sounds, not including the diphthongs (see Chapter 4).[1]

Other spelling irregularities stem from the fact that the pronunciation of English changed over time. When English was first written, *would* and *should* were pronounced with an [l] sound,[2] and *knee, know, gnat,* and *gnaw* began with the sounds [k] and [g]. The <gh> of *might, light, right,* and *enough* represented a consonant sound that can still be heard in modern German (as the final sound of the name *Bach*); however, as time went on, English speakers began to pronounce this sound as [f] in some words (*tough, rough, enough,* etc.) and dropped it from others (*light, right, night, though, thought,* etc.). Though there is no longer a [gh] sound in English, these letters remain in the spelling of words which originally contained this sound.

A third source of irregularity in our spelling is the large number of borrowings from other languages. Borrowed words such as *machine, spaghetti,* and *phlegm* still retain spelling features from their original languages. If *machine* were spelled in the English system, for example, it would be *masheen,* but this word was borrowed from French, and so it uses a French spelling, with <ch> for the sound [sh] and <i> for the sound [ē].

Despite the many irregularities in the spelling of individual words, there is, nevertheless, an overall system in our orthography; not every word has to be memorized by sight. We will begin this chapter by surveying some of the principles that must be acquired, either consciously or unconsciously, as we learn to read and write. (In most cases, this means by children in early primary school, but it can also mean adult students in adult literacy programs, or ESL students who

---

1. Latin itself had *ten* simple vowels, but they were divided neatly into pairs of long and short vowels; the long vowels were represented by means of a diacritic: ā = 'long a'; a = 'short a.' However, this system was not carried over into English.
2. The <l> of *could* was added later, by analogy with *would* and *should.*

are just learning to read English.) In the latter part of the chapter, we will consider some spelling principles that should be helpful to more advanced spellers. Pronunciations in this chapter will be represented with American dictionary symbols rather than the IPA.

5.2 Basic Spelling

This section will begin with a review of the basic spellings for consonant and vowel sounds, as well as the spelling rules for suffixes and the complex spelling conventions involving the letter <y>. In talking about spelling, it is important to be clear whether you are talking about *sounds* or *letters* (for example, the sound [k] may be represented by the letter <c>). Throughout this text, *sounds* will be represented with square brackets ([ ]), and *letters* with angle brackets (< >).

5.2.1 The Spelling of Consonant Sounds

Because of the reasonably good match between the consonant sounds of English and the consonant letters of the Roman alphabet, most consonant sounds have a fairly consistent spelling; for example, the sound [b] is spelled as <b> or <bb>, the sound [g] as <g> or <gg>, the sound [h] as <h>, and so forth. However, some consonant sounds have different spellings depending on whether they are at the beginning or the end of a word. For example, the sound [k] is spelled <c> or <k> at the beginning of a word (*cake, kite*), but as <ck> or <ke> at the end (*back, bake*, not **bac* or **bak*).

EXERCISE 1.

a. List the most common spellings for the following consonant sounds when they appear at the beginning of a word: [p], [b], [t], [d], [j], [k], [kw], [ks], [g], [f], [v], [s], [z], [l], [r], [m], [n], [w], [y], [h]. Give an example for each spelling. *Caution:* Confine yourself, in this exercise, to our basic English orthography. For example, do not worry about the fact that the sound [n] is spelled <pn> in the word *pneumonia*; this spelling is found only in words that are borrowed from Greek. Also keep in mind that some sounds in this list do not *occur* at the beginning of a word.

b. Now list the common spellings of these same consonant sounds when they appear at the *end* of a word. Which sounds have different spellings for the beginning and the end of a word?

c. Some consonants, including <l>, are normally spelled with a double letter after a single vowel (cf. *tall, hill, doll, tell, dull*). What happens if there is a two-vowel sequence before the consonant (<ee> or <ai>, for example)?

5.2.2 Digraphs

As we noted above, the Roman alphabet had no letters to spell our consonant sounds [th], [*th*], [sh], [ch], [hw], and [ng], which did not occur in Latin. The solution was to spell these consonant sounds as *digraphs* (a sequence of two letters that is used to represent one sound).[3] The diagraphs of English are set out in Table 5.1.

---

3. Don't confuse the terms *diphthong* and *digraph*. A diphthong is two vowel *sounds* that are blended together into one syllable, like the [ou] of *how*. A digraph is a sequence of two letters used to represent one sound, like <sh>.

Table 5.1   The Digraphs of English

Digraph	Pronunciation	Example
<th>[4]	[th]	*th*i*ng*, *ba*th
<th>	[*th*]	*th*i*s*, *ba*th*e*
<sh>	[sh]	*sh*ow
<ch>	[ch]	*ch*ew
<wh>	[hw] or [w]	*wh*en
<ng>	[ng]	*ri*ng

EXERCISE 2. Circle the digraphs in the following passage; each of the six digraphs appears at least once.

Fourscore and seven years ago our fathers brought forth upon this continent a new nation, conceived in liberty and dedicated to the proposition that all men are created equal.

Now we are engaged in a great civil war testing whether that nation, or any nation so conceived and so dedicated, can long endure. We are met on a great battlefield of that war. We have come to dedicate a portion of it, as a final resting place for those who died here, that the nation might live. This we may, in all propriety do. But in a larger sense, we cannot dedicate, we cannot consecrate, we cannot hallow, this ground. The brave men, living and dead, who struggled here, have hallowed it, far above our poor power to add or detract. The world will little note, nor long remember what we say here; while it can never forget what they did here.

It is rather for us the living to here be dedicated to the great task remaining before us—that from these honored dead we take increased devotion to that cause for which they gave the last full measure of devotion—that we here highly resolve that these dead shall not have died in vain, that this nation shall have a new birth of freedom, and that government of the people, by the people, for the people shall not perish from the earth.

—Abraham Lincoln

5.2.3   The Consonants <c> and <g>

The consonants <c> and <g> are especially complicated, because of a Late Latin pronunciation rule that "softened" these consonants before the vowels <i> and <e>. When English borrowed words from French and Latin, this rule was carried over into English. Thus we, also, give <c> a "hard" pronunciation ([k]) before <a>, <o>, and <u> (*cat, cot, cut*) but a "soft" pronunciation ([s]) before <i> and <e> (*city, cell*); similarly, we give <g> a "hard" pronunciation ([g]) before <a>, <o>, and <u> (*gap, got, gun*) but a soft pronunciation ([j]) before <e> and <i> (*gem, gin*).[5]

---

4. Irish monks originally used the runic letters <þ> and <ð> to represent [th] and [*th*], but these non-Roman characters were later replaced by the diagraph <th>.
5. See Exercise 3d for an exception to the softening of <g> before <i> and <e>.

EXERCISE 3.

a. Give examples to show that <c> is "hard" before <a>, <o>, and <u> and "soft" before <e> and <i>.

b. Before <i> and <e>, the sound [k] must be spelled with the letter <k> rather than <c>. Give examples.

c. Give examples to show that <g> is hard before the vowels <a>, <o>, and <u>.

d. We said that <g> is softened before <e> and <i>. Give examples. The words *get, gear, geek, gefilte fish, gift, gig, gill, gild, gilt, give,* and *gimlet* are an exception to this rule. Why? (*Hint:* It has to do with their historical origin.)

e. The sound [g] is spelled as <gu> in the words *guess, guest, guise, guilt,* and *guide.* Why is this spelling necessary?

f. The sound [j] is normally spelled <j> before <a>, <u>, and <o>. Give examples. What is strange about the word *George?*

5.2.4   The Spelling of Vowel Sounds

English vowel sounds are divided into two categories—"long" and "short." A **short** vowel ([ă], [ĕ], [ĭ], [ŏ], [ŭ], or [o͝o]) is normally spelled with a single vowel letter followed by two consonants or by a single consonant at the end of a word, as in *bag, basset, met, message, hip, listen, cod, college, rum, rustle.*[6] A **long** vowel or **diphthong** ([ā], [ē], [ī], [ō], [ô], [o͞o], [yo͞o], [oi], or [ä]) may be spelled in either of two ways:

1.   As a digraph consisting of two vowel letters or a vowel letter plus <y> or <w>,[7] as in the following spellings for the vowel sound [ā]: <ai> *paid,* <ay> *say,* <ei> *vein,* <ey> *they.*

or

2.   As a single vowel letter followed by CV (a single consonant plus a vowel—often, as in the examples, below, the silent <e>)[8]:

---

6. [o͞o], of course, is an exception. It may be spelled with <u>, as in *put,* but it is often spelled as a digraph (<oo>).

7. The long vowel [ä] is an exception, in that it is sometimes spelled with the single vowel <a>, as in *father,* but it is also often spelled as a digraph (<al>), as in *calm, palm, psalm,* and so forth.

8. This rule holds true only at the righthand edge of the stem; inside the stem of a word, a single vowel followed by CV may be either long or short:

Long vowel sound	Short vowel sound
valence	*balance*
placate	*placard*
venetian	*frenetic*
meter	*metaphysics*
miser	*commiserate*
Friday	*frigate*
solar	*solid*
omen	*ominous*
punitive	*punish*

Long vowel sound	Short vowel sound
made	*mad*
mete	*met*
fine	*fin*
hope	*hop*
tube	*tub*

EXERCISE 4.

a. Classify the vowel sound in each of the following words as long or short, and explain how the spelling indicates its length: *plan, plain, plane, planning, planing.*

b. When the plural suffix *-s* is added to a word like *potato, hero,* or *go,* an *e* must be added between the stem and the suffix: *potatoes, heroes, goes.* Why? (*Hint:* What would happen if the <s> were added alone, without the <e>?)[9]

c. Find as many spellings as you can, using digraphs, for the following long vowel sounds: [ē], [ī], [ō], [ô], [o͞o], and [yo͞o].

5.2.5   The Silent <e>

As we saw in Section 5.2.4 above, a silent <e> is sometimes added to a word to indicate that the vowel sound is long. In all, there are four uses of silent <e> in English:

1.   As part of the spelling of the consonant sound [v] at the end of a word: *give, love, have.* (<v>, for some reason, is not allowed to stand by itself at the end of a word: **giv.*)

2.   To make a <c> or <g> "soft": *silence, peace, courage, large.*

3.   To make the preceding vowel long: *made, mete, fine, hope,* and *tube.*

4.   For no purpose at all: *some, none, there.*

EXERCISE 5.

a. Account for the silent <e> in each of the following words, using one of the four reasons listed just above: *ride, sieve, once, ledge, name, cede, dove, bone, rube, these, whole, fumes, one.*

b. Uses (2) and (3) of the silent <e> sometimes collide. What is the motivation for the *dg* spelling in the following words: *badge, ridge, edge, lodge, judge.* (*Hint:* What would happen if the [j] sound were spelled simply as <ge>)?[10]

---

9. But note *ratios, radios,* and *rodeos,* where the final <o> is preceded by a vowel. In this case, the <o> stays long.

10. Because the <dg> spelling is used *only* to represent the sound [j], the silent <e> is, strictly speaking, no longer needed in words with this spelling. The silent <e> is retained at the end of a word: *judge, acknowledge,* not **judg, *acknowledg,* but in American spelling, it is dropped before a suffix: American *judgment,* British *judgement*; American *acknowledgment,* British *acknowledgement.* This textbook uses the British spelling in order to cast one small vote in favor of spelling regularity; with this spelling, <g> is soft only if it is followed by <i>, <e>, or vocalic <y>.

5.2.6 Adding Suffixes

When a suffix is added to a word that ends with a silent <e>, the <e> is retained if and only if it is still needed. For example, if the silent <e> is serving to soften a <c> or <g>, then it must be retained before a suffix that begins with a consonant or with <a>, <o>, or <u>; otherwise the <c> or <g> would become hard: *notice + -able* ⇒ *notic**e**able* (*noticable). When the suffix is *-ing*, however, the silent <e> is dropped, because the <i> of the suffix can take over the task of softening the <c>: *notice + -ing* ⇒ *noticing*, (*noticeing). The same principle holds when the silent <e> acts to make a vowel long. The <e> is dropped before a suffix that begins with a vowel, because the vowel of the suffix will take over the function of lengthening the vowel: *elope + -ing* ⇒ *eloping* (*elopeing). However, if the suffix begins with a consonant, the silent <e> must be retained, so that the vowel will continue to be long: *elope + -ment* ⇒ *elopement* (*elopment).

When a word with a *short* vowel adds a suffix beginning with a vowel, the final consonant must be *doubled*, to keep the vowel short; for example, *bag + -ed* ⇒ *bagged*; *sin + -er* ⇒ *sinner*; *fit + -ing* ⇒ *fitting*. If the consonant were not doubled, then the vowel sound would become long (*baged, *siner, *fiting), There is one exception to this rule: The final consonant is *not* doubled if its syllable is unstressed. This is because unstressed syllables are pronounced with a "reduced" vowel sound ([ĭ], [ə], or [ər]; thus an unstressed vowel *cannot* be long, and so no signal is needed in the spelling: *pro·ʹfit + -ed* ⇒ *profited*. In contrast, *re·mitʹ + -ed* ⇒ *remi**tt**ed* and *ben·ʹe·fitʹ + -ed* ⇒ *benefi**tt**ed*, because these words have a stress on their final syllable and so must double the final consonant in order to keep the vowel short.

Notice the common principle that underlies these two rules: When adding a suffix, a silent <e> is retained (or a final consonant is doubled) if and only if this is necessary to preserve the pronunciation.

EXERCISE 6.

a. Add suffixes as indicated and explain why the silent <e> is dropped or retained:

hope + -ful	*enlarge + -er*	*note + -able*	*rope + -like*
-ing	*-ing*	*-ation*	*-er*
-ed	*-ment*	*-ing*	*-ing*

b. Why is the silent <e> dropped in *notable* (*note + -able*), but not in *noticeable* (*notice + -able*)?

c. Explain why <k> is inserted in the following words: *picnic + -ing* ⇒ *picnicking*; *mimic + -ed* ⇒ *mimicked*.

d. Add suffixes as indicated, and explain why the final consonant is or is not doubled:

travel + -ing[11]	*rebel + -ing*	*abet + -ed*	*picket + -ed*
-er	*-ious*	*-or*	*-er*

begin + -ing	*beckon + -ing*
-er	

---

11. In British spelling, a final <l> is doubled even when the syllable is not stressed: British *travelling*; American *traveling*.

5.2.7   The Letter <y>

The letter <y> is used in three ways:

1. **As a consonant:** At the beginning of a word or syllable, the letter <y> represents the consonant sound [y]: *yes, yippee, yellow, young, be·yond.*
2. **As part of a digraph:** Some long vowels and diphthongs may be spelled with <*y*>, as we saw above: *day, key, buy, boy.*
3. **As a vowel:** At the end of a word, after a consonant, <y> represents the vowel sound [ē] or [ī]: *worry, baby, happy, friendly, sky, identify.* If a suffix is added to a word that ends with vocalic <y>, then the <y> changes to <i>: *baby* + *s* ⇒ *babies; hurry* + *-ed* ⇒ *hurried.* This spelling rule preserves the generalization that, in native English words, vocalic <y> normally appears only at the end of a word.[12]

EXERCISE 7.

a. What vowel sound is represented by the <y> in each of the following words: *baby, reply, funny, sky?*
b. Add suffixes, as indicated, and explain what happens to the <y> and why. You will find one exception to the <y> ⇒ <i> rule. What is it and why does it occur?

pity +	*-ed*	*happy* + *-er*	*identify* + *-able*
	-ful	*-ness*	*-er*
	-ing		*-ing*

c. *Pity* + *-s* ⇒ *pities:* The <y> changes to <i>, and the <s> is the 3rd person singular present tense suffix, but why do we also have to add <e>?

5.3   For Advanced Spellers

So far we have been looking at the system that students must master, whether consciously or unconsciously, in order to begin reading and writing in English. In the remainder of the chapter we will consider some features of English spelling that are useful for advanced spellers.

5.3.1   Words Borrowed from Other Languages

As we noted earlier, words that were borrowed from other languages often retain (some part of) the spelling of the original language. Advanced students, who have need of these words, should develop a sense of the spelling characteristics of the languages that have contributed to our vocabulary. The students who compete in regional and national spelling bees are well aware of these regularities; that is why you will hear them asking for the historical origin of the words they are given to spell.

---

12. Words borrowed from Greek do not conform to this principle: *psychology, type, rhyme,* etc.

EXERCISE 8. Using the examples below as a springboard, discuss the spelling characteristics of words that were borrowed into English from French, Greek, Italian, Spanish, and German. Your answer should take the form of generalizations like the following: "The [f] sound is normally spelled <f> in English, but in words borrowed from Greek, it is represented <ph>." Or "<ch> normally represents the sound [ch], but in words borrowed from Modern French, it represents the sound [sh]."

> **French:** *chic, beige, quiche, mauve, bureau, hour, savoir-faire*
> **Greek:** *pneumonia, psychology, rhythm, telegraph, euphony*
> **Italian:** *spaghetti, gnocchi, pizza, bologna*
> **Spanish:** *hombre, adobe, marijuana, tortilla, tequila*
> **German:** *sauerkraut, waltz*

5.3.2   The Morphological Basis of English Spelling

Except for changes that are introduced by the rules of Section 5.2.6 above, each morpheme in a complex word retains its own spelling. The spelling of the whole word is obtained by spelling its component parts, one after the other: *un-* + *easy* ⇒ *uneasy*; *book* + *keeping* ⇒ *bookkeeping*; *final* + *-ly* ⇒ *finally*.

EXERCISE 9.

a. Write out the spelling of each of the following complex words:

un + necessary	*dis + obey*	*under + rate*
over + rule	*dis + satisfied*	*under + take*
over + eat	*in + expensive*	*sole + -ly*
mis + inform	*in + numerable*	*mis + spell*
magical + -ly	*accidental + ly*	

b. The words *happiness* (*happy* + *-ness*) and *taking* (*take* + *-ing*) are not simply the sum of their component morphemes. Why not?

5.3.3   Another Consequence of Morphological Spelling

Despite the existence of sound-letter correspondences in English, our spelling system is not directly phonetic; in some ways, it is morphological, like Chinese: we are more concerned with providing a consistent spelling for each morpheme than with representing the exact pronunciation of the word. Prefixes and suffixes maintain a constant spelling despite what are sometimes radical changes in pronunciation from one word to another. For example, consider the past tense suffix *-ed*. This morpheme has three distinct pronunciations—[ĭd] (in words like *waited*), [d] (in words like *jogged*), and [t] (in words like *jumped*)—but it is spelled consistently as <ed>. Similarly, the plural suffix *-s* is given the same spelling (<s>) whether it is pronounced as [s] (*cats*) or [z] (*dogs*).

The principle of morphological spelling holds, also, for irregularly-spelled morphemes like *-tion*. This suffix has a crazy spelling, but it has the *same* crazy spelling every time it appears.

Roots and stems, also, generally maintain a consistent spelling from word to word.[13] This is particularly significant for the spelling of vowel sounds. Because of the pronunciation rule called *Vowel Reduction* (Section 4.7.4 above), unstressed vowels are usually pronounced as [ĭ] or [ə]. For example, in the word *chrysanthemum*, only the second (stressed) syllable is given a full vowel sound [ă]; the other three vowels, being unstressed, are pronounced as [ĭ] or [ə]: [krĭ.săn´thə.məm]. Notice, however, that we have no standard spelling for the vowel sound [ə]; it can be spelled with *any* vowel letter:

rel<u>a</u>tive	[rĕl´ə.tĭv]	([ə] spelled \<a>)
arithm<u>e</u>tic	[ə.rĭth´mə.tĭk´]	([ə] spelled \<e>)
ind<u>i</u>cation	[ĭn.də.kā´shən]	([ə] spelled \<i>)
dem<u>o</u>crat	[dĕm´ə.krăt´]	([ə] spelled \<o>)
inj<u>u</u>re	[ĭn´jər]	([ə] spelled \<u>)

Clearly, writers cannot depend on auditory cues to determine the spelling of [ə]. Fortunately, we can sometimes find a morphological justification for the spelling of this sound in a particular word, by finding a related word in which the vowel can be heard in its full form. For example, the \<a> of *rel<u>a</u>tive* can be heard in the word *rel<u>a</u>ted*, the \<e> of *arithm<u>e</u>tic* in the word *arithm<u>e</u>tical,* the \<i> of *ind<u>i</u>cation* in the word *ind<u>i</u>cative,* the \<o> of *dem<u>o</u>crat* in the word *dem<u>o</u>cracy,* and the \<u> of *inj<u>u</u>re* in the word *inj<u>u</u>rious*. Because morphemes maintain a consistent spelling from one word to another, the vowel will be spelled the same way whether it is pronounced as a full vowel or as [ə].

Word families like these can also help with the spelling of silent consonants. For example, the silent \<g> of *malign* shows up in the related word *malignant*, and the silent \<n> of *condemn* shows up in the related word *condemnation*.

EXERCISE 10.[14]

a. Write out pronunciations for several of the following words, using dictionary symbols. Mark the stressed vowels, and notice that the underlined *un*stressed vowels are pronounced as [ĭ] or [ə]:

magn<u>e</u>t	*def<u>i</u>nite*	*<u>a</u>ccuse*	*disp<u>o</u>sition*	*absent*
profess<u>o</u>r	*fin<u>a</u>l*	*dec<u>o</u>rate*	*photograph*	*indic<u>a</u>te*
gramm<u>a</u>r	*comp<u>o</u>sition*	*exist<u>e</u>nce*	*influ<u>e</u>nce*	*symb<u>o</u>l*
coll<u>e</u>ge	*family*	*degr<u>a</u>dation*	*num<u>e</u>rous*	*acad<u>e</u>my*

b. Find related words that justify the spelling of the underlined [ə]/[ĭ] sound in the words of (a).

---

13. English being English, there are, of course, a few exceptions to this rule. For example, words spelled with \<ou> (= [ou]) change their spelling to \<u> when they add a suffix. Thus we have *pronounce ~ pronunciation* and *denounce ~ denunciation* not *pronounciation and *denounciation.

14. Students who did the "Applications for ESL" exercises in Chapter 4 will already have done an exercise that is similar to this one.

   c. Underline the silent consonant in each word below; then find a related word in which that consonant is no longer silent:

bomb	*autumn*	*solemn*	*sign*
iamb	*column*	*hymn*	*resign*

   d. If, like the author of this text, you are sometimes tempted to spell *rhythm* as **rhythmn*, how can you remember not to do this?

_____

5.3.4 Latin Prefixes

Prefixes borrowed from Latin are a special case, in that the final consonant of the prefix often assimilates to (i.e., changes to agree with) the initial consonant of the stem; for example, when the prefix *ad-* is added to the stem *fect,* the <d> of the prefix changes to <f>: *affect.* Examples are given in Table 5.2, with the assimilated forms marked with an asterisk.

Except for this assimilation rule and other spelling rules we observed in Sections 5.2.6 and 5.2.7, the spelling of a complex word is just the sum of its component morphemes—prefix(es) + root(s) + suffix(es).

Table 5.2   The Spelling of Latin Prefixes

ad- 'toward'	*con-* 'together'	*in-* 'not'	*sub-* 'under'
ad-apt	**co-alesce*	*in-appropriate*	*sub-alpine*
*ab-breviate	**com-bat*	**im-balanced*	
*ac-cept	*con-cur*	*in-conceivable*	**suc-ceed*
ad-dict	*con-duct*	*in-direct*	*sub-due*
ad-ept	*co-efficient*	*in-ept*	
*af-fect	*con-fection*	*in-formal*	**suf-fuse*
*ag-gregate	*con-gress*	*in-glorious*	**sug-gest*
ad-here	**co-here*	*in-hospitable*	
ad-it	**co-incide*	*in-imitable*	
ad-junct	*con-jecture*	*in-justice*	*sub-ject*
*al-lege	**col-lect*	**il-legible*	*sub-lime*
ad-mit	**com-mit*	**im-measurable*	*sub-merge*
an-nex	*con-nect*	*in-nocuous*	
ad-opt	**co-opt*	*in-oper-ative*	*sub-orn*
*ap-point	**com-pose*	**im-possible*	**sup-port*
*ac-quiesce	*con-quer*		
*ar-rive	**cor-rect*	**ir-reverent*	*sub-rogate*
*as-sist	*con-sensus*	*in-satiable*	*sub-sist*
*a-scribe	*con-scription*	*in-scribe*	*sub-scribe*
*at-test	*con-tact*	*in-testate*	*sub-tract*
ad-ulation			*sub-urb*
ad-vance	*con-vert*	*in-voluntary*	*sub-vert*

5.3.5 Double Consonants: A Summary

One common issue for advanced spellers is when to double a consonant. As we have seen in this chapter, there are four main sources of double consonants in English:

1. Some consonants, including <l> and <s>, are doubled when they appear at the end of a word after a single vowel letter; for example, *bill* not **bil* and *mess* not **mes*.[15]
2. A consonant may be doubled with the addition of a suffix in order to keep a vowel short: *hop + -ing* ⇒ *hopping* (**hoping*).
3. When a word contains two morphemes, each with an instance of a given consonant, both consonants are retained in the spelling: *book + keeping* ⇒ *bookkeeping*; *un- + necessary* ⇒ *unnecessary*.
4. The Latin prefixes *ad-, con-,* and *in-* sometimes assimilate to the initial consonant of the stem, creating a double consonant, as in *in + logical* ⇒ *illogical*.

Of these double consonants, only those of type 3 are pronounced with a double consonant *sound*.

EXERCISE 11.

a. Account for the double consonant in each of the following words:

admitted	*hugged*	*connect*	*irresponsible*	*illegal*
unnatural	*interrupt*	*kiss*	*immodest*	*jabbed*
approve	*buzz*	*roommate*	*really*	*running*

b. (*Advanced*) Account for the spelling of *accommodate*.

5.4 Applications for Teachers

Beginning literacy students who are native speakers of English—whether children or adults—have already developed a large vocabulary in English, and they already know how these words are pronounced. Now they must learn how spoken words are represented on paper, by written symbols. For words like *one* and *would*, which have irregular spellings, this is a matter of remembering how the words look on the page; words of this type are called "sight" words because they have to be learned by sight. However, many English words have more transparent spellings, and this is where "phonics" comes in. Beginning readers should be taught how to break words down into their component sounds ([b] [ĭ] [g] ⇒ [bĭg])[16] and should be taught the most common spellings for each consonant and vowel sound of English.

---

15. There are a few exceptions such as *until, wonderful,* and *bus*.
16. The author's grandson, whose teacher is using this method, calls it "pound and blend." He enthusiastically pounds out the individual sounds ([b], [ĭ], [g]) and then, with a great swoop of his arms, "blends" them into the completed word ([bĭg]).

In current methodology, students are encouraged to try out their developing knowledge by using "invented spelling"[17] to write stories of their own, making the best guess they can about how each word is spelled. By applying the phonics rules they have learned, however imperfectly, students solidify their understanding of these rules and put themselves in a better position to "sound out" the words they encounter in reading. Students' invented spellings also provide valuable information to the teacher, who can use these spellings to determine what the students do and do not understand and to plan her lessons accordingly.

Figure 5.1 displays spellings of English words by first-grade children. Each horizontal row represents the spellings of one child; each vertical row represents the spellings that were given for a particular word. Notice that one of the children ("Student 9") focuses on just the first and last sounds of the word, omitting the sounds in the middle. This does not necessarily indicate a learning problem; most children begin in just this way. Notice, also, that two of the children (Students 8 and 9) are not simply "sounding out" the words; these two are already fluent readers who have seen these words in print and remember how they look.

EXERCISE 12. The following questions are based on the data in Figure 5.1.

a. We said above that Students 7 and 8 are already fluent readers who know how these words appear on paper. Give three pieces of evidence that these students are not simply "sounding out" the words.

b. The other children in this set are depending more on their ear than on their memory of the words' appearance. Give three pieces of evidence to support this statement.

c. Why do many of the children begin *camp* and *quick* with the letter <k>? Why do they put a <w> in *quick*?

d. Why do some of the children begin *zero* with the letter <s>?

e. Why do some of the children begin *job* with the letter <g>?

f. Why do some of the children spell *camp* with the letter <b> and *muffin* with the letter <v>?

g. Why do many of the children end *tack* and *quick* with <c>, <k>, or even <g> rather than <ck>? Why do they end *hill* with <l> rather than <ll>?

h. Leaving aside Students 6, 7, 8, and 9, what do these children understand about the spelling of vowel sounds? What about Student 6? Do any of the students other than 7 and 8 know anything about the silent <e>?

i. Choose any one of these children other than 7 and 8, and write a one-page essay describing what that child does/does not understand about the spelling system of English. Imagine that you are this child's reading teacher, and set out some immediate goals for him/her. (Decide, arbitrarily, on the sex of your child so that you don't have to go through your essay saying "he or she.")

---

17. "Invented spelling" is sometimes criticized in the public press by people who think it is a license for incorrect spelling. In fact, when used properly, it is a technique for *beginning* writers who are learning to match spoken sounds with written symbols. As the students begin to read, they combine the evidence from their eyes with the evidence from their ears to gradually come closer to conventional spellings.

Figure 5.1   Spellings of first-grade children

Correct spelling	camp	zero	hill	tack	five	pickle	muffin	wife	job	quick
Student 1	kip	siro	hl	tak	fifv	pikl	mifn	wif	gob	kwik
Student 2	kmb	zoz	el	tgk	vin	plp	mad	woe	gbo	uew
Student 3	kap	zao	hla	tak	fiv	pegl	mife	wif	job	kwe
Student 4	kip	sit	hill	tag	foif	pigll	maf	wuf	job	qic
Student 5	cap	sro	hill	tac	fiv	pagl	mvn	wru	job	qcic
Student 6	kamb	zero	hlri	tac	fiv	pikl	mifn	wif	job	kwak
Student 7	camp	zero	hill	tack	five	pickel	muffin	wife	jobe	quic
Student 8	camp	zero	hill	tack	five	pickle	muffin	wife	job	quick
Student 9	kp	sro	ul	tk	ff	pl	mfa	waf	gb	kwk
Student 10	cep	zeo	hel	tac	fiv	peg	muf	wif	gob	wec

Teachers of beginning readers need a thorough understanding of the relationship between sound and spelling. It is confusing to children when they are advised by adults to "listen" for the [l] in *would* or for the [d] sound in *walked*; such erroneous advice undermines their confidence in their own observation. A teacher who understands the spelling system of English will be able to tell the student that he is *correct* in his judgement that there is no [l] sound in *would* and that the -ed of *walked* does, indeed, sound like a <t>. Children can understand, if it is explained to them, that *would* has a strange spelling because many years ago it *used* to be pronounced with an [l], and that the -ed ending on verbs[18] like *walked,* which tell us something that happened in the past, is sometimes pronounced as [t].

Beginning writers have many other things to learn about the orthography of English, in addition to the spelling of the words. They struggle, at first, simply to form the letters and situate them properly on the lines; that's why young students are given special lined paper with a dotted line down the middle of each space. The orientation of the letters is also difficult. Because we write from left to right, English letters normally open to the right, but the orientation of <S> and <Z> is not clear, and <J>, exceptionally, opens to the left. Among the lower-case letters, <b> and <d> are notoriously confusing. The spacing between words is also difficult; because children have difficulty controlling the spaces between their letters, they sometimes resort to hyphens or periods to mark the boundaries between words. Even writing from left to right is something that has to be learned. Beginning writers sometimes work from right to left, by mistake, or do one line left to right and then come back the other way. And then there is the matter of punctuation—when to use upper and lower case, when to put a period or question mark, when to use commas, when to use apostrophes, when to use quotation marks.

---

18. Of course, it isn't necessary to use the word "verb," but my first-grade grandson has, in fact, been taught this term in school and, to my surprise, seems to understand it pretty well.

EXERCISE 13. Write a one-page essay discussing the spelling and punctuation of the first-grade writers in Appendix Section II. **Note:** In the examples in the Appendix, only the first-grade children seem to lack proficiency in spelling and punctuation. Don't be fooled! Before these writing samples were published in a local newspaper, the samples from the older children were edited by the teachers. While members of the public are amused by unorthodox spelling and punctuation in first-grade children, they can be rather critical if these imperfections continue into the later grades.

For teachers of older students, the lesson to be taken from this chapter is that spelling is not a subject only for grade-school children; many aspects of our spelling system are worthy of study in high school and beyond. Older students can benefit from learning about the historical development of our spelling system and how the spelling of a word relates to its etymology. Most of all, older students can benefit from an understanding of the morphological basis of our spelling; the single best strategy for improving spelling at the intermediate and advanced levels is to become more aware of the internal structure of words.

5.5 Applications for ESL Teachers

ESL students, if not literate in their first language, have all the same challenges as native-speaking students, but the task is made more difficult by their weaker control of the vocabulary and pronunciation of English. Studies show that learning to read and write in English is easier and faster if the student is already literate in her own language. Even if the orthography of the student's first language is quite different from that of English, there are important aspects of the reading process that carry over from one language to another.

The orthography of the student's first language is, however, a consideration, since students who come from a different writing system must begin by learning the Roman alphabet. It might seem that Chinese students would have the greatest difficulty, since their own writing system is not alphabetical.[19] However, Chinese students develop prodigious visual memories as they memorize thousands of characters, and a strong visual memory turns out to be very helpful with the spelling system of English. Students who are already familiar with the Roman alphabet have an advantage to start with, but they struggle with the fact that our vowel letters have different values from other languages, with <i> representing [ī] rather than [ē], and <e> representing [ē] rather than [ā]. It's confusing!

In teaching ESL students to read and write in English, it is important to give serious attention to *meaning*. Even more than native-speaking students, ESL students need to be prepared in advance for the content of a reading (by building "schemata") and to be monitored closely to be sure they understand the meaning of what they have read. We have probably all had the experience of reading a text aloud in a foreign language, giving our very best effort to the pronunciation of the words, and understanding nothing at all of the content. Students who continue to struggle with meaning can often benefit from hearing the text read out loud as they follow along silently with the text. At the same time, ESL teachers must also keep a close watch on their students'

---

19. In the Chinese writing system each character represents a morpheme, with no systematic relationship to the *pronunciation* of that morpheme.

pronunciation, because ESL students are easily led by an irregular spelling into an incorrect pronunciation of a word, pronouncing *walked,* for example, as a two-syllable word.

5.6   Summary of the Chapter

Our English orthography is based on the Roman alphabet, which we borrowed from Latin. The Roman alphabet worked fairly well for our consonant sounds, since these are mostly the same in English and Latin; for English consonants that did not exist in Latin, the monks who created our writing system invented digraphs such as <sh>, <ch>, <th>, <gh>, <wh>, and <ng>.

Our vowel spellings are a different matter. The Roman alphabet did not provide enough vowel letters to cover all our vowel sounds, and we have not developed a consistent way to deal with the problem. In one of the systems we employ, long vowels are distinguished from short vowels by spelling them as digraphs: *gr__eat__, expl__ain__, s__ay__*, etc. However, we also use another, more complex system which relies on the number of consonants that follow the vowel: A single vowel letter is given its "long" pronunciation if and only if it is followed by a single consonant letter plus a vowel letter (*pl__a__ne, r__i__ding*, etc.); otherwise the vowel is short. This system gives rise to further complications involving the silent <e> and the use of double consonants, making literacy a far more difficult task in English than in languages like Spanish, which have one spelling for each sound.

Our habit of borrowing words from other languages, often with their original spelling, has created additional confusion. Over the centuries, we have taken in spelling conventions from French, Spanish, Italian, German, and Greek to add to our own already very complex system.

Students should be aware that English spelling is not directly phonetic; our system is more concerned with maintaining a consistent spelling for each morpheme than with representing the pronunciation of the word. Thus, except where specific rules have applied, the spelling of a complex (polymorphemic) word is simply the sum of its parts: *illogically* = *i__n__-* + *logic* + *-al* + *ly,* with the underlined *n* assimilating to *l* by the Latin prefix rule. Another consequence of morphological spelling is that a morpheme generally maintains the same spelling in all the words in which it appears, even if its pronunciation changes. For example, the past tense suffix is always spelled *-ed*, even when it is pronounced as [t] or [d], and the stem *photograph* has the same spelling in *photograph* and *photographer* even though it is pronounced very differently in these two words.

In the final sections of the chapter, we looked at some of the steps that children go through in learning to read and write, and we considered some of the particular difficulties that our system presents to ESL learners.

113

CHAPTER 6

The Dictionary

Lexicographer: A writer of dictionaries; a harmless drudge that busies himself in tracing the original, and detailing the signification of words.
—Samuel Johnson's *Dictionary of the English Language,* 1775

Did you eat a balti before 1984 or have a mullet before 1994? And do you know how they got their names?
—*Questions from the* BBC Wordhunt *website*

Please do not annoy, torment, pester, plague, molest, worry, badger, harry, harass, heckle, persecute, irk, bullyrag, vex, disquiet, grate, best, bother, tease, nettle, tantalize or ruffle the animals.
—Sign on display at the San Diego Zoo.

6.1   Introduction[1]

The first English language dictionaries, in the 17th century, were lists of "hard words." John Kersey's *New English Dictionary*, published in 1702, was the first to attempt a complete list of the vocabulary of English, including ordinary words like *tree* and *have*. Kersey's dictionary was followed in 1734 by Bailey's *An Universal Etymological English Dictionary,* which contained about 40,000 entries and exhibited many of the features of a modern dictionary: etymologies (often incorrect), position of accent, and division into syllables.

Samuel Johnson's famous *Dictionary of the English Language,* also with about 40,000 entries, was published in 1755. Although some of Johnson's definitions were unorthodox, they were, for the most part, clearer and more complete than Bailey's, with illustrative quotations from reputable authors. Johnson also began the tradition of making judgements on the proper use of words.

The first comprehensive American dictionary, *An American Dictionary of the English Language*, was published in 1828 by Noah Webster. Webster pointed out differences between British and American usage, often drawing his illustrative quotations from American authors. He also introduced spelling reforms that were intended to simplify the system: *honor* (for *honour*), *center* (for *centre*), *tire* (for *tyre*), and *draft* (for *draught*). It is because of Noah Webster that the American spelling of words like these differs from that of the British.

The Oxford English Dictionary (OED) was put together over a seventy-year period, between 1858 and 1928. It contained thirteen volumes, with 414,000 entries organized in such a way as to illustrate the history and development of each word since the time of King Alfred (899 AD). Dated quotations were provided to illustrate the use of each word at various times. A second edition, in ten volumes, came out in 1989, and an online edition was introduced in 2000. The online edition

---

1. This information about the history of English dictionaries is taken from Lodwig and Barrett's *Words, Words, Words: Vocabularies and Dictionaries*, Boynton/Cook, 1981.

is a work in progress, with approximately 1000 new and revised words added each quarter. You yourself can become part of this process by logging onto the BBC Wordhunt website (http://dictionary.oed.com/bbcwordhunt/index.html), where you can contribute any information you have about the date of origin, historical source, and exact meaning of words that the dictionary editors are currently investigating

The G. & C. Merriam Company's *Webster's Third New International Dictionary,* published in 1959, was the descendant of Noah Webster's dictionary of 1828. It contained some 450,000 entries, based on ten million "citations" collected between 1934 and 1959. When this dictionary was first published, there was heated controversy over its policy of simply recording current usage without making judgements about whether the usage is good or bad; for example, it listed the word *irregardless,* which is considered by many to be incorrect. It also substituted the usage labels *substandard* 'not used by cultivated speakers of the language' and *nonstandard* 'not recognized in standard usage, but used by some speakers of cultivated English' for more judgemental earlier terms such as *vulgar, illiterate,* and *erroneous.*

In response to the controversy over *Webster's Third,* recently-published dictionaries have included more information about usage. For example*, The American Heritage College Dictionary* employs the usage labels *informal* ('wish list'), *slang* ('cool'), *nonstandard* ('anyways'), *offensive* (racial, ethnic, and gender slurs), *vulgar,* and *obscene.* Special problems, discussed in a "Usage Problem" section, provide advice to the reader based on the judgements of a Usage Panel that includes such members as Julian Bond, Alistair Cooke, John Kenneth Galbraith, Charles Kuralt, Nina Totenberg, and Eudora Welty. We are told, for example, that eighty-nine percent of the Usage Panel rejects the use of the word *disinterested* to mean 'not interested' (rather than 'unbiased').

6.2 What Dictionaries Contain

Dictionaries list words (including compound words such as *ice cream*), prefixes and suffixes, abbreviations, and lexicalized (i.e., idiomatic) phrases such as *trial and error.* Many dictionaries also list proper names, including names of famous people and geographical place names.

EXERCISE 1.

a. Find in your dictionary an example of each of the following: a compound word, a prefix or suffix, an abbreviation, a proper name, and a lexicalized phrase.

b. Explain the ambiguity in the sentences below. Which *down hill* and which *red tape* are lexicalized phrases? (That is, which meanings of these expressions are listed in the dictionary?)

    i. From a selectman at town meeting: *"A lot of our roads have been going down hill lately."*

    ii. From *The Daily Messenger,* quoted in *The Columbia Journalism Review*, September 1997: *"Red tape holds up outlet bridge."*

Look closely at some of the individual entries in your dictionary. Each entry begins with the spelling and syllabification of the word, followed by its pronunciation and then its definitions, which are the heart of the entry. The etymology (the origin) of the word may appear near the beginning of the entry or at the end. The definitions are numbered, with closely related definitions under a single number; for example, for the word "ground," *The Concise Oxford Dictionary* provides two definitions under the number 1:

> *1a. the surface of the earth.*
> *1b. a part of this surface, qualified in some way (low ground).*

Other, more distinct meanings are listed under separate numbers:

> *2. Soil; earth.*
> *3. a limited or defined area (the ground beyond the farm).*
> *4. (often pl.) a foundation, motive, or reason (excused on the grounds of ill health).*

Short lexicalized phrases (for example, *mother tongue*) are given their own entries, but longer ones are listed under one word of the phrase;[2] for example, in *Webster's New World College Dictionary* the phrases *get hold of (one)self, hold a candle to, hold one's own, hold out on (someone), hold (someone's) feet to the fire, hold the fort, hold the line, hold water, no holds barred,* and *on hold* are listed at the end of the entry for *hold*.

Dictionary definitions are organized by syntactic category (V, N, Adj, and so forth). In the *Merriam Webster* dictionaries each part of speech is given a separate listing, but most dictionaries group related noun and verb meanings under a single entry, starting with the most "basic" part of speech. For example, the entry for *motor* begins with the noun meanings, and the verb meanings come later, but the entry for *start* begins with the verb meanings. American dictionaries use the traditional category labels; for example, the word *those* is identified as an adjective or definite article rather than as a determiner, the word *very* is identified as an adverb rather than as an intensifier, and no distinction is made between coordinating conjunctions like *and* and subordinating conjunctions like *that* and *if*. The *American Heritage* and *Merriam Webster* dictionaries use the following category labels:

adjective	*(adj.)*
adverb	*(adv.)*
conjunction	*(conj.)*
definite article	*(def. art.)*
indefinite article	*(indef. art.)*
interjection	*(interj.)*
noun	*(n.)*
preposition	*(prep.)*
pronoun	*(pron.)*
verb	*(v.).*

The Concise Oxford Dictionary adds the labels *auxiliary (aux.)* and *determiner (det.)*.

---

2. It can be hard to decide where to look; for example, in one dictionary, the phrases *take advantage of* and *take charge* are both listed under *take*; in another, these phrases are listed under *advantage* and *charge*, and in a third *take advantage of* is listed under *advantage,* while *take charge of* is listed under *take*.

Verbs are further classified as *transitive (tr.)* or *intransitive (intr.)*, depending on whether the verb does or does not take a direct object. (*Close the door* is transitive, whereas *Stop!* is intransitive.) Inflectional forms (past tense, perfect participle, present participle, and the third person singular present tense) are listed for verbs; the plural form is given for irregular nouns such as *foot~feet,* but not for "regular" nouns such as *tree.* The *Oxford Learners' Dictionary,* which is intended for students of English as a foreign language, gives more detailed information about the syntactic properties of nouns and verbs.

Dictionaries also list *phrasal verbs* (sometimes called "two-word verbs") such as *give away, give back, give in, take off, throw up,* and *set out.* These are usually listed under the entry for the head word; for example, *give in, give off, give up,* and *give out* are listed under the entry for *give.* However, nouns formed from phrasal verbs by category shift are listed separately: *a giveaway, a giveback.*

Words formed by *affixation* are listed at the end of the entry for the base word if the meaning is predictable; for example, *adaptability* and *adaptableness* are listed at the end of the entry for *adaptable.* However, if the meaning is idiosyncratic a separate entry is provided; thus, *adaptable* itself is listed as a separate word rather than under the entry for *adapt,* because its meaning, when applied to a person, is 'able to adapt,' rather than the expected meaning 'able to *be adapted*' (cf. *washable* 'able to be washed,' *lockable* 'able to be locked,' *doable* 'able to be done,' and so on). A useful feature of American dictionaries is the list of synonyms at the end of some entries; for example, at the end of the listing for *fat, The American Heritage College Dictionary* provides the synonyms *obese, corpulent, fleshy, portly, stout, pudgy, rotund, plump,* and *chubby,* with a helpful discussion of the differences in meaning.

Finally, dictionaries also give information about usage, if only a labeling of some uses of a word as *informal, slang, nonstandard, offensive, vulgar,* or *obscene.* (Recall that this was the source of much of the controversy surrounding the publication of *Webster's Third International.*) Some examples from *The American Heritage College Dictionary* are given below; see if you agree with their usage labels:[3]

informal	*egghead, slob, fix up* 'provide with a date,' *give (someone) the slip, mug* 'face'
slang	*nerd, wimp, cat* 'person,' *kiddo, bitch* 'complain'
nonstandard	*ain't, anyways, irregardless*
vulgar slang	*prick* 'penis'/'contemptible man,' *bastard* 'mean, disagreeable person,' *suck*
obscene	*shit, fuck*
offensive	*Jap, kike, broad* 'woman,' *bitch* 'a spiteful or overbearing woman,' *queen* 'homosexual man'

The usage information for the word *queer* is particularly interesting. This word was formerly labeled *offensive* when used to refer to gays, lesbians, and transsexuals, but it has now been "reclaimed." The *AHD* defines a *reclaimed* word as "a word that was once used solely as a slur but has been semantically overturned by members of the maligned group, who use it as a term of defiant pride."

---

3. The dictionary editors themselves have apparently re-thought this classification; in the dictionary's fourth edition, which came out in 2002, *shit* has been downgraded to *vulgar slang.*

EXERCISE 2.

a. Check the words above with one or two other dictionaries. Usage labels are one of the places where dictionaries often disagree. Which dictionary seems to be the most conservative?

b. If you were writing a dictionary, what usage labels, if any, would you apply to the following words? *Clueless, veggies, cough up* 'give up unwillingly,' *whitey,* and *screw up?*[4] Look to see what your dictionary says about these lexical items.

6.3 Word Meaning: Referential Meaning vs. Affective and Social Meaning

Referential meaning is the part of the word's meaning that indicates what object(s), event(s), or qualiti(es) the word indicates or refers to; for example, the referential meaning of the word *dine* is 'to eat dinner.' *Affective* meaning (or *connotation*) is the information the word provides about the speaker's attitude; the word *dine* indicates a positive attitude on the part of the speaker, as opposed to 'eat dinner,' which is neutral. The *social meaning* or *register* of a word is the social context in which the word is normally used. *Dine* has a slightly formal register, and I was startled when a Burger King employee asked whether I would be *dining* in the restaurant. The basic choices for register are formal, informal, and neutral, but there are also more specific registers such as medical (*laringology*), legal (*habeas corpus*), or educational (*heterogeneous grouping*).

To give another example, the expressions *live together, cohabit,* and *shack up* can all have the same referential meaning—that a man and woman are living in the same house and enjoying a sexual relationship without the benefit of marriage. But these phrases have very different *affective* meanings. If I say that a man and woman are *living together,* then I am describing the situation in neutral terms, but if I say they are *shacking up,* then I am indicating my disapproval of their behavior. The term *cohabiting* has a neutral affective meaning, but a formal, technical register: it is used in scholarly contexts such as a sociology report. *Living together* is neutral in register, while *shacking up* is informal—even slang. In other words, the three expressions have identical referential meanings, but quite different affective and social meanings.

EXERCISE 3. Discuss the referential meaning, affective meaning, and register of the following words.[5]

a. *fat, obese, corpulent, portly, stout, pudgy, plump, chubby*

b. *talk, converse, gossip, gab, prattle, yak*

c. *man, guy, dude, jock, gentleman, hunk, boy*

d. *stupid person, idiot, nerd, ass, jerk, turkey, wimp, punk, airhead, bastard*

Most of the time when we consult a dictionary, it is the *referential* meaning of the word that we are after. Unfortunately, referential meanings are not easy to pin down, even for lexico-

---

4. Based on an exercise from Frommer, Paul R., and Edward Finegan, 1994, p. 297.
5. Based on an exercise from Finegan, Edward (1999, 218).

graphers. To see how difficult this can be, try Exercise 4, based on an experiment by the socio-linguist William Labov (1978), in which he asked his subjects to think about the meanings of the words *cup, bowl, glass,* and *bottle*:

EXERCISE 4.

a. Look closely at the drawings of containers in Figure 6.1 and decide which containers could be called *cups,* which could be called *glasses,* and which could be called *bowls*. Then use this classification to determine what properties are essential or desirable in a *cup, bowl,* or *glass*. In doing the exercise, you should consider not only the shape of the container, but also what it is composed of and what it might contain. Here are some results you may find:

    i. It is easy to list *desirable* properties of cups, bowls, and glasses, but harder to find properties that are *essential*; the absence of some properties can be forgiven if enough other relevant properties are present.

    ii. Different speakers have slightly different definitions for these terms.

    iii. Our definition of a particular term depends partly on what other terms we use. For example, speakers who customarily use the word *tumbler* for a drinking glass that is not made of glass may be reluctant to apply the term *glass* to such a container. Similarly, speakers who use the term *mug* for a cup with straight-up-and-down sides may hesitate to call such a container a *cup*.

b. When you have finished the *cup/bowl/glass* exercise, try the exercise in Figure 6.2; here you are to decide whether a given container is or is not a bottle. After you have made your classification, try to determine what properties a container must have to be a bottle.

Given the difficulty we find in determining the exact referential meanings of simple words like *glass* and *bottle*, you will not be surprised to learn that dictionary definitions are not completely reliable. For example, *The American Heritage College Dictionary* gives, as one meaning of the verb *paint*, the definition 'coat with paint,' but the linguist Jerry Fodor has pointed out that if we spill a can of paint, thereby coating a large section of the floor, we would not then say that we had *painted* the floor. In response to a suggestion that what is missing from the definition is the notion of *deliberateness*, Fodor pointed out that if I deliberately stick my brush into the paint can and coat its bristles with paint, I cannot say that I have *painted* my paintbrush bristles. Apparently, something must also be said about the *purpose* of the paint-coating—it must be done for the purpose of decoration or protection. Look to see what your dictionary says about the meaning of the word *paint*.

To give another example, consider the word *water*. *The American Heritage College Dictionary* defines water as 'a clear, colorless, odorless, and tasteless liquid, H_2O.' In fact, however, the meaning of this word can be shown to vary according to the purpose for which the liquid is used. If we are concerned with *drinking*, then lack of color and odor are, indeed, important; even a small number of tea molecules introduced by dipping a teabag for 30 seconds or so is sufficient to change *water* into *tea*. However, chlorine or other chemicals that are added for the purpose of killing germs do not have the same effect—chlorinated water is still water. If the water is *not* for

Figure 6.1 Containers used in the cup/bowl/glass experiments (from Labov, 1978, 222).

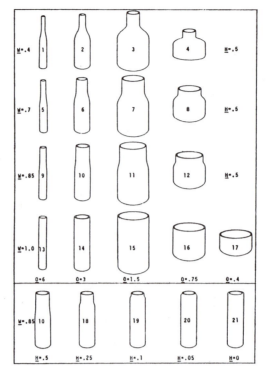

Figure 6.2 Series of bottle-like containers from Harmon S. Boertien, *Vagueness of Container Nouns and Cognate Verbs*. Unpublished University of Texas dissertation, 1975. Reprinted in Labov (1978, 230).

drinking, but is flowing in a river, then it may contain almost anything; certainly it does not have to be 'clear, odorless, and tasteless,' nor does it have to consist entirely of 'H_2O.'

6.4 Homonyms and Polysemous Words

What looks like a single word from the point of view of spelling and pronunciation may sometimes be given multiple dictionary entries. For example, *The Concise Oxford Dictionary* lists three words *bank*:

>*bank*[1]: 'the sloping edge of land by a river'
>*bank*[2]: 'a financial establishment'
>*bank*[3]: 'a set of similar objects, esp. of keys, lights, or switches'

Sets of words like this, with identical spelling and pronunciation, are called *homonyms*.[6] The motivation for representing the three *banks* as distinct words is partly semantic (the meanings

---

6. Students sometimes ask about the terms *homophone* and *homograph*. Homophones are words like *their* and *there*, which have identical pronunciations; homographs are words like *read* (present tense) and *read* (past tense), which have identical spellings. Words that have identical spelling *and* identical pronunciation are called *homonyms* (= same name).

seem not to be related to one another) and partly etymological: *bank*[1] is a borrowing from Old Norse, *bank*[2] was borrowed during Middle English times from the Old French word *banque* or the Old Italian word *banca*, and *bank*[3] was borrowed into Middle English from the Old French word *banc*.[7]

Dictionaries make a distinction between homonyms, which have separate entries, and *polysemous words* like *platform* and *eye*, which have multiple meanings listed under one entry. The meanings of the word *platform* include 'a horizontal surface raised above the level of the adjacent area,' and 'a formal declaration of the principles on which a group makes its appeal to the public'; the meanings for the word *eye* include 'an organ of vision,' 'the faculty of vision,' and 'a detective.'

EXERCISE 5.

a. The distinction between homonyms and polysemous words is not easy to make. Try your hand on the words below: Are these separate words (homonyms) or different meanings of a single polysemous word? After making your best guess, check with a dictionary. On what basis does the dictionary make this decision?

sound 'a sensation perceived by the sense of hearing'; *sound* 'healthy'; *sound* 'a long body of water'

shark 'a species of fish'; *shark* 'a person who preys greedily on others'

fire 'to set on fire'; *fire* 'to inflame with passion'; *fire* 'to hurl or throw'; *fire* 'to dismiss from a job'

bill 'a statement of money owed'; *bill* 'parts of a bird's jaw'; *bill* 'a written or printed public notice'

b. Ambiguity in the meaning of words is sometimes the basis of jokes. Explain the jokes below, and determine whether the semantic ambiguity is a matter of homonymy or polysemy:

  i. Q: *Why don't you get hot at a baseball game?*

     A: *Because there are so many fans there.*

           —From a children's joke book

  ii. Headline from the *San Francisco Business Times*, quoted in *The New Republic*, 4/1/96: *Del Monte Foods to can 150 employees.*

c. Most words are polysemous—that is, they have more than one meaning, sometimes a very large number of meanings. Thus the words *cup, bowl,* and *glass* each have several other meanings in addition to the "container" meanings that you defined above. List as many definitions as you can think of for each of these words. Then consult your dictionary to find additional meanings you may have missed.

It is often possible to identify one meaning of a word as the central meaning from which other meanings have derived. What would you consider to be the central meanings for the words *cup, bowl,* and *glass?*

---

7. The *Merriam Webster* dictionaries provide a separate entry for each part of speech; thus *Webster's* lists *five* words *bank,* with the verb 'to raise a pile or mound' listed separately from the noun 'a pile or mound,' and the verb 'to carry out the business of banking' listed separately from the noun meaning 'an establishment where money is kept.' Look to see how many *bank*s your own dictionary lists.

6.5   How Words Acquire New Meanings

There are four common methods by which new meanings are added to a word:

a.   **Generalization.** A word with a specific meaning begins to be applied more generally, as when a copy machine is called a "xerox machine" or the word *kleenex* comes to mean "tissue."

b.   **Narrowing.** A word with a general meaning is applied more specifically, as when the verb *drink* is used to mean "drink alcohol" or the word *smoke* to mean "smoke cigarettes." (*She neither drinks nor smokes.*)

c.   **Metaphor.** A word is applied to something that it *resembles* in some way, as when the words *bright, brilliant,* and *dim* are used to refer to intelligence (or its opposite), based on the underlying simile "Intelligence is like light."

d.   **Metonymy.** A word is applied to an event or object with which it is associated, as when the word *ears* is used to refer to hearing (*I'm all ears*), or the word *wheels* is used to refer to a car, or the word *bench* is used to refer to a court of law, or the word *moonlight* is used to mean "work at night" (*How long have you been moonlighting?*).

These methods may be combined with **category shift** (the use of the word as a different part of speech).

EXERCISE 6.   *The Oxford English Dictionary* (OED) gives detailed information about the history of words in English, with examples from original texts. Look up one word that interests you in the OED. State (in one sentence) how the word came into English, and then write a one-page essay describing, as simply as you can, the development of the word after it entered the English language. You should pay particular attention to the development of extended meanings for the word, but you may also mention changes in spelling or the incorporation of the word into compounds and/or lexicalized phrases. If you can, identify extensions of meaning as instances of generalization, narrowing, metaphor, or metonymy. *Caution:* The OED provides very detailed, technical information about the history of words. Your assignment is to condense that information into a brief, readable account that an ordinary reader will be able to follow.

6.6   The Ordering of Definitions

Dictionaries follow three systems for the ordering of definitions in polysemous words: The *Merriam Webster* dictionaries list the historically oldest definition first. Other dictionaries start with the most *common* use of the word or with a *central* meaning from which other meanings seem to be derived. Look to see what system your dictionary follows. (You'll find it in the explanatory material at the beginning of your dictionary.)

EXERCISE 7. Definitions for the words *drip, skirt,* and *tough* are set out below, with the order scrambled. How would you order the definitions if you were compiling a dictionary? This question has two parts:

a. Which part of speech would you list first?

b. How would you order the definitions within each category? What principle(s) are you following in ordering your definitions?

skirt (skûrt)

n. _____. The lower outer section of a rocket vehicle.

n. _____. An outer edge; a border.

n. _____. A garment hanging from the waist and worn by women and girls.

n. _____. **skirts.** The edge, as of a town; the outskirts.

n. _____. *Offensive slang.* A girl or woman.

n. _____. The part of a garment, such as a dress, that hangs freely from the waist down.

tr. v. _____. To pass along or around the border or edge of.

tr. v. _____. To lie on or along the border of.

tr. v. _____. To evade, as by circumlocution: *skirted the issue.*

drip (drĭp)

n. _____. The process of falling in drops.

n. _____. *Slang.* A tiresome or annoying person.

n. _____. The sound made by liquid falling in drops.

tr. v. _____. To let fall in or as if in drops.

intr. v. _____. To shed drops.

intr. v. _____. To fall in drops.

tough (tŭf)

v. _____. *Idiom.* **tough it out.** *Slang.* To get through despite hardship; endure.

adj. _____. Hard to cut or chew.

adj. _____. Able to withstand great strain without tearing or breaking; strong and resilient.

adj. _____. Demanding or troubling; difficult: *tough questions.*

adj. _____. Severe; harsh: *a tough winter.*

adj. _____. Physically hardy; rugged.

adj. _____. Aggressive; pugnacious.

adj. _____. *Slang.* Unfortunate; too bad.

adj. _____. Strong-minded; resolute.

n. _____. A violent or rowdy person; a hoodlum or thug.

6.7 Learning New Vocabulary

People learn new words with astonishing speed; the linguist Steven Pinker has estimated that children learn a new word every two hours, up until the time they start school. However, although children are very good at figuring out the meanings of words, they often fail at first to understand the *entire* meaning of a word. Underextensions are common, as when a three-year-old child refused to accept the expression *ready for action* except in the context of a firehouse, where he had first encountered the term. Overextensions are also frequent; a child may apply the word *doggie* to every four-legged animal, or say "up" when going either up or down the stairs. Children may also misunderstand idiomatic expressions, as when a two-year-old of the author's acquaintance ran to her mother one evening, crying "Dad said a bad word!" "What did he say?" the mother asked. "Time for bed," answered the child, thereby revealing her less-than-complete understanding of the lexicalized phrase *bad word*.

Words whose meaning is relative to the context are particularly difficult. Young children sometimes use the word *daddy* to refer to any adult male, not understanding that a man is a *daddy* only in relation to his own children. Similarly, a three-year-old may not understand that a glass may be *little* for the child, but *big* for the dolls who are to "drink" out of it.[8] Primary-school children may have difficulty with the words *before* and *after,* and even university students sometimes confuse words like *precede* and *follow* when asked, for example, whether a given consonant agrees in voicing with the consonant that *precedes* it or the consonant that *follows* it.

EXERCISE 8.

a. In the selection from the speech of a young child in Appendix Section VIII, Eve at 27 months asserts that her ice cubes are "in the refrigerator, cooking." Which word does Eve not completely understand? Does she understand *anything* about the meaning of this word?

b. When a two-year-old, pretending to read a newspaper, was asked what she was doing, she replied, "Watching the newspaper." What does this child not understand about the meaning of the word *watching*?

Adults also learn new vocabulary and, just as we saw with children, they sometimes fail to comprehend the complete meaning of a new word. One of the most common writing errors is the use of a word that is almost, but not quite, appropriate, as in the examples below, which were collected from college students' papers:

a. *American Sign Language is an **ample** form of communication.*
b. *When criticized about the grammatical error, Winston **countered right back** with the slogan, "What do you want, good grammar or good taste?"*
c. *The English language has **transformed** considerably over the past five centuries.*
d. *I'm **apt** to agree with Chomsky's contention that language is innate.*

---

8. From the wonderful film *Early Language*, by Jill and Peter DeVilliers.

e. ***Abolishing*** *the importance of correct spelling would . . .*

f. *If we spent more time **revising** our mistakes . . .*

g. *The **fact** that one doesn't think in sentences is true.*

h. *The demand for jobs has **prolifically** declined.*

i. *My knowledge of grammar is a little **sparse.***

j. *Unless precautions are **formulated**, dozens of animal species will die out. More thought and research needs to be **enacted**.*

k. *Baseball has always been **commonplace** to me every year as summer rolls around.*

l. *(In a note from a local elementary school) Children may not play in the gym in sock feet. Socks **enhance** slipping.*

EXERCISE 9.   If you agree that the boldfaced words in the examples above are misused, try to say exactly what is wrong (and right) about the use of the word in that context.

Having noted how difficult it is to define the meaning of a word (see Section 6.3 above), I was curious to see whether my students' errors could have been avoided by consulting a dictionary. Based on definitions from the *Merriam Webster's* and *American Heritage* dictionaries set out in Table 6.1, I decided they sometimes could not. Clearly, when we learn a word by hearing or reading it in context, we learn more about its meaning than can be found by consulting a dictionary. Dictionary writers do their best to represent the word meanings that *people* know, but they do not completely succeed.

Table 6.1   Dictionary Definitions vs. Students' Usage of Words

Dictionary definition	Student's use of word
ample 'generously sufficient to satisfy a requirement or need.'	*American Sign Language is an **ample** form of communication.*
counter, intr. 'to adduce an answer'	*When criticized about the grammatical error, Winston **countered right back** with the slogan, "What do you want, good grammar or good taste?"*
transform, intr. 'to become transformed; change.'	*The English language has **transformed** considerably over the past five centuries.*
apt 'ordinarily disposed; inclined.'	*I'm **apt** to agree with Chomsky's contention that language is innate.*
abolish 'do away with.'	***Abolishing** the importance of correct spelling would . . .*

6.8 Specialized Dictionaries

In addition to the general dictionaries that we have been discussing so far, there are also many specialized dictionaries such as those that are included in the following list. For the convenience of readers who want to look at these dictionaries, the Library of Congress call number is provided for each item.

a. Dialect Dictionaries

Blevins, W. *Dictionary of the American West*: Facts on File, 1993. PE 2970.W4 B5 1993

Cassidy, F.G., ed. *Dictionary of American Regional English* 2 vols.: Belknap Press, 1985. PE 2843.D52 1985

A Dictionary of Canadianisms on Historical Principles: W.J. Gage, 1967. PE 3243.D5

Holloway, J.E., and W.K Vass. *The African Heritage of American English*: Indiana University Press, 1993. PE 3102.N4 H65 1993

Hughes, J.M., et al., eds. *The Australian Concise Oxford Dictionary*: Oxford University Press, 1992. PE 3601.Z5 A863 1992

Major, C. *Juba to Jive*: Viking, 1994. PE 3727.N4 M34 1994

Ramson, W.S. *The Australian National Dictionary*: Oxford University Press, 1988. PE 3601.Z5 A97 1988

Smitherman, G. *Black Talk*: Houghton Mifflin, 1994. PE 3102.N4 S65 1994

b. Dictionaries of Foreign Words and Phrases in English

Bell, A.J. *A Dictionary of Foreign Words and Phrases in Current English*: E.P. Dutton, 1966. PE 1670.B55 1966a

Guinagh, K. *Dictionary of Foreign Phrases and Abbreviations*: H.W. Wilson, 1972. PE 1670.G8 1972

Newmark, M. *Dictionary of Foreign Words and Phrases*: Philosophical Library, 1950. PE 1582. A3 N4

c. Dictionaries of New Words

Barnhart, R., and Sol Steinmetz, with Clarence Barnhart. *The Third Barnhart Dictionary of New English*: H.W. Wilson, 1990. PE 1630.B3

The Oxford Dictionary of New Words: Oxford University Press, 1991. PE 1630.094 1991

d. Dictionaries of Slang

Ayto, J., and J. Simpson. *The Oxford Dictionary of Modern Slang*: Oxford University Press, 1992. PE 3721.94 1992

Lightner, J. E., ed. *Random House Historical Dictionary of American Slang* 2 vols.: Random House, 1994. PE 2846.H57 1994

Partridge, E. *A Dictionary of Slang,* 8th ed.: Macmillan, 1984. PE 3721.P3 1984

e. Etymological Dictionaries

Klein, E. *A Comprehensive Etymological Dictionary of the English Language* 2 vols.: Elsevier, 1966. PE 1580.K4

Morris, W., and M. Morris. *Dictionary of Word and Phrase Origins* 2 vols.: Harper & Row, 1962. PE 1580.M6

Onions, C.T., ed. *The Oxford Dictionary of English Etymology*: Clarendon Press, 1966. PE 1580.05

Partridge, E. *Origins: A Short Etymological Dictionary of Modern English*: Macmillan, 1958. PE 1580.P3

Shipley, J.T. *Dictionary of Word Origins*: Philosophical Library, 1945. PE 1580.S45

Shipley, J.T. *The Origins of English Words*: Johns Hopkins, 1984. PE 1571.S46 1984

f. Pronouncing Dictionaries

Bollard, J.K., ed. *Pronouncing Dictionary of Proper Names*: Omnigraphics, 1993. PE 1137.982 1993

Jones, D. *Everyman's English Pronouncing Dictionary,* 14th ed.: E. P. Dutton, 1977. PE 1137. G53 1977

Kenyon, J.S., and T.A. Knott. *A Pronouncing Dictionary of American English*: G. & C. Merriam, 1944. PE 1137.K37

Pointon, G.E., ed. *BBC Pronouncing Dictionary*. Oxford University Press, 1990. PE 1660.B3 1990

g. Rhyming Dictionaries

Lees, G. *The Modern Rhyming Dictionary*: Cherry Lane Books, 1981. PE 1519.L37

Stillman, F. *The Poet's Manual and Rhyming Dictionary*: Thos. Y. Crowell, 1965. PE 1505.S8

Young, S. *The New Comprehensive American Rhyming Dictionary*: Wm. Morrow, 1991. PE 1519.Y68 1991

h. Other Specialized Dictionaries

Barlough, J.E. *The Archaicon: A Collection of Unusual, Archaic English*: Scarecrow Press, 1974. PE 1667.BC

Cowie, A.P., et al. *Oxford Dictionary of Current Idiomatic English* 2 vols.: Oxford University Press, 1983. PE 1460.87

Cowie, A.P., and R. Mackin. *Oxford Dictionary of Phrasal Verbs*: Oxford University Press, 1993. PE 1319.C69 1993

Maggio, R. *The Dictionary of Bias-Free Usage*: Oryx Press, 1991. PE 1460.M26 1991

McCutcheon, M. *Descriptionary: A Thematic Dictionary*: Facts on File, 1992. PE 1591.M415 1992

Smith, R.W.L. *Dictionary of English Word-Roots*: Littlefield, Adams, and Co., 1967. PE 1580.S65

Taylor, M. *The Language of World War II*: H.W. Wilson, 1948. PE 3727.S7 T3 1948

EXERCISE 10.   Find three dictionaries from the list above and write down one interesting fact you learn from each one.

6.9 Applications for Students and Teachers of Writing

One of the most important observations of this chapter is that we learn vocabulary by hearing and using it in context: Looking up words in dictionaries is not an efficient way to develop one's vocabulary and can sometimes even be misleading, since dictionary writers are not always able to put their finger on the exact meaning of a word. However, despite their limitations as a vocabulary-learning tool, dictionaries contain a great deal of interesting and useful information; every secondary and college student should own a good college dictionary and know how to use it. Students and teachers should also know how to use the *Oxford English Dictionary* (the *OED*), which is useful for tracing the historical development of words and for finding out what they meant in earlier times. Students should also be made aware of the existence of specialized dictionaries that provide information about particular dialects or registers of English, as well as "backwards" dictionaries for budding poets who want help in finding a rhyme.

In addition to the referential meanings of words, students must also be taught to pay attention to register; expressions such as "cool" or "fabulous" are fine for conversation, but not for formal academic writing.

EXERCISE 11.   The best way to understand how something is done is to do it yourself. You can learn a lot about the workings of the dictionary by creating your own dictionary of slang.[9] Begin by collecting slang words that are used in a group you belong to, such as a fraternity or sorority, an athletic team, or simply a group of friends. When you have collected twenty words or more, compile your words into a dictionary. Be as professional as possible: include a pronunciation, inflectional forms, part-of-speech labels, and an etymology. (If you can't figure out the etymology, do what the dictionary writers do—put [origin unknown].) Write definitions and, if the word has more than one definition, organize them in a logical sequence, with numbers. Include usage labels where relevant. If appropriate, provide a list of synonyms at the end of the entry, with discussion of differences in their meaning and usage.

6.10 Applications for Students of Literature

There are many things to notice about the words of a literary passage—not only their register and referential meanings, but also their affective and social meanings, and even their sound. For example, in the passage from James Joyce's *Araby*, Appendix Section I, the author has chosen vocabulary from the poetic register (*dusk, sombre, ever-changing violet, lamps, feeble, ever (to mean 'constantly'*). The poetic tone is enhanced by the use of figurative language such as the personification in the third line "The lamps lifted . . ." Meaning is carried by all parts of speech—nouns (*winter, dusk, violet, lanterns,* etc.); verbs (*ever-changing, stung, played, glowed, echoed*);

---

9. This exercise suggests a dictionary of slang, but there may be other appropriate topics for your students. For example, a teacher from West Virginia told me that his students had put together a dictionary of mining terms. The important thing is to take the dictionary seriously and include all the information that real dictionaries contain.

and adjectives (*sombre, feeble, silent*); and the words invoke all the senses: sight (*colour, violet, dusk*, etc.), hearing (*shouts, echoed, silent*), and the kinesthetic (*cold, stung, feeble*). The author sets up a series of oppositions between light and darkness (*ever-changing violet, lamps, lanterns, glowed* vs. *short days, dusk, sombre*), between sound and silence (*shouts, echoed* vs. *silent street*), and between cold and warmth (*cold air* vs. *stung, glowed*).

In keeping with the poetic tone, the passage is filled with sound effects: alliteration (*days, dusk, dinners*; *when, winter, we, well*; *street, sombre, space of sky*); consonance (*colour, violet, lamps, lifted, feeble, lanterns, cold, glowed, silent*); rhyme (*well, fell*); and assonance (*space, changing*; *sky, violet*; *street, feeble*; *cold, glowed, echoed*). These sound patterns enhance the poetic tone and draw attention to important words in the passage and to the connections between them—notice, for example, how the words that refer to light are linked by the repetition of [l]: *colour, violet, lamps, lifted, feeble, lanterns, glowed*.

EXERCISE 12. Discuss the vocabulary of one of the literary passages in Appendix Section I. Some questions you might consider are listed below, but choose questions that are relevant to the passage you are discussing; not all questions are relevant to every passage. Write your answer as a coherent essay, with references to the selection you are discussing. **Warning:** Confine this discussion to issues of *word choice*; you will have opportunities to discuss the sentence structure of the passages in future exercises.

a. Consider the *register* of the words: Are they formal, informal, or neutral; conversational or literary? Are they characteristic of a particular mode of discourse, such as poetry or legal language? Is there a relationship between the register of the words and their historical origin?

b. Consider the author's dependence on certain syntactic categories. Some writers rely heavily on adjectives for description, while others use nouns and verbs with strong meanings.

c. Now consider the meanings of the words: Are the nouns concrete or abstract? Do the adjectives describe qualities that could be measured objectively, or are they entirely subjective (a judgment by the narrator)? Do the nouns, verbs, and adjectives rely primarily on a particular sense such as sight or hearing? Do the verbs express actions or states? Is there any figurative language? Are there particular semantic concepts or images that re-occur in the words of the passage?

d. Are there repetitions of sounds, and are they connected to meaning?

6.11 Applications for Students and Teachers of ESL

ESL students have to learn not only formal, academic vocabulary, but also ordinary conversational expressions such as *pay attention, turn in, make up for, think over, try out*, etc. In planning vocabulary lessons for ESL students, you will want to be aware of their language background, as well as their language goals. Students who come from Romance languages such as French or Spanish have a head start with Latinate vocabulary such as *conversational, academic* and *applications*, but they may tend to use Latinate vocabulary in places where English speakers would use native English: "Please extinguish the lights," for example, instead of "Please turn out the lights."

ESL students and teachers should be familiar with the dictionaries that have been created especially for them, including *Longman's Dictionary of American English,* the *Cambridge Advanced Learner's Dictionary,* the *Oxford Advanced Learner's Dictionary of English*, and the *American Heritage Dictionary for Learners of English*. Dictionaries for ESL students ignore less common usages and focus, instead, on the most frequently used words and word meanings. The space that is gained in this way is used to provide information that is needed by second language learners, such as whether a noun with a particular meaning functions as a count noun or a mass noun. For example, learners' dictionaries, unlike dictionaries for native speakers, make it clear that the count noun *pie* ("a pie") refers to an entire pastry, not to a single *piece* of pie. These dictionaries also provide useful information about choosing complements for verbs—for example, that the verb *like* can be followed by an infinitival clause (*I like **to play the piano***), but the verb *enjoy* cannot (*I enjoy **playing the piano***, not **I enjoy **to play the piano***).

6.12 Summary of the Chapter

In this chapter, we have traced the history of dictionaries and have taken a close look at what they contain—what items they list and what information is provided in each entry. We examined three kinds of meaning that can be found in words: referential meaning, affective meaning, and social meaning or register, and we took note of the fact that human beings, even dictionary writers, are not very good at defining words. Luckily, we *are* good at figuring out the meanings of words that we hear or read in context; young children learn a new word every two waking hours, on average, and middle-school children acquire thousands of Latinate words from their reading. We ended the chapter by reviewing some of the many specialized dictionaries that provide information about particular registers or geographical regions.

For students and teachers of literature and writing, we pointed out the importance of learning words in context, rather than from a dictionary, and reviewed some of the observations that can be made about the vocabulary of a literary selection. For ESL teachers, we noted that their students must learn conversational vocabulary as well as academic vocabulary and we discussed, briefly, the influence of the student's first language. Finally, we talked about learners' dictionaries, which contain information that is particularly useful to ESL students.

CHAPTER 7

The Structure of Simple Declarative Sentences

7.1 Introduction: What Is a Sentence?

This is an important theoretical question, because the sentence is the basic unit of written discourse (though not necessarily of spoken discourse, as we will see), and it is also an important practical question: Teachers spend countless hours trying to help children understand what units should be punctuated as sentences. Notice, for example, that the first-grade author of "Mafin" (Appendix Section II) has misjudged the punctuation of the sentence

> *When my mom washsi mafin. he scashed my mom and it hse [hurts] a lot.*

And the second-grade author of "Your Own Monster" has written two sentences together as one:

> *I like him he's just kind of hard to take care of.*

In the examples in Appendix Section II, the children seem to be identifying sentences correctly by third or fourth grade, but don't be fooled! These compositions have been edited with the help of the teacher. In their study of freshman writing errors, Connors and Lunsford (1988) found that even college students sometimes have difficulty identifying sentences; improper identification of sentences was the fourth most frequent error in freshman writing. (See Table 7.1.)

Teachers traditionally give two sorts of definitions for the sentence:[1]

1. *A sentence is a group of words that expresses a complete thought.*
2. *A sentence is a group of words that contains a subject and a predicate.*

These definitions address different issues. The following sentence from "My Nightmare" (Appendix Section II) is a "run-on" sentence which violates the first definition above; it is grammatically well-formed, but contains too many unrelated thoughts for one sentence:

> *They put me in a space jail, but I had a good idea and all I had to do is get that space gun.*

---

1. Notice that we are actually talking not about sentences in general, but about *statements*: Questions like "What are you doing?" and imperatives like "Please shut the door" will have to be approached in a slightly different way; we'll return to that issue in Chapter 11.

Table 7.1 Categories of Grammatical Errors in Freshman Compositions, in the Order of Their Frequency (Connors and Lunsford (1988))[2]

Spelling

Punctuation, especially commas and apostrophes

Use of inflectional forms such as past tense and subject-verb agreement

Formation of complete sentences (vs. fragments, fused sentences, and comma splices)[3]

Word choice

NP reference, especially pronouns

Consistency of verb tense

This is a different problem from the writing of fragments or fused sentences, which violate the second definition:

> *When my mom washsi Mafin.* (an incomplete sentence or "fragment")
>
> or *I like him he's just kind of hard to take care of.* (two sentences written together as one—a "fused" sentence)

The first problem—too many thoughts in one sentence—lies outside the purview of a textbook on English grammar. How many thoughts should be included in one sentence is a matter of judgement and taste, not grammatical structure. But the second problem—whether a given sequence of words has the necessary structure to be punctuated as a sentence—is a proper subject of discussion for this text. This issue is addressed by the second definition above: *A sentence is a group of words that contains a subject and a predicate.* In this chapter, we will explore this definition and introduce some revisions to make it more consistent with current thinking about the structure of sentences.

EXERCISE 1. Find other examples of fragments, fused sentences, comma splices, and run-ons in the samples of children's writing in Appendix Section II.

---

2. Connors and Lunsford provide a more specific list of writing errors; for our purposes here, I have collapsed errors of the same general type into a single category. Thus, the fourth category is a combination of four types of errors having to do with the formation of sentences: fragments, fused sentences, run-ons, and comma splices.

3. A comma splice is two sentences separated by a comma rather than a conjunction or semi-colon:

> *I like him, he's just kind of hard to take care of.*

7.2 The Structure of a Sentence

Traditionally, as we have said, a statement is divided into two parts, a subject and a predicate:

Subject	**Predicate**
Gaul	*is divided into three parts.*
People who live in glass houses	*shouldn't throw stones.*
My mom	*gets mad at Muffin.*

In this section, we will show that a statement is better analyzed as having *three* parts rather than two. Let's begin with the following set of very simple sentences:

An intelligent dog would bark.
The old girl should find a good bike.
A conscientious teacher will sit on this soft bench.

These sentences could serve as models for other sentences, as in Tables 7.2a, 7.2b, and 7.2c on the following page. If we don't worry about whether the statement makes sense, we can create a large number of well-formed statements from each table by choosing one word—any word—from each column in the table. (Stop here and try this before reading on.) Now observe that each of these tables is based on a sentence "formula" that consists of a string of categories, and that additional statements like those of Tables 7.2a–c can be constructed by following these formulas:

Table 7.2a: S(entence) = D + Adj + N + AUX + V
Table 7.2b: S = D + Adj + N + AUX + V + D + Adj + N
Table 7.2c: S = D + Adj + N + AUX + V + P + D + Adj + N

EXERCISE 2.

a. Give the full names of the categories in these formulas.
b. Generate three sentences from each formula.

7.3 Words Are Grouped into Phrases

Although the three formulas at the end of the previous section will generate a very large number of sentences (2,346,875 of them, using just the words that are listed in the tables), they hardly scratch the surface of the sentence-making capacity of English speakers. Formulas of this type, which assume that sentences consist of individual words strung together one by one, will not get us very far in understanding how sentences are constructed. Words do not enter sentences one by one, but as groups of words called *phrases*. In this section, we will revise our sentence formulas to reflect this insight.

Table 7.2a   Sentence Pattern 1

D	Adj	N	AUX	V
A(n)	intelligent	dog	would	bark
Any	healthy	teacher	can	swim
The	lucky	girl	could	laugh
Your	pesky	computer	should	run
This	old	man	will	talk

Table 7.2b   Sentence Pattern 2

D	Adj	N	AUX	V	D	Adj	N
The	old	girl	should	find	a(n)	good	bike
Any	conscientious	teacher	would	remove	this	old	hat
A(n)	good	computer	can	ruin	your	dependable	car
Your	pesky	cat	could	disturb	any	tired	man
This	lucky	man	will	steal	the	helpful	cat

Table 7.2c   Sentence Pattern 3

D	Adj	N	AUX	V	P	D	Adj	N
A(n)	conscientious	teacher	will	sit	on	this	soft	bench
Any	old	girl	can	recline	in	a(n)	old	chair
The	good	computer	could	play	by	your	dependable	car
Your	pesky	cat	would	run	near	any	large	tree
This	lucky	man	should	hide	under	the	helpful	hat

7.3.1 The Noun Phrase (NP)

The sequence "D Adj N" occurs in all three tables (7.2a–7.2c), and twice in Table 7.2b. If we pull out this sequence and identify it as a *noun phrase* (NP), then our formulas will be greatly simplified, as shown below:

Table 7.2a: S = NP AUX V   (*An intelligent dog would talk.*)
Table 7.2b: S = NP AUX V NP   (*A conscientious teacher would remove this old hat.*)
Table 7.2c: S = NP AUX V P NP   (*The lucky dog will hide under a helpful tree.*)
             where NP = D Adj N

Linguists use tests called *constituency tests* to determine whether a given string of words constitutes a phrase.[4] The following constituency tests show that we were correct to identify the sequence D Adj N as a phrase:

1. The Pro-form Test

If a string of words can be replaced with a pro-form, then it is a phrase.

   A conscientious teacher *would remove* ***this old hat.*** → ***She*** *would remove* ***it***.

The pro-form test shows that the sequences *a conscientious teacher* and *this old hat* are both phrases.

2. The Movement Test

If a string of words can be moved, as a unit, to another position in the sentence, then it is a phrase.

   This old hat, *any conscientious teacher would remove.*

The movement test shows that the sequence *this old hat* is a phrase.

3. The Short-Answer Test

If a string of words can serve as the short answer to a question, then it is a phrase.

   Q: *What would a conscientious teacher remove?*   **A:** *This old hat.*
   Q: *Who would remove this old hat?*   **A:** *A conscientious teacher.*

The short-answer test shows that the sequences *this old hat* and *a conscientious teacher* are both phrases.

---

4. Notice that these tests depend on the assumption that speakers of English already know, intuitively, how words are grouped into phrases. Otherwise, we couldn't make use of the constituency tests; we wouldn't be able to judge whether the string of words we are testing passes the tests or not.

4. The Cleft Test

If a string of words can be placed in focus position in a *cleft,* as in the example below, then it is a phrase:

Original sentence: *A conscientious teacher would remove this old hat.*

Cleft 1: *It's* | *this old hat* | *that a conscientious teacher would remove.*

Cleft 2: *It's* | *a conscientious teacher* | *that would remove this old hat.*

The cleft test shows that the sequences *this old hat* and *a conscientious teacher* are both phrases.

Although the constituency tests tell us whether a given string of words is or is not a phrase, they do not tell us what sort of phrase it is. The *category* of the phrase is determined by the head word—the word around which the phrase is built: *this old hat* is a kind of *hat* and a conscientious teacher is a kind of *teacher.* Since the nouns *hat* and *teacher* are the central elements of these phrases, they are the "heads" of their respective phrases, and these phrases are therefore *noun* phrases, or NPs.

7.3.2 The Prepositional Phrase (PP)

A preposition together with the NP that follows it (called the *complement* of the preposition) also creates a phrase: *in the house, about social security, by the author, under the sink, near Chicago, around the block,* and so on are all prepositional phrases (PPs).

EXERCISE 3. Consider the following sentences from Table 7.2c:
a. *A conscientious teacher should recline in this old chair.*
b. *The lucky man will hide under a helpful hat.*

First identify the PP in each sentence. Then use the pro-form test, the movement test, the short answer test, and the cleft test to show that the sequence of words you have identified is a phrase. *Hint:* The pro-form for a PP is *then* or *there.*

Now that we have identified the phrasal category PP, the formula of Table 7.2c can be simplified as follows:

S = NP AUX V PP, where NP = D ADJ N and PP = P NP
(*The lucky man will hide under a helpful hat.*)

7.3.3 The Verb Phrase (VP)

You are probably already familiar with NPs and PPs, from the traditional grammar that you studied in school. But our constituency tests also identify another sort of phrase that was not recognized in traditional grammar, namely, the sequence of words that consists of the verb plus the phrase that follows it:

*An intelligent dog can **talk**. She will **steal your car**. He should **sit in that chair**.*

Because the central word of this phrase is the verb, the phrase is called a *verb phrase* (VP).[5] The string of words that *follows* the verb (*your car; in that chair*) is called the "complement" of the verb.

EXERCISE 4. In each of the boldfaced VPs above, first find the verb and then the "complement" of the verb. Then identify the category of the complement (NP or PP).

Our constituency tests show that the VP is a phrase:

1. The Pro-form Test

Given an appropriate context such as the parenthesized material in the examples below, a VP can be replaced by the pro-form *do so*:

> *(Most animals cannot talk, but) an intelligent dog can* **do so.**
> > *Talk* has been replaced, in the second clause, by the proform *do so*.
> *(I said she would steal your car, and) she will* **do so.**
> > *Steal your car* has been replaced, in the second clause, by the proform *do so*.
> *(I told him to sit in that chair, and) he should* **do so.**
> > *Sit in that chair* has been replaced, in the second clause, by the proform *do so*.

2. The Movement Test

Given an appropriate context such as the parenthesized material in the examples below, the VP can be moved to the beginning of its clause:

> *(I said this dog could talk, and)* **talk** *he can.*
> > *Talk* has moved to the front of its clause.
> *(I said she would steal your car, and)* **steal your car** *she will.*
> > *Steal your car* has moved to the front of its clause.
> *(I said he should sit in that chair, and)* **sit in that chair** *he should.*
> > *Sit in that chair* has moved to the front of its clause.

3. The Short-Answer Test

A VP can serve as the short answer to a question:

> **Q:** *What can an intelligent dog do?*   **A:** *Talk.*
> **Q:** *What will she do?*   **A:** *Steal your car.*
> **Q:** *What should he do?*   **A:** *Sit in that chair.*

---

5. Unfortunately, the term *verb phrase* is used in traditional grammar with a different meaning, to designate the string of words consisting of the auxiliary verb plus the main verb: *should have gone; will notice; was decapitated*. In this course, we will use the term *verb string* rather than *verb phrase* for sequences of this sort. In the sense in which we are using the term *phrase*, the verb string is not a phrase at all.

4. The Cleft Test

VPs will not participate in clefts of the sort we saw above. [Remember that the asterisk (*) indicates that the sentence is not well-formed.]

It's | steal your car | that she will.

It's | talk | that an intelligent dog can.

But there is another type of cleft, called a *WH-cleft,* that *does* allow a VP in focus position:

What an intelligent dog can do is | talk |

What she will do is | steal your car |

We see, then, that strings like *talk, steal your car,* and *sit in that chair* do satisfy at least one form of the Cleft Test, and we conclude that the Cleft Test, like the other constituency tests, identifies these strings as phrases. Phrases of this type are called *verb phrases* (VPs), because the head word (*talk, steal, sit*) is a verb.

With the recognition of the phrasal categories NP, PP, and VP, the formulas of Tables 7.2a–c can be reduced to a single formula, shown in the righthand column of Table 7.3 below. Formulas like those of Table 7.3, which specify what elements can combine to form a sentence or phrase, are called *phrase structure rules.* We have now identified four phrase structure rules for English:

S   =   NP AUX VP
NP =   D Adj N
VP =   V *or* V NP *or* V PP
PP =   P NP

Table 7.3   Sentence Formulas: A New Version

	Original formula	New formula
Table 7.2a	S = D + Adj + N + AUX + V	S = NP AUX VP
	(*An intelligent dog can talk.*)	
Table 7.2b	S = D + Adj + N + AUX + V + D + Adj + N	S = NP AUX VP
	(*The old girl will steal your car.*)	
Table 7.2c	S = D + Adj + N + AUX + V + P + D + Adj + N	S = NP AUX VP
	(*This conscientious teacher should sit in that chair.*)	
where	NP = D Adj N,	
	VP = V *or* V NP *or* V PP	
	PP = P NP	

Note that the term "NP" appears in all three rules. The NP at the beginning of the sentence (**NP AUX VP**) is called the *subject* of the sentence; a NP that follows the verb within the VP (V **NP**) is called *the object of the verb;* a NP that follows the preposition within a PP (P **NP**) is called *the object of the preposition.*[6]

7.4 Tree Diagrams

The structure of a statement can be represented schematically by means of a tree diagram, as shown in Figure 7.1, where S = statement, NP = noun phrase, and VP = verb phrase:[7]

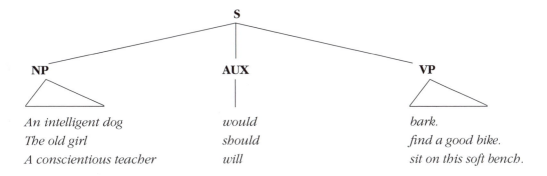

Figure 7.1   A tree diagram.

The triangles under the labels **NP** and **VP** are an abbbreviatory device which indicates that we could say more about the internal structure of these phrases but have chosen not to do so. This use of triangles is called th*e triangle notation.*

EXERCISE 5. Draw tree diagrams of the following sentences, following the model in Figure 7.1. (That is, divide the sentences into NP + AUX + VP and use the triangle notation for the NP and VP.)

   a. *This old man can swim.*

   b. *A conscientious cat would find an old bike.*

   c. *The lucky girl should sit near the old tree.*

   d. *Choosy mothers will choose Jiff.*

   e. *The cow would jump over the moon.*

---

6. The reader may be wondering about the difference between a *complement* and an *object. Complement* is a general term for the phrase that follows a particular verb or preposition. For example, in the VPs *close the door* and *look at the camera,* the NP *the door* is the complement of the verb *close* and the PP *at the camera* is the complement of the verb *look.* A complement which is a NP is also called an *object.* Thus, for example, the NP *the door* can be called either the complement or the object of the verb *close,* and the NP *the camera* is both the complement and the object of the preposition *at.* But the PP *at the camera* cannot be called the object of the verb *look*—it is the complement of the verb, but not an object (because it is not an NP).

7. In sentences like *Beth gets a haircut* and *The dog ate my homework,* the tense marker [present tense] or [past tense] serves as the AUX. Sentences of this type will be discussed in Section 7.7.

Caution: Draw your tree diagrams *very neatly* and exactly as shown above. For example, do not draw the tree upside down or put the labels inside the triangles rather than on top. A notation like this is useful only if it is applied in a uniform way, so that we become accustomed to it and recognize it immediately, rather than having to puzzle out the notation each time.

A note about diagrams: The practice of diagramming sentences has gained a bad reputation as a result of the traditional practice of asking students to do Kellogg-Reed diagrams such as the following:

Students and their teachers have pointed out that the notational conventions for these diagrams are arbitrary and difficult to learn, and that learning to diagram sentences does not help students become better writers. Let me say at the outset that I am under no illusion that diagramming sentences will greatly improve your writing. However, if we want to talk about the *structure* of sentences, then we need a way to illustrate that structure—a way to draw a picture of a sentence. Diagrams are very useful for that purpose. Tree diagrams are more logical and easier to learn than the traditional Kellogg-Reed diagrams, and their usefulness is enhanced by the triangle notation, which allows us to omit irrelevant details.

7.5 "Families" of Sentences

In the previous sections, we saw that a statement has three parts rather than two, with the auxiliary (AUX) as a separate, independent constituent: NP, AUX, VP. This section will give further evidence that the AUX is an independent element, separate from the verb. The evidence comes from observation of other sentence types such as emphatics, negatives, and *yes/no* questions. Let us begin by noting that for each affirmative statement we can construct a family of corresponding sentences, as follows:

Affirmative Statement:	*This old man can swim.*
Emphatic Statement:	*This old man **can** swim.*
Negative Statement:	*This old man can not swim.*
	(or, with contraction, *This old man can't swim.*)
***Yes/no* question:**	*Can this old man swim?*

EXERCISE 6. Give the emphatic, negative, and *yes/no* question that corresponds to each of the statements in Exercise 5. Then state a rule for forming each type of sentence.

If you did Exercise 6, you will have seen that our three-part analysis of the sentence allows a simple statement of the relationship among the various members of a sentence "family":

1. Emphatic statement: Emphasize AUX.

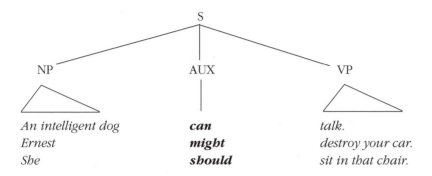

2. Negative statement: Place the negative particle *not* immediately after AUX.

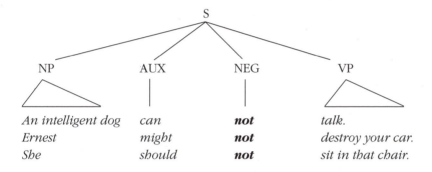

3. *Yes/no* question: Move AUX to the left of the subject NP.

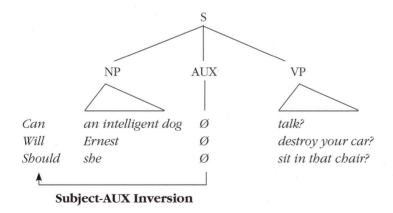

Note that the original position of the AUX is marked in the diagram with a null sign—Ø. The idea is that, in sentences of this type, the auxiliary in some sense occupies *two* positions: its basic position between the subject NP and the VP, and the position before the subject of the sentence. The rule that moves the AUX to the position preceding the subject is called *Subject-AUX Inversion.* Rules of this type, which make adjustments in the structure that is created by the phrase-structure rules, are called *transformations.*

7.6 Sentential Adverbs

In addition to its usefulness in elucidating the relationship among the members of a sentence family (statement, emphatic statement, negative statement, question), our three-part analysis of the sentence also allows a simple description of the distribution of sentential adverbs like *probably, surely,* and *sometimes:* Adverbs of this type can be placed at the boundary of any of the major constituents of the sentence (that is, in any of the positions labeled *ADV* in the tree diagram in Figure 7.2).

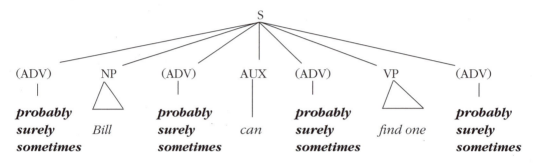

Figure 7.2 The positions for sentential adverbs.

Notice how difficult it would be to understand the position of these adverbs if we were assuming the traditional view that the sentence has only two parts—subject and predicate, and that the auxiliary is part of the verb (*can find, will destroy, should sit*). We would have to say that an adverb can be placed right in the middle of the verb (. . . *can probably find* . . .).

7.7 Sentences with No Visible AUX

We are now ready to deal with sentences like *Beth got a haircut* and *The dog ate my homework,* which have no visible AUX. To understand the structure of these sentences, consider what happens when they are converted into emphatics, questions, or negatives.

Emphatic statement

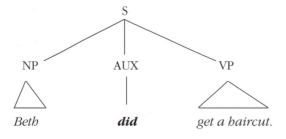

144

Question

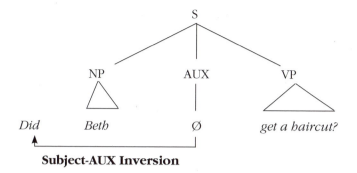

Subject-AUX Inversion

Negative statement

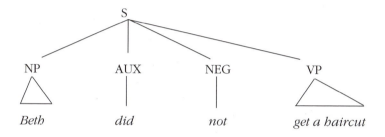

These examples show that when the statement *Beth got a haircut* is converted into one of its related forms, it *does* have an auxiliary, the "dummy" auxiliary *did*. This auxiliary is present in all forms of the sentence except the affirmative statement, and it, rather than the main verb, carries the tense marker—in this case [past tense]. This suggests that the tense marker belongs, inherently, to the AUX position. In other words, the sentence *Beth got a haircut* has the underlying structure:

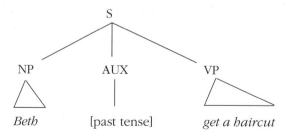

The affirmative statement is created from this underlying structure by means of a transformation called *Tense Hopping,* which attaches the tense marker to the main verb:

Affirmative statement

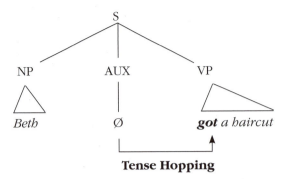

Tense Hopping

However, in emphatic sentences, questions, and negatives, which require an independent AUX, the tense marker is pronounced as *did*, by a rule called "*Do*-Support":

Emphatic statement:

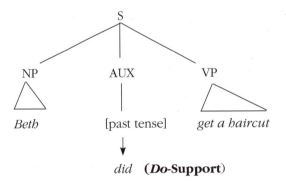

did   (***Do*-Support**)

***Yes/no* question:**

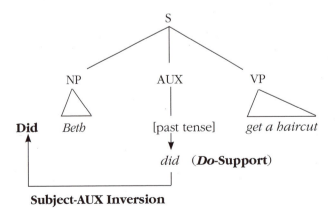

Subject-AUX Inversion

Negative statement:

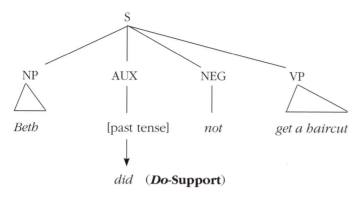

did (**Do**-Support)

A further transformation called *Contraction* converts the negative statement (optionally) to

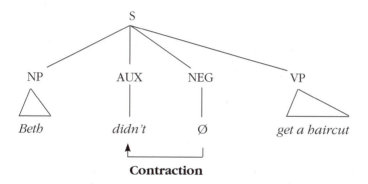

Contraction

Note that the underlying position of the *not* is marked with Ø in the tree diagram.

In conclusion, sentences like *Beth got a haircut* do have an AUX—the tense marker [past tense], which takes either of two forms: (1) It attaches to the verb by Tense Hopping, or (2) it is pronounced as *did* by the transformation of *Do*-Support. English has three tense markers, shown below, each of which can be pronounced either as part of the verb or separately, as a form of *do*:

Tense Marker	With *Do*-Support	With Tense Hopping
[past tense]	*did*	*-ed*
[general present tense]	*do*	Ø
[3rd singular present tense]	*does*	*-s*

EXERCISE 7.

a. Give tree diagrams for the sentences *The dog ate my homework, Did the dog eat my homework? The dog didn't eat my homework,* and *The dog **did** eat my homework,* showing the effects of Tense Hopping, *Do*-Support, Contraction, and Subject-AUX Inversion, as in the models above.

b. Give tree diagrams for the sentences *Beth gets a haircut, Beth **does** get a haircut, Does Beth get a haircut?* and *Beth doesn't get a haircut,* showing the effects of Tense Hopping,

Do-Support, Contraction, and Subject-AUX Inversion, as in the models above. What is the AUX in these sentences ([past tense], [general present tense], or [3rd singular present tense])?

c. Give tree diagrams for the sentences *Some people like squash, Some people **do** like squash, Do some people like squash?* and *Some people don't like squash*, showing the effects of Tense Hopping, *Do*-Support, Contraction, and Subject-AUX Inversion, as in the models above. What is the AUX in these sentences ([past tense], [general present tense], or [3rd singular present tense])?

7.8 Applications for Teachers

In his book *Grammar and the Teaching of Writing,* Rei Noguchi (1991) suggests the rule of Subject-AUX Inversion (SAI) as a test for the completeness of a statement: If the statement is complete, then it can be converted to a *yes/no* question, by Subject-AUX Inversion:

Statement to be tested: *A trained chimpanzee can change the oil in a car.*

Yes/no question: ***Can** a trained chimpanzee Ø change the oil in a car?*

SAI

Since the statement above has a corresponding *yes/no* question, it must be complete. In contrast, the statement below is *not* a complete sentence, and it has no corresponding *yes/no* question:

Which is more than I can say for some people!
(There is no corresponding *yes/no* question, so it must be a fragment.)

Notice the principle that underlies the Noguchi test: A well-formed statement contains a subject (usually a NP), AUX, and VP. By applying the rule of Subject-AUX Inversion, we locate two of the major parts of the statement—subject and AUX—and establish that both are present. If a string of words contains a subject, AUX, and VP and does not begin with a subordinating conjunction such as *although* or *because*, then the transformation of Subject-AUX Inversion will convert it into a *yes/no* question, showing that it is a complete sentence.[8]

---

8. The Noguchi test is actually a test for an *independent clause* rather than for a sentence. Compound sentences like the following contain two independent clauses connected by a coordinating conjunction (*and, but, or,* or *yet*):

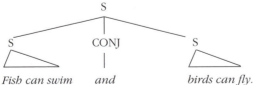

In a sentence of this type, each independent clause can undergo Subject-AUX Inversion:

Can fish Ø swim and can birds Ø fly?

but it is impossible to apply Subject-AUX Inversion just once to the entire sentence:

**Can fish Ø swim and birds can fly?*

148

EXERCISE 8.   Use the Noguchi test to determine which of the "statements" below are complete and which are only fragments. Identify the subject, AUX, and VP of each complete statement. (Examples based on Noguchi 1991, p. 88)

    a. *Sam ended up cleaning his room.*
    b. *Which he doesn't like.*
    c. *The soldiers were marching straight ahead.*
    d. *Into an ambush.*
    e. *Arthur will miss a surprise quiz.*
    f. *If he skips class.*
    g. *It should soon become obvious.*
    h. *That we aren't going to Chicago.*

Fragments are common in conversation, but in formal writing we are usually expected to use complete sentences. However, writers sometimes employ fragments deliberately to create a special effect. For example, there are several fragments in the following advertisement for Papermate pens:

> *Air-cushioned grip. Smooth Lubriglide™ ink system. Bold, vivid lines.*
> *Does all this make Dynagrip the perfect pen? In a word, yes.*

In fact, in this advertisement there is only one sentence that is *not* a fragment—the *yes/no* question, *Does all this make Dynagrip the perfect pen?*

EXERCISE 9.

a. Find the fragments in the following narrative from an article by Paul Brown entitled "The Night I Befriended the Fog," which appeared in *Points East Magazine* (2001). Would you consider these fragments to be errors, or are they an effective use of the fragment? You should also be able to find a comma splice (independent clauses joined together with nothing but a comma).

> *I stepped up onto the lazarette and let down the boarding ladder at the tran-*   1
> *som. I was slightly apprehensive about this impulse. Was I being foolish? Had*   2
> *I had too much to drink? No matter. When my toes touched the water, it was*   3
> *as any Mainer would expect; not your average bath water, but not shockingly*   4
> *cold. Actually, rather refreshing.*   5
>   *I lowered myself into the water, holding onto a rung of the ladder, then I*   6
> *kicked my legs and stroked gently with my free arm. Millions of luminescent*   7
> *globules swirled about me. Then, holding with both hands to the bottom rung,*   8
> *I kicked my feet forward and watched the cascade of glitter trailing from each*   9
> *individual toe.*   10

> *It was, as they say, almost a religious experience. Does an angel reclining* 11
> *on a soft, fluffy cloud, plunking on his harp, enjoy the same sensuous feeling?* 12
> *I'm not ready to find out, but I can tell you that this earthly experience was* 13
> *one not to be forgotten.* 14
> *Presently, I hauled myself out of the radiant brine, clambering slippery-wet* 15
> *and panting slightly from my exertion into the cockpit. One more deep inhala-* 16
> *tion and a silent thanks for a few moments to remember.* 17
>
> —Paul Brown, "The Night I Befriended the Fog"

   b. We said that fragments are common in conversation. Look over the sample of conversational English that you inserted in Appendix Section VI. To what extent do the participants in your conversation employ fragments rather than complete sentences?

   c. "Realistic" representations of conversation in literature also use fragments. Turn to the dialog passage from Ernest Hemingway's "Hills Like White Elephants" in Appendix Section VII. Find as many fragments as you can (I found eight), and use Subject-AUX Inversion to *show* that they are fragments.

7.9 Applications for ESL Teachers

The use of *Do*-Support to form questions and negatives is one of the most difficult constructions for beginning and intermediate-level ESL students. To establish a mental picture of the overall pattern, ESL students can benefit from doing three-part tree diagrams like those of Exercises 5 and 7 above, or they can do the same exercise more graphically with colored index cards, as shown in Exercise 10 below.

EXERCISE 10.

   a. Take a yellow index card and write a singular NP on one side and its plural form on the other—for example, *the candidate* on one side and *the candidates* on the other. Then take a white card and write a modal auxiliary on each side—for example, *can* and *would*. Take a pink card and write a VP to finish your sentence—for example, *climb onto the podium* on one side and *give impassioned speeches* on the other. Put the cards together to make sentences such as *The candidate would give impassioned speeches*, each with the three parts—subject, AUX, VP.

   b. Now take your AUX and move it to the left of the subject NP, to form a *yes/no* question such as *Can the candidate give impassioned speeches?*

   c. Now take a green card and write a sentential adverb on each side—for example, *probably* on one side and *of course* on the other.[9] Add your sentential adverb to your core sentence, and notice that it can be placed in any of four positions—at the beginning of the sentence, at the end, or at the boundary between any of the three major constituents.

---

9. Notice that *probably* can be inserted into the sentence without pauses, but that *of course* will need pauses in speech and a comma in writing.

d. Now take a blue card and write *not* on one side and *n't* on the other. Remove the sentential adverb and insert your blue card into the sentence. Notice that it goes in just one position—between the AUX and the VP. Try the negative in both its full form and its contracted form. Notice that when the negative contracts, it will, in some cases, cause a pronunciation change in the AUX itself, so that, for example, *will* + *n't* ⇒ *won't*. Notice, also, that when the negative is contracted onto the AUX, it becomes part of the AUX, so that Subject-AUX Inversion moves the entire unit: **Can't** *the candidate Ø climb onto the podium?* (vs. **Can** *the candidate Ø* **not** *climb onto the podium?*)

e. Now take three more white cards and write *do* on one card, *does* on another, and *did* on a third. Label the cards "present tense *-s* form," "present tense general form," and "past tense." Turn the cards over, and write *-s, Ø,* and *−ed* on the appropriate cards.

f. Insert one of these white cards into your sentence, in place of the modal auxiliary. Start with the side that says *do, does,* or *did*. Notice that, with the past tense auxiliary *did*, it makes no difference whether you choose the singular form of your subject (*The candidate did give impassioned speeches*) or the plural form (*The candidates did give impassioned speeches*). However, if you choose *does* as your AUX your subject must be singular, while if you choose *do,* your subject must be plural. This rule is called Subject-AUX agreement (or, more commonly, Subject-verb agreement). English requires agreement between the subject and auxiliary only in the present tense.[10]

g. Now create a negative sentence (by putting in the *not* card) and a *yes/no* question (by performing Subject-AUX Inversion).

h. Finally, turn over your AUX card and create an ordinary affirmative statement by "hopping" the AUX (Ø, *-s,* or *-ed*) onto the verb. Notice that, for irregular verbs, the addition of the past tense causes a change in the verb itself; for example, *hold* + past tense becomes *held,* not *holded.*

The index-card procedure in Exercise 10 is a good way to give ESL students a feel for the role of the AUX in English, but they will also need a great deal of practice in forming questions and negatives. English language curricula for ESL students usually take the students through the various verb forms of English, with practice in making questions and negatives in each form. To give the students still more practice, look for games like "Twenty Questions" that require them to form questions. Another exercise is to go through a reading passage that the students already understand thoroughly and have them turn every statement into a question. Or have them create "comprehension" questions to test their classmates on the content of the passage. In normal classroom procedure, the teacher asks most of the questions, and students give the answers. Knowing that ESL students need extra practice with questions, teachers can be on the lookout for strategies to reverse this imbalance.

Subject-AUX agreement is also tricky for ESL students; the fact that we have an agreement marker only in one place (3rd-person singular present tense) makes our system harder to learn, not easier.

---

10. In earlier times, English required subject-verb agreement in past tense, as well, and one verb, *be,* still maintains that requirement: *He/she/it* **was** *here; They* **were** *here.*

EXERCISE 11. Look through the examples of ESL writing in Appendix Section V and find five examples of problems with subject-AUX agreement.

7.10 Summary of the Chapter

In this chapter, we have established that a sentence has three basic parts: NP, AUX, and VP. The NP that appears at the beginning of the sentence is called the *subject*. Some sentences also contain the negative particle *not,* or a sentential adverb such as *probably* or *certainly*. In the examples we have seen so far, the AUX is either a modal auxiliary (*can, could, will, would, shall, should, may, might,* or *must*) or a tense marker ([past tense], [general present tense], or [3rd singular present tense]).[11]

We have also identified four "transformations" that adjust the word order or insert/alter words in certain types of sentences:

***Do*-Support**	In questions, negatives, and emphatics, pronounce the tense marker as *did* ([past tense]), *do* ([general present tense]), or *does* ([3rd singular present tense]).
Negative Contraction	(Optional) Contract the negative particle *not* onto the AUX.
Subject-AUX Inversion (SAI)	To form a question, move AUX to the left of the subject NP.
Tense Hopping	If AUX is a tense marker ([general present tense], [3rd singular present tense] or [past tense]), and if the sentence is an ordinary affirmative statement, then pronounce the AUX on the main verb.

For students whose first language is English, the information in this chapter can help them learn to recognize complete sentences (as opposed to fragments and fused sentences), and to identify the **subject**, which is important for subject-verb agreement. These two issues are also important for students of English as a second language, but, in addition, ESL students also struggle with the use of *Do*-support in forming questions and negatives.

---

11. In Chapter 10, we will consider three other auxiliaries in English—the "perfect" auxiliary *have/has/had*; the "progressive" auxiliary *am/is/are/was/were/be/been*; and the "passive" auxiliary *am/is/are/was/were/be/being/been*.

CHAPTER 8

The Structure of Phrases

8.1 Introduction

In this chapter we will delve more deeply into the grammar of English by working out the internal structure of phrases: PP (prepositional phrase), VP (verb phrase), AdjP (adjective phrase), AdvP (adverb phrase), and NP (noun phrase). The main idea we will develop is that all phrases have essentially the same structure—a *head* word (the N of a noun phrase, the P of a prepositional phrase, the V of a verb phrase, and so forth) plus the dependents of the head word—its *complements,* its *modifiers,* and its *subject* or *specifier.* (These terms will be defined in the course of the chapter.) We will begin with the three simplest phrases—the prepositional phrase, the adjective phrase, and the adverb phrase—and then move on to the verb phrase, the sentence, and, finally, the noun phrase.

8.2 The Prepositional Phrase (PP)

A prepositional phrase consists of a preposition (the head word of the phrase) together with its complement. A *complement* is a phrase that, in English, comes after the head word and completes its meaning.[1]

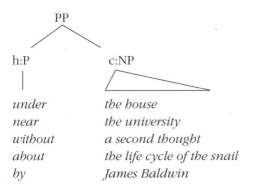

The uppercase labels (PP, P, NP) indicate the *category* of each constituent (prepositional phrase, preposition, noun phrase); the lowercase labels (h, c) indicate the *function* of the constituent (head or complement). The internal structure of the c:NP has been left unspecified, using the triangle notation.

---

1. Notice the spelling of the word *complement.* Its middle syllable is spelled with <e>, not <i>, because it is related to the word *complete.* English also has a word *compliment,* spelled with <i>, which is what you receive when people say they like your smile.

Prepositions typically take NPs as complements, as in the examples above, but it is possible for a preposition to make up a PP all by itself, as in the sentence *She ran **by***. And some prepositions take a PP complement, as in the following examples.

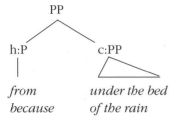

In addition to the head word and its complement, a PP may also contain a *modifier*—an optional descriptive element that is not necessary for the well-formedness of the phrase:

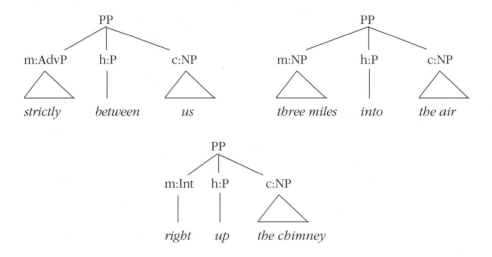

EXERCISE 1. Draw tree diagrams for the following PPs, showing the category and function of each constituent: *out the window, about the American Revolution, right around the block, completely off the mark.*

For the student who wants a challenge: *a year after the accident.*

8.3 The Adjective Phrase (AdjP)

An adjective phrase (AdjP) consists of an adjective with its complements and modifiers, if any:[2]

---

2. From this point on I will omit the label *h* for the head word and mark only the functions complement (c), modifier (m), and subject or specifier (s); in this simplified notation, the unmarked element in each phrase is the head of the phrase.

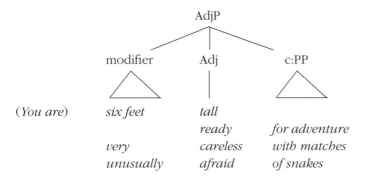

The complement of an adjective is usually a PP, as in these examples. Notice that the preposition is sometimes specific to the particular adjective; we have to be careful *with* matches rather than careful *of* matches. It appears that, as we learn the adjectives of English, we also learn which preposition goes with each adjective (but notice the usage issues of Exercise 4b below).

EXERCISE 2.

   a. Provide complements for the following adjectives, and notice that each adjective requires a PP complement with a particular preposition: *tired, interested, guilty, surprised, nervous, loyal.*

   b. Since the choice of preposition for the complement of an adjective is often arbitrary, speakers may differ in which preposition they choose, and this can sometimes become a usage issue. Some authorities object to the following choices in formal writing: *angry at (a person), different than, bored of* (cf. *tired of*). Do you consider these to be errors? If so, what would you say instead?

The *modifier* of an adjective may be an intensifier (Int), a NP, or an AdvP:

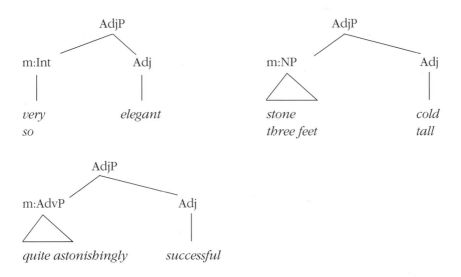

8.4 The Adverb Phrase (AdvP)

An adverb phrase (AdvP) has the same structure as an adjective phrase, except that adverbs do not take complements:

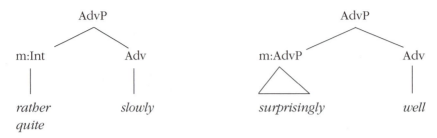

EXERCISE 3. Draw tree diagrams for the following AdjPs and AdvPs, showing the category and function of each constituent: *very excited about the game, three feet deep, incredibly naive, very foolishly.*

8.5 The Verb Phrase (VP)

A verb phrase, like the other types of phrases that we have looked at, consists of a head word (in this case, a verb) together with its complements and modifiers:

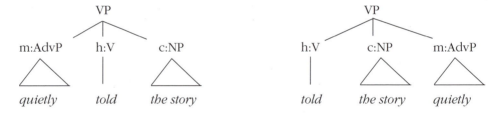

Table 8.1 Verb Phrase Patterns

Name of category	Formula			Example
Intransitive	V			*Sing.*
Transitive	V	c:NP		*Eat your vegetables.*
Prepositional	V	c:PP		*Insist on precision.*
Ditransitive	V	c:NP	c:NP	*Give the man the money.*
Transitive Prepositional	V	c:NP	c:PP	*Put your socks in the drawer.*
Linking	V	c:$\left\{\begin{array}{c} \text{AdjP} \\ \text{NP}_{pred} \end{array}\right\}$		*Be quiet.* / *Be a good sport.*
Complex transitive	V	c:NP	c:$\left\{\begin{array}{c} \text{AdjP} \\ \text{NP}_{pred} \end{array}\right\}$	*Make us rich.* / *Call me Ishmael.*

The modifier of the verb can go either at the beginning or the end of the VP; however, the complement always follows right after the head.

Verb phrases are more complex than adjective, adverb, or prepositional phrases, in that verbs take a richer variety of complements. Verbs are traditionally classified into seven categories, as shown in Table 8.1 on the preceding page, depending on what sorts of complements they require.[3]

EXERCISE 4. For each example VP in Table 8.1, draw a tree diagram showing the category and function of each constituent.

Let's go through these patterns one by one.

1. Intransitive Verbs: Verbs in this category do not need a complement:

VP
|
h:V
|
talk
run
swim
grow
etc.

---

3. Those of you who have studied traditional grammar will notice that these VP patterns correspond to the traditional seven basic sentence patterns, listed below (from Greenbaum 1989). These patterns differ from ours in that they include the subject and AUX, in addition to the VP:

SV	**Subject** *Someone*	**Intransitive verb** *is talking.*		
SVO	**Subject** *We*	**Transitive verb** *have finished*	**Direct object** *our work.*	
SVP	**Subject** *My parents*	**Intransitive verb** *are living*	**Prepositional complement** *in Chicago.*	
SVOO	**Subject** *She*	**Transitive verb** *has given*	**Indirect object** *me*	**Direct object** *the letter.*
SVOP	**Subject** *You*	**Transitive verb** *can put*	**Direct object** *your coat*	**Prepositional complement** *in my bedroom.*
SVC	**Subject** *I*	**Linking verb** *feel*	**Subject complement** *tired.*	
SVOC	**Subject** *You*	**Transitive verb** *have made*	**Direct object** *me*	**Object complement** *very happy.*

2. Transitive Verbs: Verbs in this category take a NP complement, traditionally called the *direct object* of the verb:

find   a bike
fix   your car
explain   everything
grow   tomatoes
run   the meeting
      etc.

Note that many verbs accept more than one pattern; for example, the verb *run* is listed above for both the transitive and intransitive patterns, and it also appears in the prepositional pattern below. Sometimes the verb changes in meaning from one pattern to another; for example, the intransitive *run* of *She runs* has a different meaning from the transitive *run* of *She runs the office.*

3. Prepositional Verbs: Verbs in this category take a PP complement, traditionally called the *prepositional complement*:

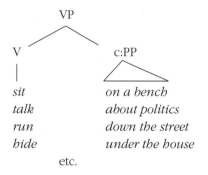

sit   on a bench
talk   about politics
run   down the street
hide   under the house
      etc.

Some prepositional verbs require a particular preposition: for example, the verb *look* wants a PP complement with *at* (*look **at** the camera*) or *for* (*look **for** your sister*); the verb *listen* wants a PP with *to* (*listen **to** the music*), the verb *decide* wants a PP with *on* (*decide **on** an answer*), and so forth. With verbs of this type, the preposition is often rather meaningless. Why do we look *at* something but listen *to* it? And what is the meaning of the preposition *on* in the VP *decide on an answer*? As we learn the prepositional verbs, we simply memorize which preposition goes with each particular verb in each of its meanings.

4. Ditransitive Verbs: Verbs in this category take *two* NP complements. The first c:NP is traditionally called the *indirect object* of the verb; the second is called the *direct object*:

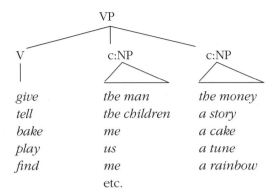

5. Transitive Prepositional Verbs: Verbs in this category also take two complements: first a NP (called the *direct object*) and then a PP (called the *prepositional complement*):

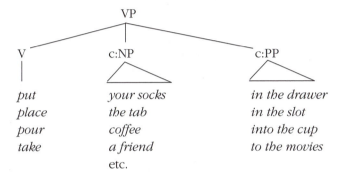

Like the intransitive prepositional verbs we looked at earlier, transitive prepositional verbs sometimes require a particular preposition: *tell your mother **about** your trip, blame somebody **for** the accident, take advantage **of** this opportunity.*

Ditransitive verbs (pattern 4 above) often allow the transitive prepositional pattern, as well, with the preposition *to* or *for: Give me the letter* or *give the letter to me; bake me a cake* or *bake a cake for me.*

6. Linking Verbs. Verbs in this category take what is called a "predicate" complement—meaning a complement that describes the subject of the sentence. Predicate complements are usually AdjPs, as in the examples below, where the subject of the sentence (*the instructor*) is described as *angry, upset, irritated,* and so forth.

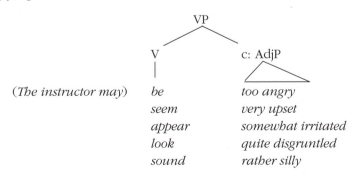

However, some linking verbs take NPs as predicate complements:

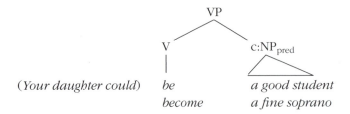

Students are sometimes confused by the fact that the linking pattern with predicate NP has the same categorical composition as the transitive pattern (V + NP). However, the two patterns differ in the meaning of the complement NP: The NP complement of a transitive verb like *meet* introduces a second participant in the situation (*Mary met **Bill***), but the predicate complement of a linking verb like *become* describes a participant that has already been introduced. For example, in the sentence above the NP *a good student* is not a participant in the situation but a (potential) description of your daughter.

7. Complex Transitive Verbs: Verbs in this category take a direct object plus a predicate complement which, in this pattern, describes the direct object of the verb:

With AdjP as predicate complement:

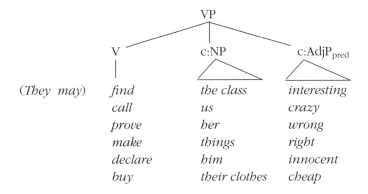

With NP$_{pred}$ as predicate complement:

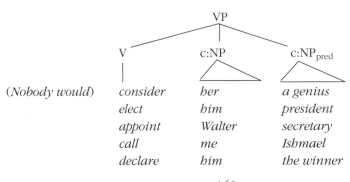

160

EXERCISE 5.

a. Find the VP in each sentence and identify its constituents (the verb plus its complements and modifiers). If you have difficulty identifying the constituents, remember the constituency tests from Chapter 7. *Caution*: Remember that the AUX is a separate constituent, not part of the VP.

   i.   *The baby was crying.*
   ii.   *The doctor abruptly cancelled his appointments.*
   iii.   *Your father may not like the house.*
   iv.   *The clinic gives elderly people free vaccinations.*
   v.   *No one could see the blackboard.*
   vi.   *We will explain the procedure to everybody.*
   vii.   *The students might take advantage of a substitute teacher.*
   viii.   *Bill can look after his own interests.*
   ix.   *This is disgusting!*
   x.   *Nobody would call her stupid.*
   xi.   *This is a difficult exercise.*
   xii.   *Your performance has made us very proud.*
   xiii.   *He looks a little upset.*
   xiv.   *She told everybody about her Irish setter.*
   xv.   *Somebody was talking very loudly.*
   xvi.   *The government was holding the prisoner illegally.*
   xvii.   *Susan doesn't speak to me.*

b. Name the "pattern" of each VP in (a). *Caution:* The pattern depends entirely on the verb plus its complements; modifiers like *slowly* or *suddenly* don't count. (Complements are constituents that are "chosen" by a particular verb; modifiers are optional elements that could go with almost *any* verb. The distinction between complements and modifiers will be discussed further in Section 8.6 below.)

c. Explain the ambiguity of the sentence *You could take her flowers*. (You should be able to draw two distinct tree diagrams for the VP of this sentence, one corresponding to each meaning.)

d. Explain the ambiguity of the sentence *Call me a taxi*. (Smart answer: *Okay, you're a taxi*.) Again, you should be able to draw two distinct tree diagrams for the VP, one corresponding to each meaning.

e. *Advanced.* Write *short, simple* sentences with the verbs in Table 8.2 on the following page, in whatever patterns they will accept, identifying the pattern of each sentence. This is a difficult exercise, so here are some cautions: (i) Don't force it; no verb will go in every pattern. (ii) Stick with simple statements in **active** voice; passive verbs and some types of questions distort the complement structure. (iii) Be careful to include only *complements* (phrases that are required by the verb in one of its meanings), not modifiers like *slowly* or *on Sunday*.

Table 8.2 Complementation Patterns for Verbs

| | Intransitive | Transitive | Prepositional | Ditransitive | Transitive Preposi-tional | Linking $V \begin{cases} \text{AdjP} \\ \text{NP}_{pred} \end{cases}$ | Complex Transitive $V\,NP \begin{cases} \text{AdjP} \\ \text{NP}_{pred} \end{cases}$ |
	V	V NP	V PP	V NP NP	V NP PP		
ask							
buy							
call							
elect							
find							
give							
grow							
make							
run							
smile							
wish							

8.6 Distinguishing Complements from Modifiers

When you did Exercise 5 above, you may have found it difficult to decide whether a particular phrase is a complement or a modifier. These two functions can be distinguished in the following ways:

1. A complement is necessary to complete the meaning of the verb. Modifiers are more loosely connected. For example, in the VP below, the c:NP *dinner* is closely associated with the verb *eat* and could not appear, for example, with the verb *wonder*. However, the m:AP *very late in the evening* could appear with almost any verb, not just with the verb *eat*:

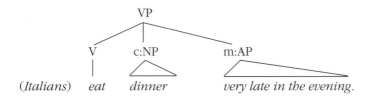

2. The verb's complements normally come first, before its modifiers:

h	c	m
raise	*your hands*	*slowly*
lock	*the door*	*with the key*
decide	*on an answer*	*this week*
look	*at the camera*	*for Daddy*

h	m	c
*raise	*slowly*	*your hands*
*lock	*with the key*	*the door*
*decide	*this week*	*on an answer*
*look	*for Daddy*	*at the camera*

3. The string of words consisting of the verb plus its complement(s) can be replaced by the pro-form *do so*. Modifiers *can* be included under the proform, but do not have to be. To apply the *do so* test, substitute *do so* for the verb plus one or more following constituents. Phrases that follow *do so* must be modifiers:

VP to be tested: *raise your hands slowly.*
Do so [slowly].   *Slowly* is a modifier; it can follow *do so*.
*Do so [my hands] [slowly].   *My hands* is a complement; it can't follow *do so*.

VP to be tested: *write often during the fall.*
Do so [often] [during the fall].   *Often* and *during the fall* are both modifiers.

VP to be tested: *run into the yard.*
*Do so [into the yard].   *Into the yard* is a complement.

EXERCISE 6. Draw tree diagrams of the following VPs, identifying the underlined constituent as a complement or a modifier and explaining how you know:

    a.   (I will) *think of a number.*
    b.   *throw the ball into the yard.*
    c.   *leave on Sunday.*
    d.   *open the door with the key.*
    e.   *stay out of trouble.*
    f.   *decide on an answer.*
    g.   *decide on the boat.*
    h.   *decide on an answer on the boat.*
    i.   *plant spinach in the spring.*
    j.   *handle this package with care.*
    k.   *bake a cake for a friend.*
    l.   *go to the movies with Susan.*

8.7 **Summary of PP, VP, AdjP, and AdvP**

As we have seen, PP, VP, AdjP, and AdvP all have the same basic structure—a head word (P, V, Adj, or Adv) with its complement(s) and modifier(s), if any:

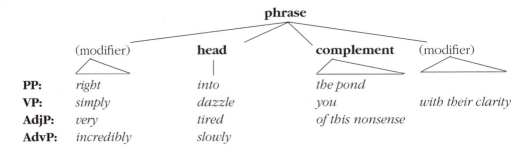

	(modifier)	head	complement	(modifier)
PP:	*right*	*into*	*the pond*	
VP:	*simply*	*dazzle*	*you*	*with their clarity*
AdjP:	*very*	*tired*	*of this nonsense*	
AdvP:	*incredibly*	*slowly*		

The head word is always present, and determines the category of the phrase. The choice of complement, if any, depends on the head word. For example, the preposition *into* and the verb *dazzle* both require NP complements (*into **the pond**, dazzle **you***), and the adjective *tired* wants a PP with *of* (*tired **of this nonsense***). The adverb *slowly* does not take a complement at all. In English, complements always follow the head word. Modifiers are added, optionally, at the beginning or end of the phrase.

8.8 **The Sentence (S)**

If we assume that the AUX is the head of the sentence (because it is the word that identifies the construction *as* a sentence rather than some other sort of phrase), then an affirmative statement has the same structure as the other phrases we have looked at, with one additional element—the *subject*. The AUX is the head of the sentence, the VP is the complement of the AUX, and our "new" constituent—the subject—comes *before* the AUX. Finally, there may be modifiers, which can appear at the boundaries between the other constituents.

A tree diagram is given below, with the statement *In the morning, the trucks would almost deafen us with their noise.* The head of this sentence is the AUX *would*, the complement of the AUX is the VP *deafen us*, and the subject of the AUX (marked "s") is the NP *the trucks*. *In the morning, almost,* and *with their noise* are all modifiers that sit at the boundaries between the major constituents of the sentence:

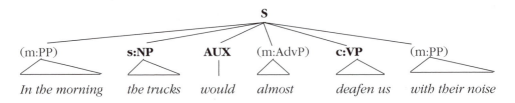

EXERCISE 7. Draw a tree diagram of every sentence in Exercise 5a, following the example above. This time, do the entire sentence—not just the VP. Don't show the internal structure of the subject, VP, or modifiers; use the triangle notation, as in the diagram above. Be careful to identify the subject (s) of each sentence; it is the string of words

that the AUX moves around to make a question (*Would **the trucks** almost deafen us with their noise?*)

8.9 The Noun Phrase (NP)

Noun phrases have the same structure as statements, in that they consist of a head word (in this case, a noun), with its complements and modifiers, and an additional element, called the "specifier," which appears to the left of the head word. The specifier of a NP is sometimes very much like the subject of a sentence:

NP, with specifier in boldface	Sentence, with subject in boldface
the speaker's *presentation of the issues*	**The speaker** *presented the issues.*
her *understanding of the problem*	**She** *understands the problem.*
their *insistence on immediate results*	**They** *insisted on immediate results.*

Because of the parallel between the specifier of a NP and the subject of a sentence, we will mark the specifier with "s", just as we did for the subject:

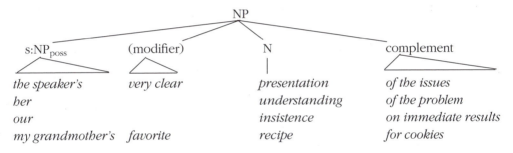

In the examples above, the specifier is a possessive NP; however, the *s* position can also be filled by a determiner (D) like *a, the* and *this*, as in the examples below:

Modifiers (m) of nouns can be AdjPs, NPs, VPs, PPs, or QPs (*quantifier phrases*) in any of several different positions, as shown in the tree diagrams below:

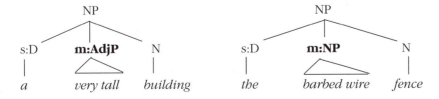

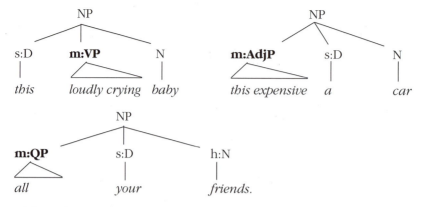

If the modifier is long, it goes after the head noun rather than before it:

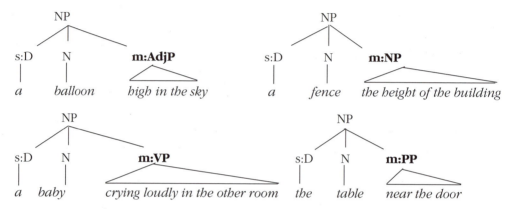

Some nouns—those that are related to complement-taking verbs and adjectives—may also take complements; for example,

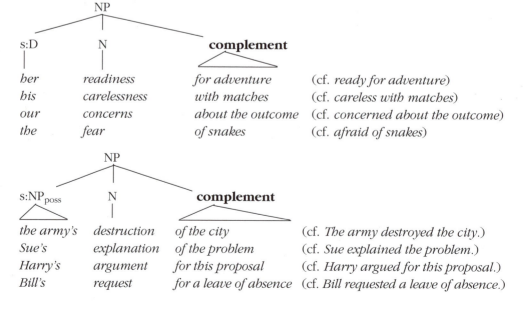

EXERCISE 8.

a. First identify the complement of each adjective or verb in the list below. Then create a corresponding NP, and notice that the noun can have the same complement as its related adjective or verb. The first one in each set is done for you, as an example:

Complement-taking adjective	Corresponding NP
extravagant with money	*extravagance with money*
thoughtful towards others	
honest about her opinions	
loyal to her friends	
polite to her teachers	
interested in biology	

Complement-taking verb	Corresponding NP
The school board *dismissed the teacher.*	The school board's *dismissal of the teacher.*
We *anticipated the results.*	
Some people *prefer chocolate.*	
John *returned to Chicago.*	
John *fled to Chicago.*	
The parents *quarreled with the principal.*	

b. Draw tree diagrams of the following NPs, showing the category and function of each constituent: *my earliest memories, the daring rescue of the fishermen, the trees in the park, your father's Oldsmobile, people.*

8.10 Phrases Are Nested Inside Phrases

In the end, phrases have a nested structure, with phrases inside phrases inside phrases, as shown below:

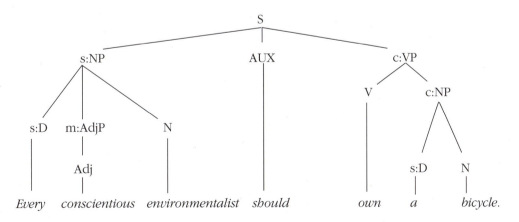

In this diagram, subjects/specifiers are identified as *s*, complements as *c*, and modifiers as *m*. The head of each phrase is left unmarked.

EXERCISE 9.

a. In the diagram above, identify the category and function of each constituent. For example, *every conscientious environmentalist* is an NP that functions as the subject of the sentence, and *should* is an AUX that functions as the head of the sentence.

  i.   *own a bicycle*
  ii.   *a bicycle*
  iii. *every*
  iv.   *conscientious*
  v.   *bicycle*

b. Draw complete tree diagrams for the following sentences, following the example on the previous page:

  i.   *The baby was crying.*
  ii.   *The doctor abruptly cancelled his appointments.*
  iii. *Your father may not like the house.*
  iv.   *The clinic gives elderly people free vaccinations.*
  v.   *No one could see the blackboard.*
  vi.   *We will explain the procedure to everybody.*
  vii. *Bill can look after his own interests.*
  viii. *This is disgusting!*
  ix.   *Nobody would call her stupid.*
  x.   *This is a difficult exercise.*
  xi.   *He looks rather upset.*
  xii. *She tells everybody about her Irish setter.*
  xiii. *Somebody was talking very loudly.*
  xiv. *The government was holding the prisoner illegally.*

  Caution: In this exercise you are asked to draw complete tree diagrams so that you can be sure you understand how to do it. In the end, however, there are very few circumstances in which you will need to draw a complete tree diagram of a sentence. Normally, we show the part of the structure in which we are interested and then abbreviate the rest, using the triangle notation. There is no virtue in showing more structure than is necessary.

8.11 Category ≠ Function

An important point to take from this chapter is the distinction between **category** and **function**. The **category** of a phrase is determined by its head word; for example, the phrase *this old house* belongs to the category NP because it has a noun (*house*) as its head word. Like other NPs, it may serve any of several different **functions**:

Subject of sentence:[4]	*This old house* must be theirs.
Complement of V:	They bought *this old house* in 1985.
Complement of P:	They moved into *this old house* in 1985.

4. Strictly speaking, this is the subject of AUX (since the AUX is the head of the sentence); however, we will stay with the more standard terminology *subject of the sentence*.

The converse is also true: a given function can be performed by any of several different categories. For example, while the subject of a sentence is usually a NP, other types of phrases can also act as subject:

NP as subject: *This old house* must be his.
PP as subject: *In front of the library* would be a good place for the statue.
VP as subject: *Sail across the Atlantic* is what he'd like to do.

To give another example, nouns are typically modified by adjectives. However, other categories, also, can act as modifiers of nouns:

AP as modifier of N: a *very high* fence
PP as modifier of N: the fence *around the pasture*
NP as modifier of N: a *barbed wire* fence
Sentence (clause) as modifier of N: the fence *we built*

EXERCISE 10. Identify the category and function of each constituent; for example, you would say that *the hills across the valley of the Ebro* in example (a) is a NP which functions as the subject of the sentence.

a. *The hills across the valley of the Ebro were very white.*
   i. *across the valley of the Ebro*
   ii. *very white*
b. *Accompanied by a plague of robins, Sula returned to Medallion.*
   i. *a plague of robins*
   ii. *accompanied by a plague of robins*
   iii. *came back*
   iv. *to Medallion*
c. *The sky was black for hours.*
   i. *the sky*
   ii. *black*
   iii. *for hours*
d. *The morning's post had given the final tap to the family fortune.*
   i. *the morning's post*
   ii. *the morning's*
   iii. *the final tap*
   iv. *final*
   v. *to the family fortune*
   vi. *family*

8.12 Determining the Structure of a Sentence

As we begin dealing with more complicated sentences, you may sometimes be unsure where a particular constituent fits into the syntactic structure. For example, consider the two sentences below:

a.   *They bought a house with three bedrooms.*
b.   *They bought a house with their savings.*

The PP in the first sentence—*with three bedrooms*—is a modifier of the noun *house*, and it therefore hangs from the NP in the tree structure:

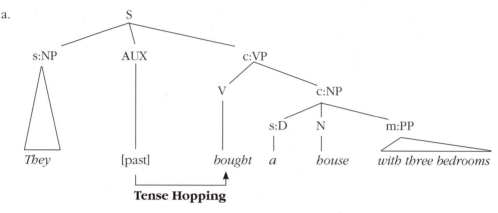

However, the PP in the second sentence—*with their savings*—is a modifier of the verb *bought*, and it therefore hangs from the VP:

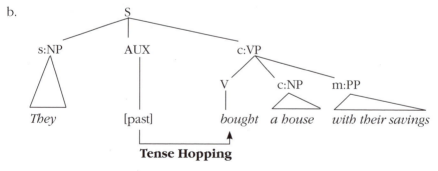

To determine where a PP should be placed in the tree, you can rely partly on the meaning of the sentence, as we did above. In addition, you can also make use of the constituency tests that were described in chapter 7: the cleft test, the pro-form test, and the short-answer test. The string *a house with three bedrooms* in sentence (a) above is a constituent—a NP—and it therefore passes the constituency tests:

The cleft test:	*It was* $\boxed{\textit{a house with three bedrooms}}$	*that they bought.*
WH-cleft:	*What they bought* *was* $\boxed{\textit{a house with three bedrooms.}}$	
The pro-form test:	*They bought* **one.** (where **one** = *a house with three bedrooms*)	
The short-answer test:	Q: *What did they buy?* A: ***A house with three bedrooms.***	

The constituency tests show that *a house with three bedrooms* is a phrase, thereby confirming our hypothesis that the PP *with three bedrooms* is part of the NP.

In contrast, the string *a house with their savings* in sentence (b) above is *not* a constituent, and so it does not pass the tests:[5]

The cleft test:	*It was	a house with their savings	that they bought.
WH-cleft:	*What they bought	was	a house with their savings.

The pro-form test: *They bought **one.** (where **one** = *a house with their savings*)
The short-answer test: Q: *What did they buy?*   A: ***A house with their savings.***

The constituency tests show that *a house with their savings* is not a constituent, thereby confirming our hypothesis that the PP *with their savings* is not part of the NP.

EXERCISE 11.

a. Draw tree diagrams showing the position of the PP in each of the following sentences. Then support your answer, using the cleft test, the pro-form test, and the short-answer test:

   (i)   *I put your socks in the drawer.*
   (ii) *I like the sparkle in his eye.*

b. *Advanced.* The following VP has a sensible meaning and a silly meaning. Draw two different tree diagrams to show the ambiguity. Which tree corresponds to which meaning?

   Try on that dress in the window.

8.13   Phrasal Verbs: An Exercise in Constituent Structure

English, like other Germanic languages, has a large class of *phrasal* or *two-word* verbs which consist of a verb plus a *particle* (an intransitive preposition). Examples are *break up, put on, take off, take over,* and so forth. Verbs of this type are often ignored in traditional grammars, perhaps because they tend to be conversational in register; however, they are very important in the grammar of English.

EXERCISE 12.

a. List five additional phrasal verbs.

b. Most phrasal verbs are polysemous (that is, they have more than one meaning). Find as many meanings as you can for the phrasal verbs *break up, put on, take off,* and *take over.*

---

5. The asterisk, you will recall, indicates that the sentence is ungrammatical.

Phrasal verbs take the same complementation patterns as simple verbs:

Intransitive:	*The plane <u>took off</u>.*
	I think I'm going to <u>throw up</u>.
Transitive:	*Please <u>take off your shoes</u>.* or *Please <u>take your shoes off</u>.*
	He <u>brought in the pie</u>. or *He <u>brought the pie in</u>.*
Prepositional:	*I won't <u>put up with this nonsense</u>.*
	<u>Look out for the cars</u>!
Ditransitive:	*<u>Pick me up some milk</u>, please.*
	Would you <u>throw me down a towel</u>?
Transitive prepositional:	*We <u>handed over our notes to the authorities</u>.*
	Please <u>turn in your paper to the instructor</u>.
or	*We <u>handed our notes over to the authorities</u>.*
	Please <u>turn your paper in to the instructor</u>.
Linking:	*Everybody <u>called in sick</u>.*
	Your brother <u>came in drunk</u>.
Complex transitive:	*You shouldn't <u>put your shoes on wet</u>.*
	I wouldn't <u>turn a child away hungry</u>.

There is a surface similarity between a simple verb in the prepositional pattern and a phrasal verb in the transitive pattern, as shown below:

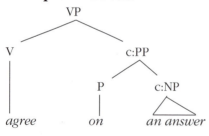

a. Prepositional verb

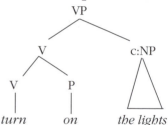

b. Transitive phrasal verb

To distinguish these constructions, you can make use of the following properties: First, if the preposition is part of a phrasal verb, then it can move to the right of its direct object by a transformation called *Particle Movement*.

The Particle-Movement Test:

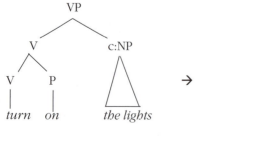

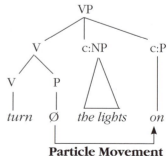

Particle Movement

In contrast, a preposition that is part of a PP cannot be moved; its position is fixed:

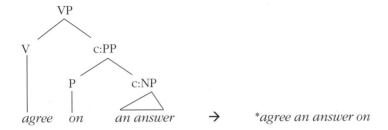

$\rightarrow$ \quad *agree an answer on*

Secondly, these constructions can also be distinguished by the constituency tests of chapter 7; for example, they can be distinguished by the Short-Answer Test:

The Short-Answer Test: *What did they agree on?* <u>*An answer*</u> or <u>*On an answer*</u>

In this construction, the NP *an answer* and the PP *on an answer* are both constituents [see diagram (a) above]; therefore, either phrase can serve as a short answer.

Compare the transitive phrasal pattern:

The Short-Answer Test: *What did they turn on?* <u>*The light*</u> but not *<u>*On the light*</u>

In this construction the P NP sequence (*on the light*) is not a constituent [see diagram (b) above]; consequently, it cannot serve as a short answer.

EXERCISE 13.

a. [*Based on an exercise from Farmer and Demers (2001).*] Use the particle-movement test and the short-answer test to determine whether the VP in each of the following sentences follows the prepositional pattern [diagram (a) above] or the transitive phrasal pattern [diagram (b) above]. Draw a tree diagram for each VP.

   i. *The witch turned into a bat.*
   ii. *The car turned into the road.*
   iii. *I put on my jacket.*
   iv. *Little Miss Muffet sat on a tuffet.*
   v. *We threw out the trash.*
   vi. *We climbed out the window.*
   vii. *The applicants must fill in all the blanks.*

b. Find VP patterns in the following poem by Robert Frost. (Your choices are intransitive, transitive, prepositional, ditransitive, transitive prepositional, linking, and complex transitive.) *Hint:* These are imperative sentences which consist of nothing but a VP; you can think of them simply as VPs, or, if you prefer, you can assume an understood subject and AUX: *you will.* There are four lines (4, 6, 7, and 8) that you may not know how to handle, but you should be able to do the rest. There is one instance of a phrasal (*two-word*) verb.

To the Thawing Wind

Come with rain, O loud Southwester!	1
Bring the singer, bring the nester;	2
Give the buried flower a dream;	3
Make the settled snowbank steam;	4
Find the brown beneath the white;	5
But whate'er you do tonight,	6
Bathe my window, make it flow,	7
Melt it as the ice will go;	8
Melt the glass and leave the sticks	9
Like a hermit's crucifix;	10
Burst into my narrow stall;	11
Swing the picture on the wall;	12
Run the rattling pages o'er;	13
Scatter poems on the floor;	14
Turn the poet out of door.	15

—Robert Frost

8.14 Building Phrases in Other Languages

As we have seen, phrases are constructed according to a consistent pattern:

PP, VP, AP:[6]   **head + complement   (plus modifiers)**

NP, S: $\begin{Bmatrix} \textbf{subject} \\ \textbf{specifier} \end{Bmatrix}$ **+ head + complement   (plus modifiers)**

The presence and nature of the complement(s) depends on the head word. (For example, the verb *enjoy* takes a NP complement, but the verb *elapse* does not.) Modifiers are optional and may be placed at various points within the phrase.

All languages construct their phrases with the same ingredients, but the *order* of elements may differ somewhat from language to language. English is an *s h c* language, because our phrases follow the order *specifier head complement*. The great majority of human languages employ one of the following three word orders:[7]

s c h   This is the most common order, found in Japanese, Turkish, and Korean.
s h c   This is the second most common order, found in English, Swahili, and Chinese.
h s c   This is a less common order, found in Welsh and Arabic.

In many languages, word order is consistent for all phrases. For example, in English the complement always follows the head word, but in Japanese, where the complement *precedes* the head,

---

6. AdjP and AdvP are collapsed here into a single "super" category, AP.
7. Klingon, a language spoken by nonhuman inhabitants of a far-distant planet, has the order *c h s*, but this order is almost never found in *human* languages.

all phrases are turned around backwards from our point of view: Instead of *shut that door,* Japanese speakers say *that door shut,* instead of *on that table, that table on,* instead of *You should go, You go should.* (Of course, they use Japanese words, rather than English!) In languages such as Latin, where word order is fairly free, it is harder to be sure about the basic order.

EXERCISE 14.

a. We can write "phrase-structure rules" for S, VP, and PP in English, as follows:

$$S = \text{s:NP AUX c:VP}; \quad VP = \text{c:} \begin{Bmatrix} NP \\ PP \end{Bmatrix}; \quad PP = \text{P c:NP}$$

How would these rules be stated for Japanese?

b. What word order would we find in the Japanese sentence for *I am speaking to the teacher?* Draw tree diagrams for the English and Japanese versions of this sentence.

c. The Japanese version of this sentence is *Watashi-wa sensei ni hanashite imasu.* What is the meaning of each Japanese word? (Hint: Japanese has no word corresponding to English *the.*)

8.15 Applications for Teachers

8.15.1 The Development of Phrases

Learning to combine words to form phrases is a basic step in the acquisition of language. In tracing the development of children's language, scholars identify a one-word stage, in which the child speaks just one word at a time, and a two-word stage in which two words are combined to form a phrase (Eve [Appendix Section VIII] has reached this stage by 18 months). However, there is no such thing as a three- or four-word stage; once the child understands the nested structure of language—that phrases can be used as constituents of larger phrases—there is no limit to the length of the utterances she can produce (though limitations on memory and pronunciation keep her sentences fairly short at first). By three years of age, Julia (Appendix Section VIII) is constructing utterances that match those of the adults around her in the complexity of their structure, though she is still working out details such as the inflection of irregular verbs (*growed* rather than *grew*).

By the age of five or six, children have essentially mastered the spoken language, though they still have a limited vocabulary, and are beginning to read and write. For English speakers, this involves learning to recognize the letters of the alphabet and to identify individual words in print. But recognizing individual words is not enough; in order to make sense of what they have read, readers must group the words into meaningful phrases. In spoken language, the phrasing is partly indicated by the inflection of the voice, but written language is less helpful. Studies have shown that children who read poorly may be helped by having the words grouped *for them* into meaningful phrases:[8]

> *The dog   bit the man   on the leg.*

---

8. See Perera (1984), p. 304.

Although reading materials for young children do not usually go to this extreme, they commonly avoid line breaks that disrupt the phrasing, especially if they occur at the beginning of the sentence where the structure is still highly unpredictable:

> *The*
> *dog bit the man on the leg.*

An arrangement like the following is easier to read, because the NP *the dog* is kept together on one line.

> *The dog*
> *bit the man on the leg.*

The breaking of a phrase is less disruptive if it occurs towards the end of the sentence, when the structure of the sentence has already been worked out:

> *The dog bit the man on the*
> *leg.*

Throughout our lives we find it helpful to have some assistance with phrasing when the language is difficult; that is why it is so much easier to understand a Shakespeare play or a passage in a foreign language if we can listen to the words read aloud as we read along from the printed page.

8.15.2   Elaboration of Phrases in Writing

The writing samples in Appendix Sections II and III provide a brief illustration of the stages children go through in learning to construct written discourse. In the early stages (kindergarten through second grade), they struggle just to form the letters correctly, arrange the letters on the lines, and make spaces between the words.[9] One hurdle, as we have discussed, is learning to recognize and punctuate sentences, a concept which the younger children of Appendix Section II have not yet mastered (*When my mom washsi mafin; Once upon a time there was boy he was mene*).

Because it is difficult simply to get the letters onto the paper, young children initially write very simple sentences with only the essential constituents.[10] Each clause has a subject, a verb, and a complement for the verb, but there are almost no adverbial modifiers (*I hvie a cat, Jessie is my first puppy*). Noun phrases tend to be short, with only a head noun and its specifier (*my mom, one day, hes friends*). Although there are a few hints of an emerging written register (*Once upon a time, …*), the child's sentences mostly follow the patterns of spoken English, with adjectives in predicate position (*he was **mene**; he wanted to be **fames**; he was **nice** agen*) rather than inside a

---

9. Children who are unable to control their spacing sometimes resort to hyphens or periods or some other device to mark the boundaries between words.

10. They sometimes string these sentences together with conjunctions, as they would do in speech (*They put me in a space jail, **but** I had a good idea **and** all I had to do is get that space gun*), but the individual clauses are still very simple.

noun phrase (*a famous man*). Only in the fourth- and fifth-grade samples do we begin to see significant numbers of adverbial modifiers (*... a boy went to the counter and **obnoxiously** said ...*), as well as adjectives and other modifiers inside noun phrases (a **pink** suit **with a pink chiffon skirt**). We will have more to say about the development of the written register in Chapter 14.

8.16   Applications for Students and Teachers of Literature

8.16.1   The Use of Phrasing in Poetry

Some poems, such as the following sonnet by William Shakespeare, have *end-stopped lines*, meaning that the ends of the lines coincide with the boundaries of major phrases, often marked by a comma, semicolon, or period:

My Mistress' Eyes Are Nothing like the Sun

My Mistress' eyes are nothing like the Sun,	1
Coral is far more red, than her lips red,	2
If snow be white, why then her breasts are dun:	3
If hairs be wires, black wires grow on her head:	4
I have seen Roses damasked, red and white,	5
But no such Roses see I in her cheeks,	6
And in some perfumes is there more delight,	7
Than in the breath that from my Mistress reeks.	8
I love to hear her speak; yet well I know,	9
That Music hath a far more pleasing sound:	10
I grant I never saw a goddess go,	11
My Mistress when she walks treads on the ground.	12
And yet by heaven I think my love as rare,	13
As any she belied with false compare. (she = woman)	14

—William Shakespeare

In modern poetry, however, there is often a mismatch between the ends of phrases and the ends of lines, so that the lines break in the middle of a phrase. The running over of a phrase from one line to another is called *enjambment*. You saw an instance of enjambment in lines 9 and 10 of the Robert Frost poem "To a Thawing Wind" (in Exercise 13b), where line 10 completes the VP that begins in the middle of line 9:

Melt the glass and leave the sticks	9
Like a hermit's crucifix;	10

This mismatch between line-end and phrase-end creates a momentary confusion in the mind of the reader: Is the VP *leave the sticks* or is it *leave the sticks like a hermit's crucifix?*—a small puzzle that adds to the interest of the poem.

EXERCISE 15. Consider the following poem by Gerard Manley Hopkins. How many sentences are there in this poem? (For the purposes of this question, count the semicolon [;] and the colon [:] as marking the ends of sentences.) Where does each sentence begin and end? Locate the line ends that do not coincide with major phrase boundaries. What is the effect of breaking the lines at these points?

Spring and Fall
To a young child

Márgarét, are you grieving		1
Over Goldengrove unleaving?	*(unleaving = losing its leaves)*	2
Leáves, like the things of man, you		3
With your fresh thoughts care for, can you?		4
Áh! Ás the heart grows older		5
It will come to such sights colder		6
By and by, nor spare a sigh		7
Though worlds of wanwood leafmeal lie;	*(leafmeal = with leaves on*	8
And yet you will weep and know why.	*the ground)*	9
Now no matter, child, the name:		10
Sórrow's springs áre the same.		11
Nor mouth had, no nor mind, expressed	*(Nor = neither)*	12
What heart heard of, ghost guessed:	*(ghost = spirit)*	13
It is the blight man was born for,		14
It is Margaret you mourn for.		15

—Gerard Manley Hopkins

8.16.2 Word Order in Poetry

Students are often confused by sentences in poetry that do not follow the standard *s h c* order. For example, in Christopher Marlowe's poem *The Passionate Shepherd to His Love*, there are five lines that have a non-standard word order:

The Passionate Shepherd to His Love

1	*Come live with me and be my love,*	
2	*And we will all the pleasures prove*	*(prove = try)*
3	*That valleys, groves, hills, and fields,*	
4	*Woods, or steepy mountain yields.*	
5	*And we will sit upon the rocks,*	
6	*Seeing the shepherds feed their flocks*	
7	*By shallow rivers, to whose falls*	
8	*Melodious birds sing madrigals.*	

9	*And I will make thee beds of roses*
10	*And a thousand fragrant posies,*
11	*A cap of flowers and a kirtle*
12	*Embroidered all with leaves of myrtle;*

(kirtle = gown)

13	*A gown made of the finest wool*
14	*Which from our pretty lambs we pull;*
15	*Fair-lined slippers for the cold,*
16	*With buckles of the purest gold;*

17	*A belt of straw and ivy buds,*
18	*With coral clasps and amber studs,*
19	*And if these pleasures may thee move,*
20	*Come live with me and be my love.*

21	*The shepherds' swains shall dance and sing*
22	*For thy delight each May morning:*
23	*If these delights thy mind may move,*
24	*Then live with me and be my love.*

— Christopher Marlowe

The lines with non-standard order are (2) *And we will all the pleasure prove*; (14) *Embroidered all with leaves of myrtle*, (14) *Which from our pretty lambs we pull*, (19) *If these pleasures may thee move*, and (23) *If these delights thy mind may move*. Changed to normal order, these lines would read (2) *And we will prove all the pleasures*, (12) *All embroidered with leaves of myrtle*, (14) *which we pull from our pretty lambs*, (19) *if these pleasures may move thee*, and (23) *If these delights may move thy mind*.

When I ask my students why poets use nonstandard word order, they tell me that it is to make the words rhyme; if Marlowe had put the word *pleasures* at the end of line (2), it wouldn't rhyme with *love*! That may have something to do with it, but this feature of poetic language also follows a historical tradition that harks back to Old English times, when English word order often placed the verb at the end of the clause rather than in the middle, where it is today.

8.17 Applications for ESL Teachers

In addition to the applications above, which are relevant to ESL students as well as native speakers, there are two important ESL issues that pertain to the material in this chapter.

8.17.1 Choosing the Complement

ESL students often make errors in choosing the complement(s) for a verb. Meaning is of some help here—for example, after the verb *close*, we expect to be told the object that is to undergo the closing (*close **your eyes***). Unfortunately, however, verbs with very similar meanings sometimes have different requirements for their complements; for example, the verb *see* requires a NP as its complement (*see **the moon***) while the verb *look*, with almost the same meaning, requires a PP (*look **at the moon***).

EXERCISE 16. Consider the sentences below (based on an exercise from O'Grady, Archibald, Aronoff, and Rees-Miller (2001)). First, decide which sentences are ungrammatical and explain why (that is, say what complement(s) the student has chosen and what complement(s) are actually required. Then explain why an ESL student might be confused:

i. *We will drink to your victory.*
ii. *We will toast to your victory.*
iii. *He gave the church $500.*
iv. *He donated the church $500.*
v. *They told us the answer.*
vi. *They said us the answer.*
vii. *She should suggest this plan to the clients.*
viii. *She should ask this question to the clients.*
ix. *They finally got to their destination.*
x. *They finally reached to their destination.*

Dictionaries that are written for native speakers of English give very little information about the complementation patterns for verbs, because this is an issue that, for some reason, is almost never a problem for native speakers. However, dictionaries for ESL students, such as the *Longman Dictionary of American English* and the *Oxford Learner's Dictionary*, provide detailed information about the patterns each verb requires/permits and the meanings that are associated with each pattern. Teachers of ESL students should ensure that their students have access to such dictionaries and that they learn how to use them.

8.17.2   Prepositional and Phrasal Verbs

Prepositional and phrasal verbs are a never-ending source of confusion to ESL students. These two classes of verbs are often lumped together in ESL texts, under the heading "two-word verbs." Phrasal verbs are called "separable two-word verbs" because the particle can be moved to the right, by Particle Movement, as in *Look the word **up**.*[11] Prepositional verbs such as *look at* are called "inseparable two-word verbs," because the preposition cannot be moved (*Look **at** the moon*, not **Look the moon **at**.*")[12]

What makes these verbs so difficult is their meaning; because the preposition or particle is often arbitrary, it is impossible to guess the meaning of the construction from the meanings of its parts. Students have to learn the prepositional verbs *look at, look for, look into,* and *look to* as

---

11. Even native-speaking children have some difficulty with this construction, as does the second-grade author of "My Nightmare" (Appendix Section II), who says "It could suck up me," not realizing that Particle Movement is obligatory when the direct object is a pronoun (*me*) rather than a full NP such as *a boy*. Children learning English as a first language will eventually work this out on their own, but older ESL students and even children learning English outside an English-speaking environment will need some explicit teaching.
12. These labels are misleading, because if we choose an adverb rather than a NP complement for our test, then it is the prepositional verb which can be "separated" and the phrasal verb which cannot: *Look **carefully** at the moon* vs. **Look **carefully** up the word.*

distinct lexical items, and then they can go on to the phrasal verbs *look up, look out,* and *look over*!

8.18   Summary of the Chapter

In this chapter, we have shown that all phrases consist of a head word plus whatever complements the head word requires. Sentences and noun phrases contain an additional element, the subject or specifier, which, in English, comes before the head word, giving us the basic word order *s h c*. Other languages build phrases with the same ingredients as English, but may employ a different word order (most likely *s c h* or *h s c*). A phrase may also contain modifiers of the head word; modifiers are always optional and may occur in several different positions within the phrase. Every element of a phrase has a *category* (N, NP, V, VP, etc.) and a *function* (subject/specifier, head, complement, or modifier). Complex structures are created by nesting phrases inside phrases, using a phrase as one of the elements of a higher phrase.

We also revisited the constituency texts (the proform test, the movement test, the short answer test, and the cleft tests) and saw how these tests can help to resolve questions that sometimes arise about the structure of a sentence or phrase. In addition, we provided some tests to distinguish the complement of a verb from a modifier and to distinguish transitive phrasal verbs from prepositional verbs.

In the "applications" sections, we looked at the development and elaboration of phrases in children's speech and writing, at the use of phrasing and word order in poetic language, and at two special difficulties for ESL students—choosing appropriate complements for verbs and understanding the meanings of prepositional and phrasal verbs.

CHAPTER 9

Semantics: How Sentences Receive Meaning

9.1 Introduction

When we create phrases and sentences, our purpose, of course, is to express meanings that will be understood by those to whom we speak and write. In this chapter, we will consider how the meaning of a sentence is constructed. First, we will consider how the verb organizes its "arguments" (its subject and its complements) into the representation of an event or state of affairs. We will then briefly discuss the semantics of sentences with predicate complements, which work a little differently from other sentences. The final sections of the chapter are concerned with the semantics of adverbials and of noun phrases.

9.2 The Meaning of a Sentence

Every sentence contains a *predicate*—a word that indicates what event or state of affairs the sentence is depicting. Except in sentences with linking verbs (see Section 9.3 below), it is the main verb of the sentence which acts as predicate. Each predicate requires a certain number of "arguments," which name the participants in the event. For example, the verb *play*, which designates an event with one participant, is called a "one-place predicate," *choose* is then a two-place predicate, and *give* is a three-place predicate.

In addition to indicating an event or situation with a certain number of participants, the predicate also assigns each participant a role; when we know the meaning of a verb, we know what event or situation the verb depicts, how many participants are involved, and what roles the participants are performing. We also know where, in the sentence, to find each role player. For example, the verbs *hate* and *upset* each name situations with two participants—an <experiencer> of the emotion and a <stimulus> that gives rise to the emotion, but the two verbs assign these roles in opposite directions: In a sentence with the verb *hate* (The baby **hates** loud noises), the subject of the sentence (*the baby*) is the <experiencer> of the hating, while the complement (*loud noises*) is the <stimulus> to which the baby is responding. But in a sentence with the verb *upset* (Loud noises **upset** the baby), the subject of the sentence (*loud noises*) is the <stimulus>, and

Table 9.1 Predicates and Arguments

Predicate	No. of arguments	Example Sentence
play	1	_The children_ were playing.
choose	2	_Sarah_ chose _a green vegetable_.
give	3	_Sarah_ gave _Bill_ _a hug._
		Sarah gave _her name_ _to the receptionist._

the complement of the verb (*the baby*) is the <experiencer>. When we know the meaning of a verb, we know what roles its arguments will play, and where, in the sentence, each role player will be found.

It is not possible to give a complete list of the roles that predicates can assign, but the rough list in Table 9.2 on the following page will be sufficient for our purposes.

The semantic structure of a sentence can be set out as shown below, with the roles the verb assigns listed in order beneath it, and arrows to the subject and complement(s) that are assigned those roles:

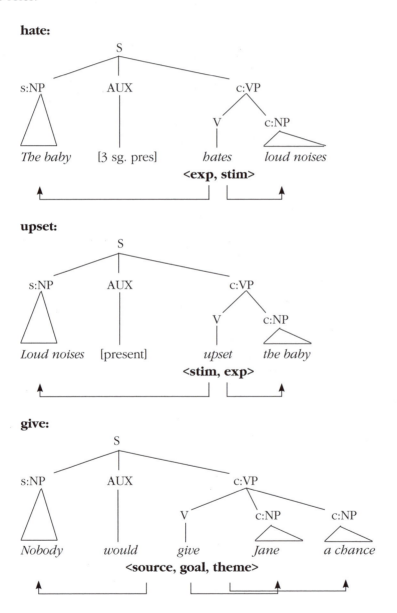

Table 9.2   Some Roles that May Be Assigned to Participants[1]

\<agent\>	The autonomous doer of an action.	*We tried to win.* *Sally looked at Jane.*
\<instrument\>	The entity used by an agent to carry out an action.	*I broke the window with a hammer.* *I used a pencil to mark the place.*
\<patient\>	The person or object that is moved to another location or that undergoes a change of state as a result of the event.	*Lightning hit the tree.* *Sue gave him a dollar.* *Bill died.*[2]
\<theme\>	A totally inert participant.	*Sally is tall.*
\<result\>	The result of an action.	*We built a house.* *Her comment caused a lot of resentment.*
\<source\>	The location from which something comes.	*We got a dollar from Sue.* *The paint fumes gave me a headache.*
\<goal\>	The person or place toward which something goes or is directed.	*I threw the ball into the yard.* *Sue gave Bill a dollar.*
\<experiencer\>	The experiencer of an emotion, thought, or perception.	*I hear you.* *The decision infuriated me.* *I understand what you're saying.*
\<stimulus\>	The thing experienced or perceived.	*She saw stars.* *Jane likes ice cream.* *We know the answer.*
\<location\>	The place where something is.	*They sat at home.*
\<possessor\>	The person who has or owns something.	*Bill has a car.* *The car belongs to Bill.*

1. Semantic roles can be assigned in other ways, as well, not just by the verb. For example, in the phrase *Bill's car*, the role of \<possessor\> is assigned by the possessive suffix *-'s*. In this text, we will concern ourselves only with semantic roles that are assigned by a verb or predicate complement.
2. Note that we are looking for the semantic roles that are assigned *by the verb*. As Bill dies he may experience great suffering, but the verb *die* does not tell us that. It will still be true that Bill died even if he was in a deep coma and experienced nothing at all.

EXERCISE 1.

a. List the predicate and the arguments in each of the example sentences of Table 9.2 and say what role is assigned to each argument. For example, for the sentence *Sally looked at Jane*, you would say that the predicate is the verb *look*. This predicate calls for two participants—an <agent> (the doer of the looking) and a <goal> (the person or place towards whom the look is directed). In the sentence in question, Sally is the <agent> and Jane is the <goal>.

b. Notice that, contrary to what you may have learned in school, the subject of the sentence is not always an <agent> (the autonomous doer of an action). Many verbs assign the role of <agent> to their subject, but there are also verbs like *see, receive, die,* and *undergo* whose subjects receive other roles. What role is assigned to the subject of each of these verbs?

c. The sensory-perception verbs *look* and *see*; *listen* and *hear*; *touch* and *feel* go in pairs: In each pair, there is one verb that assigns the role of <agent> to its subject and one that assigns its subject the role of <experiencer>. Say what role each of these verbs assigns to its subject.

d. As we observed above, verbs of emotion and perception assign the roles of <experiencer> and <stimulus> in different directions: For verbs like *see,* the subject is the <experiencer> and the complement is the <stimulus> (*I see you*). For other verbs, such as *frighten,* the subject is the <stimulus> and the complement is the <experiencer> (*The thunder frightened the cat*). Specify the role assignment for the following verbs: *hear, like, astonish, surprise, perceive, annoy, irritate, please, bore.*[3]

9.3　When the Predicate Is Not a Verb

In most sentences, as we have said, it is the verb that acts as predicate—by identifying an event or situation and assigning roles to its subject and complement(s). However, linking verbs, exceptionally, do not act as predicates; instead, it is the predicate complement that identifies the situation and assigns a role to the subject (hence the name *predicate* complement). In the examples below, the subject NP *the instructor* receives the role of <experiencer> from the predicate AdjP *more excited* in (a) and the role of <patient> or <theme> from the predicate AdjP *taller* in (b):

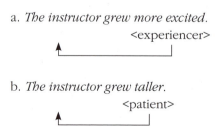

a. *The instructor grew more excited.*
　　　　　　　　　　<experiencer>

b. *The instructor grew taller.*
　　　　　　　　　<patient>

---

3. Young children sometimes mix up the role assignment for these verbs and make statements like *I'm so boring!* when they mean *I'm so bored!*

EXERCISE 2. Find the predicate complement in each sentence below, and say what semantic role it assigns to the subject:

a. *Some of us had grown sleepy.*
b. *The children seemed bored.*
c. *The children seemed boring.*
d. *Ferdinand Magellan was an explorer.*
e. *Ferdinand Magellan was a Spaniard.*

Sentences in the complex transitive pattern have a "complex" semantic structure, in that the predicate complement assigns a role to the direct object of the verb, and the verb then establishes a relationship between the subject of the sentence and the proposition that is created by the application of the predicate complement to the direct object. For example, in the sentence *The farmer painted the barn red*, the predicate AP *red* takes *the barn* as its argument and assigns it the role of <theme>, while the verb *painted* acts as a two-place predicate linking *the farmer* (the <agent> of the painting) to the proposition that the barn is red (the <result> of the painting). Readers who wish to pursue the semantics of sentences of this type should consider taking a course in semantics!

9.4 Adverbials

Modifiers of V and AUX are called *adverbials*. (Don't confuse this term with the term *adverb*. The term *adverb* names a syntactic category, while *adverbial* names a syntactic function [modifier of V or AUX].) AdvPs, NPs, PPs, and subordinate clauses can all function as adverbials. For example, in the sentence below, the AdvP *wildly* and the PP *with her handkerchief* are both adverbials:

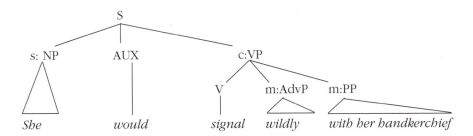

Adverbials (modifiers of the verb or AUX) differ from the "arguments" of the verb in how they receive their semantic roles. An argument NP like *John* has no semantic role of its own; it takes whatever role it is assigned by the predicate. For example, in the sentence *John ate most of the pie*, *John* is assigned the role of <agent> by the predicate *eat*, while in the sentence *John likes pie*, he is given the role of <experiencer> by the predicate *like*.

Adverbials, in contrast, have their own inherent semantic roles; they don't need a predicate to assign them roles. If I asked you the semantic role of the AP *carefully* or the PP *on Thursday*, you would tell me that *carefully* is an adverbial of manner, and *on Thursday* is an adverbial of time; you don't need to know the sentence in which they appear. Adverbials are traditionally grouped into the semantic categories that are listed in Table 9.3 on the following page.

Table 9.3 Semantic Categories of Adverbials

manner	*awkwardly, frugally, well, lengthwise, like an expert, with great courtesy, the same way I did, as if they meant it*
degree	*very much, completely, absolutely, enormously, scarcely, kind of, almost, more or less, barely, practically*
purpose	*for dinner, to get some bread, for your mother*
instrument	*with a key, by car, by pressing this button, microscopically*
accompaniment	*with a friend*
place	*in Massachusetts, somewhere*
time	*last night, on Sunday, the next day, later, now, tomorrow, during the week, three years ago, eventually, once upon a time*
duration	*for three weeks, since September*
frequency	*once a week, every Sunday, usually, often, occasionally, frequently*
attitude of subject	*deliberately, intentionally, accidentally, reluctantly, eagerly, fervently, carefully, enthusiastically*
opinion of speaker	*surprisingly, tragically, luckily, fortunately, regrettably, hopefully, apparently, truly, in fact, certainly, probably, possibly, obviously, frankly, to be honest, personally, apparently, in my opinion, wisely, understandably*
connective	*first, secondly, finally, in conclusion, however, nevertheless, moreover, consequently, hence, on the other hand, in other words*

EXERCISE 3. Give semantic analyses of the following statements, following the model in Table 9.4:

a. *The baby was crying loudly for its dinner.*

b. *The doctor reluctantly cancelled her appointments.*

c. *Your father may not like the house very much.*

d. *On Tuesdays, the clinic gives elderly people free vaccinations.*

e. *Unfortunately, no one could see the blackboard.*

f. *Bill can look after his own interests.* (The predicate is "look after.")

g. *In my opinion, this room is disgusting!*

h. *Unfortunately, Jen couldn't open the door with her key.*

i. *On the other hand, this exercise is always difficult.*

j. *Somebody should discuss the issue with Bill.*

Table 9.4   Model Answer for Sentence (a) in Exercise 3

The predicate	The arguments of the predicate	The semantic role that is assigned to each argument	Adverbial modifiers, if any	The semantic category of each adverbial
cry	*the baby* *(for) its dinner*	<agent> <goal>	*loudly*	manner

9.5   The Semantics of NPs

Except for *predicate* NPs, which act as predicates, noun phrases normally serve as *arguments* of predicates—that is, they name the *entities* (people, places, things, ideas, etc.) that participate in the event or state of affairs that is indicated by the predicate. NPs are classified as definite or indefinite, depending on whether the referent of the NP is already known to the hearer or reader of the sentence.

Indefinite NPs introduce persons, places, things, or ideas whose identity is not yet known to the hearer or reader. The following types of NPs are all indefinite:

- indefinite pronouns (*somebody, anybody, anything, one,*[4] *etc.*)
- "generic" NPs with no determiner (*We saw **stars** everywhere*)
- NPs with indefinite determiners (*an apple, some money, any luck, every student, a few good ideas*)

Definite NPs refer to entities whose identity is already known; for example, the definite NP *the old barn* can be used appropriately only if the hearer or reader already knows which old barn is being discussed. The following types of NPs are all definite:

- proper names (*Bill*)
- personal pronouns (*he, she, it, they*)
- common nouns with definite specifiers (*the moon, this week, these earrings, that scarf, those people, my brother, your house, our parents' house,* etc.)

EXERCISE 4.   Find the NPs in the following passage from "Little Red Cap" (better known as "Little Red Riding Hood") from *The Complete Fairy Tales of the Brothers Grimm*. Classify each NP as definite or indefinite, and explain why the writer has chosen a definite (or indefinite) NP. *Caution:* Remember that a NP is definite or indefinite by virtue of its *form*—whether it has a definite or indefinite determiner, is a proper name, and so forth.

---

4. English has several different *one*'s. The indefinite pronoun is the *one* that appears in the sentence "I'd like a green one."

In this exercise, you should *first* identify the NP as definite or indefinite and *then* consider why the writer has chosen that type of NP.

> *Once upon a time there was a sweet little maiden. Whoever laid eyes upon her could not help but love her. But it was her grandmother who loved her most. She could never give the child enough. One time she made her a present, a small, red velvet cap, and since it was so becoming and the maiden insisted on always wearing it, she was called Little Red Cap.*

In addition to the head noun and its specifier, a NP may also contain modifiers which provide additional information about the entities to which the NP refers—not just ***an*** *apple*, but *a **crisp, juicy** apple*, not just *those people* but *those people **standing over there near the courthouse***.

9.6 Applications for Students and Teachers of Literature

The material in this chapter has several applications for literary analysis, including (1) the unconventional use of definite NPs at the beginning of literary narratives, (2) the assignment of semantic roles to literary characters, and (3) the choice of adverbial modifiers.

9.6.1 An Unconventional Use of Definite NPs

In conversational language and in traditional storytelling, definite NPs are used to refer to entities whose identity is already known to the listener or reader. However, modern fiction writers often begin a narrative *in media res*, using definite NPs in an unconventional way, as if the characters and setting were already familiar to the reader. For example, in his story "Hills Like White Elephants" (Appendix Section I), Hemingway begins by describing ***the*** *hills across the valley of **the** Ebro* and ***the*** *American and **the** girl with him,* though the reader at this point knows nothing about these characters or this setting (What hills? What American?).

EXERCISE 5.

a. Rewrite the first paragraph of "Hills Like White Elephants" in a more traditional way, using indefinite NPs to introduce characters and features of the setting that the reader is hearing about for the first time. What is the effect of this change? What do writers gain by using definite NPs, unconventionally, at the beginning of a narrative?

b. All the literary selections in Appendix Section I are first paragraphs. Find at least one other selection in this section that uses definite NPs as Hemingway does, to refer to characters or elements of the setting that have not yet been introduced to the reader. Then find one selection that does *not* make use of this technique.

9.6.2 Semantic Roles for Literary Characters

Fictional characters are sometimes assigned rather consistent roles, sentence by sentence, throughout a narrative: one character is consistently an <agent>, another is a <patient> (things always happen to him or her); another is an <experiencer> or a <possessor>. For example, in the selection from Rachel Carson's *The Sea Around Us*, Appendix Section I, the human character in the narrative (*you*) is consistently in the role of <observer>[5]—*you* look down, *you* see, and *you* notice the phenomena around you, all of which are described in visual terms.

EXERCISE 6. Choose one of the other literary selections in Appendix Section I and, keeping in mind that this is only a very brief segment of the story, identify the roles that are assigned, so far, to each character. Be sure to say what verb, adjective, or preposition is assigning each role. In some cases, you may also want to mention the roles that are assigned to inanimate "characters." For example, the express from Barcelona is the closest to an <agent> in the passage from "Hills Like White Elephants." The American is just sitting (that is, he is a <theme>), and the preposition *with* places the "girl" in the role of <companion>. The only active entity in the passage is the express from Barcelona, which *comes, stops*, and *goes*.

9.6.3   Adverbial Modifiers

It can be interesting, also, to consider the adverbial modifiers in a literary passage. For example, in the selection from "Hills Like White Elephants," repeated below, the underlined adverbials belong almost entirely to the categories *time* and *place*. That is appropriate for a passage like this one, which sets the scene for a narrative, especially a static scene like this one:

> *The hills across the valley of the Ebro were long and white. On this side there was no shade and no trees and the station was between two lines of rails in the sun. Close against the side of the station there was the warm shadow of the building, and a curtain, made of strings of bamboo beads, hung across the open door into the bar, to keep out flies. The American and the girl with him sat at a table in the shade, outside the building. It was very hot and the express from Barcelona would come in forty minutes. It stopped at this junction for two minutes and went on to Madrid.*
>
> —Hemingway, "Hills Like White Elephants"

EXERCISE 7.

a. One of the underlined adverbials in the Hemingway passage is not an adverbial of time or place. Find it and identify its category.

b. Consider the (underlined) adverbials in the selection from Lewis Thomas's *Lives of a Cell*. (The double underline indicates that there is an adverbial *inside* an adverbial.)

---

5. The role of <observer> is not listed in Table 9.2, but it seems an appropriate label for the role that is played by the "you" of Carson's passage. The list in Table 9.2 is not intended to be exhaustive.

What are the semantic categories of these adverbials, and why are they so different from those of the Hemingway passage?

> *Ants are so much like human beings as to be an embarrassment. They farm fungi,*   1
> *raise aphids <u>as livestock</u>, launch armies into wars, use chemical sprays <u>to alarm</u>*   2
> *<u>and confuse enemies</u>, capture slaves. The families of weaver ants engage in child*   3
> *labor, <u>holding their larvae like shuttles to spin out the thread that sews the leaves</u>*   4
> *<u>together for their fungus gardens</u>. They exchange information <u>ceaselessly</u>. They*   5
> *do everything but watch television.*   6
>
> —Lewis Thomas, *The Lives of a Cell*

9.7 Applications for Teachers of Young Children

The use of definite NPs can be tricky for young (and, sometimes, older) students. Young children are notorious for their overuse of definite NPs—because they are egocentric and believe that other people have access to the same information that they have. For example, the second-grade author of "My Nightmare" (Appendix Section II) writes, "but I had a good idea and all I had to do is get **that space gun**. . . When I got out, I saw **the alien**," using two definite NPs (*that space gun* and *the alien*) whose referents have not yet been identified.

EXERCISE 8. Find definite NPs whose referent is not clear in "My Favorite Puppy," Appendix Section II.

9.8 Applications for Writing

This chapter relates to two points of interest for writers: (1) effective positioning of adverbials, and (2) clear assignment of semantic roles.

9.8.1 Positioning Adverbials

Adverbials can be placed in any of the positions marked 1, 2, 3, and 4 in the diagram below:

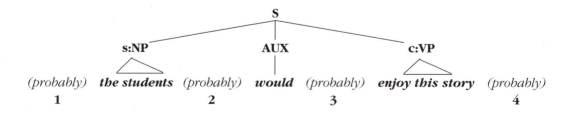

However, although adverbials are flexible in their position, there may be differences in meaning from one position to another. For example, the sentences below do not have exactly the same meaning:

1. **Erroneously,** she wrote the total on the third line.
2. She **erroneously** wrote the total on the third line.
3. She wrote the total **erroneously** on the third line.
4. She wrote the total on the third line **erroneously**.

In my reading, sentences (3) and (4) can have either of two meanings—that the total was written incorrectly, or that it should not have been written on the third line, but sentences (1) and (2) have only the second meaning—that the total should not have been written on the third line.

Even if there is no change of meaning when the adverbial shifts position, there may be significant changes in emphasis; for example, it would be better to say *His lawyer claims that he is being **illegally** held*, rather than *His lawyer claims that he is being **illegally** held,* as I heard on the news one morning. Here is another example, from a *New York Times* column: *Justice Powell proposed that universities could consider an applicant's race as long as they did not establish racial quotas, a term he inexactly defined.* The meaning of this sentence would come through more clearly if the adverb *inexactly* were moved to final position: *a term he defined inexactly.*

In another issue regarding the placement of adverbials, we were told, traditionally, not to "split" an infinitive such as *to know* or *to go* by placing an adverbial between the two words. However, this is a rule that was based on the grammar of Latin, and it has never really applied to English; there are many instances in English where an infinitive can be split: *To **really** understand this passage . . .* , or *to **boldly** go where no one has gone before* (the Star Trek motto). Unfortunately, there are no reliable rules to determine where an adverbial should be placed; the careful writer should be aware of adverbials and try them in different positions to see what works best.

EXERCISE 9.

a. Explain the difference in meaning between the following sentences:
   i. *Some White House workers improperly conducted government business on Republican party e-mail accounts.*
   ii. *Some White House workers conducted government business improperly on Republican party e-mail accounts.*
   iii. *Sadly, he read three verses before we could tell him to stop.*
   iv. *He read three verses sadly before we could tell him to stop.*

b. Find poorly placed adverbials in the following sentences, and improve the sentence, if necessary, by moving the adverbial to a different position:
   i. *The president candidly answered questions for more than an hour.*
   ii. *Police believe that someone took steps to carefully hide Holloway's body in the dunes.*
   iii. *Now she had time to more thoroughly observe the ants' behavior.*
   iv. *Nissan says that electric cars will be quickly profitable.*

    v.   *The candidate still regularly participates in town-hall style meetings. Reporters are routinely invited to ride with him on his bus.*

    vi.   *The fence is intended to keep people and vehicles from illegally crossing the US-Mexico border.*

9.8.2   When Semantic Roles Are Assigned by Nouns

As we discussed in Section 9.2 above, it is verbs and predicate complements that normally indicate what event or situation is being depicted and that assign roles to the participants. However, nouns that are semantically related to verbs or adjectives (they are called *nominalizations*) may also represent events or situations and may assign semantic roles, as in the examples below:

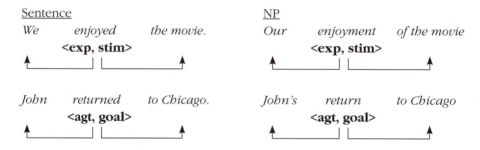

Williams (1994) calls attention to an unfortunate tendency in academic and bureaucratic writing to substitute nominalizations for verbs and adjectives; this gives the sentence a more formal register but makes it more difficult to follow. Consider the following contrasts pointed out by Williams (pp. 43–51):

a.   *The police conducted an **investigation** into the matter.*
    vs.   *The police **investigated** the matter.*

b.   *We request that on your **return** you should conduct a **review** of the data and provide an immediate **report**.*
    vs.   *When you **return**, please **review** the data and **report** immediately.*

c.   *The first step was a **review** of the **evolution** of the dorsal fin.*
    vs.   *First, we **reviewed** how the dorsal fin **evolved**.*
    or   *First, we **reviewed** the **evolution** of the dorsal fin.*

While nominalizations are an efficient way of referring to an event or situation that is already familiar (as, for example, the second nominalization in (c) above), the overuse of nominalization can seriously obscure the meaning of the sentence. It is easier to understand who is doing what to whom when the semantic roles are assigned by a verb or predicate adjective rather than by a noun.

EXERCISE 10.

a. Revise the following sentences by changing the boldfaced nominalizations to verbs or adjectives. Notice how much more clearly the role players emerge:[6]

   i.   *We received an **order** from the doctor for an **analysis** of the blood sample.*

   ii.   *The President's **impeachment** by the Senate did not lead to his **removal** from office.*

   iii. *Sally's **disagreement** with her employer was the cause of her **dismissal**.*

   iv.   *There were **charges** by the panel regarding **misappropriation** of funds on the company's part.*

   v.   *The camp's **inability** to enforce safety regulations led to its **closure** by the Department of Health.*

   vi.   ***Written cancellation** of the student's housing application by August 15 will result in **forfeiture** of the deposit only, with no additional charge.*

   vii. *Our **recommendation** is for **completion** of the core curriculum by the end of the second year.*

   viii. *Ms. Bush was given a $600 **fine** for the **use** of someone else's ID for the **purchase** of alcohol.*

   ix.   *This office has the **responsibility** for making prompt **responses** to inquiries from prospective students.*

b. Look over the passage from the University of New Hampshire catalog (Chapter 2, Exercise 7). How many nominalizations can you find? (I counted nine.) Can you find ways to eliminate some of these?

c. Look over the Samuel Eliot Morison passage in Appendix Section I. Can you find any nominalizations in this passage? (I couldn't.) Try changing some of Morison's verbs to nominalizations and see what happens.

9.9 Applications for ESL

Two topics in this chapter that are of particular interest to teachers and students of English as a Second Language are (1) the placement of adverbials, and (2) the distinction between definite and indefinite NPs.

9.9.1 The Placement of Adverbials

In most European languages, an adverbial can be placed between the verb and its direct object, a position that is not possible in English; students from these language backgrounds will tend to construct English sentences like the following:

She speaks **always English.*	(for *She **always** speaks English.*)
They called **immediately an ambulance.*	(for *They **immediately** called an ambulance.*)

---

6. This exercise is patterned after an exercise in Williams (1994).

The reason for this difference is that European languages are subject to a rule of Verb Raising, which moves a tensed verb out of the VP and into the AUX position:

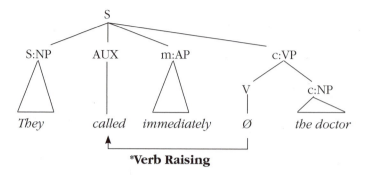

*Verb Raising

This transformation does not apply in English (see Chapter 11, Section 11.3 for further discussion), but it requires direct instruction and repeated reminders to eliminate it from the English of European students.

9.9.2   Definite and Indefinite NPs

We have already discussed (Chapter 3, Section 3.6.3) some of the difficulties that our determiner system presents for ESL students. We observed there that many languages lack our requirement that a singular count noun must have a determiner (*Please give me **pencil**). An additional difficulty for ESL students is the fact that, in English, every NP must be marked as either definite or indefinite.

In Section 9.5 of this chapter, we observed that common nouns whose referent is already known to the listener or reader are marked as definite, while those that are new and unfamiliar are marked as indefinite:

> Once there was **a sweet little maiden** [indefinite] called "Little Red Cap."
> **Her grandmother** [definite] loved her very much and could never give
> **the child** [definite] enough.

However, the system is actually more complicated than is suggested by this simple rule.

First, for those who have not grown up with the distinction between definite and indefinite NPs, it is difficult to determine what counts as "already known." Entities such as *the moon* and *the earth* are considered to be universally "known"; they do not require previous mention in the discourse. But the "universally known" status may also be extended to less obvious cases, as when the second-grade author of "My Favorite Puppy" (Appendix Section II) says, *We got her at* **the pound**. *They found her in the middle of* **the road.** Furthermore, an entity that has not yet been introduced can sometimes be treated as "already known" by virtue of its association with an entity that *has* been introduced, as when the same author says that her puppy was hit on **the** tail, though the tail itself has not been mentioned previously. In fact, we can say that ***the** tail of a dog* was found in the road, when neither the tail *nor* the dog has been previously introduced (that's why the NP ***a** dog* has an indefinite determiner). The logic, apparently, is that the tail is identifiable in relation to the dog—once we know what dog, we will also know what tail. You can see why an ESL student might be confused!

Proper names add an additional complexity. Many proper names do not use a definite determiner—we speak of George Washington, not *the* George Washington; of Canada, not *the* Canada; of Mount Washington and Lake Winnepesaukee, not *the* Mount Washington and *the* Lake Winnepesaukee; and of the languages English and French, not *the* English and *the* French. But the *people* of England and France are, indeed, *the* English and *the* French, and although mountains and lakes have no definite determiner in their names, oceans and rivers do (*the* Atlantic Ocean, *the* Mississippi River). Furthermore, *plural* proper names always use the definite determiner—*the* Joneses, *the* United States, *the* White Mountains.

Finally, as we discussed in Chapter 3, Section 3.6.3, English uses indefinite NPs to identify general *categories* of objects, in contrast to other European languages, in which generic NPs are definite:

> *Horses have four legs.*
> vs. *Los caballos tienen cuatro piernas.*   '(The) horses have four legs.' (Spanish)
>   *Les chevaux ont quatre jambes.*   '(The) horses have four legs.' (French)

ESL students beyond the early primary years should be told the basic rules for choosing articles, but I doubt that anyone has ever learned to use articles correctly simply by following the "rules." Because the use of determiners is so closely related to content, I suggest that exercises on this topic should be constructed from connected texts with which the students are already familiar. A useful exercise can be created, as shown in Exercise 11, by removing all instances of *a/an* and *the* and inserting a blank before every noun in the passage (including those which need no determiner).

EXERCISE 11. Insert *a/an* or *the*, as needed, in each of the blank spaces in the Lewis Thomas passage below.

Then try to explain the reason for each choice. (*Note*: The purpose of this part of the exercise is for you to see that it may not always be possible to give a satisfactory explanation; that is a useful thing for an ESL teacher to know!)

_____ *ants are so much like* _____ *human beings as to be* ___ *embarrassment.*	1
They farm ___ *fungi, raise* _____ *aphids as* _____ *livestock, launch* _____ *armies*	2
into _____ *wars, use* _____ *chemical sprays to alarm and confuse* _____ *enemies,*	3
capture ___ *slaves.* _____ *families of* _____ *weaver ants engage in* _____ *child labor,*	4
holding their larvae like _____ *shuttles to spin out* _____ *thread that sews* _____ *leaves*	5
together for their fungus gardens. They exchange _____ *information ceaselessly.*	6
They do everything but watch _____ *television.*	7
—Lewis Thomas, ___ *Lives of* _____ *Cell*	

Because of the great difficulty of this part of our grammar, many ESL students never completely master the use of articles.[7] Luckily, the misuse of an article does not, in most cases, interfere with intelligibility. Students should be encouraged to be as accurate as they can, and, in situations where total accuracy is required, to seek the assistance of a native-speaking editor.

9.10 Summary of the Chapter

In this chapter, we have shown that the meaning of a statement is built around the predicate (usually a verb, but sometimes a predicate complement). The predicate indicates what event or situation the sentence is depicting, and leads us to expect a particular number of participants or "role players," which are presented in the subject and complement positions. The predicate also tells us where to find each role player; for example, in a sentence with the verb *love,* the <experiencer> will be found in subject position, while in a sentence with the verb *annoy*, the <experiencer> is in complement position, after the verb.

Subjects and complements (the "arguments" of the predicate) do not have semantic roles of their own; they get their roles from the predicate. In this way, they differ from adverbial modifiers, which have their own inherent semantic roles. For example, *on Tuesday* is always an adverbial of time and *once a week* is always an adverbial of frequency, no matter what sentence they are placed in.

Except for predicate NPs, which act as predicates, NPs normally name the *arguments* of a predicate. NPs may be definite (*the president, George Washington*) or indefinite (*a politician, people*). New entities are introduced into the conversation with indefinite NPs (*a sweet little maiden*), but once the referent of the NP has been established the speaker will, on subsequent mention, use definite NPs to refer to that entity (*the maiden, Little Red Cap*).

As applications for teachers, we have pointed out the tendency of younger writers to overuse definite NPs (because it is hard for them to judge what their reader already knows). For older writers, we have talked about the positioning of adverbials, and about the advantages of verbs rather than deverbal nouns to represent events (***investigate** the matter* vs. ***conduct an investigation** of the matter*). Finally for ESL teachers, we have pointed out a tendency for speakers of European languages to place an adverbial between the verb and its direct object (**We speak **always** English*) and have described the difficulty that ESL students experience in learning to distinguish definite and indefinite NPs in English.

---

7. It is a mystery to me why articles are *not* a source of difficulty to children who learn English as a native language, in early childhood.

CHAPTER 10

Tense, Aspect, Voice, and Modality

10.1 Introduction

Traditional descriptions of the tense system of English identify three tenses—past, present, and future—each of which can be combined with the *perfect* and *progressive aspects*, as shown in Tables 10.1a and 10.1b. The verb forms in Table 10.1a are in *active voice*; their *passive* counterparts are given in Table 10.1b. Tables 10.1a and 10.1b follow traditional terminology in identifying the *will* form as future tense; however, it is more accurate, for English, to speak of the *modal* form, because the other modals can occupy the same position as *will*.[1] For example, corresponding to the "future" form *they will try*, we can create the modal forms *they would try, they can try, they could try, they should try, they may try, they might try,* and *they must try*.

EXERCISE 1.

a. Give the full name of each form in Tables 10.1a and 10.1b; for example, *It has been being repaired* is in the present perfect progressive passive form.

b. In order to see for yourself that the other modals occupy the same position as *will*, try substituting the modals *would, can, could, should, may, might,* and *must* for the modal *will* in Tables 10.1a and 10.1b. (You can also try the modal *shall*, but it will not work well; this modal has a very restricted distribution in Modern English.)

c. To practice the names of the tense forms, start with the sentence *The cat chased the mouse.* What form is this? Then follow the directions below:

Change to the simple present.
Change to a modal form.
Change to the present progressive.
Change to the past progressive.
Change to a modal progressive form.
Change to the present perfect.
Change to the past perfect.
Change to a modal perfect form.
Change to the present perfect progressive.
Change to the past perfect progressive.
Change to a modal perfect progressive form.
Change to the simple present passive.
Change to the simple past passive.
Change to a modal passive form.

---

1. Other languages that you may have studied—French, Spanish, and Italian, for example—have a real future tense, which is created by adding a suffix to the verb. English doesn't actually have a future tense, though, like all other human languages, we have ways to talk about the future, including the modal forms that are mentioned in the text, and forms with *going to* (*They are going to try*).

Change to the present perfect passive.
Change to the past perfect passive.
Change to a modal perfect passive form.
Change to the present progressive passive.
Change to the past progressive passive.
Change to a modal progressive passive form.
Change to the present perfect progressive passive.
Change to the past perfect progressive passive.
Change to a modal perfect progressive passive form.

10.2 The Structure of the Verb String

The verb string is created by combining the following elements, in the order specified, where MV stands for *main verb*:

MODAL or [tense/agreement marker] (*have*$_{\text{perf}}$) (*be*$_{\text{prog}}$) (*be*$_{\text{pass}}$) MV

The only obligatory elements in this string are the main verb (MV) and either a modal (*will, would, can, could,* etc.) or a tense/agreement marker ([*past tense*], [*general present tense*], or [*3rd singular*

Table 10.1a The Active Voice

	Past	Present	Future
Simple	They **tried.**	They **try**.	They **will try.**
Perfect	They **had tried.**	They **have tried.**	They **will have tried.**
Progressive	They **were trying.**	They **are trying.**	They **will be trying** (to finish**).**
Perfect progressive	They **had been trying** (to finish**).**	They **have been trying** (to finish**).**	They **will have been trying** (to finish**).**

Table 10.1b The Passive Voice

	Past	Present	Future
Simple passive	It **was repaired.**	It **is** (often) **repaired.**	It **will be repaired.**
Perfect passive	It **had been repaired.**	It **has been repaired.**	It **will have been repaired.**
Progressive passive	It **was being repaired.**	It **is being repaired.**	It **will be being repaired.**
Perfect progressive passive	It **had been being repaired.**	It **has been being repaired.**	It **will have been being repaired.**

present tense]). The other elements are all optional, as indicated by the parentheses, but whatever elements are chosen, they always follow the order that is specified in this formula. (See Table 10.2a on pages 202–203.) The tense/agreement marker appears on the first item in the string; for example, in the verb string *has been singing*, the marker [*3rd singular present*] appears on the first auxiliary (*have*_perf), causing it to be pronounced as *has*. If we left out *have*_perf, then the first element of the string would be *be*_prog, and the tense/agreement marker would attach to it: ***is** singing*. If there were no auxiliary at all, then the tense/agreement marker would attach to the main verb: *sings*. If a modal were chosen instead of a tense marker, then there would be no tense/agreement marker.[2]

EXERCISE 2.

a. Find and identify the tense/agreement marker in each verb string of Table 10.1a. Your choices are [modal], [general present tense], [3rd sg. present tense], or [past tense].

b. Fill in the blanks in Table 10.2b on pages 204–205.

We saw in previous chapters that a modal auxiliary occupies the head (AUX) position in the sentence:

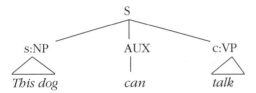

As evidence, we observed (1) that the negative particle *not* goes right after the modal, (2) that adverbials like *probably* can go before or after the modal, and (3) that the modal undergoes Subject-AUX Inversion in *yes/no* questions:

1. Position of *not*:

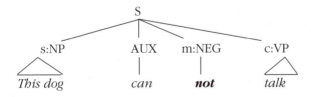

2. Position of adverbials:

An intelligent dog	***probably***	*can*		*talk.*
An intelligent dog		*can*	***probably***	*talk.*

---

2. The modal does carry a sort of tense marker; for example, the modal *would* is, in some sense, the past tense form of the modal *will*. However, the tense marker that is attached to a modal does not usually carry a past time meaning, and modals are never marked for agreement (*I will go, you will go, he/she/it will go*—not *wills go).

Table 10.2a Table of the Verb Forms

Sentence	Name of Construction
She **plays** the piano.	simple present
They **lived** in Maine.	simple past
You **should enjoy** yourself.	modal[a]
The building **is sinking**.	present progressive (or present continuous)
We **were listening**.	past progressive(or past continuous)
You **should be studying**.	modal progressive (or modal continuous)
Things **have changed**.	present perfect
Nobody **had noticed**.	past perfect
You **should have said** something.	modal perfect
Things **have been deteriorating**.	present perfect progressive
Nobody **had been listening**.	past perfect progressive
They **may have been sleeping**.	modal perfect progressive
The toaster **is broken**.	present passive
The money **was stolen**.	past passive
The patient **should be examined**.	modal passive
The patient **is being examined**.	present progressive passive
The idea **was being considered**.	past progressive passive
The idea **may be being considered**.	modal progressive passive
The jewels **have been stolen**!	present perfect passive
The jewels **had been stolen**!	past perfect passive
The jewels **might have been stolen**!	modal perfect passive
The idea **has been being considered**.	present perfect progressive passive
The idea **had been being considered**.	past perfect progressive passive
The idea **should have been being considered**.	modal perfect progressive passive

a. If the modal is *will*, the form is traditionally called *the future*.

Constituents				
modal	**have**perf	**be**prog	**be**pass	**MV**
				plays
				lived
should				*enjoy*
		is		*sinking*
		were		*listening*
should		*be*		*studying*
	have			*changed*
	had			*noticed*
should	*have*			*said*
	have	*been*		*deteriorating*
	had	*been*		*listening*
may	*have*	*been*		*sleeping*
			is	*broken*
			was	*stolen*
should			*be*	*examined*
		is	*being*	*examined*
		was	*being*	*considered*
may		*be*	*being*	*considered*
	have		*been*	*stolen*
	had		*been*	*stolen*
might	*have*		*been*	*stolen*
	has	*been*	*being*	*considered*
	had	*been*	*being*	*considered*
should	*have*	*been*	*being*	*considered*

Table 10.2b   Fill in the Blanks

Sentence	Name of Construction
The birds **are singing.**	
Birds **sing.**	
The leaves **were falling.**	
The leaves **had been falling.**	
No one **knew** the answer.	
You **should be studying.**	
Somebody **must have been listening.**	
Everybody **likes** ice cream.	
The car **had disappeared.**	
Nobody **can sing** "The Star Spangled Banner."	
They **will have left.**	
The noise **has stopped.**	
The lights **had been turned** out.	
The roof **was blown** off.	
The prisoner **is being questioned.**	
The prisoner **has been questioned.**	
The prisoner **should be questioned.**	
The prisoner **was questioned** very carefully.	
The police **will have questioned** the prisoner.	
The police **are questioning** the prisoner.	
The police **have questioned** the prisoner.	

Constituents				
modal	**have**$_{\text{perf}}$	**be**$_{\text{prog}}$	**be**$_{\text{pass}}$	**MV**

3. Subject-AUX Inversion:

Subject-AUX Inversion

The auxiliary verbs *have_perf*, *be_prog*, and *be_pass* can also occupy AUX position, as shown below:

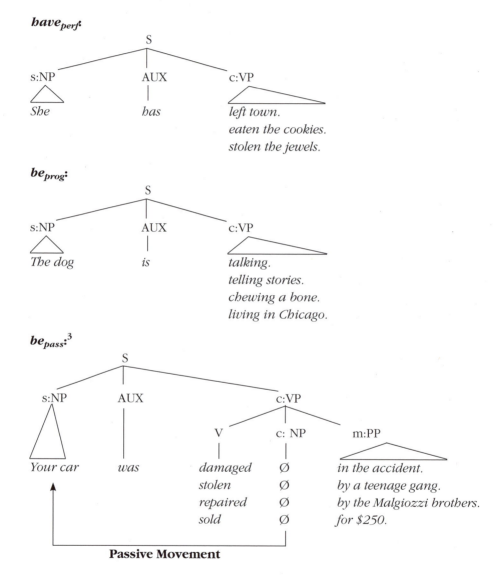

Passive Movement

---

3. Notice that sentences with the auxiliary *be_pass* undergo a transformation called *Passive Movement*, as shown in the diagram. This transformation moves what would normally be the complement of the verb out of the VP into subject position; we will have more to say about this in Section 10.5.4 below.

EXERCISE 3. Use *not, probably,* and subject-AUX Inversion to verify that the auxiliary verb occupies AUX position in the following sentences:

a. *She has left town.*
b. *The dog is talking.*
c. *Your car was damaged in the accident.*

What if the sentence has more than one auxiliary? In that case, only the first auxiliary occupies AUX position (that is, it is the head of the sentence); the second auxiliary is the head of the VP complement, and so on down the line:

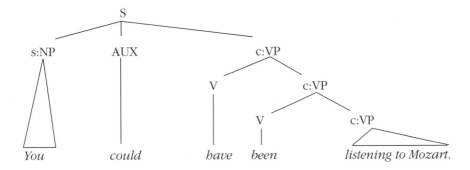

However, for the purposes of this text, it will be acceptable to abbreviate the structure in the following way:

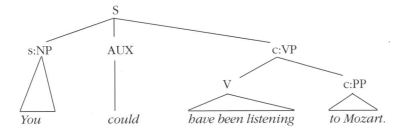

EXERCISE 4.

a. Use *not, probably,* and Subject-AUX Inversion to show that we were correct in our decision to put only the first auxiliary (*could*) in AUX position in the sentence above (*You could have been listening to Mozart*).

b. Draw a tree diagram of the sentence *They will be looking for you,* in either the full version or the abbreviated version, as you prefer.

10.3 Determining the Inflectional Form for Items in the Verb String

We observed above that the first member of the verb string, if not a modal, carries a tense/agreement marker ([*past tense*], [*general present tense*], or [*3rd singular present tense*]). For each subsequent item in the string, the form of that item is determined by the auxiliary that precedes it:

After a modal, the verb is in base form:	*George should **go**.*
After *be*$_{prog}$ the verb is in present participle form:	*George is **going**.*
After *have*$_{perf}$ the verb is in perfect participle form:	*George has **gone**.*
After *be*$_{pass}$ the verb is in passive participle form:	*George was **fired**.*

Tables 10.3a and 10.3b provide analyses of more complex verb strings.

EXERCISE 5. Choose five verb strings from Table 10.2b. For each item in the string, determine (a) its inflectional form, and (b) why it has that form. Set out this information in a chart like the ones in Tables 10.3a and 10.3b below. *Caution*: Before doing this exercise, please review the names of the inflectional forms in Figure 3.2 at the end of Chapter 3.

Table 10.3a The Inflectional Form of Items in the Verb String

Example:	*should*	*have*	*been*	*studying*
What is it?	modal	*have*$_{perf}$	*be*$_{prog}$	MV
What is its inflectional form?	base	base	perfect participle	present participle
Why is it in that form?	Modals have only one form, the base form.	It follows a modal.	It follows *have*$_{perf}$.	It follows *be*$_{prog}$.

Table 10.3b   The Inflectional Form of Items in the Verb String

Example:	*was*	*being*	*renovated*
What is it?	*be*~prog~	*be*~pass~	MV
What is its inflectional form?	3 sg. past tense	present participle	passive participle
Why is it in that form?	When there is no modal, there must be a tense/agreement marker on the first item of the string. *Was* carries the tense marker [past tense] and the agreement marker [3rd sg.], to agree with the subject NP, *the building*.	It follows *be*~prog~.	It follows *be*~pass~.

10.4   The Semantics of the Auxiliaries

The auxiliary system makes four contributions to the meaning of the sentence:

time reference	past, present, or future
aspect	how an event or situation fits into its time frame
modality	degree of certainty or strength of obligation
voice	how the verb distributes semantic roles to its arguments

10.4.1   Time Reference

One purpose of the auxiliary system is to assign a situation or event to past, present, or future time. Past and present time are usually indicated by the past and present tense markers:

Present time:	*People have strong feelings about Hillary Clinton.* (general present tense)
Past time:	*Marie and Pierre Curie discovered radium.* (past tense)

Modals characteristically refer to the future (*It **may** rain tomorrow; nobody **will** hear you; you **should** take your umbrella*).

However, time reference is more complex than is generally acknowledged. First, the forms that are called past, present, and future *tense* do not always refer to past, present, and future *time*:

If I **had** a hammer right now, I would ...	(past tense referring to present time)
If I **won** the lottery next week, I would ...	(past tense referring to future time)
The plane **leaves** at 10 o'clock tomorrow.	(present tense referring to future time)
And while I'm standing here, this guy **comes** in and **says** ...	(present tense referring to past time)
The male of the species **will** sometimes **guard** the nest while ...	(the modal *will* referring to a habitual occurrence in the present)

Secondly, we have other conventional expressions, apart from the auxiliary system, to indicate time:

She **used to** smoke.	(past habitual)
We're **about to** leave.	(immediate future)
It's **fixin' to** rain.	(immediate future)
I'm **going to** tell her.	(future)

EXERCISE 6.

a. Identify the dominant tense (past, present, or future) of each of the eight literary passages in Appendix Section I.

b. The Samuel Eliot Morison passage is predominantly in past tense, but it contains one sentence in present tense. Find that sentence and explain why Morison changes tense at this point in his narrative.

10.4.2 Aspect

The term "aspect" refers to the way an event or situation fits into its time frame. For example, expressions like *be about to* and *be fixin' to* are examples of what is called "inchoative" aspect, meaning that the event or situation will be starting immediately with its time frame:

Past inchoative:	The band **was about to** play.
Present inchoative:	The band **is about to** play.
Future inchoative:	The band **will be about** to play.

English also has forms to indicate that an event is repeated, habitually, within its time frame:

Past habitual:	The band **used to play** in the park.
	The band **would play** in the park.
Present habitual:	The band **plays** in the park.

However, only two of our aspects are marked by auxiliaries—the progressive and the perfect. The progressive auxiliary *be*$_{prog}$ indicates that an action is in progress within the time that is indicated by the tense marker:

Past progressive:	*The band **was playing**.*
Present progressive:	*The band **is playing**.*
Future progressive:	*The band **will be playing**.*

The perfect auxiliary *have*$_{perf}$ indicates that an event or situation began *before* the time that is indicated by the tense marker:

Past perfect:	*The band **had played*** The Star Spangled Banner.
Present perfect:	*The band **has played*** The Star Spangled Banner.
Future perfect:	*The band **will have played***.

Aspect markers (especially *have*$_{perf}$) are often used to indicate past, present, and future *within* a given time frame, as shown in Figure 10.1 on the following page.

EXERCISE 7.   In the following selection from James Joyce's story "The Dead," the central character, Gabriel, reflects on the past, present, and future. Set out these references in a chart like the one that is started for you at the end of this exercise, and observe the grammatical forms that Joyce uses to make these time distinctions, all within a past time framework.

Gabriel, leaning on his elbow, looked for a few moments unresentfully on her tangled hair and half-open mouth, listening to her deep-drawn breath. So she had had that romance in her life: a man had died for her sake. It hardly pained him now to think how poor a part he, her husband, had played in her life. He watched her while she slept as though he and she had never lived together as man and wife. His curious eyes rested long upon her face and on her hair: and, as he thought of what she must have been then, in that time of her first girlish beauty, a strange friendly pity for her entered his soul. He did not like to say even to himself that her face was no longer beautiful but he knew that it was no longer the face for which Michael Furey had braved death.

Perhaps she had not told him all the story. His eyes moved to the chair over which she had thrown some of her clothes. A petticoat string dangled to the floor. One boot stood upright, its limp upper fallen down: the fellow of it lay upon its side. He wondered at his riot of emotions of an hour before. From what had it proceeded? From his aunt's supper, from his own foolish speech, from the wine and dancing, the merry-making when saying good-night in the hall, the pleasure of the walk along the river in the snow. Poor Aunt Julia! She, too, would soon be a shade with the shade of Patrick Morkan and his horse. He had caught that haggard look upon her face for a moment when she was singing Arrayed for the

211

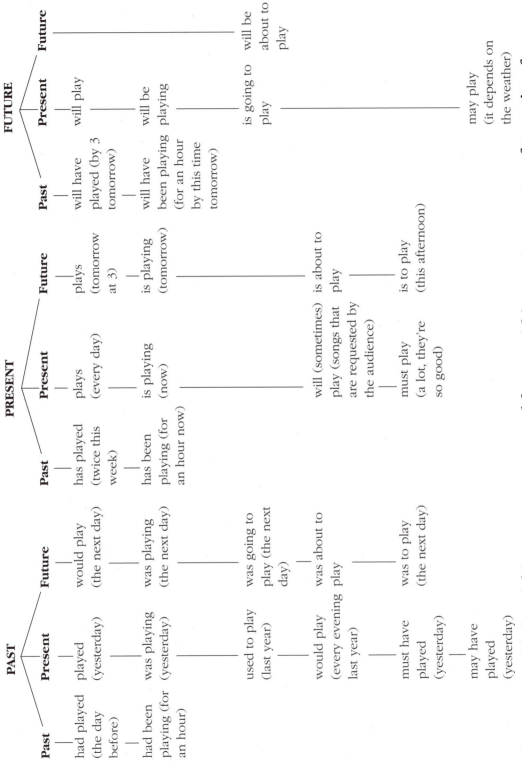

Figure 10.1 Distinguishing past, present, and future *within* a past, present, or future time frame.

> *Bridal. Soon, perhaps, he would be sitting in that same drawing-room, dressed in black, his silk hat on his knees. The blinds would be drawn down and Aunt Kate would be sitting beside him, crying and blowing her nose and telling him how Julia had died. He would cast about in his mind for some words that might console her, and would find only lame and useless ones. Yes, yes: that would happen very soon.*

"The Dead," from DUBLINERS by James Joyce, copyright 1916 by B. W. Huebsch. Definitive text Copyright © 1967 by the Estate of James Joyce. Used by permission of Viking Penguin, a division of Penguin Putnam, Inc.

Here is the beginning of an answer to Exercise 7:

Past from Gabriel's point of view	Present from Gabriel's point of view	Future from Gabriel's point of view
	Gabriel looked on her hair and mouth	
She had had that romance in her life.	*It hardly pained him now to think [about it].*	
A man had died for her sake.		
He, her husband, had played a poor part in her life.		
	He watched her while she slept.	
	His eyes rested upon her face and hair.	
He and she had lived together as man and wife.		
	Pity for her entered his soul.	
She must have been beautiful.		
Her face was no longer beautiful.		
Michael Furey had braved death for her face.		

10.4.3 Modality

Modality indicates degree of certainty or strength of obligation. If you have studied other European languages, you will have encountered the "subjunctive mood," a set of verb forms that are used to show that a statement is hypothetical or based on personal judgement. Statements that describe real, objective events or situations are in the "indicative mood." English, like other European languages, had a subjunctive mood historically; however, our subjunctive has now been almost entirely lost.[4] Instead, in Modern English, we use modal auxiliaries or, as we will

---

4. The two subjunctive forms that still exist in English are the conditional subjunctive (*I wish **I were** an apple, hanging on the tree*) and the mandative subjective (*The professor insists that **every student be** present for every class*). Notice that these subjunctive forms lack the agreement marker that is found on the first item of the verb string in the indicative forms.

see below, the past tense, to indicate the sorts of meaning that are expressed, in other languages, by the subjunctive mood.

Modal auxiliaries (*can, could, may, might, shall, should, will, would,* and *must*) express two sorts of modality, which the philosophers call "deontic modality" and "epistemic modality":

1. Deontic modality, or degree of obligation:

*You **will** do as I say.*	requirement
*You **must** do as I say.*	obligation
*You **should** do as I say.*	weaker obligation
*You **may** leave now.*	permission
*I **will** help you.*	promise

2. Epistemic modality, or degree of certainty:

*That **will** be George now.*	logical deduction
*That **must** be George now.*	logical deduction
*That **may** be George now.*	less certain logical deduction
*It **will** certainly snow in December.*	future certainty
*It **may** snow in November.*	future possibility

Doubtfulness—an instance of epistemic modality—may also be indicated by the past tense marker, as in the examples below:[5]

> *If I **won** the lottery, I would buy a vacation home in the Bahamas.*
> (The past tense indicates that I'm not optimistic about my chances.)
> *If I **had won** the lottery, I would have bought a vacation home in the Bahamas.*
> (The past perfect indicates that this did not happen.)

Similarly, past tense forms are used after the verb *wish* to indicate the unreality of the wished-for event:[6]

> *I wish I **knew** the answer to the question you are asking.*
> (The past tense indicates that I don't know the answer.)
> *I wish I **had finished** the assignment.*
> (The past perfect form indicates that I didn't finish.)

---

5. Compare the present-tense forms:
   *If I **win** the lottery, I will buy a vacation home in the Bahamas.*
   (The present tense indicates that I think I have a good chance.)
   *If I **have won** the lottery, I will buy a vacation home in the Bahamas.*
   (The present perfect indicates that I think I may have won.)
6. Compare *hope,* which is more optimistic, and which therefore uses present tense forms:
   *I hope I **know** the answers to the questions they will ask me.* (present tense)
   *I hope I **have answered** the questions correctly.* (present perfect)

These two ways of expressing doubtfulness—by using a modal auxiliary and by using the past tense marker—can be combined, by using a past tense modal to express uncertainty about the future:[7]

<u>Present-tense modals showing confidence about the future</u>
*They **will** leave this afternoon.*
*I **can** help you later.*
*It **may** rain tomorrow.*   (That's what the forecasters are predicting.)

<u>Past-tense modals showing doubt about the future</u>:
*They **would** leave this afternoon (if they could).*
*I **could** help you (if I had the right tools).*
*It **might** rain tomorrow.*   (But we think the rain will pass to the south of us.)

When past tense modals combine with the perfect auxiliary *have,* they create a "counterfactual" (a statement that isn't true):

*You **should have** said something.*   (But you didn't.)
*I **would have** said something.*   (But I didn't get the chance.)
*I **could have** danced all night.*   (If only the musicians hadn't gotten tired and gone home.)

EXERCISE 8.

a. The Samuel Eliot Morison passage (Appendix Section I) uses the past perfect form in three places. Write out these three verb strings and explain, in each case, why Morison uses this form. (*Hint:* There are two different reasons.)

b. Find an example of the *modal + have_perf* construction in the Morison passage. What does this form indicate?

10.4.4 Voice

Changes of tense, aspect, and modality do not affect the assignment of semantic roles. The verb distributes its semantic roles in the same way, without regard to tense (past or present) or the presence of auxiliaries. For example, in all the sentences below, the verb *eat* assigns the role of **<agent>** to its subject and the role of **<patient>** to its complement:

Somebody   ate   my porridge.
        <agt, pat>

---

7. We have not been treating the modals *would, could,* and *might* as "past tense" forms, but facts like these suggest that *would* is, in some sense, the past tense of *will; could* the past tense of *can,* and so forth.

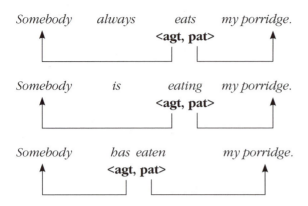

The passive is the one exception to the generalization that changing the form of the verb does not affect the assignment of semantic roles. A verb in the passive participle form loses the semantic role that would normally be assigned to its subject; instead, the subject receives the semantic role that would normally be assigned to the verb's complement:

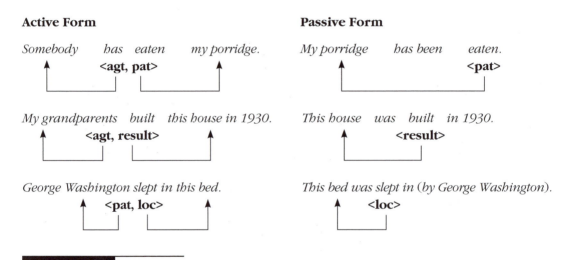

Active Form

Passive Form

EXERCISE 9.

a. Change the tense of the following sentences from present to past or past to present, and observe that the assignment of semantic roles remains unchanged:

i. *Horror movies frighten some children.*

ii. *Somebody took the coffee urn from the office.*

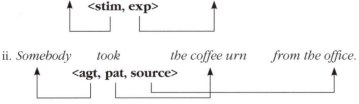

b. Insert a modal auxiliary, or the auxiliary be_{prog} or $have_{perf}$ into the sentences of (a) and notice that the assignment of semantic roles remains unchanged.

216

c. Change the sentences of (a) to passive and show what happens to the semantic roles, using diagrams like those that are given just above the exercise.

10.4.5 How Tense, Aspect, Modality, and Voice Affect the Meaning of a Sentence

As we saw in Chapter 9, the meaning of a sentence is organized around the predicate (the verb or predicate complement), which indicates the occurrence of an event or state of affairs and assigns "roles" to its subject and complements, if any. The tense, aspect, and modality of the sentence do not affect this core meaning, but, instead, indicate whether the event or state of affairs is located in past, present, or future time, how it is situated within its time frame, and whether it is a real event or only hypothetical. Thus the meaning of the sentence *Scientists have understood this principle since the 17th century* could be illustrated as shown in Table 10.4a.

Passive voice works differently from tense, aspect, and modality, in that it affects the way roles are assigned by the verb. A representation of the passive sentence *This principle has been understood since the 17th century* is given in Table 10.4b.

Table 10.4a Semantic Representation of a Declarative, Active-Voice Statement: *Scientists have understood this principle since the 17th century.*

Predicate	Arguments	Semantic roles assigned by predicate	Adverbial modifiers	Semantic roles of adverbials
understand	*scientists* *this principle*	<experiencer> <stimulus>	*since the 17th century*	duration

Tense: The present tense marker on *has* indicates that the situation is true at the present time.

Aspect: The perfect auxiliary *has* indicates that this state of affairs began before the time that is indicated by the tense marker.

Modality: The absence of a modality marker indicates that this is a statement of fact, not a hypothetical.

Table 10.4b Semantic Representation of a Declarative, Passive-Voice Statement: *This principle has been understood since the 17th century.*

Predicate	Arguments	Semantic roles assigned by predicate	Adverbial modifiers	Semantic roles of adverbials
understood (passive)	*this principle*	<stimulus>	*since the 17th century*	duration

Tense: The present tense marker on *has* indicates that this situation is true at the present time.

Aspect: The perfect auxiliary *has* indicates that this situation began before the time that is indicated by the tense marker.

Modality: The absence of any modality marker indicates that this is a statement of fact, not a hypothetical.

EXERCISE 10. Give semantic representations for the following sentences, following the model in Tables 10.4a and 10.4b:

a. *We have discussed this decision carefully.*
b. *The decision has been discussed carefully.*
c. *The professor is giving the lecture in room 16.*
d. *The lecture is being given in room 16.*
e. *They may suspect something.*
f. *They might suspect something.*
g. *They must suspect something.*

10.5 Applications for Writing

In this section, we will discuss four issues for writers and teachers of writing: (i) choosing the appropriate inflectional form for verbs, (ii) making the verb agree with the subject, (iii) maintaining consistency of tense, and (iv) using the passive voice appropriately.

10.5.1 Inflectional Forms of Verbs

The auxiliary system operates the same way in all varieties of English,[8] but there are dialect differences in subject-verb agreement and in some inflectional forms. Some dialects do not use an agreement marker for 3rd-person singular subjects: *He don't know* instead of *He doesn't know*. Students who use such forms are not being "lazy" or "illogical"; subject-verb agreement has been almost entirely lost in Modern English, and speakers of these dialects are simply taking this historical trend to its logical conclusion. Similarly, some dialects use nonstandard past tense and past participle forms for some verbs. For example, some speakers use *went* rather than *gone* as the perfect participle for *go* and *brang* rather than *brought* as the past tense for *bring*: *We had **went** there once before* and *He **brang** me a glass of water.* A speaker who uses such forms is not "confused" about tense and aspect (all native speakers of English make these distinctions), but is using a nonstandard inflectional form for a particular verb. Teachers have a responsibility to teach Standard English, but they must be careful not to belittle the dialects that their students have learned at home. The goal should be not to "stamp out" the student's home dialect, but to add Standard English as a second dialect. See Chapter 12 for further discussion of this issue.

10.5.2 Agreement Issues for Speakers of Standard English

Even speakers of Standard English have difficulty with subject-verb agreement in some constructions. It is sometimes difficult to find the subject of a sentence,[9] and sometimes it is unclear

---

8. There are some dialects that allow two modals: *We might could go*, and African-American Vernacular English has some additional auxiliaries that are not found in Standard English; these will be discussed in Chapter 12.

9. *Reminder:* To find the subject of a statement, change the statement into a *yes/no* question. The string of words between the two AUX positions is the subject of the sentence:

> *Does **drinking and driving** Ø remain a major cause of highway fatalities?*
>   SAI

whether the subject is singular or plural. For instance, consider the following examples from Lunsford and Connors (1995, p. 236):

a. *Tony and his sister commute every day from Louisville.*
AUX = [general present] because the subject, *Tony and his sister,* refers to more than one person.
b. *Drinking and driving remains a major cause of highway fatalities.*
AUX = [3 singular present], because the subject, *drinking and driving,* is intended to refer to a situation in which drinking and driving occur together, as a single event.

As these examples show, there is no consistent rule for subjects that consist of two NPs joined together by *and*; the choice of verb form depends on whether the conjoined subject refers to two separate entities or one collective entity.

EXERCISE 11. Identify the subject and the agreement marker in each sentence below, and explain the relationship, following the model above:

i. *Bacon and eggs is still one of our most popular breakfasts.*
ii. *Ham and Swiss has always been my favorite sandwich.*
iii. *The Yankees and the Red Sox are long-time baseball rivals.*

Collective nouns like *family* and *group* and "measure" phrases like *three miles* follow a similar system, with either a singular or a plural verb depending on whether the group is understood as a (plural) set of individuals, or as a single unit acting in concert.[10] For example, we would say

*Three miles **is** a long way to walk.*[11]   (not **Three miles are a long way to walk.*)
The Curl family have sold their home.   (not **The Curl family has sold their home.*)

In the second example, it is the pronoun *their* which forces the choice of a plural verb; without that pronoun it would, of course, be possible to understand the Curl family as singular:

The Curl family has moved to Massachusetts.

---

10. British speakers are more likely than Americans to treat collective nouns as plural. For example, British speakers say *Belgium have defeated the Netherlands* (meaning the Belgian soccer team), a usage that sounds very strange to the American ear.
11. Notice that you would say *It is a long way to walk,* not **They are a long way to walk.*

EXERCISE 12.   Identify the subject and the agreement marker in each sentence below, and explain why that marker is chosen. If you do not like the choice of agreement marker, explain the source of your discomfort. Notice that in some sentences more than one choice is possible, depending on the speaker's exact meaning:

i.   *A group of Mainers were thwarted in their attempt to transport medical supplies bound for Cuba across the Canadian border.*

ii.   *Pastors for Peace has been given a license to transport supplies.*

iii.   *Ten gallons of oil was pumped out of the bilge.*

iv.   *Last year at this time, the couple was headed for the altar.*

v.   *Now the same couple have decided on divorce.*

vi.   *The law firm of Dewey, Cheatam, and Howe, who have brought you this program, are the legal advisors for the radio show "Car Talk."*

Indefinite pronouns and determiners are particularly confusing. In informal writing and speech, many (most?) people say *Every one of the students **were** present* and *None of the pies **were** hot*, but we are sometimes advised to say *Every one of the students **was** present* and *None of the pies **was** hot*. To add to the confusion, we now know that the traditional admonition to treat *none* as singular was based on a mistaken etymology—that it is a reduced form of *not one*. In fact, the [n] at the end of *none* is the same as the [n] at the end of *mine*. *Mine* can be singular or plural, depending on whether it refers to one thing or more than one (*Mine is red* (my sweater) or *mine are red* (my toenails)) and there is no reason why *none* should not behave the same way.

EXERCISE 13.

a. Identify the subject and the agreement marker in each sentence below, and explain why that marker was chosen. If you do not like the choice of agreement marker, explain the source of your discomfort.

i.   *All of the students have passed an exam.*

ii.   *Each of the students has passed an exam.*

iii.   *Some of the questions were very difficult.*

iv.   *Some of the material was very difficult.*

v.   *One of the questions was very difficult.*

vi.   *None of the questions were very difficult.*

vii.   *None of the material was very difficult.*

viii.   *Not one of the questions was difficult.*

ix.   *Every one of the questions was difficult.*

x.   *Every question was difficult.*

xi.   *Every student has passed the exam.*

    xii.   *Every Tom, Dick, and Harry has passed the exam.*
    xiii. *No student has ever passed this exam.*
    xiv. *No students have ever passed this exam.*

  b. Consult at least two usage handbooks to see what they tell you about the treatment of *every one* and *none* as singular or plural.

Still another source of confusion is the fact that some statements have an unusual word order, with the subject buried somewhere inside the sentence, rather than in its normal position at the beginning. To find the subject of an inverted statement, convert the sentence to a *yes/no* question: The word order will normalize automatically, and the subject will become apparent. For example, *Down the hill come the skiers* is an inverted sentence, with the subject NP (*the skiers*) at the end of the sentence. To find the subject, turn the sentence into a *yes/no* question:

      ***Do** the skiers Ø come down the hill?*

The subject of the sentence—*the skiers*—is the string of words that is surrounded by the two positions for the auxiliary.

EXERCISE 14. Use Subject-AUX Inversion to identify the subject and AUX in each of the following sentences. Once you have identified the subject, explain the choice of agreement marker:

    i.   *Near the intersection was a small cross.*
    ii. *Attached to the cross were the dog tags of the soldiers who were buried there.*

10.5.3 Problems with Tense

    A common fault in student writing is inconsistency of tense: A passage should normally maintain the same tense throughout.[12] One good way to practice this rule is by transposing a passage from one tense to another. For example, the James Joyce passage in Appendix Section I is written in past tense, but it can be transposed to present tense, as shown below. (Verbs whose tense has been changed from past to present have been highlighted in bold):

> *When the short days of winter **come**, dusk **falls** before we **have** well eaten our dinners. When we **meet** in the street the houses **have** grown sombre.*

12. But notice the use of present tense in the second sentence of the Samuel Eliot Morison passage in Appendix Section I: *For we now **admit** that the people whom **Columbus** mistakenly named Indians. . . .* This is because the author has momentarily stepped out of his past-tense narrative in order to make a comment about the beliefs of present-day historians.

*The space of sky above us **is** the colour of ever-changing violet and towards it the lamps of the street **lift** their feeble lanterns. The cold air **stings** us and we **play** till our bodies **glow**. Our shouts **echo** in the silent street.*

EXERCISE 15.

a. Change the Hemingway and Toni Morrison passages (Appendix Section I) from past tense to present tense. *Caution:* In each verb string, change *only* the element that carries the present or past tense marker (the first element of the verb string). Leave the rest of the verb string as it is. For example, you would change the verb string

> ***had*** *been crying*

to ***has*** *been crying*

Also, participles remain unchanged. For example, the passive participle *encouraged* does not change when the following sentence is changed to present tense:

Past tense: ***Encouraged*** *by her test results, she **applied** to dental school.*

Present tense: ***Encouraged*** *by her test results, she **applies** to dental school.*

b. The Rachel Carson and Lewis Thomas passages (Appendix Section I) are written in present tense. Change them to past tense.

c. The James Joyce passage (Appendix Section I) is written in past tense; change it to future.[13]

10.5.4 Passive Voice

Students are sometimes advised to avoid passive voice, as being *weaker* than the active (because of its suppression of the **<agent>** role). In fact, however, passive voice is common, particularly in expository writing. Contrary to what you may have been told, good writers do not avoid the passive voice, though they take care to use it appropriately. One purpose of the passive is to avoid mentioning the doer of an action—sometimes because this information is already known, sometimes because it is unnecessary or uninteresting, and sometimes because it might be embarrassing. The examples below are from Williams 1994, 72:

> *Valuable records should always be **kept** in a fireproof safe.*
> (We already know who should do this.)
> *Once this design was **developed** for our project, it was quickly **applied** to others.*
> (We already know who developed it, and we don't really care who applied it elsewhere.)
> *Those who are **found** guilty can be **fined**.*
> (We know who will do this—the court.)

---

13. In order to do this exercise, you will need to be aware that time clauses do not accept future forms but, instead, use present tense to refer to the future:

<u>When she **comes in**,</u> *we'll jump out and sing "Happy Birthday."*   (*when she **will come in**)
<u>Before we **know** it,</u> *it'll be summer.*   (*before we **will know** it)
<u>After they **leave**,</u> *we'll clean up the mess.*   (*after they **will leave**)

EXERCISE 16. Find the passive participle in each sentence below and say, in each case, what **\<agent\>** has been suppressed by the use of the passive, and why:

a. *The President has been criticized for his decision.*

b. *Although the windows had been left open, no one entered the premises.*

c. *No decision has been made yet about George.*

d. *Children are raised differently in other parts of the world.*

e. *Although we had not been invited to the meeting, we went anyway.*

Another common use of the passive is to move old information to the beginning, so that the sentence connects smoothly with the sentence before it. (This issue will be discussed further in Chapter 15.) For example, if we were talking about naval exploration in the 15th century, we might say (using active voice):

> *Then, in 1492, Columbus discovered America.*

But if we were talking about the situation of the Indians in America and how that was affected by the arrival of the Europeans, we would use passive voice, in order to put *America* in subject position:

> *Then, in 1492, America was discovered by Christopher Columbus.*

EXERCISE 17. You should be able to find eleven passive participles in the following excerpt from "The Rats on the Waterfront," by Joseph Mitchell. Be prepared to say something about why the passive voice is appropriate in each case. *Hint:* In order to find all the passive participles in the passage, you will need to be aware that passive participles appear not only as complements to *be*~pass~, but also as noun modifiers, as in line 6 below: *tightly **packed** clay.*

1   *The brown rat is distributed all over the five boroughs [of New York City]. It*
2   *customarily nests at or below street level—under floors, in rubbishy basements,*
3   *and in burrows. There are many brownstones and red-bricks, as well as many*
4   *commercial structures, in the city that have basements or sub-basements with*
5   *dirt floors; these places are rat heavens. The brown rat can burrow into the hard-*
6   *est soil, even tightly packed clay, and it can tunnel through the kind of cheap*
7   *mortar that is made of sand and lime. To get from one basement to another,*
8   *it tunnels under party walls; slum-clearance workers frequently uncover a*
9   *network of rat tunnels that link all the tenements in a block. Like the magpie,*
10   *it steals and hoards small gadgets and coins. In nest chambers in a system of*
11   *tunnels under a Chelsea tenement, workers recently found an empty lipstick*
12   *tube, a religious medal, a skate key, a celluloid teething ring, a belt buckle,*
13   *a shoehorn, a penny, a dime, and three quarters. Paper money is sometimes*
14   *found. When the Civic Repertory Theatre was torn down, a nest constructed*

15 *solely of dollar bills, seventeen in all, was discovered in a burrow. Extermina-*
16 *tors believe that a high percentage of the fires that are classified as "of undeter-*
17 *mined origin" are started by the brown rat. It starts them chiefly by gnawing the*
18 *insulation off electric wires, causing short circuits. It often uses highly inflam-*
19 *mable material in building nests. The majority of the nests in the neighbor-*
20 *hood of a big garage, for example, will invariably be built of oily cotton rags.*

From Up in the Old Hotel by Joseph Mitchell, copyright © 1992 by Joseph Mitchell. Used by permission of Pantheon Books, a division of Random House, Inc.

10.6 Applications for ESL Teachers

For speakers of other languages, our tense and auxiliary system is one of the most difficult parts of our grammar. Traditional ESL curricula were built around the tense/auxiliary system, beginning with the present progressive and simple present and working through the other forms one by one. Modern communicative approaches take a less systematic approach, but there are parts of the system that will still need direct, conscious attention. Here are some areas of difficulty:

1. Agreement. English subject-verb agreement is difficult even for students with agreement systems in their own languages: Because we have no subject-verb agreement in past tense,[14] or when the verb string begins with a modal, it is hard to remember the *-s* suffix on present-tense verbs with a 3rd-person singular subject. Students will say *She **know** the answer* instead of *She **knows** the answer*, or, conversely, will apply the *-s* suffix, erroneously to a verb string that begins with a modal: *He **cans** swim* instead of *He can swim*. *Yes/no* questions add an additional confusion, with the agreement marker on the auxiliary rather than on the main verb; students may write *__Does__ she **knows** the answer* instead of ***Does** she **know** the answer*. Pronunciation adds another difficulty; students whose languages do not allow final consonant clusters will find it hard to pronounce consonant clusters like the [mps] at the end of the verb *jumps*. Finally, there are three irregular 3rd-person singular forms—*has* (not **haves*), *is* (not **bes*),[15] and *does*, pronounced [dʌz] not [du:z].

2. Present Tense. In addition to the agreement marking in this tense, ESL students also have difficulty with its *meaning*. Unlike most other languages, English does not use the simple present tense to talk about an action that is taking place at the present moment; the sentence *Farhat speaks English* refers to an action that Farhat performs regularly and habitually, not one that he is performing right now. To talk about an event that is taking place in the present moment, we use the present progressive (*He **is speaking** English right now*) not the simple present (**He **speaks** English right now*).

But there is an exception: "Stative" verbs such as *know, have,* and *see,* which indicate states of affairs rather than events or actions, *do* use the simple present tense to refer to the present moment: *I know the answer (right now); She has a cut on her cheek (right now); We see the*

---

14. Except for the verb *be*, which does make a singular/plural distinction in past tense (*was* vs. *were*).
15. Of course, the verb *be* is irregular in almost *all* its forms.

entrance (*right now*). Stative verbs do not normally accept progressive aspect: **I'm knowing the answer; *She's having a cut on her cheek; *We're seeing the entrance.*

3. Past Tense. The past tense is relatively simple in its meaning—it refers to an event that took place either once or repeatedly at some time in the past, or a state of affairs that was true in the past. The chief difficulty of this tense is the fact that many common verbs have irregular the past-tense forms: *held, knew, ran, spoke, fell, slept, swam,* etc., not **holded, *knowed, *runned, *speaked, *falled, *sleeped,* or **swimmed*). In addition, students from most language backgrounds have difficulty pronouncing the complex consonant clusters that arise in the regular past tense forms: *rubbed* [rʌbd], *asked* [æskt], etc.

4. Perfect Aspect. The perfect forms (*have left, had left*) share the same difficulty as the past tense, namely that many verbs are irregular in this form (*have held, have known, have spoken, have fallen, have slept,* etc.), and those that are *regular* are often difficult to pronounce. In addition, it is hard to understand the *meaning* of the construction. The present perfect is like the past tense in that it refers to an event or situation that began in the past, but it contains an additional meaning, namely, that the situation or event—or at least the effects of the situation or event—continues into the present. For example, if I say *I lost my wallet* (past tense), I am simply telling you something that happened in the past, but if I say *I have lost my wallet*, I have added the additional information that I am still suffering from the effects of this loss: I have not yet replaced my drivers' license or my credit cards, and I may need to borrow some money to pay for dinner.

EXERCISE 18. Explain the difference in meaning between the following pairs of sentences, including when you might use each one:
a. *It rained all afternoon* vs. *It has rained all afternoon.*
b. *I had two years' experience as a teachers' aide* vs. *I have had two years' experience as a teachers' aide.*

5. Passive Voice. The passive participle (which is homonymous with the perfect participle) is frequently irregular (*was held, was known, was spoken, was slept in,* etc.). In addition, ESL students have the same difficulty as native speakers in knowing how to use passive voice appropriately. (See Section 10.5.4 above).

6. Modality. The meanings of the modals are often very subtle and, to make things more difficult, each modal has several *different* meanings: *We thought it **would** rain; she **would** sometimes sing us to sleep; **Would** you hand me that towel?* The use of modals in conditional sentences is often taught explicitly, as follows:

The "first" conditional:	*If I **pass** the exam, I **will apply** to dental school.*
The "second" conditional:	*If I **passed** the exam, I **would apply** to dental school.*
The "third" conditional:	*If I **had passed** the exam, I **would have applied** to dental school.*

EXERCISE 19.

a. Explain the meaning of the modal *would* in each of the following sentences: *We thought it **would** rain; she **would** sometimes sing us to sleep; **Would** you hand me that towel?*

b. Rank the following sentences in order of the probability they express; that is, which is most certain and which is most hypothetical?

   i.   *That will be Bill coming in now.*
   ii.   *That must be Bill coming in now.*
   iii. *That might be Bill coming in now.*
   iv.   *That should be Bill coming in now.*
   v.   *That could be Bill coming in now.*
   vi.   *That may be Bill coming in now.*
   vii. *That would be Bill coming in now.*

c. Translate each sentence of (b) into another sentence that expresses approximately the same degree of certainty but without a modal. For example, you might translate sentence (i) as follows: *Because I was expecting Bill to arrive at exactly this time, I have absolutely no doubt that he is the person we hear coming through the door.*

10.7 Summary of the Chapter

In this chapter we have observed that the main verb of an English sentence may be preceded by one or more auxiliaries, in the following order:

modal or tense/agreement marker   ($have_{perf}$) (be_{prog}) (be_{pass}) MV

The only obligatory elements are the main verb (MV) and either a modal auxiliary or a tense/agreement marker ([*past tense*], [*general present tense*], or [*3rd sg. present tense*]).

The tense/agreement marker, if present, appears on the first element of the verb string, whatever that may be. The form of each subsequent element is determined by the element that precedes it—the verb that follows a modal is in base form, the verb that follows $have_{perf}$ is in the perfect participle form, the verb that follows be_{prog} is in the present participle (-*ing*) form, and the verb that follows be_{pass} is in the passive participle form.

Semantically, the tense marker usually indicates the time frame in which the event or situation takes place, and the aspect marker, if present, indicates how that event or state of affairs is situated within its time. The modal auxiliaries indicate that an event or situation is not an objective fact, but is hypothetical in some way (*It might rain*). However, tense, aspect, and modality are very complex in English: Time can be indicated in other ways than by a tense marker—for example, by the modal auxiliary *will*; aspects such as the inchoative or the habitual are indicated by expressions such as *be about to* or *used to*, rather than by auxiliaries; and modality may be expressed by the past tense marker (*I wish I **knew***) or by an adverb such as *probably*, rather than by a modal auxiliary. The aspect marker $have_{perf}$ is often used to create a time sequence within a past-time narrative; this use of $have_{perf}$ is sometimes called "the past from the past."

The passive auxiliary be_{pass} has a different sort of meaning from the other auxiliaries, in that it does not refer to time or certainty but, instead, signals a change in the way the main verb (the predicate) passes out its semantic roles.

As applications for writers and teachers of writers, we have discussed some common issues concerning subject-verb agreement and inflectional forms for verbs, as well as consistency of tense and the appropriate use of the passive voice. For ESL teachers, we have discussed the considerable difficulty that this system poses for speakers of other languages—in memorizing our many irregular verb forms and learning what the various constructions mean.

CHAPTER 11

Interrogatives, Exclamatives, and Imperatives

11.1 Introduction

English, like other languages, has four types of sentences, classified according to function, as shown in Table 11.1. Up to now, we have been concerned, primarily, with declarative sentences. In this chapter, we turn to interrogatives, imperatives, and exclamatives.

11.2 *Yes/No Questions*

As we saw in Chapter 7, *yes/no* questions are formed by a transformation called *Subject-AUX Inversion* (SAI) which moves the head of the sentence (the AUX) to a position before the subject, identified here as C:

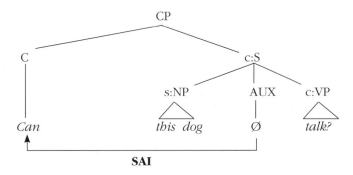

What is new in this diagram is the claim that the auxiliary moves into a position called *C*, which is the head of a higher-level constituent called *CP* or "clause." Note that the CP follows the normal

Table 11.1 Types of Sentences, According to Function

Declaratives		*Today is Tuesday.*
Imperatives		*Close the window.*
Exclamatives		*What big teeth you have, Grandmother!*
Interrogatives	*yes/no* questions	*Would you like another cookie?*
	WH-questions	*What are you doing?*

phrase structure for English, in that it consists of a head word *C* plus its complement *S* (a slightly defective *S* with a Ø where its AUX used to be).

Students often ask why this higher-level phrase is called *CP*. This notation developed in recognition of the similarity between the structure of a question and that of a dependent or subordinate clause:

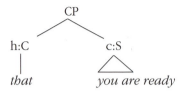

A subordinate clause is called *CP* (= clause) because its head word is a *C* (= subordinating conjunction). The "C" word gives two pieces of information about its clause:

1. Whether the clause is a main (independent) clause or a subordinate (dependent) clause.[1]
2. Whether the clause is declarative or interrogative.

If the "C" word is *that*, as in the example above, then the clause is a dependent, declarative clause. To create a dependent *interrogative* clause, we would need a different "C" word—*if* or *whether*. (*I wonder*) *if this dog can talk*. An independent declarative clause has nothing in the C position (*This dog can talk*), and an independent interrogative clause has its AUX in the C position. These four possibilities are set out in Table 11.2 on the following page.

EXERCISE 1. Draw tree diagrams of the interrogative sentences below, following the model on the preceding page:
a. *Can you find an answer?*
b. *Has the jury reached a verdict?*
c. *Is your refrigerator running?*
d. *Were the paintings stolen?*

11.3 The Main Verb *be*

The normal position for the verb is inside the VP, as in the sentence below, where the tense marker has attached to the verb by the transformation of Tense Hopping:

---

1. Main, or independent, clauses can stand alone as complete sentences. Subordinate, or dependent, clauses cannot stand alone; rather, they serve a function such as complement or modifier within a larger sentence. For example, in the sentence *I hope that you are ready*, the dependent clause *that you are ready* is the complement of the verb *hope*. The independent clause in this example is the whole sentence: *I hope that you are ready*.

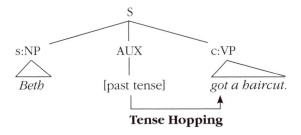

Tense Hopping

To convert this statement to a question, we pronounce the tense marker as *did* (by the rule of *Do*-Support), and move it to the C position (by Subject-AUX Inversion):

yes/no Question:

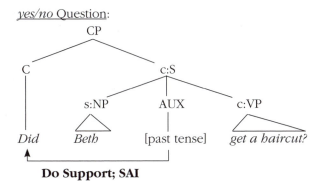

Do Support; SAI

Table 11.2 The "C" word determines the status of the clause

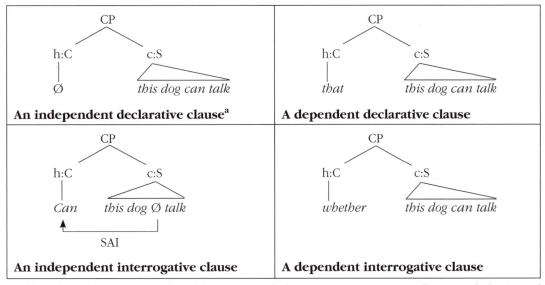

a. Although we have now established that ordinary declarative sentences are actually CPs with the C-word Ø, we will continue, for convenience, to represent them simply as S.

The verb *be* is an exception: If the verb is *be* and there is no overt auxiliary, then the verb *be* joins the tense marker in the AUX position, by a transformation called *Be* Raising:

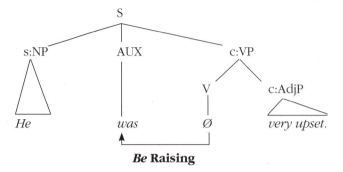

Be Raising

As a result of this transformation, the verb *was* is now the AUX as well as the main verb of the sentence.

To show that *was* is in AUX position, consider the emphatic and negative versions of this sentence: *He **was** very upset* (*emphatic*); *He was **not** very upset*. These sentences show that *was* behaves like any other AUX: To create the emphatic form, we stress the AUX (=*was*), and to create the negative form we insert the negative particle *not* right after the AUX (i.e., after *was*). The possible positions for the adverb *probably* (on either side of AUX) also support our contention that *was* is in AUX position (see Chapter 7, Section 7.6):

> *He **probably** was very upset.*
> *He was **probably** very upset.*

Finally, when we create a *yes/no* question from this sentence, it is the verb *was* (now in AUX position) that undergoes Subject-AUX Inversion:

yes/no Question:

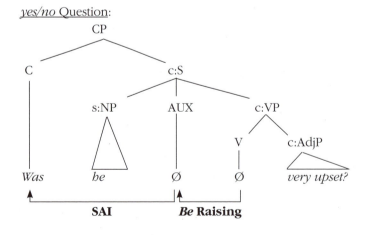

SAI   **Be Raising**

EXERCISE 2.

a. Draw tree diagrams for the following sentences, showing the effects of *Be* Raising and Subject-AUX Inversion:

   i.   *This is obviously a serious mistake.*

ii. *Is this a serious mistake?*

iii. *This is not a serious mistake.*

b. (Advanced) We said above that *be*-Raising does not take place if the AUX position is already occupied by an auxiliary, as in the sentence *This will be a serious mistake.* Use the emphatic, negative, and *yes/no*-question versions of this sentence to show that the verb *be* has not moved to the AUX position in this sentence. Give the relevant tree diagrams.

Historical Note

In most Indo-European languages, *all* verbs behave like the verb *be* in English. For example, in French and Spanish questions, the main verb moves to AUX and then to C.

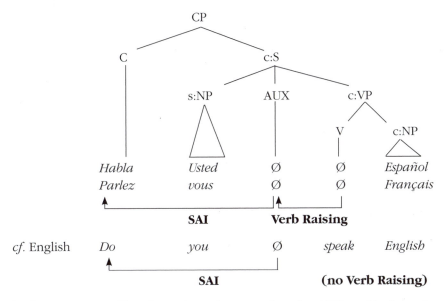

In French, the same point (that the main verb moves into the AUX position) can be made with the negative:

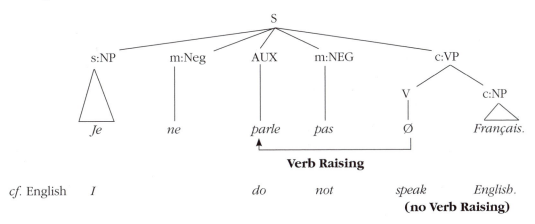

233

English was once like French and Spanish. That is why, in older versions of English, we find the negative particle *not* after the main verb, as in Patrick Henry's words:

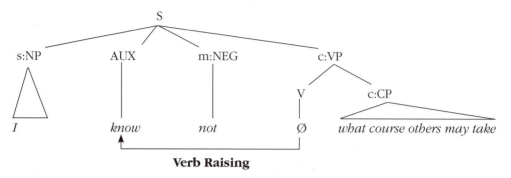

Verb Raising

(*but as for me, give me liberty or give me death.*)

The verb also moved to the front in questions, as in the following question from the *King James Bible* (Jesus speaking to Peter):

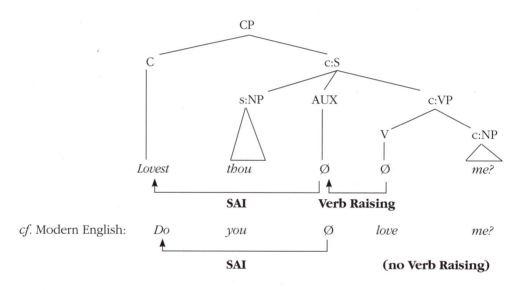

In present-day American English, the verb *be* is the only main verb that undergoes Verb Raising. However, the British maintain the old system with the main verb *have* as well as the main verb *be*; thus, where Americans say

> *Do you have the time?*　　and　　*I don't have the time.*

the British say

> *Have you the time?*　　and　　*I haven't the time.*

EXERCISE 3.

a. Draw tree diagrams for the British and American sentences above: *Have you the time? Do you have the time? I haven't the time. I don't have the time.*

b. Draw tree diagrams for the following sentences, showing what transformations have taken place. The transformations are as follows: *Be* Raising, Subject-AUX Inversion, Tense Hopping, *Do* Support, and Contraction.

i.	*Should we go?*	vi.	*I don't hear you.*
ii.	*Have they finished?*	vii.	*Do you hear me?*
iii.	*Will they have finished?*	viii.	*We are ready.*
iv.	*They will not have finished.*	ix.	*We are not ready.*
v.	*I hear you.*	x.	*Are we ready?*

11.4 WH-Questions

WH or *information* questions contain *WH-words* such as *who, whom, whose, what, which, where, why,* and *how.* In one type of WH-question, called an *echo* question, the WH-phrase maintains its normal position in the sentence:

> *You went **where**?*
> *You borrowed **whose** car?*
> *She said **what**?*
> *Your grandmother is **how** old?*

Echo questions are used to express puzzlement or dismay at what someone has just said.

Neutral WH-questions—simple requests for information—have a different structure: Here, the WH-phrase (the phrase containing the WH-word) is required to occupy initial position in the sentence:

> ***Where*** *did you go?*
> ***Whose car*** *did you borrow?*
> ***What*** *did she say?*
> ***How old*** *is your grandmother?*

If this requirement is not met by the normal word order,[2] then the WH-phrase must be *moved* to the front, by a transformation called *WH Fronting,* and the AUX must be moved into C position, to show that the clause is a question:

---

2. If the WH-phrase is the subject of the sentence, then the requirement that it must occupy first position is met automatically, and no transformation is needed:

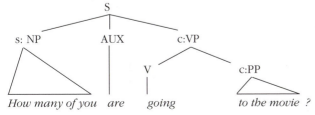

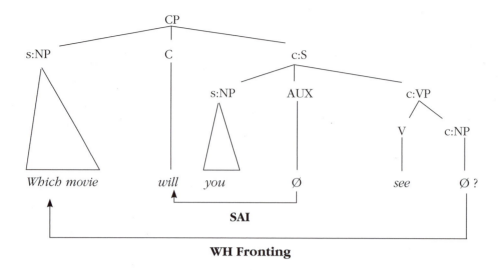

In the example above, the WH-phrase is a NP that originates as the complement of the verb *see*. However, AdjPs, AdvPs, and PPs can be moved, as well, as in the examples below:

WH-phrase = AdjP:

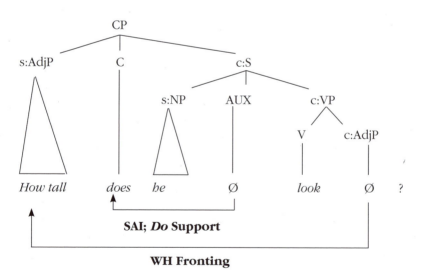

WH-phrase = AdvP:

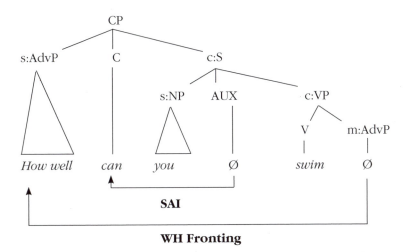

WH-phrase = PP:

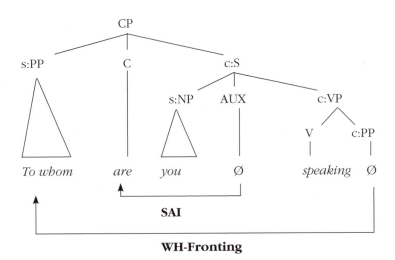

In the example above, the entire PP *to whom* is moved to the front; however, it is more common, in conversational English, to front just the *complement* portion of the PP, leaving the preposition *stranded*:

WH-phrase = NP:

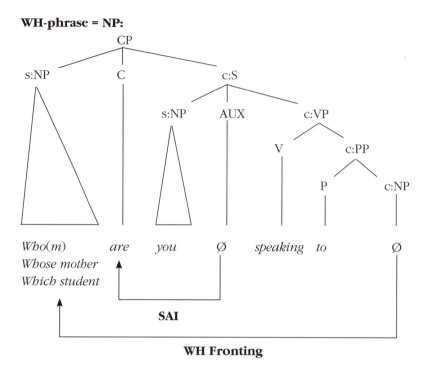

WH Fronting

EXERCISE 4. Draw tree diagrams of the following sentences, which have undergone WH Fronting and SUBJ-AUX Inversion:

a. *Who(m) should the parents call?*
b. *How old does he seem?*
c. *Who(m) will you stay with in Chicago?*
d. *What did Terry find?*
e. *What are you looking at?*
f. *What verdict did the jury reach?*
g. *What time is it?*
h. *How many hot dogs do you want?*
i. *What grade is she in?*
j. *How reliable are you?*

11.5 Exclamatives

Exclamatives such as *What big teeth you have, Grandmother!* also undergo WH-Fronting, but not Subj-AUX Inversion. Exclamatives have a "silent" C which we will represent as Ø:

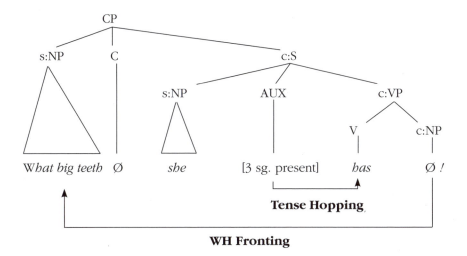

EXERCISE 5. Draw tree diagrams of the following exclamative sentences:

a. *What a nice job you did with this report!*

   (Caution: The *did* in this sentence is the past tense form of the main verb *do*.)

b. *How discouraged he looks!*

c. *How quickly they grow up!*

11.6 Imperatives

Imperatives have the same structure as statements, except that they have a silent AUX, and the subject may also be silent, in which case it is understood as *you*:

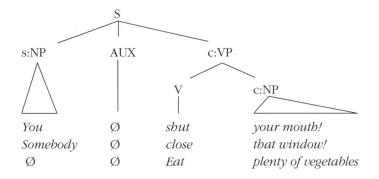

Notice that there is no Subj-AUX agreement in Imperatives; we say *Somebody please close that window,* not **Somebody please closes that window* (which would be a statement, rather than an imperative).

EXERCISE 6. Draw tree diagrams of the following imperative sentences:

a. *Have another cookie.*
b. *Give the man the money.*
c. *Everybody hold up your hands!*

11.7 Speech Acts: The Semantics of Declaratives, Interrogatives, Exclamatives, and Imperatives

When we speak directly and literally, the sentence-types *declarative, interrogative, exclamative*, and *imperative* are used to carry out the *speech acts* that are shown in Table 11.3. There are other speech acts, also, such as giving permission, making a request, giving a compliment, making a promise, and so forth, but those are not linked to particular sentence types.

When a speech act is performed by a sentence of the designated type—for example, when the interrogative sentence *Do you have a ballpoint pen?* is used to ask a *yes/no* question—the utterance is called a *direct speech act*. But in real conversation sentences are often used *indirectly*, to perform speech acts other than the ones they represent literally. For example, if you tell me that you couldn't turn in your assignment because your printer is not working, I might use the sentence *Do you have a ballpoint pen?* not as a question, but as a suggestion that there are alternative methods for producing an assignment. This is called an *indirect speech act*. Because my sentence isn't intended as a request for information, I don't expect you to respond with a *yes* or *no* answer, but with an apology for having made so little effort to carry out your assignment. The contrast between direct and indirect speech acts is illustrated in Table 11.4.

Table 11.3   Speech Acts and Sentence Types

Sentence Type	Speech Act	Example
Declarative	Stating a fact	*Christmas comes but once a year.*
Interrogative	Asking a question	*Do you live on campus?*
Imperative	Giving a command	*Close the door.*
Exclamative	Making an emotional comment	*What nice children you have!*

Table 11.4   Direct and Indirect Speech Acts

Purpose of Speech Act	Direct Speech Act	Indirect Speech Act
To ask the time	*What time is it?*	*I wonder what time it is.* *Do you know what time it is?*
To ask someone to pass the salt	*Please pass the salt.*	*Can you reach the salt?* *Is there any salt?* *I wonder if I could have the salt.*
To state a fact	*There are 4617 islands in Maine.*	*Did you know that there are 4617 islands in Maine?*

EXERCISE 7. Give the literal meaning of each sentence in the Indirect Speech Act column in Table 11.4. For example, the sentence *I wonder what time it is* is literally a statement indicating that a certain question is present in my mind.

Indirect speech acts are a puzzling phenomenon. If I want to ask you what time it is, why don't I just say *What time is it?* And if I ask *Do you know what time it is?*, how do you know that I will not be satisfied with the answer *Yes, I do?* In the theory developed by the philosopher John Searle, our ability to use and understand indirect speech acts derives from our knowledge of a set of *appropriateness conditions* that define when each speech act can be performed. Some appropriateness conditions for statements are listed below:

Appropriateness conditions for stating a fact
(*S* = *speaker*, *H* = *hearer*)
1. S knows this fact to be true.
2. The fact is relevant to the conversation.
3. S believes H does not know this fact.
4. S believes H will be interested.

Thus, for example, if I (the speaker) state that there are 4617 islands in Maine, then, by Condition 1, you (the hearer) have a right to assume that I have obtained this information from some reliable source—in other words, I know what I am talking about. Furthermore, by Condition 2, the statement must be relevant to our conversation—I can't make a statement like this right out of the blue. Condition 3 says that you, the hearer, are not an expert on Maine geography, since in that case you would know this fact already, and I would have no business telling it to you. However, by Condition 4, you must have some sort of interest in islands or in the state of Maine—otherwise I would have no *reason* to tell you.

Some appropriateness conditions for questions and commands are listed below:

Appropriateness conditions for asking a question
1. S does not know the answer to the question.
2. S believes H knows the answer.
3. S believes that H is willing to tell him/her.
4. S wants to know the answer.
5. S would like H to tell him/her.

Appropriateness conditions for giving a command
1. S has authority over H with respect to this matter.
2. S believes H is capable of carrying out the command.
3. S wants H to do this.

EXERCISE 8. Following the models above, list appropriateness conditions for two other speech acts: giving permission and making a request.

Following Searles's (1974) theory, we can explain an indirect speech act as an attempt to avoid one or more of the appropriateness conditions for the speech act that the speaker intends to perform. For example, if I ask *Do you know what time it is?* instead of *What time is it?*, that may be because I am uneasy about Appropriateness Conditions 2 and 5 for questions (*S believes that H knows the answer*; *S wants H to tell him/her*); I don't want to put you on the spot by demanding information that you cannot give me. By asking a *yes/no* question, instead, I make it possible for you to give an appropriate answer (*No, I don't*) even if you don't have the information I want.

Turning now to the other participant in the conversation, how do you, the hearers, know that when I ask, *Do you know what time it is?* I really mean *What time is it?* In other words, how do you know to respond *It's three o'clock* rather than *Yes, I do*? The answer lies, again, in the appropriateness conditions for questions. According to Appropriateness Condition 4, I would not *really* ask a question unless I wanted to know the answer. But why would I care whether you know the time or not? The only reason I would be interested in this information is that I want to know whether you can tell me the time. So, you conclude, that is what I really want, and you respond accordingly: *Yes, it's three o'clock.*

EXERCISE 9.

a. The imperative form can seem abrupt and rude, and even a *request* may seem somewhat demanding in American culture, where people are normally expected to accede to requests. Thus we are likely to speak indirectly when giving commands or making requests, using a question or statement that the hearer *interprets* as a command or request.

All the following sentences can be interpreted as commands or requests. For each sentence, explain first the literal meaning of the sentence; then say what request the sentence can be understood to make and how H knows to interpret the sentence as a request. For example, sentence (i) is literally a *yes/no* question inquiring about H's ability to reach the salt, but it can be understood as a request to pass the salt. The reason is that sentence (i) does not meet Appropriateness Condition 4 for questions, because the information is of no possible interest unless S wants H to pass the salt.

   i.   *Can you reach the salt?*
   ii. *It's awfully hot in here.*
   iii. *You've already had three beers.*
   iv. *The garbage is full.*
   v.   *Would it be out of your way to stop by the grocery store?*

b. Sometimes a question acts indirectly as a statement, or a statement acts indirectly as a question. For the following sentences, first identify the literal meaning of the sentence; then explain its *understood* meaning and what the speaker gains by speaking indirectly. In other words, if I want to tell you how many islands there are in Maine, why don't I say so directly, using a declarative sentence?

   i.   *Did you know that there are 4617 islands in Maine?*
   ii. *I wonder what time it is.*

c. What is the literal meaning of the sentence below, and how is it understood in conversation? Why do you think the speaker chose to speak indirectly? Why isn't it rude to use the imperative form in this situation?

   Have another piece of cake! (as he passes you the plate)

d. Since the usual purpose of a question is to gain information, one of the appropriateness conditions for a question is that the speaker does not know the answer. However, this condition is sometimes violated. One thing children have to learn when they go to school is that *teachers* often ask questions whose answers they already know; these are not real questions, but rather a teaching technique that many teachers use. What is the purpose of the questions in the Samuel Eliot Morison passage in Appendix Section I?

11.8 The Cooperative Principle of Conversation

When people communicate with one another, they follow a *cooperative principle* which, according to the philosopher H. Paul Grice (1975), includes a tacit understanding between speaker and hearer that the speaker will be truthful, relevant, concise, and clear, and will give all the information that is necessary for the situation. In addition, speakers and hearers usually cooperate by taking turns as they converse, by being as agreeable as they can, and by trying to understand and respond to the speaker's *intended* meaning, rather than what he literally said. (That is why, when someone asks you *Do you know what time it is?*, you cannot answer simply *Yes, I do.* You have to answer *Yes, I do; it's three o'clock* or *No, I'm sorry, I don't.*)

EXERCISE 10. Read through the conversation from Hemingway's "Hills Like White Elephants" in Appendix Section VII. Although the participants in this conversation take turns, as they should, their conversation is not very cooperative in other respects. Something is clearly wrong between them.

Go through the conversation to find instances where the speakers do or do not respond cooperatively to one another. (That is, look carefully at each utterance to see what the speaker intended to say; then look to see whether the other participant responded appropriately to that intent.) For the responses that you identify as uncooperative, say what is uncooperative about them, and suggest what the speaker might have said if he/she were in a more cooperative mood.

11.9 Applications for Teachers

In this section we will look first at some issues in the acquisition and usage of questions, and then at some possible applications of the notion of Speech Acts.

11.9.1 The Development of Interrogatives

Statements and imperatives come easily to children, and they can also ask questions at an early age, using the intonation of their voice. But the grammatical form for questions is slower to emerge—perhaps because it depends on the acquisition of auxiliary verbs, which children take a long time to acquire.

EXERCISE 11. Look at the examples of children's speech in Appendix Section VIII.

a. At 18 months Eve already knows how to ask *yes/no* and WH-questions. Give examples. How can you tell that she is asking a question?

b. One example from Eve's 27-month sample suggests that she is now learning how to apply Subject-AUX Inversion and WH-Fronting in interrogative sentences. Find that example, and give a diagram to show that Eve has apparently applied these two transformations.

c. Julia, at 36 months, knows how to form both *yes/no* and WH-interrogatives (with a variety of WH words). Give examples. However, like many children of this age, she sometimes forgets to perform Subject-AUX Inversion in WH-questions. Give examples to show this immaturity in Julia's mastery of question formation in English.

11.9.2 Two Usage Issues in WH-Questions

Older students, even adults, still struggle with two issues in forming WH-questions—(a) when/whether to use *whom*, and (b) whether a preposition can be left stranded at the end of the sentence. With regard to *who* vs. *whom*, this choice is traditionally determined by the basic position of the WH-word in the sentence: If the WH-word comes from a subject position, choose *who*; if it comes from a complement position, choose *whom*. For example, the traditional rule tells us to choose *whom* in (a) (***Whom** should the parents call Ø?*) and (b) (***Whom** will you stay with Ø in Chicago?*) because in (a) the WH-word is the complement of the verb *call,* and in (b) it is the complement of the preposition *with*. But in the sentence *Who do you think Ø will call me first?*, the only possible choice is *who*, because the WH-word is the subject of the dependent clause *(who) will call me first*. However, if you find it difficult to follow this rule, my advice is to choose *who*, because ****Whom** do you think Ø will call me first?* is a seriously malformed sentence, while ***Who** should the parents call?*, though it violates the traditional rule, is not malformed but only informal. In present-day English, *whom* is absolutely obligatory only when it immediately follows the preposition of which it is the complement: ***With whom** have you discussed your plans?*, not ****With who** have you discussed your plans Ø?*

EXERCISE 12. Choose *who* or *whom* in each of the following sentences, and explain the reason for your choice:

a. *Who/whom are you staring at?*

b. *Who/whom do you think is better qualified for the position?*

c. *Who/whom will be chosen as "best-dressed student in the class"?*

d. *To who/whom have you disclosed this information?*

e. *Will whoever/whomever left this message on the blackboard please contact the English Department Office?*

f. *Who/whom is bringing the refreshments?*

g. *Who/whom should I say is calling?*

h. *I'll go with whoever/whomever is kind enough to invite me.*

Our second question—whether a preposition can be left "stranded" at the end of the sentence—is an issue that often worries writers. For many of my students, *Never end a sentence with a preposition* is the one grammatical "rule" they remember from their schooldays. Luckily they do not always recognize a preposition when they see one! (You may have heard Winston Churchill's famous rejoinder when he was criticized for violating this "rule": *This is nonsense, up with which I will not put.*)

In fact, the treatment of prepositional phrases in WH-fronting is more complicated than most people realize. When the prepositional phrase is a *complement* of the verb, the preposition is usually left behind: ***Which formula** are they looking **at?*** rather than ?***At which formula** are they looking?*[3] This is especially true if the question is embedded inside a larger sentence: *I wonder* [***which formula** they are looking **at**], not **I wonder* [***at which formula** they are looking*]. However, when the prepositional phrase is an adverbial modifier, it is often better to front the entire phrase, especially in formal English; ***At what concentration** does this substance become toxic?* is much better than *****What concentration** does this substance become toxic **at?***, and this is true even when the question is embedded in a larger sentence: *We wanted to know* [***at what concentration** this substance becomes toxic*], not ??*We wanted to know* [***what concentration** this substance becomes toxic **at**].*[4]

The rule we have arrived at—*When performing WH-fronting, leave the preposition behind if the PP is a complement; bring it along if the PP is a modifier*—is, unfortunately, not an easy rule to follow, given the difficulty of distinguishing complements from modifiers (see Chapter 8, Section 8.6), and there are other complicating factors that have not been mentioned here. My advice to student writers, therefore, is to be aware of this issue and to try the sentence both ways: First move the entire PP and then try leaving the preposition behind; then choose the version that sounds better to your ear. If you are a native speaker of English, or even an advanced ESL learner, then, except for constructions where you *know* that your intuitions are unreliable, your sense of how a sentence sounds is almost always a better guide than a grammatical rule you think you know.[5] Human beings are extraordinarily talented at *using* grammatical systems, but not so talented at applying consciously learned grammatical rules.

11.9.3   Applications of Speech Act Theory

By the time they enter primary school, children can usually form interrogative sentences accurately, but they may not be familiar with all the ways that interrogative sentences are used in conversation. For example, when parents ask "Are you ready to go?" as a way of suggesting (indirectly) that it is *time* to go, young children may interpret this question directly and answer, simply, "No." Similarly, young children may be puzzled by the "display" questions that teachers

---

3. A question mark at the beginning of a sentence indicates that the sentence is unnatural, but not absolutely ungrammatical.

4. Preposition stranding is less acceptable in relative clauses than in interrogative clauses. The issue of preposition stranding in relative clauses will be discussed in Chapter 14 below.

5. There may be places where your ear is *not* a reliable guide for formal English. For example, the author of this text, who grew up in the South, is inclined to accept sentences such as *I told the children **for them** to move their toys off the front porch*, but she has learned from experience that this construction is not acceptable in New England, even in conversation.

ask in school. Since the normal function of an interrogative is to request information that the speaker does not know, the child may be puzzled when the teacher asks questions to which she clearly knows the answer, such as, "Which of these words begins with the letter <t>?" Parents and teachers should be aware of these potential misunderstandings and should not jump to the conclusion that the child is being uncooperative.

EXERCISE 13. "Rhetorical" questions are another exceptional use of the interrogative form—not to request information, but to draw attention to a topic that the speaker or writer is about to address. "What is causing this turmoil in the stock market?" the politician asks, to introduce the hypothesis that s/he is just about to propound. Find a rhetorical question in the passage from Samuel Eliot Morison in Appendix Section I, and explain its purpose.

English teachers have a responsibility to teach their students not only standard grammar and vocabulary, but also how to use language effectively to perform a variety of language functions: asking for information, making requests, apologizing for error, turning down invitations. Students can be asked to identify situations where they struggle with what to say—for example, what to say in a job interview, how to ask for a raise in pay, how to say "no" to a request—and teachers should also take note of problem areas that they observe in class: how to speak to the principal, how to give constructive criticism of a classmate's work, how to disagree with an opinion that has been expressed by a classmate. Teachers can talk with students about these issues, have them observe how various speech acts are carried out (often indirectly) in literature and in real life, and give them opportunities to practice in the classroom—by role plays, dramatic skits, formulating "rules" for class discussion, and so forth.

11.10 Applications for ESL Teachers

ESL students have the same issues as native-speakers in forming interrogative sentences and in learning to perform a variety of speech acts. However, ESL students encounter additional difficulties that native speakers do not.

11.10.1 Forming Interrogative Sentences

The grammar of interrogative sentences is difficult for ESL students, just as it is for children who are learning English as their first language (see Sections 11.9.1 and 11.9.2 above). For students whose first language forms questions by using special "C" words, rather than by moving constituents from one place to another, the English rules of Subject-AUX Inversion and WH-fronting will be a source of great frustration. Even students from European languages that use our same rules for question formation (see the "Historical Note" in Section 11.3a above) will struggle with our rule of *Do*-Support, which provides a pronounceable AUX for sentences which otherwise have none. ESL students will ask questions such as *Do she knows the answer? What do she wrote?* and *What means this word?*

To address this issue, students must be given models, over time, in how questions are formed in all the various verb forms, and they need a great deal of practice in order to internalize those patterns. It can be hard to practice questions in a traditional classroom, because the pattern of conversation typically flows from the teacher, who asks the questions, to the students, who try to answer. Teachers have to set up opportunities for students to practice questions by, for example, asking them to review an expository passage whose content is already familiar and write a study question for each paragraph. Or students can be asked to make a short presentation to their classmates, followed by a list of questions to test their classmates' comprehension of the talk. For *communicative* practice (exercises in which interrogative sentences are used to solicit new information), students can play games like Twenty Questions or can prepare a list of questions to ask a visitor who will be coming to their class. The teacher can also insist on accurate formulation of questions that are asked repeatedly in the classroom; for example, I would refuse to answer the question *What means this word?* until the student reformulates her question as *What does this word mean?*

Finally, it should be pointed out that ESL students find it difficult to *understand* WH-questions, because the questioned item has been moved out of its normal position in the sentence. In situations where it is important for the student to understand what is being asked, the questioner can rephrase the sentence as an "echo" question: *Which exercise did you do?* ⇒ *You did which exercise?* In the end, however, the students will have to learn to understand WH-questions in their normal word order; this will require practice and patience.

11.10.2 Speech Act Theory in ESL

An understanding of speech acts is particularly important for ESL teachers; in fact, ESL courses are sometimes *organized* around the notion of speech acts, using a "functional-notional syllabus." The term "notional" refers to concepts such as quantity, time, location, and probability, which students are taught to express in various ways, and the term "functional" refers to an extended list of the speech acts that we have been talking about—asking for information, making requests, agreeing and disagreeing, answering the telephone, etc., as well as "conversational strategies" such as how to get someone's attention, how to start or end a conversation, and how to compensate for the fact that you can't remember a word.

No matter how your own course is organized, you must find ways to teach your students how to handle common speech situations in English. For example, many ESL students assume that a simple "please" attached to an imperative sentence is enough to make a request polite (*Please sign this document for me*), and they may find it difficult to be sufficiently indirect (*I'm wondering if it might be possible for you to sign this document for me, if you're not too busy*)!

One technique is to observe how speech acts are carried out in literary selections or in films and have the students do brief dramatic performances of these scenes. (This exercise provides very good pronunciation practice, as well.) Or you can work with the students to construct a list of strategies and suggested wording for a difficult social situation such as refusing an invitation, and then let them create role plays of their own. (I would suggest reviewing the role plays with the students before they perform them for the class, so that those that are finally presented provide reasonably good models.) Wording for situations that come up frequently in class can be displayed on posters on the wall—for example, a list of expressions for disagreeing tactfully with a classmate's stated opinion. Non-verbal gestures are also important. These differ from one culture to another and can sometimes cause misunderstanding, as when a Latin American child looks away from the teacher who is talking to her. For the child, this is a sign of respect, not sullenness, as we tend to interpret it in our culture.

11.11 Summary of the Chapter

In this chapter, we have looked at interrogative, imperative, and exclamative sentences, and have concluded that they have the same structure as declarative sentences, except that some constituents of the sentence have been moved to other positions (for interrogatives and exclamatives) or have been left to be "understood" (for imperatives). We saw that declarative, interrogative, and exclamative sentences are part of a larger structure,[6] called a CP or "clause," where the "C" word of the CP (which may be Ø) indicates whether the clause is an independent or dependent clause, and whether it is declarative or interrogative.

In considering the semantics of these four sentence types, we introduced the notion of "speech acts"—how sentences are used to carry out functions such as asking for information, stating a fat, or making a request. Each of the four basic sentence types is associated with a particular speech act—declarative sentences with statements, interrogative sentences with questions, and imperative sentences with directives (commands or requests). However, as we saw, language is often used indirectly: Sentences are often used to perform speech acts other than the ones with which they are directly correlated, as when the declarative sentence "You've already had three beers" is used as a request not to have any more, or the *yes/no* interrogative "Do you have the time?" is used with the meaning of a WH-interrogative: "What time is it?" This use of language was the subject of a famous study by the philosopher John Searle, whose theory of speech acts attempts to explain why we so often speak indirectly, and how our listeners understand what we really mean.

As applications for teachers, we considered the development of interrogative sentences in children's speech, and addressed two usage issues for older students: the choice between *who* and *whom*, and whether a preposition can be "stranded" at the end of the sentence. We also discussed some applications of speech act theory—making sure that children understand what is being said to them, and helping older students develop the linguistics skills to handle difficult social situations. For ESL teachers, we pointed out the structural complexity of English questions and suggested some techniques for giving students the practice they need in forming questions. Finally, we discussed some techniques for teaching ESL students to perform various speech "functions" in American English.

---

6. Imperative sentences probably also have a "C" word (Ø), but we have ignored that possibility here.

CHAPTER 12

Variation in English

Language is not an abstract construction of the learned, or of dictionary-makers, but is something arising out of the work, needs, ties, joys, affections, tastes, of long generations of humanity, and has its bases broad and low, close to the ground.

—Walt Whitman, *Slang in America*, 1892

12.1 Introduction

In this chapter, we will take a short break from our investigation of English syntax in order to apply the concepts that we have already covered to the topic of *variation* in English—including differences between spoken and written English, and differences among regional and social dialects. We will return to our syntactic analysis in chapters 13 and 14, which deal with the grammar of compound and complex sentences.

12.2 Dialects

Language changes over time, as we have seen, because of changes in culture, influences from other languages, and, most of all, because of the adjustments children make as they acquire the language, generation after generation. When speakers of a language are in close contact with one another, changes made by one group spread to other groups as well, so that the language remains uniform despite historical change. However, if two groups become separated, then as time goes on they develop separate dialects, and if they continue to be separated, then they eventually develop separate languages. That is what happened when Indo-European divided into Celtic, Germanic, Italic, Hellenic, and so forth, and again when Germanic split into Danish, Swedish, Norwegian, German, Dutch, and English.

Whether two varieties are classified as distinct dialects or distinct languages depends, in principle, on whether they are mutually intelligible: If two speakers can understand one another, then they are speaking the same language. In real life, however, the classification of language varieties is partly a political decision. For example, Swedish and Norwegian are largely mutually intelligible, but they are classified as separate languages because they are identified, politically, with two different countries. And many of us have met speakers of English whose speech was almost unintelligible to us but whom we consider, nevertheless, to be speaking a dialect of English.

12.3 Regional Dialects

One source of dialect differences is geographical separation. American English is different from British English and Australian English, and there are further differences *within* each of these countries. These dialects differ in pronunciation, vocabulary, and syntax. For example, American English differs from British English in that (except along the East Coast) Americans pronounce [r] after a vowel, as in *car*, *poor*, and *over*. American English also exhibits a pronunciation regularity

249

called the *flap rule* which causes [t] to merge with [d] between a stressed and an unstressed vowel. Thus the word-pairs *latter* and *ladder, waited* and *waded, otter* and *odder* are homophones in American English but not in British English.

American and British English also differ in vocabulary; for example, what Americans call *gasoline,* the British call *petrol,* and what Americans call an *apartment* the British call a *flat.* Finally, there are a few syntactic differences between British and American English; for example, as we have seen, the main verb *have* acts as an AUX in British English (that is, it undergoes the rule of *Be* Raising, which we discussed in Chapter 11):

Have *you* Ø   Ø   *the time?*   (*cf.* Am. Eng   **Do** *you*   Ø   *have the time?*)

EXERCISE 1.

a. Listen to a speaker of British English in person, in a film, or on TV, and identify one or two additional differences between British and American English.

b. There are some *spelling* differences (introduced by Noah Webster) between British and American English. Give examples.

c. Translate these British vocabulary items into American English. If necessary, use your dictionary or consult a friend:

lorry	*spanner*	*bonnet* (of a car)	*knock up*
loo	*bobby*	*boot* (of a car)	*biro*
biscuits	*nappy*	*chemist's shop*	*dustbin*
pram	*pub*	*trunk call*	*cinema*

There are also regional differences *within* American and British English. People from different parts of the U.S.—Southerners, New Englanders, New Yorkers, Chicagoans, Wisconsinites, Californians—are often recognizable by their pronunciation. Those of us who live on the East Coast tend to *r*-drop, like the British. A New Yorker may make a three-way distinction among the vowel sounds [ô] *law,* [ä] *father,* and [ŏ] *box,* while a Californian pronounces all three vowels exactly the same. Southerners and Midwesterners often treat *pen* and *pin, hem* and *him* as homophones (that is, they merge the vowel sounds [ĕ] and [ĭ] before nasal consonants). For Chicagoans, the vowel sound [ă] of *bad* closely approaches the pronunciation other Americans give to the [ĕ] of *bed.* Wisconsinites have a distinctive pronunciation of the vowel sounds [ā] and [ō].

Regional dialects also differ in vocabulary; whether you say *sneakers* or *tennis shoes, a sack of groceries* or *a bag of groceries* depends primarily on where you live. If you have traveled to other regions of the country, then you can probably add examples of your own. However, American regional dialects show very little variation when it comes to syntax. A few examples that can be observed are the use of double modals in Appalachian English (*I **might could** go*), a second person plural pronoun (*y'all*) in Southern dialects, and the short answer *so don't I* instead of *so do I* in eastern New England.

EXERCISE 2.

a. Use a dictionary and/or your own experience to identify the geographical locations in which the following expressions are used:

    i.   *tennis shoes* vs. *sneakers*

    ii.   *a sack of groceries* vs. *a bag of groceries*

    iii. *a bubbler* vs. *a water fountain*

    iv. *a cabinet* vs. *a frappe* vs. *a milkshake*

    v.   *hose* vs. *stockings* vs. *nylons*

    vi. *a teeter-totter* vs. *a see-saw*

    vii. *an elastic* vs. *a rubber band*

   viii. *lightning bugs* vs. *fireflies*

    ix. *fixin' to* vs. *about to*

    x.   *sprinkles* vs. *jimmies*

    xi. *a belly buster* vs. *a belly flop*

b. List six additional regional differences that you are aware of in American English.

In Britain, with its much longer history as an English-speaking nation, rural communities were isolated for many centuries, so that regional differences had a greater opportunity to develop and become established. As a consequence, British regional dialects differ dramatically in pronunciation and vocabulary. Furthermore, unlike the situation in the United States, there are significant differences in syntax from one region to another. For example, some speakers in the north and west of England still use the old second person singular pronouns *thou, thee,* and *thy,* though these pronouns have disappeared in most other areas; in southwestern dialects, the pronouns *he, she, we,* and *they* can be used as objects of verbs, while the pronouns *him, her,* and *us* can be used as subjects:[1]

> *John saw **they**.*
> *Bill gave it to **she**.*
> ***Us** be a-goin.*
> ***Her** don't like it.*

Many dialects have nonstandard subject-verb agreement:

*He **like** her.* *She **want** some.*	East Anglia (eastern England)
*I **want**s it.* *We **like**s it.*	western and northern England
*I **like**s everybody.* *He's older than what I **be**.*	Somerset (southwestern England)

1. This information on British regional dialects is taken from Trudgill (1999) and Trudgill and Chambers, eds. (1991). The examples of the Somerset dialect are from Ihalainen (1991).

They also exhibit nonstandard past tense and past participle forms:

> *He **done** that wrong.*
> *I **give** her a birthday present yesterday.*
> *I **writ** a letter yesterday.*
> *Is that the car I **see/seed/sawed/seen**?*

and nonstandard auxiliary forms:

> **Cost** *lend us a quid? No, I **conna**.*   Staffordshire
>   'Can you (canst thou) lend me a pound? No, I can't.'
> *I **anna** done it*
>   'I haven't done it.'

> *I **divent** knao—I **might could** do it.*   Northumberland (northern England)
>   'I don't know—I might be able to do it.'
> *The girls usually make me some, but they **mustn't could've** made any today.*
>   'The girls usually make me some, but they must not have been able to make any today.'

As you can see, there is far greater regional variation in British English than in American English, especially in syntax. In American English, syntactic differences tend to be associated with social class rather than with region (see Section 12.5 below).

12.4 Spoken English *vs.* Written English

Spoken English is different from written English, and forms that are acceptable in the one are not necessarily acceptable in the other. For example, the following sentences would be decidedly odd in spoken English:

> *To whom have you given the money?*
> *They had, although they were hungry, refused all food.*
> *Behind me were my mother and my mother's friend.*
> *The quick, brown fox jumped over the lazy dog.*
> *While very hot indeed, the temperature never rose over 106°.*

Conversely, lexical expressions and syntactic constructions that are used in spoken English are not always acceptable in formal writing (unless the writer is trying to *represent* spoken English). For example, as we have seen, sentence fragments are common in conversation, but they are not always acceptable in writing. Written English also avoids slang expressions such as *awesome* 'very good' and colloquial expressions such as the word *pretty* used as an intensifier (*The play was **pretty** good*). One pervasive difference between the two varieties is the use of contractions. In spoken English, the negative particle *not* is almost always contracted onto the AUX:

	will	*not*	→	*won't*
You do the rest:	*would*	*not*	→	
	should	*not*	→	
	must	*not*	→	
	is	*not*	→	
	are	*not*	→	
	has	*not*	→	
	had	*not*	→	

The AUX (if not contracted with *not)* is contracted onto the subject:

	she	*will*	→	*she'll*
You do the rest:		*would*	→	
		is	→	
		has	→	
		had	→	
	they	*will*	→	
		would	→	
		are	→	
	they	*have*	→	
		had	→	

The AUX may also be contracted onto a preceding WH-word:

	who	*will*	→	*who'll*
You do the rest:		*would*	→	
		is	→	
		has	→	
	what	*will*	→	
		is	→	

and the auxiliary verb *have$_{perf}$* is contracted onto a preceding modal:[2]

	will	*have*	→	*will've*
You do the rest:	*would*	*have*	→	
	could	*have*	→	
	should	*have*	→	
	might	*have*	→	

---

2. Because the contracted *have* sounds like *of,* students sometimes write *would of* and *could of* instead of *would have* and *could have.*

In casual spoken English, we often use other *informal contractions* which have no standard spelling. The infinitive particle *to* may be contracted onto the preceding verb:

	have to	[hăft´ə]
You do the rest:	*has to*	
	want to	
	going to	
	got to	

A pronoun may be contracted onto a preceding verb:

	I told	*him*	[ĭm]
You do the rest:		*her*	
		them	
		you	

and a pronoun may be contracted onto a preceding AUX:

	Will	*he*	[wĭl´ē]
You do the rest:		*you*	
	Did	*he*	
		you	

Short function words, including *and, or, can,* and *of,* tend to be *reduced*:

*black **and** white*	[n̩]
*men **or** women*	[ər]
*I **can** go*	[kĭn]
*cup **of** coffee*	[ə]

and unstressed *ing* may be pronounced as [ĭn]:

something	[sŭm´ thĭn]
running	[rŭn´ ĭn]

Another common phenomenon in conversational English is the deletion of AUX in questions, and sometimes the subject pronoun *you,* as well:

Are you going?	→	*You goin'?* or *Goin'?*
Do you want another pancake?	→	*Want another pancake?*
Did you catch any fish?	→	*Catch any fish?*
Have they gone yet?	→	*They gone yet?*
Where are you going?	→	*Where you goin'?*

EXERCISE 3. Listen to the recording you made of a short conversation (Appendix Section VI). What contracted forms do you hear? Do you hear any examples of AUX Deletion in questions? What other characteristics (colloquial vocabulary and sentence structure, use of fragments, and so forth) mark your sample as spoken rather than written English?

12.5 Social-Class Dialects

12.5.1 Introduction

Geography is not the only thing that separates people; we are separated by social boundaries as well as geographical ones. Each social group has its own way of speaking. As children, we acquire the language of the group to which we belong, and unless we choose to change our station later in life, we maintain that dialect in adulthood; this is one of the ways we proclaim our identity.

As we noted earlier, social-class dialects are characterized not only by a distinctive pronunciation and vocabulary, but also, particularly, by syntax. The syntactic constructions listed in Section 12.5.2 below are characteristic of working-class dialects in both American and British English. As you read through this list, it is important to keep in mind that there is nothing inherently wrong or illogical about any of these constructions: All dialects of English follow a consistent set of rules that make sense from a linguistic point of view; otherwise, children couldn't learn to speak them! The judgements we make about these constructions are social judgements, not linguistic ones. Remember, also, that these are spoken dialects, not written ones; many people *speak* nonstandard dialects but use Standard English for writing. And many of us are bi-dialectal even in speech, switching back and forth between a standard and a nonstandard variety depending on the situation.

12.5.2 Some Characteristics of Working-Class American Dialects

a. Use of the third-person pronoun *them* as a determiner: *them shirts* for SAE *those shirts.* Standard American English (*SAE*) uses first- and second-person plural pronouns as determiners: *us kids, you students,* and so on, but does not accept third-person pronouns as determiners.

b. Nonstandard subject-AUX agreement, especially in the negative forms, as shown in Table 12.1[3]

c. Use of *ain't* where Standard English uses *am not, is not, are not, have not, has not:*

> She **ain't** here.
> He **ain't** come in yet.

Ain't was originally a contraction for *am not,* but has been extended, in some dialects, to include *is not, are not, have not,* and *has not.* It is now severely stigmatized and is no longer used in Standard English even with its original meaning, *am not.* This is unfortunate, since we *need* the contraction *ain't* in tag questions such as "I'm here, _____ I?" The banishment of *ain't* from Standard English has left us with no completely satisfactory way to complete this sentence—a fitting punishment for our snobbery!

---

3. Nonstandard subject-AUX agreement in the negative forms is a marker of social class; nonstandard subject-AUX agreement in the affirmative forms is more common in ethnic dialects (Section 12.6 below).

Table 12.1   Subject-AUX Agreement in Standard and Nonstandard English

Standard American English (SAE)	Nonstandard English		
I know	*I know*	*or*	*I **knows***
You know	*You know*	*or*	*You **knows***
*He/she/it **knows***	*He/she/it **know***	*or*	*He/she/it **knows***
We know	*We know*	*or*	*We **knows***
You know	*You know*	*or*	*You **knows***
They know	*They know*	*or*	*They **knows***
I don't smoke	*I don't smoke*		
You don't smoke	*You don't smoke*		
*He/she/it **doesn't** smoke*	*He/she/it **don't** smoke*		
We don't smoke	*We don't smoke*		
You don't smoke	*You don't smoke*		
They don't smoke	*They don't smoke*		

d. Negative Concord: Use of *no, none, nothing, nobody, no one, never* in negative contexts where SAE uses *any, anything, anybody, anyone,* and *ever:*

> *They didn't do **nothin** to **nobody**.* vs. *They didn't do **anything** to **anybody**.*
> *He ain't **never** gonna say it to his face.* vs. *He isn't **ever** going to say it to his face.*
> *We can't do **nothin.**.* vs. *We can't do **any**thing.*

The rule of Negative Concord is a sort of agreement rule: once the sentence is marked as negative, every word that can be marked as negative must be so marked. This rule is highly stigmatized in English, but it is the standard method of forming negatives in many languages of the world, including French and Spanish:

> French: *Je **ne** sais **rien**.*   Literally, 'I don't know nothing.'
> Spanish: ***No** se **nada**.*

e. Non-standard past tense or perfect participle:

> *Finally, she **come** in.*   (*come,* rather than *came,* as the past tense of *come*)
> *He **brang** me one.*   (*brang,* rather than *brought,* as the past tense of *bring*)
> *I **seen** him.*   (*seen,* rather than *saw,* as the past tense of *see*)
> *She's already **went**.*   (*went,* rather than *gone,* as the past participle of *go*)

256

f. Homonymy between adjectives and adverbs that are distinguished in SAE:

>   *You did **good**.*
>   *He talks too **slow**.*

SAE uses *fast* as either an adjective or an adverb (*A **fast** car goes **fast***), but uses *good* and *slow* only as adjectives; the adverb forms for Standard English are *well* and *slowly*.[4]

g. Object-case pronouns in subject position:

>   ***Him** and **me** are good friends.*

Native speakers of English have no intuitions about the assignment of case in coordinate structures (NPs joined with *and* or *or*). As children, we tend to use the object-case forms (*him* and *me*), and this form persists in many dialects, but in communities that speak Standard English, we are told by our parents and teachers to say ***He and I** are good friends*. We accept this correction but then make the opposite error: *This is between **he and I**.*

EXERCISE 4.   The characters in the following literary excerpts speak English that is marked by both regional and social-class features. Find examples of Negative Concord, Nonstandard Subject-Verb Agreement, *ain't*, and the use of *them* as a determiner. You should also be able to find informal contractions, as well as words and expressions that are typical of regional or social-class dialects. In what region of the country do people use the expression "fixin' to"? In what region did family members traditionally address the adult male of the family as "Father"? *Caution:* Be sure to distinguish between the language of the narrator and the language of the characters (called "dialog"). In this exercise you should concern yourself only with the quoted dialog of the characters.

1   *Anse keeps on rubbing his knees. His overalls are faded: on one knee a serge*
2   *patch cut out of a pair of Sunday pants, worn iron-slick. "No man mislikes it*
3   *more than me," he says.*
4   *"A fellow's got to guess ahead now and then," I say. "But come long and*
5   *short, it won't be no harm done either way."*
6   *"She'll want to get started right off," he says. "It's far enough to Jefferson at*
7   *best."*
8   *"But the roads is good now," I say. "It's fixing to rain tonight, too. His folks*
9   *buries at New Hope, too, not three miles away. But it's just like him to marry a*
10 *woman born a day's hard drive away and have her die on him."*
                                                    —William Faulkner, *As I Lay Dying*

---

4. According to an American Heritage Dictionary Usage Note, *slow* is coming to be more accepted as an adverb, in place of *slowly*, "when brevity and forcefulness are sought," as in *Drive slow!*

1	*"Father!" said she.*
2	*The old man pulled up. "What is it?"*
3	*"I want to know what them men are diggin' over there in that field for."*
4	*"They're diggin' a cellar, I s'pose, if you've got to know."*
5	*"A cellar for what?"*
6	*"A barn."*
7	*"A barn? You ain't goin' to build a barn over there where we was goin' to*
8	*have a house, father?"*
9	*The old man said not another word. He hurried the horse into the farm wagon,*
10	*and clattered out of the yard, jouncing as sturdily on his seat as a boy.*

—Mary E. Wilkins Freeman, "The Revolt of 'Mother'"

12.6 Ethnic Dialects

In addition to regional and social-class dialects, American English also has *ethnic* dialects such as Hispanic English, Chinese English, and African-American Vernacular (also called *Black English* or *Ebonics*). Dialects are, of course, cultural, not biological: There are African-Americans who do not speak African-American Vernacular, and members of other ethnic groups who *do* speak this dialect as a result of having lived in an African-American community. Ethnic dialects are also subject to regional variation; for example, the Hispanic English of New York City differs from that of Chicago, but both dialects show evidence of influence from Spanish.

Like other nonstandard dialects, ethnic dialects are primarily *spoken* dialects; most English speakers use Standard English for writing. Speakers of nonstandard dialects often *speak* Standard English, as well, in formal situations outside their own community. However, within the community the dialect is an important cohesive force; we establish our membership in a community by using the language of the community, whether it is a regional dialect, an ethnic dialect, college slang, or Standard American English. English teachers have a responsibility to teach their students Standard English, especially for writing, but they should not try to replace the students' home dialect—the language that connects them to their family and friends. The school's job is to give the child access to a *second* dialect (or a second language, if the child speaks another language at home) which will open the door to opportunities in the world outside his or her own community.

Ethnic dialects have a somewhat different history from other dialects, in that they have their source in the English spoken by speakers of another language. For example, Hispanic English was created by speakers of Spanish. As time went on, however, the dialect took on a life of its own; children growing up in the Hispanic community learn Hispanic English as their mother tongue even if they themselves do not speak Spanish.

African American Vernacular is believed to have originated as a *creole* spoken by African slaves on American plantations. The African people who were brought to this country as slaves spoke many different languages (Wolof, Malinke, Temne, Yoruba, and Luba, to name just a few), but they had to use English to communicate with their white masters and even with one another, when speakers of different languages were mixed together on a single plantation. The first step, in such circumstances, is the development of a *pidgin*—a simple linguistic system that allows speakers of different languages to communicate with one another for business purposes. However, when children are born into the community and hear the pidgin more than any other language, they adopt it as their mother tongue, expanding and regularizing it as they go, so that it develops the vocabulary and structure of a full-fledged language. A language that is created in this way, by a generation of children, is called a *creole*.

Creoles arose all over the world in the eighteenth and nineteenth centuries as colonialism, with its plantation economies, brought laborers from many language backgrounds to work together. Some important English-based creoles are

Jamaican Creole	Tok Pisin (Melanesia)
Bahamian Creole	Hawaiian Creole
Belizean Creole	Krio (Sierra Leone)

There are also French-based creoles, including Haitian Creole and Louisiana (Cajun) French, and Portuguese-based creoles such as Cape Verde Creole, spoken in the Cape Verde Islands and by immigrants from Cape Verde to Massachusetts and California.

The English-based creole that was used on American plantations is called *Gullah;* remnants of this creole are still spoken on islands off the coast of Georgia and South Carolina. The following is an excerpt from a Gullah folktale collected by C.C. Jones in 1888 and reprinted in Loreto Todd's (1984) *Modern Englishes: Pidgins and Creoles:*

> *Buh Elephant [Brother Elephant], him bin know Buh Rooster berry well. Dem blan [used to] roam togerrur, an Buh Rooster blan wake Buh Elephant duh mornin, so eh kin hunt eh bittle befo de jew dry.*
>
> *Dem bin a talk togerrur one day, an Buh Elephant, him bet Buh Rooster say him kin eat longer ner him. Buh Rooster, him tek de bet, an dem tun in nex mornin, wen de sun jis bin a git up, fuh see who gwine win de bet.*
>
> — C.C. Jones

African American or Black English Vernacular (AAVE or BEV) is the *de-creolized* English dialect that developed when speakers of the plantation Creole began to interact more closely with the surrounding English-speaking population. Some characteristics of BEV, especially its distinctive aspectual system, are apparently derived from Gullah, but other features are found in Southern American English generally. These features were not noticeable as long as American blacks remained in the South, but drew more attention when they migrated to northern cities in great numbers after the Second World War. Some characteristics of BEV are as follows:

12.6.1 Pronunciation

a. Substitution of [t] and [d] for initial [th] and [*th*]

thing	→	[tĭng];	*this* →	[dĭs]

Substitution of [f] and [v] for final [th] and [*th*]:

mouth	→	[mouf];	*bathe* →	[bāv]

259

b. Simplification of consonant clusters

most	→	[mōs];		*field*	→	[fēl];
told	→	[tōl] or [tō];		*ask*	→	[ăs] or [ăks];
help	→	[hĕp]				

c. [r]-dropping:

car	→	[kä];		*over*	→	[ōv´ə];
here	→	[hĭə]				

d. Pronunciation of [ī] as [ä]:

I	→	[ä];		*mine*	→	[män]

12.6.2 Syntax

a. Deletion of contracted AUX or *copula* (the main verb *be*):[5]

Standard English	**Black English Vernacular**
I'll do it in just a minute.	*I do it in just a minute*
We're on tape.	*We on tape.*
He's gonna try to get up.	*He gon try to get up.*

b. Use of "invariant *be*" to indicate habitual or durative aspect (that is, that something is *generally* true, not just on this occasion):

> *The office **be** closed on weekends.*
> *Everyday when I come home, I **be** scared.*
> *But the teachers don't **be** knowing the problems like the parents do.*
> *Everybody **be** tired from the heat.*
> *He **be** hiding when he know she's mad.*

c. *Done + past participle* to indicate perfect aspect (that is, to refer to a situation that is the result of a previous action):

> *She **done** lost her keys.*
> *We **done** told him about these pipes already.*
> *It don't make no difference, cause they **done** used all the good ones by now.*
> *Boy, you **done** done it now.*

This construction sometimes occurs in combination with uncontracted *be*:

> *They **be done** left.*
> *I **be done** bought my own radio by then.*

---

5. As we saw above, Standard English speakers also delete certain auxiliaries in questions, so that *Are you going?* → *You goin'?*

d. Inversion of a negative auxiliary with an indefinite subject pronoun (to satisfy a requirement that an indefinite negative pronoun must be preceded by the negative particle *not* or *n't*):

> ***Ain't*** *nobody seen it.*
> ***Didn't*** *nobody see it.*

e. *It* as a "dummy" subject in positions where standard English uses *there*:

> ***It's*** *a lot of people here.*   (cf. SAE ***There's*** *a lot of people here.*)

EXERCISE 5. Look through the following literary selections to find characteristics that identify the characters as speakers of African American Vernacular. (In the selection from *Huckleberry Finn*, only Jim is African American, but you may be able to find some features of African American Vernacular in Huck's speech, as well.) You should be able to find examples of [r]-dropping, consonant cluster simplification, pronunciation of [ī] as [ä], substitution of [d] for initial [*th*], *it* as a dummy subject where Standard English uses *there*, and deletion of a contracted AUX or copula. You should also be able to find general working-class characteristics, including Negative Concord, Nonstandard Subject-Verb Agreement, as well as informal (conversational English) contractions, and words and expressions that would not be found in Standard English. Notice that Hurston and Twain, but not Baldwin, use "eye dialect" (nonstandard spelling) to represent their characters' pronunciation; thus you will find pronunciation features only in these excerpts. The decision to use eye dialect is a stylistic decision by the author; some writers (and some readers) like eye dialect and others do not. Notice that some of the pronunciations that Hurston attributes to Grandma are not particular to African American Vernacular, but are informal contractions and reductions that are used by most English speakers in informal conversation. Find four pronunciations used by Grandma that speakers of Standard English would also use when speaking informally.

1 *"Come to yo' Grandma, honey. Set in her lap lak yo' use tuh. Yo' Nanny wouldn't*
2 *harm a hair uh yo' head. She don't want nobody else to do it neither if she kin*
3 *help it. Honey, de white man is de ruler of everything as fur as Ah been able*
4 *tuh find out. Maybe it's some place way off in de ocean where de black man is*
5 *in power, but we don't know nothin' but what we see. So de white man throw*
6 *down de load and tell de nigger man tuh pick it up. He pick it up because he*
7 *have to, but he don't tote it. He hand it to his womenfolks. De nigger woman*
8 *is de mule uh de world so fur as Ah can see. Ah been prayin' fuh it tuh be dif-*
9 *ferent wid you. Lawd, Lawd, Lawd."*
                                              — Zora Neale Hurston, *Their Eyes were Watching God*

1 *"Oh, honey," she said, "there's a lot that you don't know. But you are going*
2 *to find out." She stood up from the window and came over to me. "You got to*
3 *hold on to your brother," she said, "and don't let him fall, no matter what it*
4 *looks like is happening to him and no matter how evil you gets with him. You*

5   *going to be evil with him many a time. But don't you forget what I told you,*
6   *you hear? . . . You may not be able to stop nothing from happening. But you*
7   *got to let him know you's **there**."*

— James Baldwin, "Sonny's Blues"

1   *"Le's land on her, Jim."*
2   *But Jim was dead against it, at first. He says:*
3   *"I doan' want to go fool'n 'long er no wrack. We's doin' blame well, en we*
4   *better let blame' well alone, as de good book says. Like as not dey's a watch-*
5   *man on dat wrack."*
6   *"Watchman your grandmother," I says; "there ain't nothing to watch but the*
7   *texas and a pilot-house; and do you reckon anybody's going to resk his life for*
8   *a texas and a pilot-house such a night as this, when it's likely to break up and*
9   *wash off down the river any minute?" Jim couldn't say nothing to that, so he*
10   *didn't try. "And besides," I says, "we might borrow something worth having, out*
11   *of the captain's stateroom. Seegars, I bet you — and cost five cents apiece, solid*
12   *cash. Steamboat captains is always rich, and get sixty dollars a month, and they*
13   *don't care a cent what a thing costs, you know, long as they want it . . ."*

—Mark Twain, *Huckleberry Finn*

EXERCISE 6.   Here are two other ethnic varieties to consider—first, the Yiddish-influenced English of Jewish immigrants in New York City and then the Chinese-influenced English of the character Kwan from Amy Tan's novel *The Hundred Secret Senses*. Find characteristics showing that these characters are not native speakers of English. (Be as specific as you can, following the model that we have used in listing the features of working-class and ethnic dialects.)

1   *"What do we need all this for?" he would ask loudly, for her hearing aid was*
2   *turned down and the vacuum was shrilling. "Five rooms" (pushing the sofa*
3   *so she could get into the corner) "furniture" (smoothing down the rug) "floors*
4   *and surfaces to make work. Tell me, why do we need it?" And he was glad he*
5   *could ask in a scream.*
6   *"Because I'm use't."*
7   *"Because you're use't. This is a reason, Mrs. Word Miser? Used to can get*
8   *unused!"*
9   *"Enough unused I have to get used to already . . . Not enough words?" turning*
10   *off the vacuum a moment to hear herself answer. "Because soon enough we'll*
11   *need only a little closet, no windows, no furniture, nothing to make work for*
12   *but worms. Because now I want room . . . Screech and blow like you're doing,*
13   *you'll need that closet even sooner . . . Ha, again!" for the vacuum bag wailed,*
14   *puffed half up, hung stubbornly limp. "This time fix it so it stays; quick before*
15   *the phone rings and you get too important-busy."*

—Tillie Olsen, "Tell me a Riddle"

1	*"I was just making a—ah, forget it. What's a secret sense?"*
2	*"How I can say? Memory, seeing, hearing, feeling, all come together, then*
3	*you know something true in you heart. Like one sense, I don't know how say,*
4	*maybe sense of tingle. You know this: Tingly bones mean rain coming, re-*
5	*freshen mind. Tingly skin on arms, something scaring you, close you up, still*
6	*pop out lots a goose bump. Tingly skin top a you brain, oh-oh, now you know*
7	*something true, leak into you heart, still you don't want believe it. Then you*
8	*also have tingly hair in you nose. Tingly skin under you arm. Tingly spot in*
9	*back of you brain—that one, you don't watch out, you got a big disaster come,*
10	*mm-hm. You use you secret sense, sometimes can get message back and forth*
11	*fast between two people, living, dead, doesn't matter, same sense."*

— Amy Tan, *The Hundred Secret Senses*

12.7 Applications for Teachers

Everybody loves regional dialects—my students all have stories about the vocabulary and pronunciation of their cousins in other parts of the country, and my grandchildren perform improvised skits in Received Pronunciation or an Alabama drawl. However, social-class and ethnic dialects are a different matter; our view of these dialects is mixed with anxieties about race and class along with deeply ingrained beliefs that English is either "correct" or incorrect,[6] that nonstandard dialects do not follow grammatical rules, and that departures from Standard English are a sign of laziness and stupidity. Some of my students claim never to have met anyone who would say, "She don't say nothin'," while others tell me of the deep shame they feel when they hear their parents use such language. A few confess, sheepishly, that they themselves sometimes use these constructions when speaking with friends.

Because my students carry such a burden of negative attitudes, I think it is important (though difficult) to talk with them about dialects. I find it easiest to begin with regional dialects, which allow me to introduce the basic concepts in a context that is less emotionally charged. When we move on to social-class and ethnic dialects, I often make use of literary texts, for two reasons: First, my students have already learned, in other classes, to approach literary characters with empathy and respect. Secondly, the fact that the language is represented in writing makes it easier to identify particular grammatical constructions that are different from those of Standard English. In this way, the students can see that nonstandard dialects do have consistent grammatical rules, which are, in some cases, different from the rules of Standard English.

In trying to teach Standard English to students who come from nonstandard-dialect backgrounds, I would find it easiest to frame these discussions in terms of the distinction between informal and formal *registers*. All students, even those who speak Standard English at home, have to learn new vocabulary and grammatical constructions for use in formal, written English; "too conversational" is one of the most frequent comments I write in the margins of student essays. The move from a nonstandard dialect to Standard English is essentially the same problem, except that there is a bigger gap between the students' informal, conversational language and the formal

---

6. When I taught English as a Peace Corps Volunteer in Nigeria, my British school principal extended this notion to regional dialects, as well. Instead of American English vs. British English, she always spoke of American English vs. "correct" English.

register they need to acquire. Of course, there are attitudinal obstacles, as well—feelings of disloyalty and lack of authenticity in adopting the "white man's" or the "rich man's" English. To address these feelings, I would try to give students examples of fine writing by members of their own community, while assuring them that it is not necessary to abandon their home dialect; the goal is to give them competence in more than one register or dialect. Most people in the world speak two or three *languages*, and there is no reason why American students cannot learn to use two or more dialects of English.

12.8 Applications for Students and Teachers of Literature

In talking with students about register and dialect variation in English, I like to begin by looking at the representation of spoken language in literature. (If students are writing stories and dramas of their own, then they have another reason to be interested in how published authors handle spoken dialog.) Here are some observations about literary dialog:

Authors differ in their strategies for representing spoken language; for example, as was pointed out in Exercise 5 above, some authors use eye dialect to indicate a character's nonstandard pronunciation, while others represent dialect using only vocabulary and syntax. Writers from earlier times did not always attempt to give a realistic representation of their characters' speech. For example, I doubt that any actual human being ever began a sentence with "Thus, thus, and not otherwise . . . ," as the Usher does in the following excerpt from Edgar Allan Poe's "The Fall of the House of Usher." (The lack of realism in this dialog is not a failing on Poe's part; he wasn't trying to write realistic dialog, he was trying to tell a scary story.)

1	*To an anomalous species of terror I found him a bounden slave. "I shall perish,"*
2	*said he, "I must perish in this deplorable folly. Thus, thus, and not otherwise,*
3	*shall I be lost. I dread the events of the future, not in themselves, but in their*
4	*results. I shudder at the thought of any, even the most trivial, incident, which*
5	*may operate upon this intolerable agitation of soul. I have, indeed, no abhor-*
6	*rence of danger, except in its absolute effect—in terror. In this unnerved—in*
7	*this pitiable condition, I feel that the period will sooner or later arrive when I*
8	*must abandon life and reason together, in some struggle with the grim phan-*
9	*tasm, FEAR."*

— Poe, "The Fall of the House of Usher"

Modern writers usually try to give a realistic representation of their characters' speech. Thus, in the selection from Hemingway's "Hills Like White Elephants" (Appendix Section VII), the characters use contractions (*it's, let's*) and slang expressions ("*Oh, cut it out,*" ln. 35), and they sometimes speak in fragments (*Two big ones*, ln. 7; *With water*, ln. 25; *Especially all the things you've waited so long for, like absinthe*, lns. 33–34). The sentence *Just because you say I wouldn't have doesn't prove anything* (lns. 15–16) could only be found in conversation; sentences like this never appear in formal writing.

EXERCISE 7.

a. Identify the subject of the Hemingway sentence that was quoted just above (the one from lines 15–16 of the excerpt).

b. Look through the Hemingway passage (Appendix Section VII) and identify other ways in which the dialog is or is not completely realistic. Would the transcription of a real conversation look exactly like this? (You might consider, for example, whether the characters use informal contractions (Section 12.4 above).

c. Listen again to the conversation you recorded (Appendix Section VI). Choose a manageable portion of that conversation and re-write it as you might do if you were using it as dialog in a short story. What changes did you have to make in order to convert your recorded conversation into a written dialog? Did you choose to use eye dialect? Why or why not? What other decisions did you have to make (about punctuation, for example)?

d. Re-write the Edgar Allan Poe excerpt above to give Usher a more realistic style of speech.

There are many interesting issues in the representation of literary dialog, including differences in the speech of different characters, changes in the speech of a single character from one situation to another, and the relationship between the language of the narrator and the language of the characters. The sample exercises below provide some suggestions for addressing these issues.

EXERCISE 8.   In the passage from *Huckleberry Finn* in Exercise 5 above, Twain makes a contrast between the dialects of Huck and Jim. Write a one-page essay about the differences you find in the speech of these two characters, beginning with nonstandard features that you find in Huck's language and then some features that show Jim's speech to be less standard than Huck's. Keep in mind, however, that Twain is giving us an *impression* of the differences in these dialects, not an actual transcription. Certainly there would have been dialect differences in the speech of Huck and Jim, but you should be able to find some instances in which Huck's speech is represented as more standard than it would have been in real life, and some instances where Jim is given "dialect" pronunciations that would also be used by speakers of Standard English.

EXERCISE 9.   Literary characters sometimes change their speech from one point to another in a story (just as in real life). What changes do you see in Sula's speech from line 3 to line 6 in the passage below, and what causes the change?

1   *When Sula opened the door [Eva] raised her eyes and said, "I might have*
2   *knowed them birds meant something. Where's your coat?"*
3   *Sula threw herself on Eva's bed. "The rest of my stuff will be on later."*
4   *"I should hope so. Them little old furry tails ain't going to do you no more*
5   *good than they did the fox that was wearing them."*
6   *"Don't you say hello to nobody when you ain't seen them for ten years?"*
7   *"If folks let somebody know where they is and when they coming, then other*
8   *folks can get ready for them . . ."*

—Toni Morrison, *Sula*

265

EXERCISE 10.   It can be interesting to compare the language of the characters with the language of the narrator.

a. In a first-person narrative such as *Huckleberry Finn*, the narrator is a character in the story. Look again at the passage from Huckleberry Finn in Exercise 5 above, to see whether Huck's language remains the same in these two roles. Is the language of Huck the narrator the same as that of Huck the character, or are there differences?

b. In a third-person narrative, the attitude of the narrator to the characters is indicated, to some extent, by the similarities and differences in their language. Consider the following passages from Lawrence's "The Horse Dealer's Daughter" and Welty's "A Worn Path." In what ways is the narrator's language in each passage similar to/different from that of the characters, and what, if anything, does that tell you about the narrator's attitude?

1	*. . . [Fred Henry] pushed his coarse brown moustache upwards, off his lip, and*
2	*glanced irritably at this sister, who sat impassive and inscrutable.*
3	*"You'll go and stop with Lucy for a bit, shan't you?" he asked. The girl did*
4	*not answer.*
5	*"I don't see what else you can do," persisted Fred Henry.*
6	*"Go as a skivvy," Joe interpolated laconically.*
7	*The girl did not move a muscle.*
8	*"If I was her, I should go in for training for a nurse," said Malcolm, the*
9	*youngest of them all. He was the baby of the family, a young man of twenty-*
10	*two, with a fresh, jaunty <u>museau</u>.*
11	*But Mabel did not take any notice of him. They had talked at her and round*
12	*her for so many years, that she hardly heard them at all.*

                                                    — D.H. Lawrence, "The Horse Dealer's Daughter"

1	*Now and then there was a quivering in the thicket. Old Phoenix said, "Out of*
2	*my way, all you foxes, owls, beetles, jack rabbits, coons and wild animals! ...*
3	*Keep out from under these feet, little bob-whites . . . Keep the big wild hogs out*
4	*of my path. Don't let none of those come running my direction. I got a long*
5	*way." Under her small black-freckled hand her cane, limber as a buggy whip,*
6	*would switch at the brush as if to rouse up any hiding things.*
7	*On she went. The woods were deep and still. The sun made the pine needles*
8	*almost too bright to look at, up where the wind rocked. The cones dropped as*
9	*light as feathers. Down in the hollow was the mourning dove—it was not too*
10	*late for him.*
11	*The path ran up a hill. "Seem like there is chains about my feet, time I get this*
12	*far," she said, in the voice of argument old people keep to use with themselves.*
13	*"Something always take a hold of me on this hill—pleads I should stay."*

                                                    — Eudora Welty, "A Worn Path"

12.9   Applications for ESL Teachers

If students are studying English outside an English-speaking area, decisions will have to be made about whether they are to focus on spoken or written English, whether they are to learn British or American English or some other variety, and to what extent they should be made aware of regional and social-class variations in English. If the students are in a country such as India, Singapore, or Nigeria, where English is an official second language, there is a further tension between each country's tendency to develop its own variety of English (Indian English, Nigerian English, and so forth) and the desire to teach students a variety of English that will be maximally useful for international communication. In addressing these questions, it is necessary to know the policies of the host government as well as what use the students will be expected to make of their English once they have left school.

Students who are studying English in an English-speaking country will most likely be interested, primarily, in learning the standard dialect of that country. However, they may also need to understand and, sometimes, speak, the nonstandard varieties that are found in the communities where they live. All ESL students will need practice with the "informal contractions" that are discussed in Section 12.4 of this chapter. ESL students may not need to learn to say "Whaddaya doin'?" or "Didja go?", but they have to understand these questions when they hear them.

ESL teachers should pay close attention to dialect when they choose films or literature for non-native speakers. Unless the teacher has a specific reason for exposing students to a nonstandard dialect, nonstandard pronunciation in films and eye-dialect in literature serve no useful purpose for ESL students and are a serious source of confusion.

12.10   Summary of the Chapter

This chapter has been concerned with variation in English, including regional and social dialects, and changes of register as a single speaker moves from informal to formal situations and from speech to writing. We talked first about regional dialects (British vs. American as well as regional dialects in American English), then about conversational English as opposed to formal written English, and, finally, about working class and ethnic dialects, especially African American Vernacular. We looked briefly at the representation of spoken English in literature.

As applications for teachers, we talked about the importance of teaching respectful attitudes towards nonstandard social-class and ethnic dialects. For students who come from nonstandard dialect backgrounds, we discussed the need to maintain the language that connects them to their family and friends while, at the same time, acquiring the standard English that will give them entry into the wider world.

We also discussed the representation of spoken language in literature, including the techniques that writers use to represent their characters' speech, and the fact that language differences may be used to indicate relationships between characters or between the characters and the narrator.

For ESL teachers, we described some of the decisions that must be made about what variety of English to teach to students. We pointed out the need to teach informal English pronunciation, at least for comprehension, and we warned teachers to watch for nonstandard English that may be confusing to their students in films and literature.

CHAPTER 13

Coordination

13.1 Introduction

In this chapter, we return to the syntax of English and extend our analysis to sentences that contain conjoined structures—that is, constituents that are connected by the coordinating conjunctions *and, or, but, yet,*[1] and *so.*[2]

13.2 The Formation of Coordinate Structures

Coordinate or *conjoined* structures are formed by joining two or more constituents of the same category with a coordinating conjunction such as *and* or *but*, as indicated by the formula below, where the symbol $\propto$ stands for "any syntactic category," and the subscript n means "any number from one on up":

$$\propto \ \Rightarrow \ \propto_n \ \text{CONJ} \ \propto$$

The formula says that if we conjoin two or more instances of any category with a conjunction such as *and*, the result is an instance of the same category. For example, if we conjoin two NPs, the result is a NP:

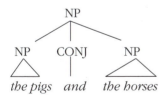

As the formula indicates, a conjoined structure can contain more than two members:

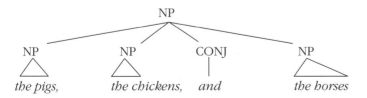

---

1. *Yet* is used as a conjunction only in formal written English: *We worked steadily all day, yet there was little to show for our efforts.*
2. *So* is often used as a conjunction in conversational English but is not completely accepted in formal written English: *I want to be there for the whole ceremony, so please don't start without me.*

A conjoined constituent can occupy the same syntactic positions as any other member of that category; for example, a conjoined NP occupies NP positions such as subject of sentence or complement of verb:

A conjoined NP as the subject of a sentence:

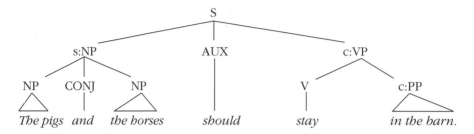

A conjoined NP as the complement of a verb:

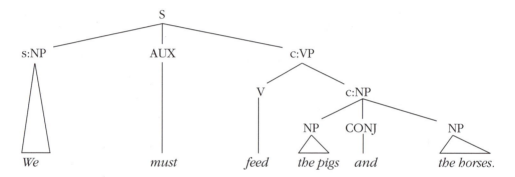

Other categories can be conjoined in the same way; in each case, the result is a member of the same category as the constituents that were conjoined:

S:

VP:

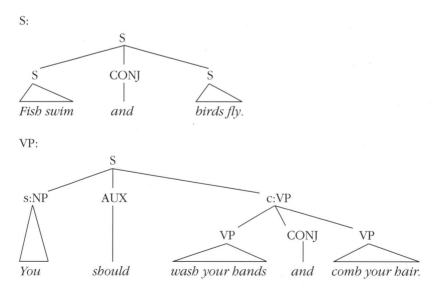

PP:

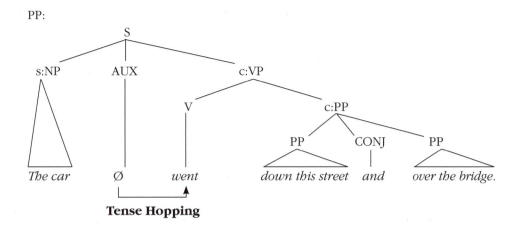

Lexical categories can be conjoined, also, as in the examples below:

N:

V:

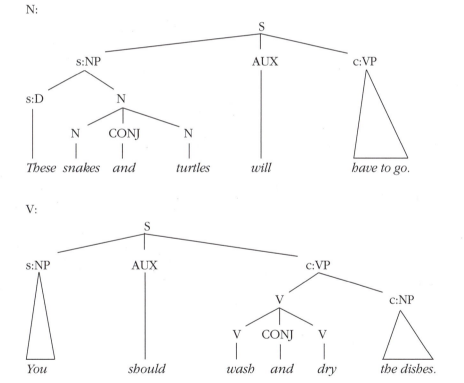

271

P:

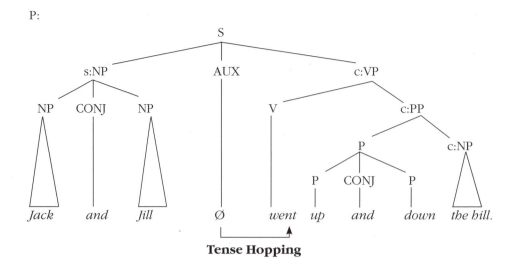

Tense Hopping

EXERCISE 1. Draw tree diagrams of the following sentences, which contain coordinate (conjoined) structures:

a. *The guests drank soda or beer.*
b. *The plane will land at the airport and taxi to the terminal.*
c. *I walked down the stairs and out the door.*
d. *We landed on the island and made a fire.*
e. *I just can't stand these snakes and turtles.*
f. *Spring will come and the gardens will flourish.*

13.3 Applications for Teachers

In this section we will look first at the development of coordinate structures in children's speech and writing, then at coordination as a characteristic of literary style, and finally at some usage issues that arise in connection with coordinate structures.

13.3.1 The Development of Coordination in Speech and Writing

Coordination is very common in spoken English, and young children soon learn how to conjoin constituents of various categories, as when Eve, at 27 months, joins two sentences with the coordinating conjunction *but* to form the compound sentence *This one better but this one not better.*

EXERCISE 2. Find coordinate structures in the speech of Eve and Julia in Appendix Section VIII, and say what constituents are being conjoined in each case (two Ss, two NPs, or what).

When children first begin to write, they follow the pattern they are accustomed to in speech, chaining sentences together with *and, but,* or *so;* thus a first-grade author in Appendix Section II writes, *He got all his friends back. and most of all they thot he was speshel and then he grew up to be a good man a varey good man.*

As their writing matures, the children will begin to rely more heavily on subordination (the use of dependent clauses introduced by subordinate conjunctions such as *if, when, although, as,* etc.). Subordinating conjunctions provide a more explicit statement of the relationship between ideas, while the coordinating conjunctions, especially *and,* leave it to the reader or listener to figure out the connection. Compare the examples below:

> With coordinating conjunction:
> *The sun rose,* **and** *the birds began singing all around us.*

> With subordinating conjunction:
> **As** *the sun rose, the birds began singing all around us.*

The grammar of subordinate clauses will be discussed in Chapter 14.

EXERCISE 3. Find other examples of the overuse of conjoined structures in the children's writing samples in Appendix Section II. Do you find changes in the children's use of coordination vs. subordination as they grow older?

13.3.2   Coordination in the Prose Style of Mature Writers

Some mature writers continue to rely heavily on coordination as a deliberate stylistic choice. For example, in the brief passage from Hemingway's "Hills Like White Elephants" (Appendix Section I), there are seven instances of the conjunction *and.*

EXERCISE 4.

a. Find the coordinating conjunctions in the Hemingway passage (Appendix Section I) and say what constituents are joined in each case (two NPs, two Ss, etc.). Then comment on the stylistic effect of coordination in Hemingway's writing. Why does he use so many coordinating conjunctions, in your view, and what is the effect of this choice?

b. Choose two other selections from Appendix Section I, and find all the coordinating conjunctions in the passage. Say what constituents are joined by each conjunction, and then compare the writer's use of coordinate structures with that of Hemingway (ex. (a) above).

13.3.3   Usage Issues in Coordinate Structures

In this section, we will look at two usage issues that arise in connection with coordinate structures—first, the choice of case for conjoined pronouns, and then—a more serious issue—parallel structure.[3]

13.3.3.1   Choosing Case for Conjoined Pronouns

One issue that arises in coordinate structures is the choice of case (subject or object) for pronouns. When a pronoun appears alone in a NP, English speakers have no difficulty in choosing its case. A pronoun in subject position has subject case:

> **We** *know the answer.*

A pronoun that is the specifier of a noun has possessive case:

> **Your** *niece is here.*

And a pronoun in complement position has object case:[4]

*We gave **her** the money.*	(complement of verb: indirect object)
*We saw **her**.*	(complement of verb: direct object)
*We will go with **them**.*	(object of preposition)

Speakers of Standard English never make mistakes with these pronouns; we are not even slightly tempted to say **Us** *will go with* **they**. However, coordination, for some reason, interferes with our intuitions about case; we are uncertain whether to use the subject or the object form, and we make mistakes in both directions:

> *Bill and* **me** *went to the movies.*
> (object case *me* wrongly chosen for subject position)

> *This story is about you and* **I**.
> (subject-case *I* wrongly chosen for object of preposition *about*)

---

3. Students are sometimes told a third conjunction rule—namely that a sentence should never begin with *and* or *but*. However, this is a "rule" that is not worth following; good expository writing is full of sentences that begin with *and* or *but*. *The American Heritage Dictionary*, in its Usage Note, states that "this rule [has been] ridiculed by grammarians like Wilson Follett and H.W. Fowler and . . . ignored by writers from Shakespeare to Virginia Woolf."

4. There is one exception to this statement. In formal register, the complement of the verb *be* takes subject case rather than object case:

> *It was* **I** *who cut down the cherry tree.*   *This is* **she** *now.*   *It's* **I**.

However, many speakers find this choice too stilted, and use object case instead—*This is* **her** *now; It's* **me**. (If you feel uneasy about this, notice that the French do the same thing: they say *C'est moi*, not **C'est je*.)

EXERCISE 5. Choose the correct pronoun to fill in the blanks in the following conjoined structures. You can find the correct form simply by eliminating the other member of the conjoined structure; once the pronoun is alone in its NP, your native-speaker intuition will choose the correct form for you. For example, if you change the sentence *This story is about you and I/me* to *This story is about I/me*, you will have no difficulty in choosing the correct form. However, because this is a course in English grammar, I would like you, in addition, to explain *why* a particular case form (subject or object) is required. For example, in this sentence, the object form *me* is the correct choice, because the conjoined NP *you and me* is the *complement* (the object) of the preposition *about*.

    a. *Helen and ___ had to stay after school because ___ and ___ were passing notes.* (I, me; she, her; I, me)

    b. *Nobody except Ann and ___ voted for Louisa and ___.* (I, me; he, him)

    c. *Between you and ___, I don't think Greg is as nice as Bill.* (I, me)

    d. *The dog comes to ___ and ___ whenever we call it.* (he, him; I, me)

    e. *The answer will be the same whether you ask Laura or ___.* (I, me)

13.3.3.2 Parallel Structure

A more serious usage issue in the use of coordinate structures is parallel structure. As we have seen, conjoined constituents normally belong to the same category and perform the same grammatical function (s, h, c) within the clause or phrase. In the case of Vs and VPs, they must also have the same inflectional form (that is, all past tense, all -*ing* form, etc.). This is called *parallel structure*. Failure to use parallel structure is a serious writing fault. Consider the following example:

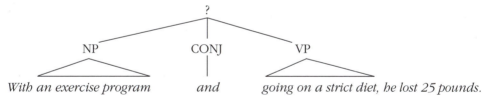

The first member of the above structure (*an exercise program*) is a NP, but the second (*going on a strict diet*) is a VP. The structure could be made parallel in either of the following ways:

    1.   Change the first conjunct to a VP:

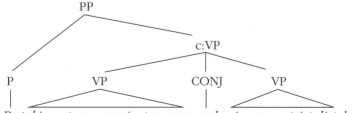

By taking up an exercise program and going on a strict diet, he lost 25 pounds.

    (two VPs, both complements of the preposition *by*)

2. Change the second conjunct to a NP:

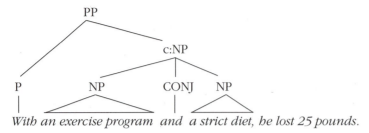

With an exercise program and a strict diet, he lost 25 pounds.

(two NPs, both complements of the preposition *with*)

EXERCISE 6. Find and correct the nonparallel structures in the following sentences, as shown in the example above. Explain what you did to correct each sentence.

a. *I enjoy swimming, jogging, and to take long walks.*

b. *In spring, summer, and in winter, I like to be outside.*

c. *On a university campus, drunkenness can lead to expulsion or even being arrested.*

d. *During the summer, we worked at the restaurant, went to the beach, and a few parties.*

e. *Dialects can be classified into three types: regional, social class, and ethnicity.*

Some conjunctions, called *correlative conjunctions*, have two parts. Examples are *both . . . and; either . . . or; neither . . . nor;* and *not only . . . but also.* The two parts of a correlative conjunction surround the first member of the conjoined structure, as shown in the tree below:

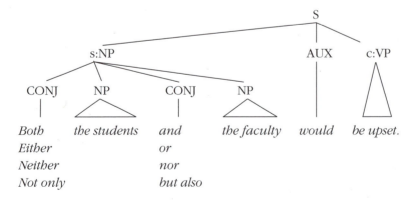

Except for *either . . . or*, which is fairly common in speech, the correlative conjunctions are used primarily in formal written English.

As with simple conjoined structures, two constituents that are joined with a correlative conjunction must match one another in category and function. For example, the following sentence is ill-formed, because the first conjunct is a PP, while the second is a NP:

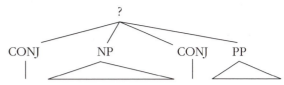

Employees are being transferred to either corporate headquarters   or   to other cities.

Again, we can correct the sentence in either of two ways.

1. Change the first conjunct to a PP (by moving the first part of the correlative conjunction to a different position):

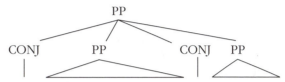

Employees are being transferred either to corporate headquarters or to other cities.

2. Change the second conjunct to a NP to match the first:

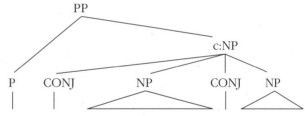

Employees are being transferred to   either   corporate headquarters or other cities.

EXERCISE 7.

a. Find the correlative conjunctions and correct the nonparallel structures in the following sentences, following the model above. Explain what you did to correct each sentence, and draw a tree diagram of the (corrected) conjoined structure.

  i.   *You can either talk to her mother or to her father.*

  ii. *This is a time not for words, but action.*

  iii. *Either you must do as he says or take the consequences.*

  iv. *The students were not only given the questions, but also the answers,*

  v.   *Some guys came into the restaurant neither wearing shoes nor shirts.*

b. The following sentence seems to me to be grammatical, but it should not be grammatical according to our rule. Can you give an explanation for this exception?

  We should be able to express ourselves both orally and in writing.

13.4 Applications for ESL Teachers

Coordination works similarly in all languages; thus coordination should not present serious difficulty for ESL students. Of course, students will have to be taught the conjunctions, especially the correlative conjunctions. In the end, however, ESL students will struggle with the same usage issues as native speakers—namely, (a) choosing the case form (subject or object) for conjoined pronouns and (b) using parallel structure.

13.5 Summary of the Chapter

In this chapter, we discussed the use of coordinating conjunctions to create conjoined structures, following the formula

$$\propto \quad \Rightarrow \quad \propto_n \quad \text{CONJ} \quad \propto$$

As the formula indicates, two or more members of a category $\propto$ (that is, any category) can be joined together by a coordinating conjunction to create a new member of the same category. Constituents that are created in this way are called conjoined constituents or coordinate structures. A sentence that consists of two sentences joined with a conjunction is called a compound sentence. Conjoined constituents occupy the same positions as simple members of their same category; for example, a conjoined NP can function as the subject of a sentence or the complement of a verb or preposition. We discussed two usage issues that are associated with coordinate structures—the choice of case for conjoined pronouns and (more importantly) the need for parallel structure.

Children very soon learn how to form conjoined constituents in spoken English. When they enter school and begin to read and write, they initially write long, conjoined sentences like those they would use in an oral narrative; with some nagging from their teachers, they eventually learn to break up these "run-on" sentences and develop more sophisticated ways of combining their thoughts. However, mature writers also use coordinate structures—some more than others; this is one characteristic that makes up a writer's style.

ESL students do not have particular difficulty with coordination, though they struggle with the same usage issues as native speakers.

CHAPTER 14

Subordination

14.1 Introduction

In the previous chapter, we saw that two or more sentences can be combined, using a coordinating conjunction, to form a compound sentence such as [*Fish swim*] *and* [*birds fly*]. In this chapter we will look at another way of combining sentences—by inserting an altered version of one sentence into a larger sentence, in such a way that it performs some grammatical function (subject, complement, or modifier) within the larger sentence. The embedded sentence is called a *subordinate* or *dependent* clause; the sentence into which the subordinate clause is embedded is called *the matrix clause*. The topmost clause in the sentence (the clause into which all subordinate clauses are embedded) is called *the main clause*.

We will begin the chapter by looking at the two forms that subordinate clauses can take—*finite* clauses (e.g., *if she wins*) and *non-finite* or "near" clauses (e.g., *for her to win*).

14.2 Finite Clauses

Finite clauses are sentences that are introduced by a subordinating conjunction ("C") such as *that, when, although*, or *because*. Except for the subordinating conjunction, a finite clause has the same structure as an independent sentence—that is, it has a subject, AUX, and VP, and the AUX contains an auxiliary or tense marker, as shown in the tree diagram below:

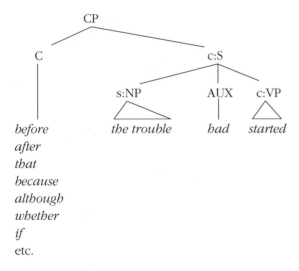

Some clauses have a *silent* C (Ø) which is interpreted as *that:*

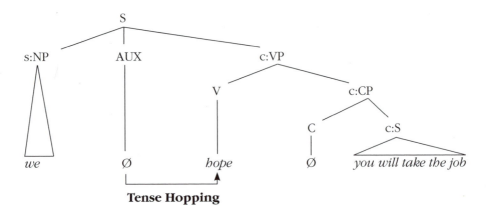

Tense Hopping

EXERCISE 1.

a. Put brackets around the subordinate clauses in the examples below, and identify the subordinating conjunction (C) in each clause. (Remember that the C-word may be Ø):

    i.   *Columbus thought he had reached the Indies.*

    ii.   *Nobody told me that the faucet was broken.*

    iii. *That enrollment is increasing is also a consideration.*

    iv. *The fact that enrollment is increasing is also a consideration.*

    v.   *Before I say anything, I should know all the facts.*

    vi. *I will talk to you after I look at the facts.*

    vii. *If it rains, we won't go.*

    viii. *I'm glad it isn't raining.*

    ix. *We can't leave until I find my keys.*

    x.   *The engine overheated because the radiator was leaking.*

b. Choose two clauses from the sentences in (a), and draw tree diagrams like the one on page 279, to illustrate their internal structure.

c. Explain why each of the CPs above qualifies as a finite clause (in other words, find the AUX in each clause and show that it contains an auxiliary or a tense marker).

In addition to ordinary finite CPs like those above, English also has WH-CPs, in which a WH-phrase has been moved to the front of the clause by WH-Fronting, as in the examples shown in the tree diagram below:

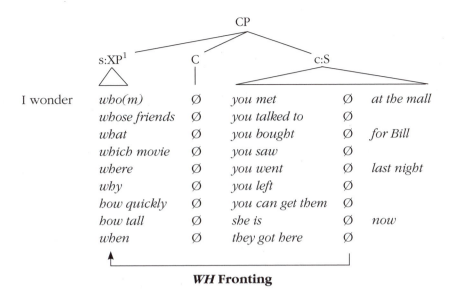

WH Fronting

There are two Øs in each tree above: The first Ø is the subordinating conjunction (C). The second Ø marks the *underlying* position of the *WH*-phrase (the position it occupied before *WH* Fronting): *You met <u>who(m)</u> at the mall; you saw <u>which movie</u>; you got there <u>when</u>; you went <u>why</u>,* and so on.

In Standard English, the C position in a *WH*-CP is always Ø. However, there are dialects, including Irish English and African American Vernacular, in which Subject-AUX Inversion is allowed to apply in *WH*-CPs:

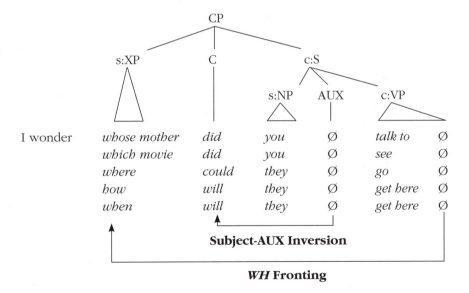

Subject-AUX Inversion

WH Fronting

---

1. *XP* is an abbreviation for *any* phrase; as the examples show, the constituent that moves to this position may be a NP, AdjP, or AdvP.

EXERCISE 2.

a. Bracket the *WH*-CP in each of the following sentences. Then underline the *WH*-phrase (the phrase that was moved by *WH*-Fronting), and mark its underlying position with Ø. The first sentence has been done for you, as an example:

i. *I wonder* [<u>*how tall*</u> *she is Ø.*]

ii. *We asked Bill when he would be ready.*

iii. *The detectives were shocked by what they found in the cellar.*

iv. *Beethoven could not hear how his compositions sounded.*

v. *Whoever goes out last should turn out the lights.*

vi. *Whatever you decide will be O.K. with me.*

vii. *Why she did it, I can't imagine.*

b. Choose two of the *WH*-clauses from (a) above and draw tree diagrams, following the model on the preceding page, to illustrate their internal structure.

c. Say why each of the *WH*-clauses in (a) counts as *finite* (that is, identify the AUX in each clause and say whether it is an auxiliary or a tense marker).

14.3 Nonfinite Clauses

English also has five types of *nonfinite* clauses, whose structure will be discussed in this section: infinitives, *WH*-infinitives, present participles (-*ing* clauses), passive participles, and absolute or *verbless* clauses. Nonfinite clauses, sometimes called "near" clauses, differ from finite clauses in that they have no modal or tense marker and the subject position is often empty.[2] However, they always have at least an understood subject.

<u>a. Infinitives.</u> The *AUX* position in an infinitival clause is occupied by the infinitive particle *to* rather than by a modal or tense marker.[3] The subject position may be filled (*for **Alice** to leave now*) or empty (*Ø to leave now*); if the subject is not specified, it must be possible to understand it from the context ((*for **you***) *to leave now*). Infinitival clauses have a special C-word, *for*, which is present only when the clause has an overt subject.[4]

---

2. Non-finite clauses with Ø subjects (e.g., [*Ø Holding her hands behind her*], *she strode into the boardroom*; *We'll try* [*Ø to find a solution*]) are traditionally called *phrases*. However, modern grammarians generally treat them as clauses, on the grounds that (a) they sometimes have overt subjects ([**Your** *holding your hands behind you*] *was what tipped off the police*), and (b) even when the subject is not overtly expressed, it can still be understood; for example, in the sentence [*Ø Holding her hands behind her*], *she strode into the boardroom*, we understand that *she* is the person who is holding her hands behind her.

3. There are also infinitival clauses without *to*, called *bare* infinitives: *We made the children* [*Ø cross the street*]; [*Ø Sail around the world*] *is what we'd like to do.* The internal structure of bare infinitives is not entirely clear, but we will assume here that they have the usual sentence structure, with Øs in both subject and AUX position.

4. In older versions of English, heard now only in folksongs, it was possible to have *for* without an overt subject: *I went to London **for** to see my love.*

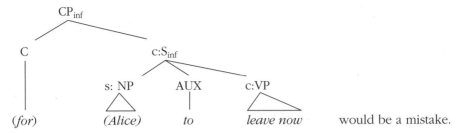

b. WH-Infinitives. A *WH*-infinitive is an infinitival clause that contains a *WH*-phrase. As always in English, the *WH*-phrase will have moved to the specifier-of-C position by the transformation of *WH*-Fronting:

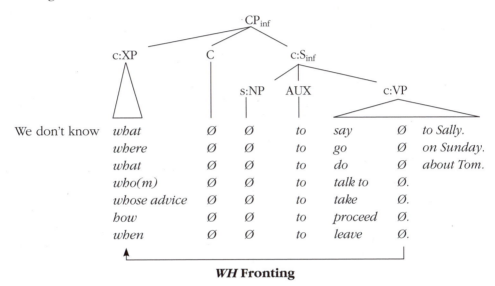

WH Fronting

There are three Øs in these diagrams: The first is the subordinating conjunction (C), which is always silent in a *WH*-infinitive. The second is the subject of the clause, which is also silent. The third is the underlying position of the *WH*-phrase: *to say **what** to Sally; to go **where** on Sunday,* and so on.

c. *ing*-Clauses. *ing*-clauses have a Ø in AUX position, with the VP in present participle (*-ing* form):

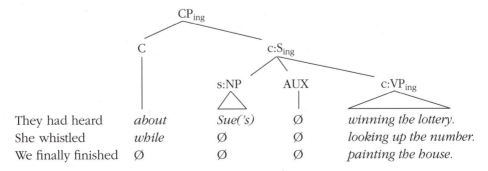

283

If the clause has an overt subject (that is, not Ø), it may be in possessive case (***Sue's*** *winning the lottery*) rather than object case (***Sue*** *winning the lottery*), especially in formal writing. However, the subject can also be Ø, as in the second and third examples above.

d. Passive Participles. Passive participles have a Ø in AUX position, with the VP in passive participle form. The subject position and the "C" position may be filled, or they may be empty (Ø):

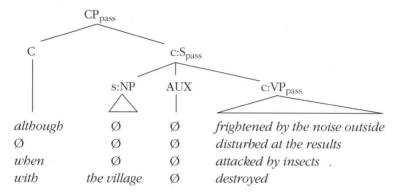

	s:NP	AUX	c:VP_pass
although	Ø	Ø	*frightened by the noise outside*
Ø	Ø	Ø	*disturbed at the results*
when	Ø	Ø	*attacked by insects* .
with	*the village*	Ø	*destroyed*

e. Absolute or Verbless Clauses. *Absolute* clauses have an overt subject but no tense or auxiliary and no verb; hence they are sometimes called *verbless* clauses. The presence of the subject is particularly important in a verbless clause; if there were no subject, there would be no reason to call the construction a clause rather than a PP, AdjP, or NP.

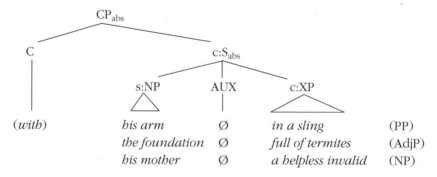

	s:NP	AUX	c:XP	
(with)	*his arm*	Ø	*in a sling*	(PP)
	the foundation	Ø	*full of termites*	(AdjP)
	his mother	Ø	*a helpless invalid*	(NP)

EXERCISE 3.

a. Find the nonfinite clauses in the sentences below, and say what type of clause each one is (an infinitive, a *WH*-infinitive, an *ing*-clause, a passive participle, or an absolute [verbless] clause):

  i. *Everybody likes to feel important.*
  ii. *I asked the children to pick up their toys.*
  iii. *The time to plant garlic is in the Fall.*
  iv. *She went to the store to get some bread.*
  v. *To open the door, you should press this knob.*
  vi. *What I want is for you to put on your coat.*
  vii. *Nobody knew what to say.*
  viii. *How to break the news to her parents was a difficult question.*

ix. *For you to come for Christmas would make your parents very happy.*
x. *They had finally saved enough money to buy a house.*
xi. *They like living in New Hampshire.*
xii. *We caught Bill sneaking out the door.*
xiii. *Everyone was surprised at Sue('s) taking such a strong stand.*
xiv. *Living in an apartment on the beach, we could watch the sunrise over the ocean every morning.*
xv. *The window got broken in the storm.*
xvi. *Driven to madness by her English grammar class, she had to spend the rest of her life in an asylum.*
xvii. *The person chosen for this job must be able to handle pressure.*
xviii. *Although terribly discouraged by the outcome, they refused to give up.*
xix. *Her heart in her mouth, she slowly turned the key.*
xx. *With the engine roaring, he zoomed out of the driveway.*
xxi. *My hands shaking, I reached towards the window.*

b. From the sentences above, choose one infinitive, one *WH*-infinitive, one *ing*-clause, one passive participle, and one verbless clause and draw a tree diagram for each one (just the clause, not the entire sentence), following the models provided earlier in this section.

14.4 The Functions of Subordinate Clauses

A subordinate (dependent) clause can perform all the same functions as any other constituent; that is, it acts as a subject, complement, or modifier within a larger constituent, as shown in Tables 14.1–14.8 below.

Table 14.1 Clause as Subject of Sentence

CP	[*That you gave up so soon*] *surprised everybody.*
CP$_{WH}$	[*What she wanted*] *remained a mystery.*
CP$_{inf}$	[*(For you) to give up now*] *would be a mistake.*
CP$_{wh-inf}$	[*What to do next*] *is a difficult question.*
CP$_{ing}$	[*Phil('s) giving you the answer*] *was dishonest.*

Table 14.2 Clause as Complement of V

CP	*We know* [*(that) you'll understand*].
CP$_{WH}$	*I wonder* [*why she said that*].
CP$_{inf}$	*We'll try* [*to understand*].
CP$_{wh-inf}$	*We wondered* [*what to do next*].
CP$_{ing}$	*The children enjoyed* [*singing madrigals*].
CP$_{pass}$	*The mail carrier got* [*bitten by a dog*].

Verbs that take clauses as complements usually require a particular type of clause; for example, the verb *wonder* takes a CP$_{WH}$: *I wonder <u>why she said that</u>*; the verb *enjoy* takes a CP$_{ing}$: *Do you enjoy <u>studying grammar</u>?*; the verb *try* takes either a CP$_{inf}$ or a CP$_{ing}$: *We tried <u>to open the window</u>; we tried <u>opening the window</u>*. A complete list of VP patterns, including verbs that take clauses as complements, is provided in Table 14.13 at the end of this chapter.

Table 14.3   Clause as Complement of P

CP$_{WH}$	(*We wondered*) *about* [*what they were doing*].
CP$_{wh\text{-}inf}$	(*We thought*) *about* [*where to go next*].
CP$_{ing}$	(*The plans called*) *for* [*going on to Miami*].

Table 14.4   Clause as Complement of N

CP	*our belief* [*that the earth is round*]
CP$_{WH}$	*no idea* [*who committed the crime*]
CP$_{inf}$	*our attempts* [*to understand*]
CP$_{wh\text{-}inf}$	*no idea* [*what to do next*]

Table 14.5   Clause as Complement of Adj

CP	*afraid* [(*that*) *we can't help you*]
CP$_{WH}$	*curious* [*why she said that*]
CP$_{wh\text{-}inf}$	*puzzled* [*what to do next*]
CP$_{inf}$	*eager* [*to go*]

Finite clauses that are subjects or complements of verbs or prepositions are traditionally called "noun clauses," because these positions are most commonly occupied by nouns. Ordinary finite clauses in these positions refer to facts, statements, or states of affairs (*I believe* [*that the President has given his approval*].). WH-clauses in these positions refer sometimes to questions (*I wonder* [*where she is*]) and sometimes to entities (*We liked* [*what we saw*]); those that name questions are called "interrogative" clauses, and those that name entities are called "nominal" or "substantive" clauses. *Ing*-clauses in subject or complement position are traditionally called "gerunds."

There is no special name for clauses that function as complements of nouns or adjectives; they are simply called "complements."

Table 14.6 Clause as Modifier of N

CP	*the information [(that) we sent for]*
	the people [(that) you talked to]
	the day [(that) we met]
	the reason [(that) I called you]
CP$_{WH}$	*the information [(which) we sent for]*
	the information [(for which) we sent]
	the students [(who(m) we met]
	the student [whose roommate we met]
	the day [when we met]
	the place [where we met]
	the reason [why I called you]
CP$_{inf}$	*a goal [(for us) to strive towards]*
CP$_{ing}$	*the child [standing near the stairs]*
CP$_{pass}$	*the banners [carried by the demonstrators]*

Clauses that modify nouns are traditionally called "relative" clauses or "adjectival" clauses. These clauses have special syntactic properties which will be discussed in Section 14.5.1 below. *Ing*-clauses that function as modifiers are traditionally called "participles."

Table 14.7 Clause as Sentential Modifier

CP	*[If you read the letter] you'll understand.*
	We bought it [because it was on sale].
	[Since you've been away], everything has changed.
	[After you left], things changed a lot.
CP$_{WH}$	*[When he took off his hat], everybody cheered.*
	[Whenever you eat Chinese food], you always feel thirsty afterward.
CP$_{inf}$	*[To understand the issue], you should first read the letter.*
CP$_{ing}$	*[Singing and carrying candles], they marched through the campus.*
CP$_{pass}$	*[Painted green], the shutters wouldn't look so bad.*

Table 14.8 Clause as Modifier of V

CP	*I called [until he came].*
CP$_{WH}$	*Do it [however you like].*
CP$_{inf}$	*Go to the store [to buy some bread].*
CP$_{ing}$	*She sat [knitting a sweater].*

It is not always easy to distinguish between a sentential modifier and a modifier of the verb. The criterion used here is that a sentential modifier can appear at the beginning of the sentence, not just at the end: If a clause prefers to stay at the *end* of the sentence, then it is a modifier of the verb, inside the VP. Clauses in either of these positions are traditionally called "adverbial" clauses and are classified into semantic categories like those shown in Table 14.9.

Table 14.9   Some Semantic Categories of Adverbial Clauses

Circumstance	[*The weather having improved*], *we decided to go ahead.*
	[*Being a woman of ingenuity*], *Sue soon rigged a replacement sail.*
Concession	[*Although we hadn't eaten*], *we felt fine.*
	[*Old as he is*], *he's still more agile than you are.*
Condition	[*If you read the letter*], *you'll see what I mean.*
	[*Unless the weather improves*], *we won't be able to go.*
	[*Painted green*], *the shutters wouldn't look so bad.*
Hypothetical Condition	[*If you listened to me*], *you wouldn't make so many mistakes.*
Counterfactual Condition	[*If you had listened to me*], *you wouldn't have made this mistake.*
	[*Had you listened to me*], *you wouldn't have made this mistake.*
Manner	*Do* [*as I do*].
	Do it [*however you like*].
	[*Singing and carrying candles*], *they marched through the campus.*
Place	*They went* [*wherever they could find work*].
Preference	[*Rather than travel by air*], *I took the bus.*
Purpose	*I was hurrying* [*to catch the train*].
	[*To understand what I'm saying*], *you'll have to read the article.*
Reason	*I'm phoning you* [*because I have some rather disturbing news*].
Time	*Buy your ticket* [*as soon as you reach the station*].
	[*When he took off his hat*], *everybody was astonished.*
	[*Since you left*], *things have changed a lot.*
	[*After you left*], *things changed a lot.*

EXERCISE 4.

a. Choose one example from each "function" table (14.1–14.8), and draw a tree diagram, using a triangle for the subordinate clause. Model answers based on examples from Tables 14.1 and 14.3 are given in Table 14.10. The purpose of this exercise is not to examine the *internal* structure of the clause, but to be sure you understand where the clause goes in the larger sentence.

b. Find the dependent (subordinate) clauses in the sentences below and identify their type (ordinary finite CP, CP$_{WH}$, infinitive, *WH*-infinitive, *ing*-clause, passive participle, or absolute) and function (subject, complement, or modifier of . . .). For example, for the first sentence, you should say that the clause is *that he had reached the Indies*, that it is a finite CP, and that it is the complement of the verb *thought*.

    i.   *Columbus thought that he had reached the Indies.*

    ii.   *Nobody told Bill that the faucet was broken.*

    iii.   *That enrollment is increasing is also a consideration.*

    iv.   *Nobody liked the speech he made.*

    v.   *I wonder how tall she is.*

    vi.   *Students who have finished the assignment should turn it in now.*

    vii.   *We asked Susan when she would be ready.*

    viii.   *The detectives were shocked by what they found.*

    ix.   *Beethoven could not hear how his compositions sounded.*

    x.   *Whoever goes out last should turn out the lights.*

    xi.   *Whatever you decide will be O.K. with me.*

    xii.   *The fact that enrollment is increasing is also a consideration.*

    xiii.   *Everybody likes to feel important.*

    xiv.   *I asked the children to pick up their toys.*

    xv.   *My first attempt to grow garlic was a complete failure.*

    xvi.   *The bus to take is Number 17.*

    xvii.   *She went to the store to get some bread.*

    xviii.   *To open the door, please press this knob.*

    xix.   *What I want is for you to put on your coat.*

    xx.   *For you to come home for Christmas would make your parents very happy.*

    xxi.   *They like living in New Hampshire.*

    xxii.   *The clothes hanging on the line should be dry by now.*

    xxiii.   *We caught Bill sneaking out the door.*

    xxiv.   *Everyone was surprised at Sue('s) taking such a strong stand.*

    xxv.   *Sue('s) taking such a strong stand surprised everyone.*

    xxvi.   *Living in an apartment on the beach, we could watch the sunrise over the ocean every morning.*

    xxvii.   *The window got broken in the storm.*

    xxviii.   *Driven to madness by her English grammar class, she had to spend the rest of her life in an asylum.*

    xxix.   *We have a lot of work to do.*

    xxx.   *The person we hire must be able to handle a lot of pressure.*

xxxi.   *Although terribly discouraged, we refused to give up.*

xxxii.   *Her heart in her mouth, she quietly turned the key.*

xxxiii.   *With the engine on fire, he leapt out of the car.*

xxxiv.   *My hands shaking, I reached towards the window.*

Table 14.10   Model Answers for Exercise 4a

Model 1, from Table 14.1

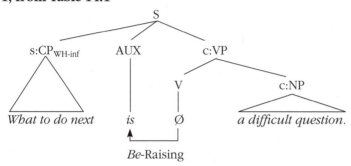

Model 2, from Table 14.3

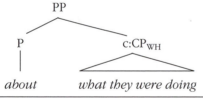

EXERCISE 5.

a. Draw a tree diagram of each sentence in the James Joyce passage in Appendix Section I, showing the position and function of every subordinate clause. Do not show the internal structure of the subordinate clauses; use the triangle notation.

b. (*For the very ambitious student*) Do the same with the Toni Morrison passage.

14.5   Two Special Types of Subordinate Clauses

In this section we will discuss two types of clauses that have special syntactic properties—relative clauses and clauses of comparison and degree.

14.5.1   Relative Clauses

Clauses that modify nouns are called *relative clauses* or *adjectival clauses*. Relative clauses have a special property that makes them different from other subordinate clauses—namely that they have a missing constituent (a Ø) that is identified with the noun that the clause modifies. For example, the Øs in the relative clauses *(that) we sent for Ø* and *(that) you talked to Ø* in the tree diagram below correspond to the nouns *information* and *students*: *we sent for the information; you talked to the students*.

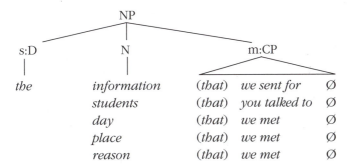

If the relative clause is a WH-clause, then the correspondence with the head noun is established through the WH-phrase at the front of the clause; the Ø in the clause marks the underlying position of the WH-phrase. Thus in the first example in the tree diagram below, Ø marks the underlying position of the WH-phrase *which*, and the WH-phrase *which*, in turn, corresponds to the NP *the information*:

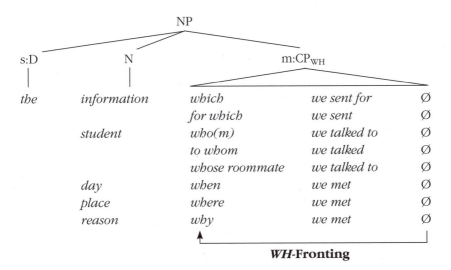

Infinitives, *WH*-infinitives, *ing*-clauses, and passive particles can also function as relative clauses (modifiers of nouns). Like the finite relative clauses that are illustrated in the tree diagram above, these clauses contain a Ø which is identified with the noun that the clause modifies:

291

Infinitive

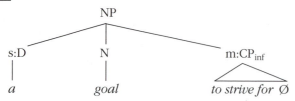

Ø = the goal

Ing-clause

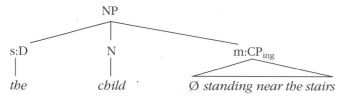

Ø = the child

Passive participle

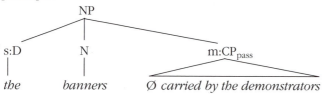

Ø = the banners

EXERCISE 6.   Combine the sentences below by forming relative clauses as indicated. Put brackets around the relative clause *and* around the NP that contains the relative clause. The first one is done for you as an example.

a.   i.   *Sarah met her boyfriend in the dorm.*
   ii.   *You lived in that dorm last year.*
   Change (ii) into a *WH*-clause (CP_WH) that modifies the noun *dorm*.
   Answer: *Sarah met her boyfriend in [the dorm [where you lived Ø last year]].*

b.   i.   *A person was crammed into the armchair.*
   ii.   *The person was Madeline.*
   Change (i) into a passive participle (CP_pass) that modifies the noun *person*.

c.   i.   *When Raoul finished talking, Steve let out a loud cough.*
   ii.   *It sounded oddly like "jerk."*
   Change (ii) into a *that*-clause (CP) that modifies the noun *cough*.

d.   i.   *He was remembering the glories of earlier days.*
   ii.   *Then his back was not yet bent with the toil of the years.*
   Change (ii) to a CP_WH that modifies the noun *days*.

e.   i.   *Jackie had sensed the terrible thing.*
   ii.   *Her warning had been shrugged off as the ranting of a hysterical woman.*
   iii.   *It was waiting out there in the darkness.*
   Change (ii) into a CP_WH that modifies the noun *Jackie*. Change (iii) into an *ing- clause* that modifies the noun *thing*.

f.　i.　　*Calvin went right ahead with his plan.*

　　ii.　　*He didn't let common sense stand in his way.*

　　iii.　　*He wasn't that sort of person.*

　　Change (ii) into an infinitival clause that modifies the noun *sort (of person).*

　　Change (iii) into a *WH*-clause that modifies the noun *Calvin.*

g.　i.　　*A broker can skin the bear market.*

　　ii.　　*He trades this way.*

　　iii.　　*We trade this way.*

　　Change (iii) into a *that*-clause that modifies the noun *way.*

　　Change (ii) into a WH-clause that modifies the noun *broker.*

h.　i.　　*Here is a porch light.*

　　ii.　　*Lovers can linger under it.*

　　Change (ii) into an infinitival clause (CP$_{inf}$) that modifies the noun *porch light.*

14.5.2　Relative Clause or Complement?

As we have seen, a clause that follows a noun may be either a *modifier* (relative clause) or a *complement* of that noun:

<u>Complement</u>　　　　　　　　　　　　　<u>Modifier</u>

a. *the belief* [*that the earth is flat*]　　b. *the belief* [*that we defend Ø most strongly*]

c. *a proposal* [*to reduce tuition charges*]　　d. *a proposal* [*to show Ø to your parents*]

Here's how to tell one from the other:

1.　A noun that takes a complement is semantically similar to a verb that takes a complement. Thus (a) above corresponds to the VP *believe that the earth is flat* and (c) corresponds to the VP *propose to reduce tuition charges.* There is no VP corresponding to (b) or (d): **believe that we defend Ø most strongly, *propose to show Ø to your parents.*

2.　Finite relative clauses can begin with *that/Ø* or with *WH*-phrases. Thus the relative clause of (b) can be changed to *the belief **which** we defend Ø most strongly.* Complements do not have this option: a noun requires a *that*-clause or a *WH*-clause as its complement and will not accept anything else. Thus the complement of (a) cannot be changed to a *WH*-clause: **the belief **which** the earth is flat.*

3.　As we saw in the previous section, a relative clause has a missing constituent (a Ø) that corresponds to the noun the clause modifies. Thus the relative clauses *we defend Ø most strongly* and *to show Ø to your parents* are understood to mean *We defend <u>that belief</u> most strongly* and *to show <u>the proposal</u> to your parents.* In contrast, the complement clause of (a) contains no Ø (*the earth is flat*), and while the complement clause of (c) does have a Ø subject, as non-finite clauses often do, this Ø understood as the university or other institution that is imposing tuition charges (*for <u>the university</u> to reduce tuition charges*); it is not identified with the head noun *proposal.*

EXERCISE 7.

a. Each of the sentences below contains a NP with a clause inside it. Put brackets around the NP and around the clause. Then identify the clause as a modifier (relative clause) or a complement and explain why. The first one is done for you as an example.

    i.   *Her claim that she had been abducted by aliens met with skepticism.*

Answer: [*Her claim* [*that she had been abducted by aliens*]] *met with skepticism.*

The clause is a complement (1) because the NP is semantically similar to a VP: *claimed that she had been abducted by aliens*, (2) because the subordinating conjunction *that* cannot be replaced by a *WH*-phrase: **her claim <u>which</u> she had been abducted . . .* , and (3) because there is no missing constituent (no Ø) in the clause (*she had been abducted by aliens*).

    ii.   *Sue reminded us of the fact that alcohol is addictive.*

    iii.   *This is certainly a day to remember.*

    iv.   *She made an enormous effort to remember.*

    v.   *Students who fail to turn in their assignments on time will be shot.*

    vi.   *We were disturbed at the suggestion that malingering students might be shot.*

b. Find the relative clauses in the literary passages in Appendix Section I. *Hint:* There are two relative clauses in the Toni Morrison passage, one in the Rachel Carson passage, three in the Samuel Eliot Morison passage, and five in the passage from Stephen Hawking. The Hawking passage also contains a finite clause acting as *complement* of a noun. Find it. The Hemingway passage has no *finite* relative clauses, but it does have a CP_{pass} functioning as a noun modifier. Find it, also.

14.5.3 Clauses of Comparison and Degree

Both finite and non-finite clauses can function as complements of intensifiers such as *so, too,* and *enough*. Clauses in this position are traditionally called *clauses of degree*:

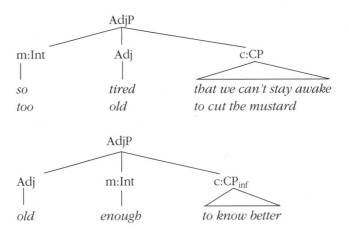

As evidence that the degree clause is a complement of the intensifier, notice that if the intensifier were not present, then the clause could not be, either: **tired that we can't stay awake* or **old to*

know better. The intensifier also determines the form of the clause; *so* requires a finite clause with the subordinating conjunction *that*; *too* and *enough* require infinitives.

The comparative elements *as*, *-er* and *-est* also take complements, traditionally called *comparative clauses*. The choice of subordinating conjunction (*than*, *that*, or *as*) depends on the comparative element: *as* takes an *as*-clause, *-er* takes a *than*-clause, and *-est* wants a clause beginning with *that* or Ø:

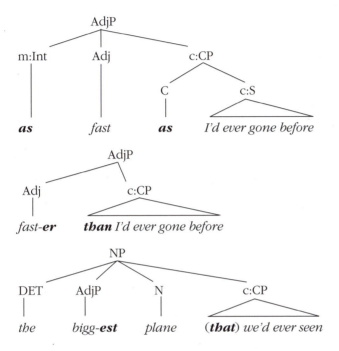

Clauses of comparison and degree are often *truncated*—that is, part of the clause is omitted. For example, the comparative clause *than you are* in the sentence below is truncated—short for *(than) you are smart:*

> *Nobody is smarter* [*than you are*].

EXERCISE 8. Combine the following sentences, following the instructions given. The first one is done for you, as an example:

a. i.   *A century ago, something so horrible happened in that house.*
   ii.   *Nobody has dared to enter it since.*
   Change (ii) to a *that* clause that is the complement of the intensifier *so*.
   Answer: *A century ago, something so horrible happened in that house that nobody has dared to enter it since.*

b. i.   *The story had been retold too many times.*
   ii.   *No one could be sure of the truth.*
   Change (ii) to an infinitive and insert it into (i) as complement of the intensifier *too*. (Hint: You will have to change *no one* to *anyone*.)

    c. i.   *She would get them out before the water rose any higher.*

        ii. *She knew he had to work quickly enough.*

        Change (i) into an infinitive that acts as complement of the intensifier *enough*.

    d. i.   *Your dad can run fast.*

        ii. *My dad can run just as fast.*

        Change (i) into a truncated *as* clause and insert it into (ii) as complement of the intensifier *as*.

    e. i.   *This is the biggest house.*

        ii. *I've never seen a bigger house.*

        Change (ii) into a truncated *that* clause and insert it into (i) as complement of the superlative suffix *-est*. (*Hint*: You will have to change *never* to *ever*.)

14.6 Applications for Teachers

In this section we will discuss two kinds of issues that are of interest to teachers—first, issues having to do with language development and then issues having to do with usage.

14.6.1   The Acquisition and Development of Subordinate Clauses

Most English-speaking children begin to use subordinate clauses by the age of three. By the time they enter school, they can handle most types of subordinate clauses that are found in adult speech, though they may still have difficulty with subtleties of meaning. For example, Perera (1984) points out that in the conditional sentences below, children may not understand the implication in (1) that we have no money, and in (2), they may not understand that they are being advised to hurry.

1. *If we had some money, we could buy some.*
2. *If we don't hurry, we'll miss the bus.*

Similarly, children as old as eleven years may not be able to recognize (1) as the bad sentence in the following pair:

1. *The meal was good although the pie was good.*
2. *The meal was good although the pie was bad.*

EXERCISE 9. Find subordinate clauses in the speech of Eve and Julia in Appendix Section VIII. Identify the type (CP, CP_{WH}, CP_{inf}, CP_{ing}, etc.) and function (subject of sentence, complement or modifier of . . .) of each clause. You should be able to find five subordinate clauses in the speech of Eve at 27 months and at least ten in the speech of Julia at age 36 months.

When children first begin to read and write, their written syntax tends to be very simple, with short sentences often strung together with *and* and *but*. As they become more fluent, their written sentences become longer, with more subordinate clauses.

EXERCISE 10. Compare the sentence structure of the second-grade author of "My Nightmare," Appendix Section II, with that of the fifth-grade author of "Shells of the Sea." First, count the number of words in each passage and divide by the number of sentences, to find an average number of words per sentence. Then list the subordinate clauses in each passage. You should find that the fifth grader is using longer sentences with more subordinate clauses, as well as more different *types* of subordinate clauses.

In a series of studies sponsored by the National Council of Teachers of English during the 1960s, Professor Kellogg Hunt of Florida State University worked to develop an objective measure of syntactic development in children's written sentences. Hunt began by observing, as we did in Exercise 10, that older children tend to write longer sentences. However, a simple count of words per sentence turned out not to be an adequate measure of syntactic sophistication, for two reasons: First, children's writing often contains idiosyncratic punctuation, so that it is difficult to decide what to count as a sentence. For example, you may have wondered whether the "Shells" sentence *You can curl your finger around the inside of the conch shell, it also has a starlike top* should count as one sentence or two. Secondly, it seems intuitively wrong that the author of "Nightmare" should improve his score with the long sentence *They put me in a space jail, but I had a good idea and all I had to do is get that space gun.* This run-on sentence should surely not count as more sophisticated than the better-formed three-sentence version: *They put me in a space jail. Then I had a good idea! All I had to do is get that space gun.*

To obtain a more accurate measure of syntactic sophistication, Hunt introduced the notion of a *T-unit,* which is defined as one main clause plus any subordinate material that is embedded within it. Stated another way, a T-unit is the smallest unit that could be punctuated as a sentence, using standard punctuation; if a sentence could be divided into two or three well-formed sentences, then each of those parts is a T-unit. To calculate the number of words per T-unit for a given piece of prose, begin by dividing the passage into T-units. Then count the number of T-units and the number of words in the passage, and divide. Using this procedure, the "Shells" sentence divides into two T-units, for an average of 9 words/T-unit:

1. *You can curl your finger around the inside of the conch shell*
2. *it also has a starlike top.*

And the "Nightmare" sentence divides into three T-units, for an average of 8 words/T-unit:

1. *They put me in a space jail*
2. *but I had a good idea*
3. *and all I had to do is get that space gun*

In a study of fourth, eighth, and twelfth graders at the Florida State University School, Hunt (1965) found that T-unit scores increased with grade level, as shown in Table 14.11.

Table 14.11   Grade Level and T-Unit Scores

Grade level	Average length of T-units
Grade 4	8.6
Grade 8	11.5
Grade 12	14.4

Hunt later extended his study to a set of eighteen "superior" adult writers who had published articles in *Harper's* and *Atlantic* magazines. In the first one thousand words of each article, Hunt found an average of 20.4 words per T-unit.

EXERCISE 11.

a. Choose one writer from each grade level in Appendix Section II, and use the following procedure to calculate a T-unit score for each child: First, count the number of words in the passage. Then divide the passage into T-units. Now divide the number of words by the number of T-units to obtain an average number of words/T-unit. Do the T-unit scores increase as the children grow older? How do your results compare with Hunt's (1965) observations at the Florida State University School?

b. Look more closely at the children's sentences to see what the older children are doing to increase their T-unit scores. Look, especially, for the following features: (i) coordination below the sentence level (rather than conjoining whole sentences), (ii) the presence of adverbial modifiers, and (iii) the presence of modifiers inside NPs.

c. If you or your parents or grandparents have saved samples of your writing throughout your school years, use these samples to trace the average length of your T-units from the early school years to the present. How does your progress compare with that of Hunt's subjects?

d. Hunt found that T-unit scores are affected not only by the maturity and linguistic sophistication of the writer, but also by *genre*, with longer T-units in expository writing than in narratives. Confirm this observation by calculating T-unit scores for the passages in Appendix Section I. There are four pieces of narrative writing (the first four) and four pieces of expository writing (the last four). How do the T-unit scores for the narrative pieces compare with those for the expository pieces?

e. If you yourself do more than one kind of writing (for example, expository writing in papers for courses and fiction writing for your own pleasure), then compare your T-unit scores for a representative sample from each genre.

The observation that T-units are affected by *genre* (Exercise 3d above) raises a question about the results of Hunt's (1965) study: Do the longer T-unit scores of older writers indicate an increasing ability to handle complex syntactic structures, or do they simply reflect a difference in *genre* and subject matter? Maybe older writers write longer T-units not because they have greater control over the syntactic structures of written English, but because they are dealing with more difficult, more abstract subject matter.

To answer this question, Hunt (1970) conducted a follow-up study in which writers of various ages and levels of experience were all given the same task—to revise a passage written in extremely short sentences. The passage and the directions for the exercise are set out below.

Aluminum

Directions: Read the passage all the way through. You will notice that the sentences are short and choppy. Study the passage, and then rewrite it in a better way. You may combine sentences, change the order of words, and omit words that are repeated too many times. But try not to leave out any of the information.

1 *Aluminum is a metal. It is abundant. It has many uses. It comes from bauxite. Bauxite*
2 *is an ore. Bauxite looks like clay. Bauxite contains aluminum. It contains several*
3 *other substances. Workmen extract these other substances from the bauxite. They*
4 *grind the bauxite. They put it in tanks. Pressure is in the tanks. The other substances*
5 *form a mass. They remove the mass. They use filters. A liquid remains. They put it*
6 *through several other processes. It finally yields a chemical. The chemical is powdery.*
7 *It is white. It is alumina. It is a mixture. It contains aluminum. It contains oxygen.*
8 *Workmen separate the aluminum from the oxygen. They use electricity. They finally*
9 *produce a metal. The metal is light. It has a luster. The luster is bright. The luster is*
10 *silvery. This metal comes in many forms.*

EXERCISE 12. Before reading any further, *stop right here* and do Hunt's exercise yourself. Take plenty of time: the children were allowed a whole hour. When you have finished, calculate your T-score, using the procedure described in Exercise 11a.

T-unit scores are not as high in this artificial exercise as in free writing, but the results of the study show, again, that T-unit length increases with age and maturity. Hunt's (1970) results are set out in Table 14.12.

Table 14.12   T-Unit Results from the "Aluminum" Experiment

Grade level	Average number of words per T-unit
Grade 4	5.42
Grade 6	6.84
Grade 8	9.84
Grade 10	10.44
Grade 12	11.30

To see whether T-unit length continues to increase after students leave school, Hunt also tested a group of twenty-five Tallahassee firemen, average age 32, who had completed twelfth grade but had not attended college. Although their occupation did not require extensive daily reading or writing, they showed a slight improvement over the twelfth graders, with a T-unit score of 11.85. To obtain a sample of "superior" adult writers, Hunt sent the Aluminum exercise to 95 authors who had recently published nonfiction articles in *Harper's Magazine* and the *Atlantic*. For the 25 writers who completed the exercise, the average T-unit score was 14.8.

In summary, Hunt's results show a steady growth in T-unit length with increased experience in writing. This growth does not stop when we finish school, but continues to develop, especially for those who continue to hone their skills. T-unit scores have also been shown to vary with *genre* and writing style (Exercise 11d above) and with the task the writer is given (higher for "free" writing than for the Aluminum exercise (Table 14.11 vs. Table 14.12)). If these limitations are kept in mind and if we are careful not to equate high T-unit scores with "good writing," then these scores can be useful in giving us an objective measure of the syntactic complexity of a student's writing.

Exercise 13 below is an example of a "sentence-combining" exercise which asks students to combine short, choppy sentences into a single well-formed structure. Exercises of this type can be used to encourage students to attempt more sophisticated sentence structures.

EXERCISE 13. Combine the short sentences in each set below to create a longer, smoother sentence. This first one is done for you, as an example:

a.   i.   *Tom called the chickens.*
    ii.   *They came to him.*
    iii.   *They squawked and flapped their wings.*
    Possible answer: *When Tom called the chickens, they came to him, squawking and flapping their wings.*

b.   i.   *Rachel's supervisor walked into her cubicle.*
    ii.   *She quickly turned off the computer game.*

c.   i.   *Rachel turned off the computer game.*
    ii.   *She had been playing the computer game.*

d.   i.   *Why did he chase the alligator in the first place?*
    ii.   *I don't understand this.*

e.   i.   *Aunt Esmeralda leapt onto the coffee table.*
    ii.   *She shrieked with fear.*

f.   i.   *Here is the house.*
    ii.   *The murder occurred here.*

g.   i.   *Rodney the beaver was nestled safely in his lodge.*
    ii.   *Rodney the beaver had no clue about this.*
    iii.   *What would the impending spring bring?*

h.   i.   *Their quarrel was finished.*
    ii.   *Cecelia kissed Brad right in front of the whole crowd.*

i.   i.   *What makes these boots so dangerous?*
    ii.   *It is this.*
    iii.   *The soles are five inches thick.*

j. i.   *Other topics for gossip ran out.*
    ii.   *We returned to the subject of Joan's strange marriage.*
k. i.   *Hedwig the woodchuck burrowed under the fence.*
    ii.   *By this method, he gained access to the succulent snap peas.*
l. i.   *He raced back to his computer.*
    ii.   *He only found this.*
    iii. *He had forgotten all his wonderful ideas.*
m. i.   *Someone might underestimate her capacity for mischief.*
    ii.   *It would be a big mistake.*
n. i.   *She had invented the story about alien abduction.*
    ii.   *The police were quite sure of this.*
o. i.   *They were married.*
    ii.   *They told me so.*
    iii. *What should I say?*
    iv.   *I had no idea.*

The usefulness of an exercise like 13 is limited by the fact that its sentences are chosen randomly, with no unifying context. To provide practice in constructing sentences within a meaningful connected discourse, teachers can create sentence-combining exercises from reading passages with which the students are already familiar. For example, from the Samuel Eliot Morison passage (Appendix Section I), we could create the sentence-combining exercise that is shown in Exercise 14.

EXERCISE 14.

a. Combine the following short sentences (based on the passage from Samuel Eliot Morison) into longer, smoother sentences. Then compare your passage with the original passage in Appendix Section I.

> *Who discovered America? Or rather, what European discovered America? Columbus found people in America. He called them Indians. This was a mistake. We now admit this. These people came over from Asia. They came via the Bering Strait. They came somewhere between 25,000 and 40,000 years ago. Then the Europeans arrived. The Indians had spread from Alaska to Tierra del Fuego. They had developed several hundred languages. In three places, at least, they had developed highly sophisticated societies. Those places were Peru, Mexico, and the highlands of Colombia. This happened before Columbus landed. What if the Spaniards had come a century later? They might have encountered a strong Aztec empire. This empire would have been defensible. It would have been a powerful nation. It would have been like Japan. Japan is in Asia.*

b. Choose another passage from Appendix Section I, or choose any appropriate passage of similar length, and use it to construct a sentence-combining like the one in (a).

14.6.2 Three Usage Issues in Relative Clauses

Writers of all ages struggle with three usage issues in the formation of relative clauses: (1) the treatment of prepositions, (2) the punctuation of "restrictive" and "non-restrictive" relative clauses, and (3) *which* vs. *that* vs. *who* in relative clauses.

14.6.2.1   The Treatment of Prepositional Phrases

In Chapter 11, Section 11.10.1, we observed that WH-fronting often leaves a preposition behind in interrogative clauses, especially when the prepositional phrase is a complement of the verb. Thus it is more natural to ask *Which volumes were you searching for?* than *For which volumes were you searching?* This is even more true when the question is embedded in a matrix sentence: *She wanted to know [which volumes I was searching for]*, not *??She wanted to know [for which volumes I was searching]*.

Relative clauses differ from questions in that WH-fronting more commonly moves the entire prepositional phrase, especially in formal writing. Thus it is entirely natural to write *She never found [the volumes [for which she was searching]]*, though in conversation we would be more likely to hear *She never found [the volumes [(that) she was searching for]]*. This is the source of the "rule" that students are often taught in school: *Never end a sentence with a preposition*. Teachers introduce this rule when they are trying to nudge students towards the more formal version of relative clauses like the one above. However, it is important to understand that this "rule" applies only in formal writing, and mainly in relative clauses, not questions. (But see Section 11.10.1 for a description of situations in which this rule applies even in questions.)

14.6.2.2   Restrictive *vs.* Non-restrictive Relative Clauses.[5]

Relative clauses are often divided into two semantically based categories, traditionally called "restrictive" vs. "nonrestrictive." Restrictive relative clauses help to define ("restrict") the class of entities that a NP refers to. For example, in the sentence [*People who live in glass houses*] *shouldn't throw stones*, the relative clause *who live in glass houses* is "restrictive" because it limits the class of people to whom the admonition applies—not *all* people, but only those who live in glass houses. If the clause were omitted, the reference of the NP would change: [*People*] *shouldn't throw stones*.

Non-restrictive relative clauses, also called "appositive" or "parenthetical" clauses, do not affect the reference of the NP; they simply add additional information. For example, in the sentence [*George Washington, who was our first president,*] *wore false teeth*, the non-restrictive relative clause *who was our first president* does not restrict the class of George Washingtons; George Washington is already fully identified by his name. If the relative clause were omitted—*George Washington wore false teeth*—there would be no change in the reference of the subject NP. A non-restrictive relative clause can, if desired, be enclosed in parentheses (hence the term "parenthetical"): *George Washington (who was our first president) wore false teeth*.

---

5. Before reading this section, please review Section 14.5.1 above, which discusses the structure of relative clauses or "adjectival" clauses.

The semantic distinction between restrictive and non-restrictive relative clauses is honored both in speech and in writing: In speech, non-restrictive relative clauses are pronounced with pauses at both ends, and these pauses are marked, in writing, by commas:

<u>Spoken form</u>: *George Washington [pause] who was our first president [pause] wore false teeth.*

<u>Written form</u>: *George Washington [,] who was our first president [,] wore false teeth.*

Restrictive relative clauses like the clause of [*people* [*who live in glass houses*]] are not surrounded by pauses in speech[6] and are not set off by commas in writing. See Chapter 16 for a more detailed discussion of the use of commas in English.

14.6.2.3 *Which* or *that* in Relative Clauses?

There is another difference between restrictive and non-restrictive relative clauses, in that ordinary finite CPs—*that*-clauses—cannot function as non-restrictive relative clauses:

[*Kendall Hall, <u>which</u> you visited the last time you were here,*] *is no longer open.*
[Kendall Hall, <u>that</u> you visited the last time you were here,] is no longer open.

Some usage authorities, including E. B. White in his deservedly popular *The Elements of Style*, have tried to apply this rule in the opposite direction, as well, by claiming that the WH-pronoun *which* should not be used in *restrictive* relative clauses. In this view, sentence (a) below is incorrect; we should write (b), instead:

a.   *This is [a rule [<u>which</u> is frequently ignored]].*
b.   *This is [a rule [<u>that</u> is frequently ignored]].*

Notice, however, that this putative rule conflicts with the don't-leave-the-preposition-behind rule:

c.   *This is [the room [in <u>which</u> they held their meetings]].*
d.   *This is [the room [<u>that</u> they held their meetings <u>in</u>]].*

And it is hard to find a writer who follows the rule consistently. In fact, E.B. White's own beautifully written essays are full of sentences like (e) below, from his short essay "The Cost of Hyphens" (*The New Yorker* 12/15/28):

e.   [*The pain* [*<u>which</u> attends all literary composition*]] *is increased, in some cases, by the writer's knowing how much per word he will receive for his effort.*

---

6. Warning: There may be a pause at the *end* of a restrictive relative clause, as in *People who live in glass houses [pause] shouldn't throw stones.* Crucially, however, there cannot be a pause at the beginning of the clause (before *who*); this is different from the non-restrictive clause, which is *surrounded* by pauses.

To complicate the matter further, some authorities recommend that a WH-clause *should* be chosen, rather than a *that*-clause, when the head noun is a person; that is, we should write (f), not (g):[7]

    f.   *This is [the thief [who stole the diamonds]].*

    g.   *This is [the thief [that stole the diamonds]].*

This rule is not only inconsistent with the *which/that* "rule," but also ensnares us in the *who/whom* dilemma when the WH-phrase comes from a complement position:

    h.   *This is [the man [whom we saw Ø at the crime scene]].*

    i.   Better: *This is [the man [(that) we saw Ø at the crime scene]].*

No wonder I so often receive e-mails and telephone calls from faculty colleagues with questions about how to word a relative clause in a paper they are sending to their publisher! Here is the advice I give them: The grammar of English allows all the sentences (a)–(i); the choice among them is a matter of taste, not grammar. In deciding among the options, I would rely on my ear, which tells me that (a), (b), (c), (e), (f), (g), and (i) are fine, but (h) is awkward, and (d) is too informal for a written essay. If your ear gives you a different result from mine, then you should choose the option that sounds best to you!

14.6.3 Dangling Participles

Because non-finite clauses often have empty subjects (Ø), the listener or reader must be able to discover the subject of the clause from the context. Participles whose Ø subjects are hard to identify are called *dangling participles*; this is a common usage error in participles that are functioning as sentential modifiers. To make the sentence maximally easy to understand, the Ø subject of a sentential modifier should be the same as the subject of the main clause. For example, the passive participle in the sentence below, cited by Greenbaum 1989, is a dangling participle because its Ø subject is not the same as the subject of the main clause:

    [*When Ø delivered*], **they** *found the merchandise to be spoiled.*

The sentence will be easier to follow if the main clause is re-worded so that its subject is the same as the Ø subject of the sentential modifier:

    [*When Ø delivered*], **the merchandise** *was found to be spoiled.*

Alternatively, the sentential modifier could be recast as a finite clause with an overt subject:

    [*When* **the merchandise** *was delivered*], *they found it to be spoiled.*

---

7. For what it is worth, E.B. White *rejects* this advice in his essay "Relative Pronouns" (*The New Yorker*, 12/25/48), citing Matthew 2:1: ". . . there came wise men from the east to Jerusalem, saying, Where is he that [not *who*] is born King of the Jews?"

Although usage handbooks focus on dangling participles, infinitives are subject to the same problem:

> [Ø *To be sure the package will get there in time*], ***express mail*** *should be used.*
> Clearer: [Ø *To be sure the package will get there in time*], ***you*** *should use express mail.*

It is important to avoid dangling participles and infinitives. For writing to be clear and crisp, readers must be able to immediately identify the Ø subjects of non-finite clauses.

EXERCISE 15. Re-write the sentences below so that the Ø subject can be identified more easily. *Hint*: The general rule is that a Ø subject in a sentential modifier should be the same as the subject of the main clause:

    i.   [*Upon Ø getting home from work*], *the dog greeted us at the door.*
    ii.   [Ø *Having finally graduated*], *his parents took him out to dinner.*
    iii.   [*Upon Ø crossing the finish line*], *the race is over.*
    iv.   [Ø *To assemble the apparatus correctly*], *a wrench or a pair of pliers will be needed.*
    v.   [Ø *Fearing that it would spoil the children's teeth*], *the candy was kept locked away in a cupboard.*
    vi.   [Ø *Originally located in Thompson Hall, the move to new office space will accommodate the program's growing staff.*]

14.7 Applications for Students of Literature

Sentence structure is an important element of a writer's style. We have already introduced Kellogg Hunt's "T-unit score" as a measure of syntactic complexity in children's writing. This measure can also be useful as a preliminary step in comparing the prose styles of adult writers.[8] For example, in looking at the passages from Rachel Carson and Lewis Thomas (Appendix Section I), you may feel, intuitively, that Carson's sentence structure is more complex than Thomas's. This intuitive observation can be confirmed by calculating T-unit scores for the two passages:

T-units in the Thomas Passage (71 words)

1   *Ants are so much like human beings as to be an embarrassment.*
2   *They farm fungi, raise aphids as livestock, launch armies into wars, use chemical sprays to alarm and confuse enemies, capture slaves.*
3   *The families of weaver ants engage in child labor, holding their larvae like shuttles to spin out the thread that sews the leaves together for their fungus gardens.*
4   *They exchange information ceaselessly.*
5   *They do everything but watch television.*

---

8. But do not use the term "T-unit" in a literature paper; this term is educational jargon and has not entered the literary register.

T-units in the Carson Passage (111 words)

1   *Nowhere in all the sea does life exist in such bewildering abundance as in the surface waters.*

2   *From the deck of a vessel you may look down, hour after hour, on the shimmering discs of jellyfish, their gently pulsating bells dotting the surface as far as you can see.*

3   *Or one day you may notice early in the morning that you are passing through a sea of microscopic creatures, each of which contains an orange pigment granule.*

4   *At noon you are still moving through red seas*

5   *and when darkness falls the waters shine with an eerie glow from the phosphorescent fires of yet more billions and trillions of these same creatures.*

Dividing the number of words by the number of T-units, we obtain a T-unit score of 14.2 for the Thomas passage vs. 22.2 for the Carson passage, thereby confirming our impression that Carson's sentences are more complex. Be careful, however, not to equate complexity with superiority. Thomas is a sophisticated and very skillful writer who is no doubt capable of constructing complex sentences when he chooses to do so. Sentence structure is one of the stylistic choices a writer makes—an expression of the writer's individual style and taste, and his/her judgement of how best to present a particular subject matter to a particular audience.

EXERCISE 16.   Look over the remaining literary passages in Appendix Section I and make a quick, intuitive judgement about the relative complexity of their sentence structure. Then look at the T-unit scores you calculated for these passages in Exercise 11d above. How well do the T-unit scores correlate with your intuitive judgment about the syntactic density of these passages?

More important than the mere length of a writer's T-units is what structures are used to make the T-units long—subordinate clauses rather than simple NPs as subjects and complements of verbs? adverbial modifiers to augment the basic subject-AUX-VP structure of the sentence? adjectival modifiers that add to the length of the NPs? conjoined constituents below the level of the sentence? Carson uses all these devices: a long *that*-clause (*that you are . . . an orange pigment granule*) as complement of the verb *notice* in sentence (3); adverbial modifiers such as *nowhere in all the sea* (sentence 1) and *when darkness falls* (sentence 3), adjectival modifiers such as *each of which contains an orange pigment granule* (sentence 3), and conjoined constituents below the level of the sentence (*yet more <u>billions and trillions</u> of these same creatures*, sentence 5). But her favorite device is the use of adjectival modifiers to create long NPs such as the following:

> *such <u>bewildering</u> abundance*
> *the <u>shimmering</u> discs <u>of jellyfish</u>*
> *their <u>gently pulsating</u> bells*
> *a sea <u>of microscopic creatures</u>, <u>each of which contains an orange pigment granule</u>*

306

an <u>orange</u> pigment granule
an <u>eerie</u> glow
the <u>phosphorescent</u> fires <u>of yet more billions and trillions of these same creatures</u>

Other writers favor other devices. For example, Hawking uses mostly short, simple NPs:

a physical theory
the sense
a hypothesis
how many times
the results of experiments
some theory
the next time

But he makes frequent use of sentential modifiers, some of them long:

in the sense that it is only a hypothesis
no matter how many times the results of experiments agree with some theory
on the other hand
in principle
by finding even a single observation that disagrees with its predictions
as philosopher of science Karl Popper has emphasized
each time new experiments are observed to agree with the predictions
if ever a new observation is found to disagree
at least

As for Thomas, he uses one long NP:

the thread that sews the leaves together for their fungus gardens

and two sentential modifiers:

ceaselessly
holding their larvae like shuttles to spin out the thread that . . .

but the primary device that lengthens his T-units is coordination:

Conjoined VPs: *farm fungi, raise aphids as livestock, launch armies into wars, use*
   chemical sprays to alarm and confuse enemies, capture slaves
Conjoined Vs: *alarm and confuse*

Preferences like these are a signature feature of a writer's style.

Tree diagrams of some selected sentences from the passages of Appendix Section I are given in Figure 14.1 at the end of this chapter.

EXERCISE 17. Choose two other passages from Appendix Section I (not Carson, Hawking, or Lewis), and compare their syntactic structure. Begin by giving the T-unit scores for the two passages you have chosen and then identify some of the syntactic devices that lengthen the T-units in each passage.

14.8 Applications for ESL Teachers

ESL students need a great deal of practice with sentence combining exercises, and, even more than for native speakers, it is important to construct these exercises from passages that are already familiar to the students (see Exercise 14a above). Meaning is hard to work out in a foreign language, and if sentences are taken out of context students may work through them in a mechanical way, with little attention to their semantic content.

Because ESL students tend to avoid constructions that are difficult for them, teachers must find ways to encourage them to attempt new structures. One technique is a "spontaneous pattern practice" in which the students are asked to construct meaningful sentences in a particular pattern. For example, to practice relative clauses, students could be asked to create original sentences telling what kinds of stories, books, songs, or movies they like, following this pattern:

> *I like [movies that have a happy ending].*
> *I like [stories that take place in far-away places].*

Once the sentences have been collected (and corrected, if necessary), they can be used as the basis for an exercise in which students are asked to remember their classmates' responses: *What kind of movies does Jaime like? He likes movies that . . . .* and to ask follow-up questions: *Why do you like [movies that have a happy ending]?* or *Tell me the name of [a movie that you liked].*

ESL students have particular difficulty in choosing clausal complements for verbs,[9] especially the choice between infinitives and *ing*-clauses:[10] Why do we say *We saw him [running down the road]* rather than *We saw him [to run down the road]*? Sometimes there is a meaning difference between these two types of clauses, with the *ing*-clause representing an *actual* situation or event, while the infinitive represents a *potential* situation or event. Thus sentence (1) below, but not (2), expresses some doubt about your ability to open the window.

> 1.   *You could try [to open the window].*
>
> *vs.* 2.   *You could try [opening the window].*

---

9. Luckily, prepositions accept only *ing*-clause complements, not infinitives, so there is a reliable rule for that part of the grammar: *before hiking in the mountains*, not **before to hike in the mountains*.

10. There is a further challenge in the fact that some verbs take "bare" infinitives rather than full infinitives: *We made her [go outside]*, not **We made her [to go outside]*. Of course, this is an exception to the usual pattern: *We forced her [to go outside]*, not **We forced her [go outside]*.

However, it is difficult to find a similar difference between (3) and (4):

3.   *We like [to hike in the mountains].*
4.   *We like [hiking in the mountains].*

and there is no obvious reason why *enjoy*, with virtually the same meaning as *like*, accepts only an *ing*-complement, and not an infinitive:

> *I enjoy [hiking in the mountains].*
> **I enjoy [to hike in the mountains].*

It seems, then, that knowing what kind of complement to put after each verb is partly a matter of memorization. Because this is not an area of difficulty for native speakers, general college dictionaries do not provide much assistance with this issue. For help in choosing the right complement, ESL students need access to learners' dictionaries such as *The Oxford Advanced Learner's Dictionary of Current English*, which specify, for every meaning of every verb, what complements the verb can take.

14.9   Summary of the Chapter

In this chapter, we discussed six types of subordinate clauses—ordinary finite clauses, finite WH-clauses, infinitives, WH-infinitives, *ing*-clauses, and absolute or "verbless" clauses. These clauses enter into the structure of larger "matrix" clauses by acting as the subject, complement, or modifier of some element in the matrix clause. We then discussed two types of clauses that have special syntactic properties—relative (or "adjectival") clauses and clauses of comparison and degree.

As applications for teachers, we looked at the development of subordinate clauses in children's speech and writing, and introduced Kellogg Hunt's notion of words-per-T-unit as a measure of syntactic complexity. We then discussed four usage issues—"dangling" participles, WH-fronting of prepositional phrases in relative clauses, the punctuation of restrictive and non-restrictive relative clauses, and the choice between *which, that*, and *who* in restrictive and non-restrictive relative clauses.

For students of literature, we pointed out some characteristics to look for in the sentence structure of literary passages. Finally, for ESL teachers, we recommended sentence-combining exercises and "spontaneous pattern practice," and we discussed the difficulty that ESL learners have in determining what sort of clause to use as complement for a particular verb.

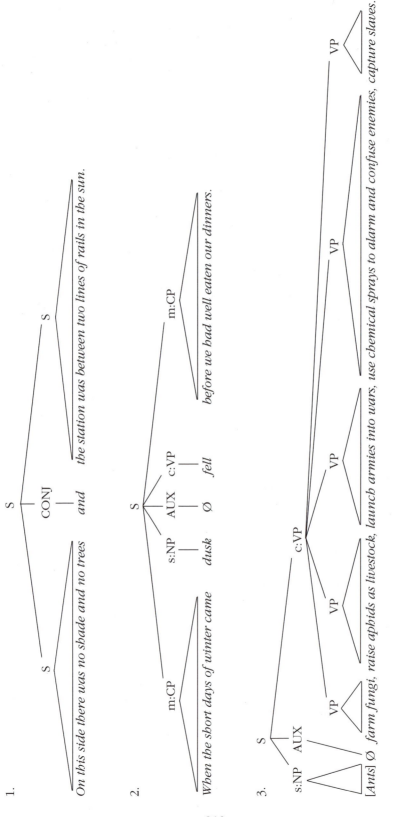

1.

```
              S
      ┌───────┴───────┐
      S              S
 ┌────┴────┐
         CONJ
          │
         and
```

On this side there was no shade and no trees   and   the station was between two lines of rails in the sun.

2.

```
                    S
          ┌─────────┼─────────┐
       m:CP         S        m:CP
              ┌─────┼─────┐
            s:NP  AUX  c:VP
              │    │    │
            dusk   Ø   fell
```

When the short days of winter came   before we had well eaten our dinners.

3.

```
        S
   ┌────┴────┐
 s:NP  AUX       c:VP
       Ø    ┌────┬────┬────┐
           VP   VP   VP   VP ...
```

[Ants] Ø farm fungi, raise aphids as livestock, launch armies into wars, use chemical sprays to alarm and confuse enemies, capture slaves.

310

4.

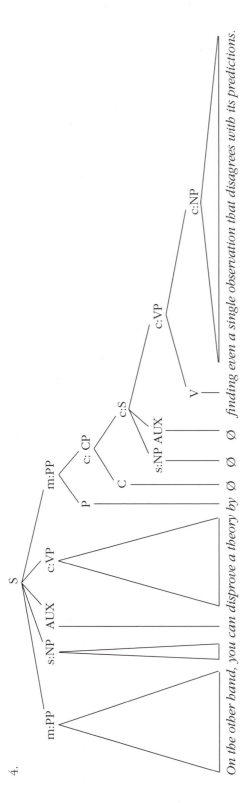

On the other hand, you can disprove a theory by Ø Ø Ø finding even a single observation that disagrees with its predictions.

Figure 14.1 Some sentences from the literary passages in Appendix Section I.

311

5.

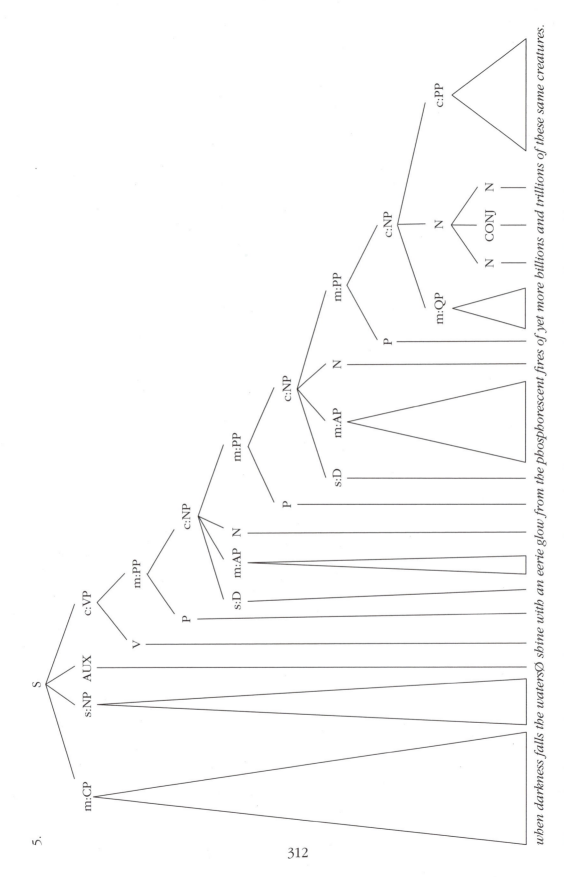

when darkness falls the watersØ shine with an eerie glow from the phosphorescent fires of yet more billions and trillions of these same creatures.

Figure 14.1 (continued)   Some sentences from the literary passages in Appendix Section I.

312

Table 14.13 Complementation Patterns for Verbs

The addition of clauses as complements for verbs gives us several new VP patterns. A complete list of VP patterns is given in this table. The second columns for patterns 12, 13, and 14 are left blank because these patterns have no traditional names.

Pattern	Traditional Name	Examples
1. VP | V	Intransitive	They *laughed*. They *frowned*. They *sang*. They *left*.
2. VP ╱ ╲ V c:NP	Transitive: The complement is called the direct object.	I *closed the door*. We *enjoyed the movie* You have *made a mistake*. She is *singing a song*.
3. VP ╱ | ╲ V c:NP c:NP	Ditransitive: The first c:NP is the indirect object; the second is the direct object.	Sue *gave Tom a kiss*. I will *make you a cup of tea*. The children *sang us a song*. Please *pass me the sugar*.
4. VP ╱ ╲ V c: { AdjP / NP$_{pred}$ }	Linking: The AdjP or NPpred is a predicate complement that describes the subject of the clause.	He *is very tall*. She *seems worried*. You *look lovely*. She *became a famous writer*.
5. VP ╱ | ╲ V c:NP c: { AdjP / NP$_{pred}$ }	Complex transitive: The first complement is the direct object; the second is a predicate complement that describes the direct object.	We *found the news very disturbing*. I *consider him a friend*. We *elected Bush president*.
6. VP ╱ ╲ V c:PP	Prepositional	We *looked at the house*. We *listened to the crickets*. They *have decided on an answer*. We *agree with you*.

Table 14.13 (continued)   Complementation Patterns for Verbs

Pattern	Traditional Name	Examples
7. VP V c:NP c:PP	Transitive prepositional	We *gave the books to the children.* They *blamed George for the accident.* We *loaded the wagon with hay.* Tell *us about your sister.*
8. VP V c:CP	Clausal	I *think (that) you're right.* She *said (that) she'd go.* I *wonder if she's ready.* We don't *know whether she's coming.*
9. VP V c:NP c:CP	Transitive clausal.	We *told Bill (that) you were here.* I'll *inform the president (that) you're here.* I *asked Sue if she was ready.*
10. VP V c:CP$_{inf}$	Infinitival	We *tried to open the window.* We *wanted you to open the window.* Birds *like to eat worms.* We *expected it to rain.* We *saw him go.* ("bare" infinitive)
11. VP V c:NP c:CP$_{inf}$	Transitive infinitival	Please *tell your brother to come in.* They *forced him to attend the meeting.* We *helped him (to) change the tire.*
12. VP V c:CP$_{ing}$		I *enjoyed playing tennis.* I *like raking leaves.* *Try opening the window.*
13. VP V c:NP c:CP$_{ing}$		They *have him bagging groceries.* We *found her painting the shutters.* We *heard Bill leaving the house.*
14. VP V c:CP$_{pass}$		The glass *got broken.* We *had the windows repaired.* We *got the house painted.* They *found the village destroyed.*

CHAPTER 15

Presenting Information

15.1 Introduction

Not *all* language is intended to convey information. The language of a love letter, a pep rally, or a political speech may be intended primarily to arouse emotion, and the language of ordinary conversation often has little purpose other than to establish or maintain social contact. Language of this sort is called *phatic* communication.

However, much of the language we use *is* intended, at least partly, to convey information—to give directions, to make a report, to orient an employee to a new job, to tell a story, to make an argument. Informative language is often planned in advance—sometimes very carefully and sometimes just by pausing for an instant to get one's thoughts together. In preparing to present information, the speaker or writer must consider such questions as the following:

    a.   *What are my main points and sub-points and how can I make these clear and salient to my audience?*

    b.   *In what order should I present my points?*

    c.   *What supporting information should I give?*

    d.   *What can I do to make the presentation flow clearly?*

    e.   *How can I word each sentence so as to make my meaning as clear as possible?*

Some of these questions belong to a course in composition rather than one on the structure of English. Grammarians do, however, have something to say about the saliency of topics, the flow of information from sentence to sentence, and the ordering of information within a sentence. These are the issues that will be addressed in this chapter. Unlike previous chapters, applications for writers and teachers will be mixed with the content of the chapter rather than placed in a separate section at the end.

15.2 Coherence: Making It Clear What a Passage Is About

A passage is said to be *coherent* when its *topic* (i.e., what the passage is about) is easily identified and when every sentence of the passage relates to that topic in a clear and logical way. In very straightforward passages such as the selection from Lewis Thomas in Appendix Section I, each clause has a topic that corresponds closely to the overall topic of the passage—in this case, ants. The Thomas passage is repeated below, with the topic of each sentence highlighted in boldface:[1]

---

1. The topic of a sentence (what the *sentence* is about) is usually in subject position, as in the Thomas passage. Some exceptions are sentences such as the following, which have overtly specified topics:

    *As for **dessert**, I'm hoping you'll serve your famous Bananas Foster.*

    ***Why she said that** I can't imagine.*

and sentences such as the following, where the topic of the sentence has been moved to a position following the verb:

    *There was **an enormous vase** on the table.*

    *It's obvious **that you don't care for my Bananas Foster**.*

315

1   [**Ants** *are so much like human beings as to be an embarrassment.*] [**They** *farm*
2   *fungi, raise aphids as livestock, launch armies into wars, use chemical sprays to*
3   *alarm and confuse enemies, capture slaves.*] [**The families of weaver ants** *engage*
4   *in child labor, holding their larvae like shuttles to spin out the thread that sews the*
5   *leaves together for their fungus gardens.*] [**They** *exchange information ceaselessly.*]
6   [**They** *do everything but watch television.*]

More typically, as in the following example from Williams (1994, 124), the clauses of a passage have different topics. However, if the passage is coherent, then the topics are few in number and are clearly related to one overall theme—in this case, the identification of topics by a reader:

1   [**Topics** *are crucial to a reader* [*because* **they** *focus attention on particular ideas*
2   *toward the beginning of sentences and thereby notify readers what a whole passage*
3   *is "about."*]] [[*If* **a sequence of topics** *seems coherent,*] *then* **readers** *will feel* [**they**
4   *are moving through a paragraph from a cumulatively coherent point of view.*]] [*But*
5   [*if* **topics** *shift randomly through the paragraph,*] *then* **the reader** *has to begin each*
6   *sentence out of context, from no coherent point of view.*] [[*When* **that** *happens,*] **the**
7   **reader** *will feel dislocated, disoriented, out of focus.*]

This paragraph has three (related) topics—(a) the topics of individual sentences and clauses, (b) the readers of the passage, and (c) the confusion that is created when topics shift randomly (this is the reference of *that*, in line 6).

EXERCISE 1.

  a. The finite clauses are blocked off for you in the following passage. Underline the topic of each clause (following the model of the "ants" and "topics" paragraphs above). Then make a list of the topics you have underlined. Is the passage coherent, in your view, with a logical sequence of topics all related to one overall theme? *Caution:* When the topic position is occupied by a pronoun such as *which* in line 3, then the topic of that clause is the referent of the pronoun; for example, for the clause that begins in line 3, you would identify the topic as "which" and say that it refers to the keyboard and screen.

1   [*E-mail derives its usefulness from the fact* [*that users are able to choose the*
2   *incoming messages to read and respond to.*]] [*Unfortunately, e-mail is limited*
3   *by its input and output devices, a keypad and a screen,* [*which are cumber-*
4   *some when large and hard to use when reduced to pocket size.*]] [*Cell phones*
5   *have the advantage of being significantly more compact.*] [*Also, spoken mes-*
6   *sages contain intonational clues about the mood of the speaker,* [*which are*
7   *missing from written messages.*]] [*Unfortunately, incoming calls are often*
8   *disruptive,*] [*and voice-mail services are inconvenient to use.*] [*What we will*
9   *see in the future is a combination of these two devices:*] [*Messages will be*
10   *spoken and stored in a voice-mail system but will be displayed and retrieved*
11   *in a fashion similar to e-mail, in a written list, accompanied by subject lines,*
12   [*so that the user can select which messages to respond to.*]]

b. Block off the clauses in the Rachel Carson and Samuel Eliot Morison passages in Appendix Section I, and identify the topic of each clause. Use your list of topics to evaluate the coherence of these passages.

15.3 Cohesion: Linking Sentences Together in Connected Discourse

Writers must also pay attention to the cohesion between sentences. A discourse is said to be *cohesive* when each sentence follows smoothly from the one that precedes it. This section will set out some strategies for creating cohesion between sentences.

Strategy 1. Begin each clause with information that was mentioned in an immediately preceding clause or sentence. For example, in Chapter 10, Section 10.5.4, we considered two versions of the same statement—one active and one passive:

1. *Christopher Columbus discovered America.*
2. *America was discovered by Christopher Columbus.*

Either of these sentences can be inserted, as a subordinate clause, in the blank space in (3):

3. *Everything changed in 1492, when _____.*

Which version we should choose depends on what we have been talking about in previous sentences: If we have been talking about the history of European exploration in the 15th century, then we should choose (1), beginning with Christopher Columbus, who was one of those explorers:

4. *Everything changed in 1492, when **Christopher Columbus** discovered America.*

But if we have been talking about the life of Native Americans on this continent, then we should choose version (2), which begins with *America*:

5. *Everything changed in 1492, when **America** was discovered by Christopher Columbus.*

To give another example, an adverbial modifier can be placed either at the beginning or the end of a sentence:

1. *Many of his customers stopped doing business with him **when he introduced his environmental service fee.***
2. ***When he introduced his environmental service fee,** many of his customers stopped doing business with him.*

But in the blank position below, sentence (2) is the better choice, because it begins with a reference to Rubin's new concern for the environment, which has just been mentioned in the previous sentence:

3. *Not everyone appreciated Rubin's new concern for the environment. _____*

EXERCISE 2.

a. (from Williams 1994, p. 116) Here are two versions of the same statement—one active and one passive. Decide which version, active or passive, is more appropriate for the blank space in the paragraph below, and say why:

    i.   *A black hole is created by the collapse of a dead star into a point perhaps no larger than a marble.*

    ii.   *The collapse of a dead star into a point perhaps no larger than a marble creates a black hole.*

Some astonishing questions about the nature of the universe have been raised by scientists exploring black holes in space. _____ So much matter compressed into so little volume changes the fabric of space around it in puzzling ways.

b. Improve the cohesion between the sentences of the following paragraph by revising each sentence so that it begins with a topic that has been mentioned in an immediately preceding sentence:

    i.   *If possible, transport the computer in its original packaging. Computer manufacturers fit the packaging material to the individual computer. During your move, your computer will be held securely by this packaging. Ask the company for similar material if you have not kept the original packaging. Alternatively, you can simply toss the computer into a box, with cables and whatnot still connected, during those last few frantic moments before the moving van arrives.*

    ii.   *In his address to the committee, Dr. Aaronsen posited that the single biggest influence on the evolution of human intelligence was a dramatic reduction in fertility rates. Diet, environment, or perhaps a virus caused this fertility reduction in pre-humans. Natural selection favored parents who were able to reproduce over a long period of time, because offspring were born later and less frequently. And greater intelligence was favored by a longer reproductive lifespan, because intelligent parents were more successful at finding food and avoiding predators. In addition, parents could devote more time to each child, because they had fewer offspring to raise. Thus knowledge, as well as instinct, could be passed along to the children by the parents.*

Strategy 2: Eliminate unnecessary repetition. Unnecessary repetition makes a passage difficult to follow, because the reader is misled into thinking that a new topic has been introduced when, in fact, the topic is still the same. The following passage contains several unnecessarily repeated NPs, marked with boldface:

> *Ireland was once a poverty-stricken nation. But today **Ireland** is experiencing a comeback, fueled in no small part by American companies. By the end of 1997, almost six hundred American companies had set up offices in **Ireland**. In 1999 **American companies located in Ireland** contributed about thirty-two billion dollars of the fifty billion dollars*

> *worth of goods and services exported from **Ireland**. Today **Ireland** is the fastest-growing nation in Europe, and **American companies** are reaping the benefits of **Ireland's** booming economy.*

The passage can be made clearer by deleting the repeated NPs or replacing them with proforms or other substitutes:

> *Ireland was once a poverty-stricken nation. But today **its** economy is experiencing a comeback, fueled in no small part by American companies. By the end of 1997, almost six hundred of **them** had set up offices **there**. In 1999 **they** contributed about thirty-two billion dollars of the fifty billion dollars worth of the goods and services **the country** exported. Today **Ireland** is the fastest-growing nation in Europe, and **American companies** are reaping the benefits of **its** booming economy.*

EXERCISE 3. Improve the cohesion of each passage by deleting unnecessarily repeated constituents or replacing them with proforms or other substitutes. Repeated NPs and VPs are highlighted in the first example:

a. *Stanley made mistakes just as everyone **makes mistakes**. Unlike other people, however, **Stanley** never apologized for **his mistakes**. Instead, **Stanley** took out his broom, swept up **his mistakes**, and tossed **his mistakes** into the trash. **The mistakes** sat in **the trash** until Tuesday morning. On **Tuesday morning Stanley** took **the mistakes** out to the curb to be picked up by the garbage collector.*

b. *The name Rudyard Kipling brings to mind jungles, boarding schools, and English soldiers. That's why many Rudyard Kipling fans are surprised to learn that the only house Rudyard Kipling ever built is located in Brattleboro, Vermont. Rudyard Kipling's wife's family lived in Brattleboro, Vermont. Rudyard Kipling was so fond of the house, which Rudyard Kipling completed in 1893 and called Naulakha, that Rudyard Kipling apparently intended to live in the house for the rest of his life.*

c. *Before 1999, most investors looking for mutual funds that invested solely in Internet companies had little to choose from. In 1999, however, Internet mutual funds began proliferating rapidly. A total of nineteen new Internet mutual funds were born in 1999. By three weeks into January of 2000, four more Internet mutual funds had been delivered, and the storks were circling with another eight Internet mutual funds. This population explosion of Internet mutual funds was inspired by an Internet mutual fund that garnered returns of close to 200 percent in both 1998 and 1999.*

d. *Do not expose your Elvis Commemorative Plate no. 1367 to direct sunlight. Exposing the plate to direct sunlight will fade the lettering. Do not expose your Elvis Commemorative Plate to extreme temperature fluctuations. Exposing the plate to extreme temperature fluctuations may result in cracking. Wipe your Elvis Commemorative Plate no. 1367 regularly with a dry cloth. Wiping the plate with a dry cloth will discourage mildew. Mildew is caused by dampness. Wiping the plate with a dry cloth will also keep the surface dust free.*

Strategy 3: Use connectives such as *first, secondly, for example, for instance, furthermore, moreover, in addition, similarly, finally, in fact, therefore, as a result, of course, consequently, in other words, yet, however, in contrast, nevertheless,* and *on the other hand,* or evaluative expressions such as *fortunately, in the view of most observers, frankly, briefly put, etc.* For example, consider the passage below, in which the connectives have been deleted:

> *E-mail derives its usefulness from the user's ability to sort incoming messages and respond at will. E-mail is limited by its input and output devices, a keyboard and a screen, which are cumbersome when large and inconvenient when reduced to pocket size. Cell phones are significantly more compact. Spoken messages contain intonational clues that cannot be obtained from a written message. Incoming calls are disruptive and voice-messaging devices are inconvenient to use. Spoken messages will be displayed and retrieved in a fashion similar to e-mail, in a written list that allows users to select which messages they wish to retrieve.*

Notice the improvement when connectives are added:

> *E-mail derives its usefulness from the user's ability to sort incoming messages and respond at will.* **However,** *e-mail is limited by its input and output devices, a keyboard and a screen, which are cumbersome when large and inconvenient when reduced to pocket size.* **In contrast,** *cell phones are significantly more compact.* **Furthermore,** *spoken messages contain intonational information that cannot be obtained from a written message.* **Unfortunately,** *incoming calls are disruptive and voice-messaging devices are inconvenient to use.* **Possibly, in the future,** *spoken messages will be displayed and retrieved in a fashion similar to e-mail, in a written list that allows users to select which messages they wish to retrieve.*

EXERCISE 4. Improve the cohesion of the following paragraphs by inserting connectives:

a. *This short quotation—insightful, amusing, and well written—gives you an idea what you can expect from the rest of the book. The first essay is a clunker. Apart from this one chapter, this is a five-star book.*

b. *The flowering herb* Buddleia *has many uses. It is a delicious flavoring for fish. It provides a perfect foil for lavender and black fennel. Butterflies love its blooms. It is often called "butterfly bush."*

c. Verre églomisé *is the technique of decorating glass by applying gold leaf to glass. The artist etches designs into it. Layers of color are added. Varnish is applied. It's a painstaking process.*

d. *Chicken makes solid nutritional sense. It is a good source of protein. Poultry with the skin removed is low in fat. Red meat can be a bit fattier. Many people on a low-fat diet avoid it.*

Strategy 4. Use coordination and parallel structure. (By *parallel structure,* we mean that the second element of a conjoined structure should mirror the structure of the first part.) Consider the following example from Daiker, Kerek, and Morenberg 1982, 290–291:

> *For the Northerners, Lincoln was a hero because he ended slavery and saved the Union. But because he threatened to destroy one of the staples of their economy, Lincoln was regarded as a villain by Southerners.*

Daiker et al. point out that this passage can be strengthened by combining the two sentences into one compound sentence, with parallel structure in the two parts:

> *For the Northerners, Lincoln was a hero because he ended slavery and saved the Union, but for Southerners he was a villain because he threatened to destroy one of the staples of their economy.*

EXERCISE 5. Improve the cohesion of the following passages by conjoining sentences, and/or using parallel structure:

a. *If possible, transport the computer in its original packaging. If you have not kept the packaging, your computer store may be able to supply similar materials. Alternatively, the computer can be tossed into a box, with cables and whatnot still connected, during the final frantic moments before the moving van arrives.*

   Hint: The first sentence is an imperative, while the second and third are declaratives. Make them all the same.

b. *Lao was responsible for transporting the general's servants. He was also responsible for transporting the general's concubines. He was also responsible for transporting the general's visitors. But, like most drivers of that era, he was also expected to keep track of the whereabouts of his charges and the conditions of their coming and going. His performance of these duties was such that he secured a prominent position in Qui's hierarchy of intrigue. And he also received a substantial income from those whose secrets he was paid to keep.*

c. *E-mail is limited by its input device, the keyboard. It is also limited by its output device, the screen. These are cumbersome at their normal size, and when they are reduced to pocket size they are hard to manipulate.*

15.4 Ordering Information in a Sentence

As we have seen in previous sections, a concern for the flow of information in a passage often dictates how items should be ordered in each sentence or clause. However, the grammar of English is based on a fixed word order—*SUBJECT AUX VP*—that gives us little choice about the ordering of constituents. Fortunately, English has several transformations—called *stylistic* transformations—that allow constituents to be moved to other positions.

15.4.1   Transformations That Move Long, Heavy Constituents to the End of the Sentence

A long, heavy constituent in the middle of a sentence disrupts the flow of information and makes the sentence difficult to follow. The heavy constituents in the examples below have been enclosed in brackets:

  a.   [*That everyone already knew what had happened*] *was obvious.*
  b.   [*A Supreme Court ruling* [*concerning racial preferences in university admissions*]] *has just been issued.*
  c.   [*A book* [*on the same topic*]] *has been published.*
  d.   *We had checked* [*every window and door on the ground floor*] *very carefully.*

English has two transformations that move long, awkward constituents to the end of the sentence:

1. <u>Extraposition</u> shortens the subject of a sentence by moving a CP or PP out of the subject to the end of the sentence. If the moved constituent *is* the subject (not just part of the subject), then a "dummy" subject, *it,* is left behind as a place-holder. Extraposition can be used to improve sentences (a), (b), and (c) above:

  a′.   [*That everyone already knew what had happened*] *was obvious.* ⇒ *It was obvious <u>that everyone already knew what had happened</u>.*
  b′.   [*A Supreme Court ruling* [*concerning racial preferences in university admissions*]] *has just been issued.* ⇒ [*A Supreme Court ruling* Ø] *has just been issued <u>concerning racial preferences in university admissions.</u>*
  c′.   [*A book* [*on the same topic*]] *has been published.* ⇒ [*A book* Ø] *has been published <u>on the same topic.</u>*

2. <u>Heavy Complement Shift</u> moves a long, heavy complement to the end of the sentence. This transformation can be used to improve sentence (d) above:

  d′.   *We had checked* [*every window and door on the ground floor*] *carefully* ⇒
        We had checked Ø *very carefully <u>every window and door on the ground floor</u>.*[2]

EXERCISE 6.

  a. Find an example of Extraposition in the Toni Morrison passage in Appendix Section I. What would the sentence be like if Extraposition had not applied?
  b. *Advanced.* Find three examples of Extraposition in the following passage from a short story by Henry James. *Hint:* In order to uncover the basic word order of these sentences, begin by crossing out the parentheticals that interrupt each sentence. (Parentheticals

---

2. Notice that the complement can move *only* if it is heavy; for example, the complement *every window* cannot be moved to the end of the sentence below:
    We had checked [*every window*] *very carefully* ⇒ **We had checked* Ø *very carefully <u>every window</u>.*

are comments by the narrator that are inserted into the middle of the sentence; the frequent use of parentheticals is a distinctive characteristic of James's style.)

1   *It was one of the secret opinions, such as we all have, of Peter Brench that his*
2   *main success in life would have consisted in his never having committed himself*
3   *about the work, as it was called, of his friend Morgan Mallow. This was a subject*
4   *on which it was, to the best of his belief, impossible with veracity to quote him,*
5   *and it was nowhere on record that he had, in the connexion, on any occasion*
6   *and in any embarrassment, either lied or spoken the truth.*

—*Henry James, "The Tree of Knowledge"*

c. *Advanced.* Find two examples of Heavy Complement Shift in the Rachel Carson passage in Appendix Section I. *Hint:* Begin by locating each verb and trying to find its complement. In two clauses, the complement does not immediately follow its verb, but has been moved to the end of the sentence. Underline the complement and mark its underlying position with Ø.

15.4.2 Transformations That Move New Information Away from the Beginning of the Sentence

We have already observed (Section 15.3 above) that a sentence should begin with "old" information that orients the hearer or reader to the preceding context. English has two transformations that rearrange constituents when normal word order would violate this principle by placing new information at the beginning of the sentence:

1. *There* Insertion moves a subject NP that introduces new information to the position following the main verb, leaving a "dummy" subject called "existential *there*" in its place. Existential *there* at the beginning of a sentence serves to warn the hearer or reader that new information is coming up:

> [*A smudge*] *is on your nose* ⇒ *There is a smudge on your nose.*
> [*A note*] *should have been attached to the paper* ⇒ *There should have been a note attached to the paper.*
> [*A day*] *came when the king could no longer govern his people* ⇒ *There came a day when the king could no longer govern his people.*

Sometimes a locative complement is fronted, as well, by a transformation called *Locative Fronting:*

> [*A large mole*] *was* [*on her cheek*] ⇒
> *There was a large mole* [*on her cheek*] (by *There*-Insertion) ⇒
> *On her cheek there was a large mole* (by Locative Fronting)

2. The Passive Transformation can be used to reverse the order of the subject and the direct object when necessary. For example, as we observed in Section 15.3, the active sentence in the example

below should be converted to passive form when *America*, rather than *Christopher Columbus*, is the "old" information in the sentence:

> *Christopher Columbus discovered America in 1492* ⇒ *America was discovered by Christopher Columbus in 1492.*

EXERCISE 7.

a. Find examples of *there*-Insertion in the Hemingway and Lawrence passages in Appendix Section I. (There are two in the Hemingway passage and one in the Lawrence passage.) Then (i) rewrite each *there*-sentence in "normal" order, with the logical subject of the sentence in first position, (ii) explain why the author found it necessary to apply *there*-Insertion, and (iii) note whether Locative Fronting has occurred as well.

b. Find four passive clauses in the Stephen Hawking passage in Appendix Section I. (If you really work at it, you may be able to find five.) Then (i) re-write the passage, changing the passive clauses to active, and (ii) decide which version—active or passive—is the better choice, and why.

15.4.3   Transformations That Place New, Interesting Information in a Position of Focus

In *speech,* new information is focused by giving it "nuclear" stress. Nuclear (i.e., heaviest) stress normally falls on the rightmost piece of new information in each intonational phrase:

> *Noam Chomsky teaches linguistics at <u>MIT</u>.*   (Nuclear stress on *MIT*.)

But it can also be placed in other positions, as in the examples below:

> Noam *Chomsky teaches <u>linguistics</u> at MIT.*   (Nuclear stress on *linguistics*)
> <u>*Noam Chomsky*</u> *teaches linguistics at MIT.*   (Nuclear stress on *Noam Chomsky*)

Because written language has no system for marking stress, a constituent must be focused in writing by moving it to a position where it will receive stress automatically.[3] English has four transformations that can be used to move constituents to stressed positions:

1. <u>Clefting</u>. The constituent in the focal position of a clefted sentence is automatically given nuclear stress. By converting the sentence to a cleft, the writer can determine which constituent will receive nuclear stress. For example, the statement *Chomsky teaches linguistics at MIT* can be clefted in any of the following ways:

---

3. Of course, it is possible to underline or italize a focused constituent, as we have done above, but overuse of this device gives one's prose style a somewhat breathless feel.

> *It's <u>Chomsky</u> who teaches linguistics at MIT.*   (focus on *Chomsky*)
> *It's <u>linguistics</u> that Chomsky teaches at MIT.*   (focus on *linguistics*)
> *It's <u>at MIT</u> that Chomsky teaches linguistics.*   (focus on *MIT*)

Read these sentences aloud and notice that the nuclear stress falls automatically on the (underlined) constituent in focal position.

2. <u>Moving a Constituent to the End</u>. Because nuclear stress normally falls on the last piece of new information in the sentence, a constituent can be focused by moving it to the end of the sentence. Besides Extraposition and Heavy Constituent Shift, which we have already discussed (Section 15.4.1), English has two other transformations that move a constituent to the end of a sentence—*WH-Clefting* and *Subject-Locative Reversal*. WH-Clefting allows us to focus the VP of the sentence, or any NP other than the subject:

WH-Clefting
Basic sentence: *Chomsky teaches linguistics at MIT.*
WH-Cleft focusing the NP *linguistics*: *What Chomsky teaches at MIT is <u>linguistics</u>.*
WH-Cleft focusing the VP *teach linguistics*: *What Chomsky does at MIT is <u>teach linguistics</u>.*

Read these sentences aloud and notice that nuclear stress automatically falls on the underlined constituent at the end of the sentence.

Subject-Locative Reversal is a transformation that interchanges the subject with a locative complement, so that the subject is now at the end of the sentence, where it will receive nuclear stress:

Basic sentence: *<u>Bill</u> came <u>around the corner</u>.*
After Subject-Locative Reversal: *<u>Around the corner</u> came <u>Bill</u>.*

Read this sentence aloud and notice the nuclear stress on *Bill*.

3. <u>Using Adverbials or Parentheticals to Break the Sentence into Separate Intonational Phrases</u>. Another way to focus the subject of the sentence is to insert an adverbial or parenthetical expression after it. The parenthetical expression causes the subject to be treated as a separate intonational phrase, with its own nuclear stress. In the examples below, intonational boundaries are marked with "/."

> a. */ Rachel, / however, / can never be counted on /.*
>   (Focus on *Rachel* and *counted on*.)
> b. */ The Bushes, / you know, / have a ranch in Texas /.*
>   (Focus on *the Bushes* and *Texas*)
> c. */ P.T. Barnum, / that wily rascal, / knew that a sucker is born every minute /.*
>   (Focus on *P.T. Barnum* and *every minute*)

Read these sentences aloud and notice (i) the pauses at the intonational boundaries, and (ii) the nuclear stress on the last constituent of each intonational phrase (except the parenthetical).

EXERCISE 8. Find a post-subject parenthetical modifier in the Hemingway passage in Appendix Section I. What constituent is put into focus by the presence of the parenthetical? Read the clause aloud, with and without the parenthetical, and listen for a difference in the stress on the subject NP.

---

4. <u>Topicalization</u>. Topicalization is a transformation that focuses a constituent by moving it to the subject-of-C position.

Basic sentence: *I like Bill.*

Topicalized version:

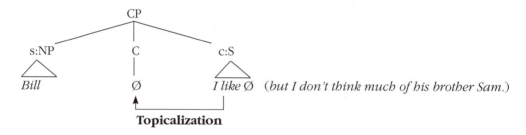

Topicalization

Because a "topicalized" NP is pronounced as a separate intonational phrase, it receives nuclear stress. Read the sentence aloud and notice the nuclear stress on *Bill* and *like*.

If the topicalized constituent is negative, Subject-AUX Inversion applies as well, as in the example below:

Basic sentence: <u>*Never have I seen such a mess!*</u>

Topicalized version:

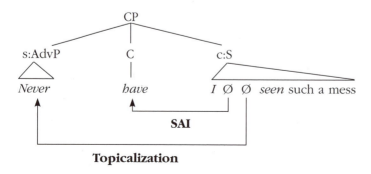

Topicalization

326

EXERCISE 9. Find instances of Topicalization in the Rachel Carson and James Joyce passages in Appendix Section I. (You should be able to find one example in each passage.) One sentence has undergone Subject-AUX Inversion as well as Topicalization. Why?

The transformations that have been introduced in this section, called *stylistic transformations*, allow flexibility in the order in which information is presented within a sentence. A summary of the stylistic transformations of English is provided in Chart 15.5 at the end of this chapter.

EXERCISE 10. (adapted from Hudson 1992) Use the stylistic transformations that have been described in this section to improve the awkward sentences below. Begin by finding the long, heavy constituent that interferes with the processing of each sentence. Then try the stylistic transformations Extraposition, Heavy Complement Shift, *There* Insertion, Locative Fronting, Passive, Clefting, and WH-Clefting. Say, for each sentence, which transformations are possible and whether they help. (You may find it useful to refer to Chart 15.5.)

a. *A long noun phrase that contained two finite relative clauses was near the end of the paragraph.*

b. *A long noun phrase that contained two finite relative clauses attracted my attention.*

c. *We found a long noun phrase that contained two finite relative clauses near the end of the paragraph.*

15.5 Summary of the Chapter

In this chapter we have discussed the presentation of information in sentences and in connected discourse, beginning with *coherence* (making it clear what the passage is about) and *cohesion* (linking sentences smoothly together). We suggested four strategies for improving cohesion between sentences: (1) Begin each sentence with information that was already mentioned in the previous sentence, (2) Eliminate unnecessary repetition, (3) Use connectives, (4) Use coordination and parallel structure.

In the final section of the chapter, we described eight "stylistic" transformations that rearrange the order in which information is presented within a sentence: (1) Extraposition, (2) Heavy Complement Shift, (3) *There*-insertion (with or without Locative Fronting), (4) Passivization, (5) Clefting, (6) WH-Clefting, (7) Subject-Locative Reversal, and (8) Topicalization. A summary of these stylistic transformations is provided in Chart 15.1.

Chart 15.1   Stylistic Transformations

Extraposition	[*That you were upset*] *was obvious.* ⇒ *It was obvious* [*that you were upset*].
Heavy Complement Shift	*We checked* [*every window and door on the ground floor of the building*] *very carefully.* ⇒ *We checked* Ø *very carefully* [*every window and door on the ground floor of the building*].
***There* Insertion** **With Locative Fronting**	[*A mouse*] *was under the chair.* ⇒ *There was* [*a mouse*] *under the chair.* ⇒ [*Under the chair*] *there was a mouse.*
Passive	[*A boy wearing jeans and a red jacket*] *took* [*my bicycle*]. ⇒ [*My bicycle*] *was taken by* [*a boy wearing jeans and a red jacket*].
Subject-Locative Reversal	[*Sue*] *came* [*down the hill*] ⇒ [*Down the hill*] *came* [*Sue*].
Cleft	[*A boy wearing jeans and a red jacket*] *took* [*my bicycle*]. ⇒ *It was* [*a boy wearing jeans and a red jacket*] *that took* [*my bicycle*].
WH-Cleft	[*That he didn't say anything*] *was surprising* ⇒ *What was surprising was* [*that he didn't say anything*].
Subject-Locative Reversal	*Then* [*Bill*] *came* [*along*] ⇒ *Then* [*along*] *came* [*Bill*].
Topicalization	*I understand* [*this one*] ⇒ [*This one*], *I understand* Ø.

CHAPTER 16

Semicolons, Colons, and Commas

16.1 Semicolons

A semicolon [;] is used to connect two independent clauses that are not joined by a conjunction:[1]

> *There are many basements in the city that have dirt floors; these places are rat heavens.*
> *To get from one basement to another it tunnels under party walls; slum-clearance workers*
> *frequently uncover a network of rat tunnels that link all the tenements in a block.*

Be careful with connectives like *however* and *nevertheless*. Although these are *logical* connectives, they are not conjunctions. Clauses that are joined by connectives need a semicolon, as well:

> *It would have been possible to adjust Ptolemy's theory so as to account for the observed*
> *facts; however, Copernicus's theory was much simpler.*
> *Composition teachers often frown upon the passive voice as being "weaker" than the*
> *active; nevertheless, passives are very common in serious expository writing.*

16.2 Colons

A colon announces a list of examples or some other expansion of what has just been said:

> *Aristotle believed that everything was made out of four elements: earth, air, fire, and water.*
> *A physical theory is . . . only a hypothesis: you can never prove it.*[2]

Note that the sentence is already grammatically complete before the colon is added. A colon should not be placed in the middle of a clause:

> **The four basic elements in Aristotle's theory were: earth, air, fire, and water.*
> **The Indo-European language family includes languages such as: Russian, Hindi,*
> *Greek, French, and English.*

Instead, these sentences should be punctuated as follows:

> *The four basic elements in Aristotle's theory were earth, air, fire, and water.*
> *The Indo-European language family includes languages such as Russian, Hindi, Greek,*
> *French, and English.*

---

1. These examples are based on sentences from the Mitchell passage found in Chapter 10, Exercise 17.
2. From the Hawking passage found in Appendix Section I. Hawking could, alternatively, have used a semicolon in place of the colon: *A physical theory is only a hypothesis; you can never prove it.*

16.3 **Commas**

There are three uses of commas in English—conventional commas, series commas, and modifier commas:

1. Conventional commas. A comma is placed, by convention, in certain positions such as between the day and year in a date: *January 4, 1937* and between the name of a town and its state: *Portland, Oregon.* I will not list these comma positions here, but would like to note one common error regarding the use of commas with quotations. A quoted utterance is set off by a comma:

> *Bill said, "Please pass the sugar."*
> *"This is a most auspicious occasion," Sally oozed.*

However, quoted words and phrases that are part of the normal structure of a sentence are not set off with commas. Thus, there is no comma before the quoted material in the following examples:

> *The word "accommodate" is spelled with two c's and two m's.*
> *According to the article, the public schools of Portland now have "over a thousand ESL students from twenty-seven different language backgrounds."*
> *Exterminators believe that a high percentage of the fires that are classified as "of undetermined origin" are started by the brown rat (Mitchell).*

2. Series commas. Commas are used to separate conjoined items or items in a series:

> *The room was filled with excited men, women, and children.*   (Conjoined Ns)
> *It was a big, mean dog with ugly, pointed teeth.*   (AdjPs in series)
> *The room was hot, noisy, and crowded.*   (Conjoined AdjPs)
> *He pulled out his gun, pointed it at the intruder, and fired.*   (Conjoined VPs)

Exceptions:

a. Items that cannot be separated by a pause in speech are not separated by commas in writing:

> *Near the old brick house was a big red barn.*
> (No comma between *old* and *brick* or between *big* and *red*.)[3]

b. *Two* constituents that are joined with a coordinating conjunction (*and, or, but*) are normally not separated by a comma:

---

3. Here is another test that is sometimes recommended for deciding whether a sequence of adjectives should be separated by commas: Adjectives that are separated by commas can be restated as conjoined predicate adjectives. *A big, mean dog* is *a dog that is big and mean,* but *an old brick house* is not *a house that is old and brick.* Hence *old* and *brick* cannot be separated by commas.

> *We ordered a hamburger and a coke.*   (Conjoined NPs)
> *The car turned down the street and into an alley.*   (Conjoined PPs)
> *The child was emaciated and very pale.*   (Conjoined AdjPs)
> *The plane landed on the runway and taxied to the terminal.*   (Conjoined VPs)
> *He called her but didn't leave his name.*   (Conjoined VPs)

However, *sentences* conjoined with *and* are separated by commas, even when there are only two:

> *I've never seen a purple cow, and I never hope to see one.*   (Conjoined sentences)

As before, if there would be no pause in pronunciation, there is no comma in writing:

> *Fish swim and birds fly.*

3. <u>Commas to Set Off Modifiers.</u> Modifiers (not subjects or complements) are set off by commas if they would be set off by pauses in speech. Note that modifier commas go in pairs; thus, the modifier *however* in sentence (a) below has commas on both sides:[4]

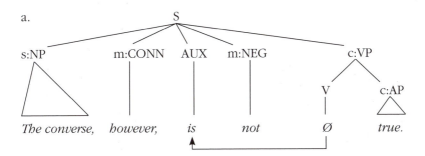

Note that the modifier *not* in (a) has no surrounding commas because it cannot be surrounded by pauses in speech. The same is true of the modifiers *physical* and *never* in example (b) below; however, the modifier *which are the basis of scientific reasoning*, which *is* pronounced with pauses, has a comma on either side:

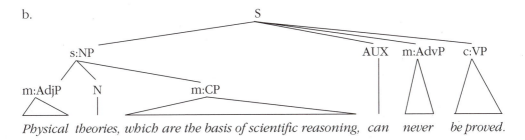

---

4. Examples (a), (c), and (d) are based on examples from the Hawking passage found in Appendix Section I.

If the modifier is at the edge of the sentence, as is the case with the first m:PP in (c) below, only one comma—the inside comma—will appear. The second m:PP in this example is not set off by commas because it would not have a pause before it in speech:

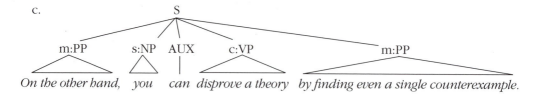

c.

On the other hand, you can disprove a theory by finding even a single counterexample.

Example (d) illustrates a modifier set off by commas at the *end* of a sentence:

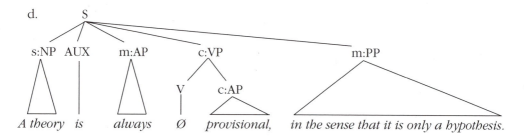

d.

A theory is always Ø provisional, in the sense that it is only a hypothesis.

A pause by itself does not justify a comma. For example, sentence (e) below might well be spoken with a pause after the subject (s:NP), but subjects are never set off by commas:

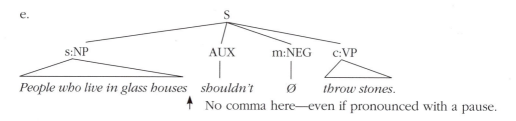

e.

People who live in glass houses shouldn't Ø throw stones.
↑ No comma here—even if pronounced with a pause.

Similarly, in example (f), there might be a pause, in speech, before the c:CP, but a complement can never be set off by a comma:

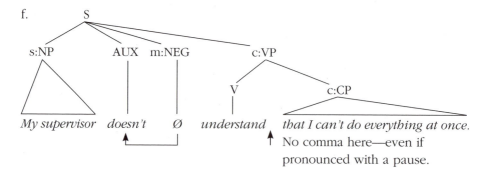

f.

My supervisor doesn't Ø understand that I can't do everything at once.
↑ No comma here—even if pronounced with a pause.

332

In other words, two conditions are required for a constituent to be set off with commas—the constituent must be a modifier, and it must be set off, in speech, with pauses.

EXERCISE 1. Decide where to put commas in the following sentences, and explain why. Remember that commas require a pause, but that subjects and complements are never set off by commas, even if pronounced with a pause.

a. *Jack and Jill went up the hill.*

b. *Jack Jill and Rudolph went up the hill.*

c. *We washed and dried the dishes.*

d. *We washed the dishes but didn't dry them.*

e. *Tomorrow I'll cry.*

f. *I'll cry tomorrow.*

g. *When the bell rang everybody stood up.*

h. *Everybody stood up when the bell rang.*

i. *Everybody came running although the bell had not yet rung.*

j. *The first person to complete the exercise will win the prize.*

k. *George Washington who was the first president of the United States wore false teeth.*

l. *Students who move into apartments off campus often need to buy a car.*

m. *Some of the parts unfortunately did not fit together.*

n. *Some of the parts really didn't fit together.*

EXERCISE 2. Punctuate the literary passages below, presented here with all their commas removed. Be able to explain the reason for each comma you put in. Then compare your punctuation with that of the originals (found in Appendix Section I). Note that fiction writers are sometimes unconventional punctuators. (In expository writing, we are expected to follow the rules more closely.) If you find instances of unconventional punctuation in the original passage, consider their effect. Is the punctuation effective as it is, or would it have been better if the author had been taken in hand by a stern copyeditor?

1	*The hills across the valley of the Ebro were long and white. On this side there*
2	*was no shade and no trees and the station was between two lines of rails in*
3	*the sun. Close against the side of the station there was the warm shadow of*
4	*the building and a curtain made of strings of bamboo beads hung across the*
5	*open door into the bar to keep out flies. The American and the girl with him*
6	*sat at a table in the shade outside the building. It was very hot and the express*
7	*from Barcelona would come in forty minutes. It stopped at this junction for*
8	*two minutes and went on to Madrid.*

—Ernest Hemingway, "Hills Like White Elephants"

1   *Nowhere in all the sea does life exist in such bewildering abundance as in the*
2   *surface waters. From the deck of a vessel you may look down hour after hour on*
3   *the shimmering discs of jellyfish their gently pulsating bells dotting the surface*
4   *as far as you can see. Or one day you may notice early in the morning that you*
5   *are passing through a sea of microscopic creatures each of which contains an*
6   *orange pigment granule. At noon you are still moving through red seas and*
7   *when darkness falls the waters shine with an eerie glow from the phosphorescent*
8   *fires of yet more billions and trillions of these same creatures.*

—Rachel Carson, *The Sea Around Us*

1   *Ants are so much like human beings as to be an embarrassment. They farm*
2   *fungi raise aphids as livestock launch armies into wars use chemical sprays to*
3   *alarm and confuse enemies capture slaves. The families of weaver ants engage*
4   *in child labor holding their larvae like shuttles to spin out the thread that sews*
5   *the leaves together for their fungus gardens. They exchange information cease-*
6   *lessly. They do everything but watch television.*

—Lewis Thomas, *The Lives of a Cell*

EXERCISE 3. The Stephen Hawking passage, repeated below with its punctuation removed, contains a colon, as well as a semicolon which the author uses, in place of a comma, to clarify the structure at a point where too many commas were starting to pile up. Try to reconstruct the punctuation of this piece:

1   *Any physical theory is always provisional in the sense that it is only a hypothesis*
2   *you can never prove it. No matter how many times the results of experiments*
3   *agree with some theory you can never be sure that the next time the result*
4   *will not contradict the theory. On the other hand you can disprove a theory*
5   *by finding even a single observation that disagrees with the predictions of the*
6   *theory. As philosopher of science Karl Popper has emphasized a good theory*
7   *is characterized by the fact that it makes a number of predictions that could*
8   *in principle be disproved or falsified by observation. Each time new experi-*
9   *ments are observed to agree with the predictions the theory survives and our*
10   *confidence in it is increased but if ever a new observation is found to disagree*
11   *we have to abandon or modify the theory. At least that is what is supposed to*
12   *happen but you can always question the competence of the person who carried*
13   *out the observation.*

—Stephen Hawking, *A Brief History of Time*

EXERCISE 4. Now try the passage that appeared in Chapter 10, Exercise 17. Here you will need two semicolons, plus lots of commas.

1	*The brown rat is distributed all over the five boroughs [of New York City]. It*
2	*customarily nests at or below street level—under floors in rubbishy basements*
3	*and in burrows. There are many brownstones and red-bricks as well as many*
4	*commercial structures in the city that have basements or sub-basements with*
5	*dirt floors these places are rat heavens. The brown rat can burrow into the*
6	*hardest soil even tightly packed clay and it can tunnel through the kind of*
7	*cheap mortar that is made of sand and lime. To get from one basement to an-*
8	*other it tunnels under party walls slum-clearance workers frequently uncover*
9	*a network of rat tunnels that link all the tenements in a block. Like the magpie*
10	*it steals and hoards small gadgets and coins. In nest chambers in a system of*
11	*tunnels under a Chelsea tenement workers recently found an empty lipstick tube*
12	*a religious medal a skate key a celluloid teething ring a belt buckle a shoehorn*
13	*a penny a dime and three quarters. Paper money is sometimes found. When*
14	*the Civic Repertory Theatre was torn down a nest constructed solely of dollar*
15	*bills seventeen in all was discovered in a burrow. Exterminators believe that a*
16	*high percentage of the fires that are classified as "of undetermined origin" are*
17	*started by the brown rat. It starts them chiefly by gnawing the insulation off*
18	*electric wires causing short circuits. It often uses highly inflammable material*
19	*in building nests. The majority of the nests in the neighborhood of a big garage*
20	*for example will invariably be built of oily cotton rags.*

—Joseph Mitchell, *The Rats on the Waterfront*

Samples for Analysis

I. Literary Passages

Literary Passages: Narrative

1   *The hills across the valley of the Ebro were long and white. On this side*
2   *there was no shade and no trees and the station was between two lines of rails*
3   *in the sun. Close against the side of the station there was the warm shadow of*
4   *the building, and a curtain, made of strings of bamboo beads, hung across the*
5   *open door into the bar, to keep out flies. The American and the girl with him*
6   *sat at a table in the shade, outside the building. It was very hot and the express*
7   *from Barcelona would come in forty minutes. It stopped at this junction for two*
8   *minutes and went on to Madrid.*

—Hemingway, "Hills Like White Elephants"

1   *The three brothers and the sister sat round the desolate breakfast table, attempt-*
2   *ing some sort of desultory consultation. The morning's post had given the final tap*
3   *to the family fortunes, and all was over. The dreary dining-room itself, with its*
4   *heavy mahogany furniture, looked as if it were waiting to be done away with.*
5   *But the consultation amounted to nothing. There was a strange air of ineffect-*
6   *uality about the three men, as they sprawled at table, smoking and reflecting*
7   *vaguely on their own condition.*

—Lawrence, "The Horse Dealer's Daughter"

1   *When the short days of winter came dusk fell before we had well eaten our*
2   *dinners. When we met in the street the houses had grown sombre. The space of*
3   *sky above us was the colour of ever-changing violet and towards it the lamps*
4   *of the street lifted their feeble lanterns. The cold air stung us and we played till*
5   *our bodies glowed. Our shouts echoed in the silent street.*

—Joyce, "Araby"

1   *Accompanied by a plague of robins, Sula came back to Medallion. The little*
2   *yam-breasted shuddering birds were everywhere, exciting very small children away*
3   *from their usual welcome into a vicious stoning. Nobody knew why or from where*
4   *they had come. What they did know was that you couldn't go anywhere without*
5   *stepping in their pearly shit, and it was hard to hang up clothes, pull weeds or just*
6   *sit on the front porch when robins were flying and dying all around you.*
7   *Although most of the people remembered the time when the sky was black*
8   *for two hours with clouds and clouds of pigeons, and although they were accus-*
9   *tomed to excesses in nature—too much heat, too much cold, too little rain, rain*
10   *to flooding—they still dreaded the way a relatively trivial phenomenon could*
11   *become sovereign in their lives and bend their minds to its will.*

—Toni Morrison, *Sula* "1937"

Literary Passages: Expository Writing

1   *Nowhere in all the sea does life exist in such bewildering abundance as in*
2   *the surface waters. From the deck of a vessel you may look down, hour after hour,*
3   *on the shimmering discs of jellyfish, their gently pulsating bells dotting the surface*
4   *as far as you can see. Or one day you may notice early in the morning that you*
5   *are passing through a sea of microscopic creatures, each of which contains an*
6   *orange pigment granule. At noon you are still moving through red seas, and*
7   *when darkness falls the waters shine with an eerie glow from the phosphorescent*
8   *fires of yet more billions and trillions of these same creatures.*

—Rachel Carson, *The Sea Around Us*

1   *Ants are so much like human beings as to be an embarrassment. They farm*
2   *fungi, raise aphids as livestock, launch armies into wars, use chemical sprays to*
3   *alarm and confuse enemies, capture slaves. The families of weaver ants engage*
4   *in child labor, holding their larvae like shuttles to spin out the thread that sews*
5   *the leaves together for their fungus gardens. They exchange information cease-*
6   *lessly. They do everything but watch television.*

—Lewis Thomas, *The Lives of a Cell*

1   *Who discovered America? Or rather, what European discovered America? For*
2   *we now admit that the people whom Columbus mistakenly named Indians came*
3   *over from Asia via the Bering Strait, somewhere between 25,000 and 40,000 years*
4   *ago, and, by the time the Europeans arrived, had spread from Alaska to Tierra del*
5   *Fuego and had developed several hundred languages. In three places at least—*
6   *Peru, Mexico, and the highlands of Colombia—the Indians developed highly*
7   *sophisticated societies before Columbus landed; and if the Spaniards had come a*
8   *century later, they might have encountered a strong, defensible Aztec empire that*
9   *would have developed into a powerful nation, like Japan in Asia.*

—Samuel Eliot Morison, "Who Really Discovered America?"

1   *A physical theory is always provisional, in the sense that it is only a hypoth-*
2   *esis: you can never prove it. No matter how many times the results of experiments*
3   *agree with some theory, you can never be sure that the next time the result will not*
4   *contradict the theory. On the other hand, you can disprove a theory by finding*
5   *even a single observation that disagrees with its predictions. As philosopher of*
6   *science Karl Popper has emphasized, a good theory is characterized by the fact*
7   *that it makes a number of predictions that could in principle be disproved or*
8   *falsified by observation. Each time new experiments are observed to agree with*
9   *the predictions the theory survives, and our confidence in it is increased; but if*
10   *ever a new observation is found to disagree, we have to abandon or modify the*
11   *theory. At least that is what is supposed to happen, but you can always question*
12   *the competence of the person who carried out the observation.*

—Stephen Hawking, *A Brief History of Time*

II. The Development of Literacy: Children's Writing[1]

Grade 1

An Invitation to the Ball

1   *Can you come to the anyoul ball at the casl tonite at 78m midnit there will*
2   *be a big ball tonite come and do not be Late Lav Julia*

Mafin

1   *I hvie a cat. It is named mafin. When my mom washsi mafin. he scashed*
2   *my mom and it hse (hurts) a lot. My mom gis mad at mafin, and he gis madr at*
3   *my mom.*

The Seal and the Fish

1   *Once there was a seal. He met a fish, "That looks good said seal. don't eat*
2   *me" said the fish. One day the seal got caught inside a pece of ice. the fish sucked*
3   *on the ice, until it turned to water so after that, he always ate ice and snow. but*
4   *never fish.*

Meanie

1   *Once upon a time there was a boy he was mene. But he wanted to be remberd*
2   *as a spashel person. He wanted to be fames. He wanted to go to oter spac. one*
3   *day somethig majecl hapeind. he was nice agen. He got all of hes friends back.*
4   *and most of all they thot he was speshel and then he grow up to be a good man*
5   *a varey good man.*

Grade 2

My Nightmare

1   *One night I was going to sleep and I had a nightmare about I was going down*
2   *the walkway and I saw space police walk toward me. They had a long mouth. It*
3   *could suck up me. They got me. I said, "Help Help." But no one heard me. They*
4   *took me to their space ship. They put me in a space jail, but I had a good idea and*
5   *all I had to do is get that space gun. I got loose. When I got out, I saw the alien. I*
6   *got the space laser and shot a hole through the alien. He melted.*

Your Own Monster

1   *I have a monster I found him at the park. He enjoys chasing cars and eats*
2   *rotten goatcheese dunked in green gunk. I don't know where he came from. He*
3   *likes playing in garbage and scaring people and I have to chain him up so he*
4   *won't chase any more cars. I like him he's just kind of hard to take care of.*

---

1. Except for the letter from the author's granddaughter Julia, these examples of children's writing are taken from *Write On!*, a supplement to the *Journal Tribune* of Biddeford, ME, which regularly publishes samples of writing from children in the local public schools.

My Favorite Puppy

1   *Jessie is my first puppy. She's going to be three years old this year. We got her*
2   *at the pound. They found her in the middle of the road. One day she ran in front*
3   *of a car and she got hit on the tail. But it didn't fall off! That's why we are happy,*
4   *very happy. When Shannon comes over, Jessie jumps on her. She loves Shannon a*
5   *lot! She is a beagle puppy. When anyone comes over she is excited. She loves kids*
6   *very much. She is a hunting dog.*

Grade 3

Specialness

1   *Once there was a bird. He was walking with his friend the frog. Then Frog*
2   *said, "I have more specialness than you, Bird." Bird said quietly, "Why?" "Well I*
3   *have more camouflage, I hop higher, and I attract people more. You have hardly*
4   *any specialness," Frog said. They kept on walking. Then Bird said, "I have better*
5   *eyesight." When Frog turned around Bird was gone.*
6   *Sometimes people are not what you think they are.*

My Dog and Me

1   *One day my dog and me were playing pass. His name is K.C. He likes to play*
2   *pass with my football. He lives at my grandmother's house. She has a big yard we*
3   *play in. K.C. is an awesome catcher. He is cute, fluffy and very loveable. He is a*
4   *good dog and he is a fun dog to be with.*

My Most Admired Person

1   *The person I admire most is my dad. I admire him because he does lots of*
2   *things with me. He passes a football, fishes, plays catch and chess. These are fun*
3   *things to do. He also is very nice to me. Sometimes on Friday we go to a place*
4   *called Federal Jacks and play pool. This is fun, a lot of fun. When we go to my*
5   *gramma's we go on a paddle boat ride on the lake and fish. We also fish at my*
6   *house in the creek in the woods. When we catch a fish we eat it. They are good*
7   *when you put salt on them. So that's why I admire my dad.*

The Mouse with Tiney Feet

1   *Once upon a time 100 years ago when mice rould the earth there was a fam-*
2   *ous mouse known as Theador mouse. Theador was a very interesting mouse he*
3   *always wanted to know everything.*
4   *One day he was walking throu the forest and he saw a mouse factory. So he*
5   *went inside. He saw tools and a lot of macheans. When he went into the next*
6   *room he saw a compactor, but Theador did not know what a compactor was. So*
7   *he asked a werker mouse what a compactor was, and the werker said it makes*
8   *thing smaller and Theador said can I try it?*
9   *Then the mouse said stik your feet in and I'll turn it on. Then the mouse*
10   *terned it on Theador's feet got smaller and smaller. Then Theador got out and*
11   *fell down because his feet wor as small as a pea. From now on Theador has to*
12   *use a wheelchair.*

Grade 4

My Bicycle Ride

1   *I press down the dusty button to open the garage. My shiny new bike sits there*
2   *waiting for me to take it on its first ride. I put on my helmet and I take out my*
3   *bike into my driveway. I stated pedaling faster and faster, the wind whirling in*
4   *my face. When I get back I put my bike away and press the dusty button.*

Respect—What It Means to Me

1   *Respect can be many things. Respect is being nice, saying "excuse me," and*
2   *not hurting other people's feelings.*
3   *If you respect someone, they will respect you. If everyone in the entire world*
4   *respect each other, there would not be any fights or wars or any argument. The*
5   *world would be nice and kind if everyone respected each other. Everyone would*
6   *be at peace, and no one will steal and no one will starve.*
7   *You can do a lot to respect. You could help an elder get around or babysit your*
8   *little brother and give your parents a break. You could do something small like*
9   *just listening and not speaking out. You can respect by respecting other people's*
10   *property, like if you see a jacket on the ground, don't step on it. Pick it up!*
11   *You don't only respect people, you need to respect the earth by not littering, or*
12   *the animals by not destroying their homes. They worked hard on them!*
13   *Don't forget, respect is the best thing you can give a plant or an animal or*
14   *another person.*

Billy's Unusual Frog

1   *Once there was an unusual frog. This frog was no ordinary frog. He lived*
2   *in a pet shop called "Frank's Unusual Pets." The pets there were very unique. The*
3   *mice did group aerobics. The cat sang jazz, the dogs played tackle football, and*
4   *the frog talked. He talked to any customer who would listen to him.*
5   *One day while the frog was talking to the customers, a boy went to the counter*
6   *and obnoxiously said, "How much is the frog?"*
7   *Before the clerk could answer, the frog answered loudly, "I'm $20.00. Do you*
8   *want to buy me?"*
9   *The boy replied, "Yes I do." He yelled to his mother who was at the other end*
10   *of the store watching the mice do aerobics, "Mom, can you give me $20.000?"*
11   *His mother said to her son "Why do you want $20.00?"*
12   *"I want to buy the talking frog," he replied. His mother gave him the money,*
13   *and he purchased the frog.*
14   *On the way home from the pet shop, the frog blurted out, "What's your name,*
15   *kid?"*
16   *"My name is Billy," responded the child. The radio was on in the car. Billy's*
17   *mom was singing along with the song, when she heard a croaking voice.*
18   *"Billy is your frog singing?" she asked.*
19   *"Yeah Mom, he is. Isn't he great?" Billy exclaimed.*
20   *"No he isn't. Make him stop," she ordered. Billy told his new frog to be quiet,*
21   *and from then on he never talked or sang again. (Not when Billy's mother was*
22   *around at least!!)*

Grade 5

The Big Box

1   *In the town of Saco there lived a toy maker.*
2   *His name was Scot. He had a little girl. Her name was Laura.*
3   *All Laura wanted was a new doll that danced like a ballerina. The doll had*
4   *a pink suit with a pink chiffon skirt. Then on Christmas morning Laura and her*
5   *dad went downstairs.*
6   *In the middle of the room was a big box. Laura couldn't believe her eyes. She*
7   *ran to the box and opened it. Inside was a ballerina bigger than her. The doll*
8   *started to spin and twirl. Her arms went up in the air. Laura's eyes sparkled as*
9   *she watched the doll. Laura was happy and content.*

A Ginger Day

1   *One snowy December day a small kitten named Nightmare decided he was*
2   *bored. He got out his old ball of string and bounced it up and down and up and*
3   *down and up so high that it landed in the food cupboard. Not wishing to miss*
4   *any excitement he jumped up as well. He could not see his ball for there was a*
5   *box, a rather large one at that, blocking his view. High in the air he soared and*
6   *he was almost over the box when he felt himself plunging through the box cover*
7   *and falling down and down. He landed on something soft.*
8   *He soon realized the softness he felt was a marshmallow. In fact he was in a*
9   *whole world of candy. He walked over to the chocolate sidewalks that had a frost-*
10 *ing of ice cream as snow. A doughnut wreath hung from every door and window.*
11 *Inside the houses were stockings hung from the chocolate brick fireplaces. There*
12 *were lampposts made of candy canes with little yellow gumdrops as lights.*
13 *Miles of people (gingerbread people) were roaming the streets. Some were*
14 *even in the windows of the three-story tall gingerbread houses that were nicely*
15 *decorated with goodies of all kinds, looking quite nice to eat. A gingerbread*
16 *mouse dashed across the street in his direction. Nightmare pounced upon it but*
17 *the mouse just crumbled to a pile of crumbs, frosting, and two little gumdrop eyes.*
18 *Not wanting to draw attention, he walked off down the street and soon came to*
19 *a frozen pond. He thought it fun to try and skate and stepped upon the delicate*
20 *ice. It did not take him long to realize it would not hold his heavy cat weight and*
21 *he broke through into a whirlpool of milk. Suddenly he opened his eyes. He was*
22 *in his own room in his own bed. "Here kitty kitty come and eat. Mommy made*
23 *you a nice gingerbread meal."*
24 *"Meeooowww," he yelled, and ran off to hide.*
25 *The End.*

Shells of the Sea

1   *Here are some similarities of a conch shell and a clam shell. Both shells have*
2   *a silky-smooth inside. The conch shell could be a home to hermit crabs and other*
3   *sea creatures. The clam shell is a home to clams. The conch shell and the clam*
4   *shell are both found in the water, and they are both shells. If you drop either one*
5   *of these shells, they will break. In both shells you can find white.*
6   *The conch and the clam shell are both admired, and sold in stores. Many*
7   *people collect them. Even though the inside is very smooth the outside is very*
8   *rough.*
9   *Here are some of the differences of a conch shell and a clam shell. The clam*
10   *shell is all white, while the conch shell is white and brown. The conch shell is also*
11   *really spiky.*
12   *You can curl your finger around the inside of the conch shell, it also has a*
13   *starlike top. It's difficult to put a clam shell flat down because the clam shell has*
14   *a little arch. The conch shell holds a hermit crab, while the clam shell holds a*
15   *clam.*
16   *Finally if you flip the clam shell upside down it looks like a bowl, and it has*
17   *a little brown spot at the end.*

III. The Writing Development of One Individual Student[2]

Grade 1

I Went to Jupiter

1   *It hapend so fast I was doing my repote on Jupiter the next minute I was*
2   *on Jupiter Reading it ther Aliens were Listening to me end they brat me to their*
3   *school they told me all abot their school they pled strr toes and they pley star rop*
4   *and the pled wih stars tan I was Bac at my school I finict it Jupiter is the largest*
5   *planet the end*

Grade 4

The Exhibit

1   *My favorite thing in the Exhibit was the sea urchin and the flounder because*
2   *the sea urchin is pircily and they feal neat in your hand and thire pretty also*
3   *I like the flounder because they are sort of flat and thire spoted and I like thire*
4   *back fins. I also like the starfish because some are pink and some are orange and*
5   *they feal neat on your hand too. On the way home we went to Riche's because*
6   *Pat needed to get some water seal for the new steps. Then we went to shaws to get*
7   *some milk. After that we went home.*

2. Thanks to my student Meredith Schofield for providing these samples of her writing over the years.

Grade 6

The Classiest Cars of the 60's

1   *There were quite a few changes in cars during the sixties. The British invented*
2 *the sports car in the early sixties. The most popular color of cars was blue. Another*
3 *change in cars was the Lotus Elite, the first Lotus made for the road instead of rac-*
4 *ing from 1957 to 1963. The MGA was built from 1955 to 1962, all though there*
5 *are a couple of things that stayed the same, like the Mazda Mx-5 from today is*
6 *a lot like the Lotus Elan from the sixties. Though cars had changed through the*
7 *sixties, all of the changes were improvements and anything that stayed the same*
8 *was good enough to begin with.*

Grade 9

Running

1   *It is cold and raining. I'm on my third mile. I ask myself why I do this and*
2 *reply with, "I have to." For some people, running is something that they just have*
3 *to do, not because someone makes them, but because they owe it to themselves*
4 *to do their best. On a track team, you also have coaches and teammates to run*
5 *for. Running consists of stretching, knowing what events you are suited for as a*
6 *runner, and training.*
7   *Before you go out and run, you need to stretch. If you don't stretch and warm*
8 *up you could seriously injure yourself. . .*

Grade 12

Bernard A. Schofield, The man who never left the table

1   *As I walked into the kitchen the smell of dogs and cigarette smoke hit my face.*
2 *Though my grandfather had been gone for almost a month, the odor was as strong*
3 *as I had always remembered. When I was younger my mother would not allow*
4 *my sisters and I to wear our good clothes and our coats were left in the car when*
5 *we went to visit, for the smell would cling. All of his belongings had absorbed the*
6 *stench, a brown scum coating everything in the house. All of the faces of his an-*
7 *tique clock collection had thick layers of residue, which hid the numbers. Every*
8 *pendulum was still, for the clocks' owner had not been there to wind them. I ran*
9 *my finger across one of the faces, but the film remained. There must have been at*
10 *least twenty years worth of smoke that had seeped into all of this belongings and*
11 *as we packed his clocks, coins and albums our hands became dry from the dust*
12 *and residue, which left us awkwardly avoiding contact with our own hands.*

College sophomore

Down with Sentimentality: The use of irony in *Shapes of a Soul*

1   *At first one may argue that Platt's poem is simply the product of a female*
2   *imagination, which places the female subject in the role of the "snowy dove" and*
3   *"flush'd flower" (lines 4,8). This is understandable considering the first two stanzas*
4   *of the poem. The use of words such as "nesting timidly" suggests that the narrator*
5   *of the poem is indeed the ideal feminine, angelic wife (line 2). A vision of white*
6   *with "starlight folded in its wings" suggests the image of an angel (line 1).*
7   *The "You" in the poem is assumed to be a male counter part, such as the*
8   *narrator's husband. In the first two stanzas she is describing what he calls her.*
9   *For example in the second stanza the narrator states, "You'll say my soul buds*
10   *as a small flush'd flower." This comparison of the narrator's soul to something*
11   *as delicate and frail as a flower creates the image of a woman who needs to*
12   *be protected. Not to mention that the use of "bud" and "flush'd" give a sense of*
13   *sexual innocence. These hackneyed images of birds and flowers create a sense*
14   *the "poetess" is indeed creating a ridiculous image of the perfect wife. This is*
15   *true in a sense, for in the first two stanzas Platt attempts to show what the man*
16   *expects the woman to be.*

IV. A Writing Sample from an Older Student

Here you should insert a brief sample of your own writing. If possible, include two samples—one from a piece of narration and one from a piece of expository writing.

V. ESL Writing

Learning English

1   *wen i was a little boy with only 12 years old, my mom thinks "maybe is good*
2   *for nicolas learn other lenguage" and her pay for my class in a institude. my*
3   *first word in english "please set down" don't liked because i beleaved that i never*
4   *needed speak other language, and now you can see my breaking my head trying*
5   *to learn english.*

         —A Spanish-speaking student at the beginning level

Malcolm X

1   *After I saw the passage that wrote from Malcolm X, I think I am really one*
2   *of the lucky girls in the world. I can get the education when I was small, started*
3   *at three years old. From kindergarten, primary school, secondary school, high*
4   *school until university, I didn't have a really big problem let me to stop my study-*
5   *ing. However, the child life of Malcolm X is very poor. He didn't have enough slept*
6   *and stay in streets on night. Even more he didn't have chance to study in school*
7   *because he is black. He couldn't study until he was in prison.*

—A Chinese student at a low intermediate level

A Review of the Film "Baraka"

1   *When I watched Baraka, I am not surprise that this world been changed so*
2   *much. In that movie people change from respect nature power and their life to*
3   *ignore nature power and their life. I think it is because human are the most self-*
4   *ish creature in the world. We forget how to life with this world because we only*
5   *care about ourselves. Few years ago, I heard some environmental groups said*
6   *that we need to protect our environment because we need to leave our children*
7   *a great earth. When I heard that, I don't understand why we need to protect our*
8   *environment just because our species. How about other living things? However, I*
9   *still and must have faith in human because if we are completely selfish, we won't*
10   *know how to cooperation and then the world will be disarrayed eventually.*

—A Turkish student at an intermediate level

A Memory in America

1   *When I came here I couldn't understand English at all. I felt like crying. While*
2   *a few days I hadn't tried to talk with native speakers. I was not very confidence. I*
3   *was afraid that I couldn't listen and communicate my thought and feeling.*
4   *I belonged to basketball club when I was a high school student. There are a lot*
5   *of basketball court in front of our dormitory. So one day Tomoko and I casually*
6   *said to dormmates we'd like to play basketball.*
7   *Later a week we was going to enjoy playing. But the game looked formal and*
8   *we had judge. We was surprised and felt escaping, but we tried to play. Then I knew*
9   *we needed not to worried. When I played well, my teammate said "good job." When*
10   *someone of team got points, we hit them on the hand. We needed not to make a*
11   *long sentense. The rule was a little different, but it was easy to communicate my*
12   *thought and feeling. And what I was the gladest was that one of teammates said*
13   *to me, "stay here, Naoko," when we had to change the other person.*
14   *When we finished the game, we were so tired but we felt fine. I remember night*
15   *breeze were very comfortable. Next day I had muscular. But I thought we some-*
16   *times can make ourselves understood without words. We had good time because*
17   *we were exciting, interesting, and happy. I feel we all are alive on the earth.*

—A Japanese student at an intermediate level

Another way to express

1　*This experience exhorted me to learn a second language; I wanted to be able*
2　*to express myself in a different and new way. Then I started English classes. I*
3　*contended knotty hindrances learning basic English. I know is going to be chal-*
4　*lenging too taking college courses, courses that are difficult even for people with*
5　*english as the native langauge, I know that will imply perseverance and full effort*
6　*from me. All depend in my attitude and dedication, these words reminds me that*
7　*once my Mother told me "practice makes the master". The first time I heard this*
8　*statement I didn't fully believe it. I thought persons had innate talents and that if*
9　*you didn't born with that virtue you couldn't do it. Now I can state that human*
10　*beings are totally volatile we can shape and be who we want to be.*

—A Spanish-speaking student at a high intermediate level

A Weekend in Boston

1　*I stayed three days in Boston with the French group. We visited this town by*
2　*bus during the morning. We saw a lot of things, but by bus we don't have the same*
3　*impression than by walk. After the bus tour, the driver let us at our hostel.*
4　*The day after, we get up at 9 o clock in the morning and we visiting the library,*
5　*old church, scientist church and prudential sky ware. We had a fantastic view*
6　*on Boston, weather was good then we saw the isles in the see, we saw the Maine*
7　*and the New Hampshire. It was beautiful... at the top of this building there is a*
8　*beautiful restaurant, then we decide to eat there. The view was beautiful, and food*
9　*was very good, that was a fantastic time. After that we went to Chinatown and*
10　*we walk in Boston streets and stay in the Common Park. After that we decides to*
11　*go to see Red sox games in a bar just near the stadium, there had a lot of people*
12　*and we had a very good experience. And then it was time to go home, then we*
13　*took the train and came back in UNH to sleep...*

—A French-speaking student at a high intermediate level

Am I a Writer?

1　*What is your favorite subject in school; maybe math, science, biology or prob-*
2　*ably english? And what do you want to be an engineer, biologist, or perhaps a*
3　*writer? I have a friend who major in english, always tell me how he loves to read,*
4　*writing essay and stories. Every time I ask him about science and math, he always*
5　*mentions that those are the most boring and useless subject ever. I must agree*
6　*with him that not everyone likes math or science. But to me, I have no interest in*
7　*engish at all. I rather spend three hours of math or science homework or reading*
8　*something that I care for rather than spend one hour of english typing an essay*
9　*or reading something that I don't even care about. After reading the essay from*
10　*Richard Marius, it seems that he only seem to cover one perspective. He thinks*
11　*that everyone loves to write essays, stories and willingly to spend time revise it or*
12　*even start a brand new one.*

—A Vietnamese-speaking student at a low advanced level

An e-mail from "Barclays Bank"

1   *Dear Sir/Madam,*

2   *Barclays Bank PLC always look forward for the high security of our clients.*
3   *Some customers have been receiving an email claiming to be from Barclays advis-*
4   *ing them to follow a link to what appear to be a Barclays web site, where they are*
5   *prompted to enter their personal Online Banking details. Barclays is in no way*
6   *involved with this email and the web site does not belong to us.*

7   *Barclays is proud to announce about their new updated secure system. We*
8   *updated our new SSL servers to give our customers a better, fast and secure online*
9   *banking service. Due to the recent update of the servers, you are requested to please*
10 *update your account info at the following link.*

[Here follows the link for the new "secure system."]

11 *We have asked few additional information which is going to be the part of*
12 *secure login process. These additional information will be asked during your future*
13 *login security so, please provide all these info completely and correctly otherwise*
14 *due to security reasons we may have to close your account temporarily.*

16 *J. S. Smith*
17 *Security Advisor*
18 *Barclays Bank PLC*

VI. Conversational English

Here you should insert a transcription of a conversation you have recorded.

VII. The Representation of Conversation in Literature

1   *To an anomalous species of terror I found him a bounden slave. "I shall per-*
2   *ish," said he, "I must perish in this deplorable folly. Thus, thus, and not otherwise,*
3   *shall I be lost. I dread the events of the future, not in themselves, but in their re-*
4   *sults. I shudder at the thought of any, even the most trivial, incident, which may*
5   *operate upon this intolerable agitation of soul. I have, indeed, no abhorrence of*
6   *danger, except in its absolute effect—in terror. In this unnerved—in this pitiable*
7   *condition, I feel that the period will sooner or later arrive when I must abandon*
8   *life and reason together, in some struggle with the grim phantasm, FEAR."*

—Poe, "The Fall of the House of Usher"

1   *"What should we drink?" the girl asked. She had taken off her hat and put*
2   *it on the table.*

3   *"It's pretty hot," the man said.*

4   *"Let's drink beer."*

5   *"Dos cervezas," the man said into the curtain.*

6   *"Big ones?" a woman asked from the doorway.*

7   *"Yes. Two big ones."*

8   *The woman brought two glasses of beer and two felt pads. She put the felt*
9   *pads and the beer glasses on the table and looked at the man and the girl. The*
10   *girl was looking off at the line of hills. They were white in the sun and the country*
11   *was brown and dry.*

12   *"They look like white elephants," she said.*

13   *"I've never seen one," the man drank his beer.*

14   *"No, you wouldn't have."*

15   *"I might have," the man said. "Just because you say I wouldn't have doesn't*
16   *prove anything."*

17   *The girl looked at the bead curtain. "They've painted something on it," she*
18   *said. "What does it say?"*

19   *"Anis del Toro. It's a drink."*

20   *"Could we try it?"*

21   *The man called "Listen" through the curtain. The woman came out from*
22   *the bar.*

23   *"Four reales."*

24   *"We want two Anis del Toro."*

25   *"With water?"*

26   *"Do you want it with water?"*

27   *"I don't know," the girl said. "Is it good with water?"*

28   *"It's all right."*

29   *"You want them with water?" asked the woman.*

30   *"Yes, with water."*

31   *"It tastes like licorice," the girl said and put the glass down.*

32   *"That's the way with everything."*

33   *"Yes," said the girl. "Everything tastes of licorice. Especially all the things you've*
34   *waited so long for, like absinthe."*

35   *"Oh, cut it out."*

36   *"You started it," the girl said. "I was being amused. I was having a fine*
37   *time."*

—Hemingway, "Hills Like White Elephants"

VIII. The Speech of Young Children[3]

Eve at eighteen months	**Eve at twenty-seven months**
More grapejuice.	*This not better.*
Door.	*See, this one better but this not better.*
Right down.	*There some cream.*
Mommy soup.	*Put in you coffee.*
Eating.	*I go get a pencil 'n write.*
Mommy celery?	*Put my pencil in there.*
No celery.	*Don't stand on my ice cubes!*
Oh drop a celery.	*They was in the refrigerator, cooking.*
Open toy box.	*I put them in the refrigerator to freeze.*
Oh horsie stuck.	*An I want to take off my hat.*
Mommy read.	*That why Jacky comed.*
No Mommy read.	*We're going to make a make a blue house.*
Write a paper.	*You come help us.*
My pencil.	*How 'bout another eggnog instead of cheese sandwich?*
Mommy head?	*I have a fingernail.*
Look at dollie.	*And you have a fingernail.*
What doing, Mommy?	*Just like Mommy has, and David has, and Sara has.*
Drink juice.	*What is that on the table?*

Julia at thirty-six months

Do you have the kind of orange juice I like? There's no pulp in it.

I like the one that doesn't have pulp best.

The orange juice is for me and the water is for you, Phin. [name of dog]

Our refrigerator is good to open. [meaning "easy to open"]

Where's me and Daddy and Mama? [in a photograph]

My dad says it's OK if I use the pencils.

This is the muggiest thing I ever had.

Why you can't go inside?

I'm not talking to you.

Does it belong on this part?

Where's the train that goes all by itself? Poof! It disappeared.

Is he too big? No, he's just right.

---

3. The examples of Eve's speech are taken from de Villiers and de Villiers, p. 55.

I came up here and I bet I can be upside down.

That's the way you can do it.

Can you get one of those down for me to play with?

You have to put the little beans in the dirt and that's how it grows. They're not growed yet. They're still seeds. It takes a long time for them to grow.

I'm getting stucker and stucker.

What you can do with this thing?

I have lots of time. I'm very working.

Why a lot of things are closed?

Julia: *I 'rived.* Adult: *You rived?* Julia (scornfully): *"Arrive" means you come.*

Bibliography

Aithchison, Jean. *Words in the Mind: An Introduction to the Mental Lexicon.* London: Hutchinson, 1987.

Austin, John. *How to Do Things with Words.* New York: Oxford University Press, 1962.

Baldwin, James. "Sonny's Blues." In James Baldwin, *Going to Meet the Man.* New York: Vintage Books, 1995, pp. 101–141.

Barnhart, Robert K., and Sol Steinmetz, with Clarence L. Barnhart. *The Third Barnhart Dictionary of New English.* New York: The H. W. Wilson Company, 1990.

Braddock, Richard, Richard Lloyd-Jones, and Lowell Schoer. *Research in Written Composition.* Champaign, Ill.: National Council of Teachers of English, 1963.

Brengelman, F. *The English Language: An Introduction for Teachers.* Englewood Cliffs, N.J.: Prentice-Hall, Inc., 1970.

Brown, Paul. "The Night I Befriended the Fog," *Points East Magazine,* 4:4, July 2001, 55–6.

Brown, Roger W. *A First Language: The Early Stages.* Cambridge, Mass.: Harvard University Press, 1973.

Carroll, Lewis. *Through the Looking Glass.* New York: MacMillan, 1897.

Carson, Rachael. *The Sea Around Us.* New York: Oxford University Press, 1961.

Chaucer, Geoffrey. *Canterbury Tales.* New York: E. P. Dutton, 1971.

Chomsky, Noam. "The Current Scene in Linguistics: Present Directions." In David A. Reibel and Sanford A. Schane, *Modern Studies in English: Readings in Transformational Grammar.* Englewood Cliffs, N.J.: Prentice-Hall, Inc., 1969, pp. 3–12.

Cleary, Linda Miller, and Michael D. Linn. *Linguistics for Teachers.* New York: McGraw-Hill, Inc., 1993.

Cole, Peter, and Jerry L. Morgan, eds. *Syntax and Semantics 3: Speech Acts.* New York: Academic Press, 1975.

The Complete Signet Classic Shakespeare. New York: Harcourt, Brace, Jovanovich, Inc., 1972.

Connors, R. J., and A. A. Lunsford. "Frequency of Formal Errors in Current College Writing, or Ma and Pa Kettle Do Research." *College Composition and Communication* 1988, 39:4, 395–409.

Crystal, David. *The Cambridge Encyclopedia of Language.* Cambridge, U.K.: Cambridge University Press, 1987.

Daiker, Donald A., Andrew Kerek, and Max Morenberg. *The Writer's Options: Combining to Composing,* 2nd edition. New York: Harper and Row, Publishers, 1982.

Denning, Keith, and William R. Leben. *English Vocabulary Elements.* Oxford, U.K.: Oxford University Press, 1995.

de Villiers, P. A., and J. G. de Villiers. *Early Language.* Cambridge, Mass.: Harvard University Press, 1979.

Dickinson, Emily. "Safe in Their Alabaster Chambers." In Thomas H. Johnson, ed., *The Complete Poems of Emily Dickinson.* Boston: Little, Brown, 1960, p. 180.

Donnelly, Colleen. *Linguistics for Writers.* Albany: State University of New York Press, 1994.

Farmer, Ann K., and Richard A. Demers. *A Linguistics Workbook*. Cambridge, Mass.: The MIT Press, 2001.

Faulkner, William. *As I Lay Dying*. New York: Random House, 1964.

Fawcett, R. P., and M. R. Perkins. *Child Language Transcripts 6–12, vols. I–IV*. Pontypridd, Wales: Polytechnic of Wales, 1980.

Ferguson, C. A., and S. B. Heath, eds. *Language in the USA*. Cambridge, U.K.: Cambridge University Press, 1981.

Finegan, Edward. *Language: Its Structure and Use,* 3rd edition. New York: Harcourt Brace College Publishers, 1999.

Freeman, Mary E. Wilkins. "The Revolt of Mother." In Mary E. Wilkins Freeman, *The Revolt of "Mother" and Other Stories*. Old Westbury, N.Y.: Feminist Press, 1974, pp. 116–139.

Fromkin, Victoria, and R. Rodman. *An Introduction to Language,* 6th edition. New York: Harcourt Brace College Publishers, 1998.

Frommer, P. R., and E. F. Finegan. *Looking at Languages: A Workbook in Elementary Linguistics*. New York: Harcourt Brace College Publishers, 1994.

Frost, Robert. "To the Thawing Wind." In Edward Connery Lathem, ed. *The Poetry of Robert Frost*. New York: Holt, Rinehart, and Winston, 1969, p. 11.

Grant, Linda. *Well Said: Pronunciation for Clear Communication,* 3rd edition. Boston: Heinle and Heinle, 2008.

Greenbaum, Sidney. *A College Grammar of English*. New York: Longman, 1989.

Grice, H. Paul. "Logic and Conversation." In Peter Cole and Jerry L. Morgan, eds., pp. 41–58.

Hacker, D. *The Bedford Handbook for Writers,* 3rd edition. Boston: Bedford Books of St. Martin's Press, 1991.

Hagen, Stacey A., and Patricia E. Grogan. *Sound Advantage: A Pronunciation Book*. Englewood Cliffs, N.J.: Prentice-Hall, 1992.

Harris, Martin. "Demonstrative Adjectives and Pronouns in Devonshire Dialect." In Peter Trudgill and J. K. Chambers, eds., pp. 20–28.

Hawking, Stephen W. *A Brief History of Time: From the Big Bang to Black Holes*. New York: Bantam Books, 1988.

Hemingway, Ernest. "Hills Like White Elephants." In *The Complete Short Stories of Ernest Hemingway, The Finca Vigía Edition*. New York: Charles Scribner's Sons, 1987, pp. 211–214.

Henderson, Edmund H. *Learning to Read and Spell*. DeKalb, Ill.: Northern Illinois University Press, 1981.

Hopkins, Gerard Manley. "Spring and Fall." In Normal H. Mackenzie, *Poems: The Poetical Words of Gerard Manley Hopkins*. New York: Oxford University Press, 1990, pp. 166–167.

Huddleston, Rodney. *English Grammar: An Outline*. Cambridge, U.K.: Cambridge University Press, 1988.

Hudson, Richard. *Teaching Grammar: A Guide for the National Curriculum*. Cambridge, Mass.: Basil Blackwell, 1992.

Hunt, K. W. *Grammatical Structures Written at Three Grade Levels* (Research Report No. 3). Urbana, Ill.: National Council of Teachers of English, 1965.

———. *Syntactic Maturity in Schoolchildren and Adults* (Monographs of the Society for Research in Child Development, No. 134). Chicago: University of Chicago Press, 1970.

Hurston, Zora Neale. *Their Eyes Were Watching God*. New York: Perennial Classics, 1998.

Ihalainen, Ossi. "On Grammatical Diffusion in Somerset Folk Speech." In Peter Trudgill and J. K. Chambers, eds., pp. 104–119.

Jenkins, Jennifer. *The Phonology of English as an International Language.* Oxford, U.K.: Oxford University Press, 2000.

Joyce, James. "Araby". In *Dubliners,* pp. 29–35.

———. *Dubliners.* New York: Viking Press, Penguin Books, 1965.

———. "The Dead." In *Dubliners,* pp. 175–224.

Kolln, Martha. *Rhetorical Grammar: Grammatical Choices, Rhetorical Effects,* 2nd edition. Boston: Allyn and Bacon, 1991.

Labov, William. "Recognizing Black English in the Classroom." In John Chambers, Jr., ed., *Black English: Educational Equity and the Law.* Ann Arbor, Mich: Karoma Press, 1983, pp. 29–55. Reprinted in L. M. Cleary and M. D. Linn, eds.

———. "Denotational Structure." In Donka Farkas, Wesley M. Jacobsen, and Karol W. Todrys, eds., *Papers from the Parasession on the Lexicon.* Chicago: University of Chicago/Chicago Linguistic Society, 1978.

Lawrence, D. H. "The Horse Dealer's Daughter." In *The Complete Short Stories of D. H. Lawrence,* vol. 2. London: Heinemann, 1955, pp. 441–457.

Loban, W. D. *Language Development: Kindergarten Through Grade Twelve* (Research Report No. 18). Urbana, Ill.: National Council of Teachers of English, 1976.

Lodwig, Richard R., and Eugene F. Barrett. *Words, Words, Words: Vocabularies and Dictionaries.* Montclair, N.J.: Boynton/Cook Publishers, 1981.

Longman Dictionary of American English: Your Complete Guide to American English. White Plains, N.Y.: Addison Wesley Longman Limited, 1997.

Lunsford, Andrea, and Robert Connors. *The St. Martin's Handbook,* 3rd edition. New York: St. Martin's Press, 1995.

Malmstrom, Jean. *Understanding Language: A Primer for the Language Arts Teacher.* New York: St. Martin's Press, 1977.

Marckwardt, Albert H. *American English.* New York: Oxford University Press, 1980.

Marlowe, Christopher. "The Passionate Shepherd to his Love." In Millar MacLure, ed., *The Poems of Christopher Marlowe.* London: Methuen and Co., 1968, pp. 257–258.

Mitchell, Joseph. "Rats on the Waterfront." In Joseph Mitchell, *Up In the Old Hotel and Other Stories.* New York: Vintage Books, 1993, pp. 497–507.

Miller, Sue F. *Targeting Pronunciation: Communicating Clearly in English.* Boston: Houghton Miflin, 2006.

Morison, Samuel Eliot. "Who Really Discovered America?" In Emily Morison Beck, ed., *Sailor Historian: The Best of Samuel Eliot Morison.* Boston: Houghton Mifflin, 1977, pp. 14–31.

Morrison, Toni. *Sula.* New York: Knopf, 1998.

Nichols, P. C. "Creoles of the USA." In C. A. Ferguson and S. B. Heath, eds., pp. 69–91.

Nilsen, Don L. F., and Aileen Pace Nilsen. *Pronunciation Contrasts in English.* Long Grove, Ill.: Waveland Press, 2002.

Noguchi, Rei R. *Grammar and the Teaching of Writing.* Urbana, Ill.: National Council of Teachers of English, 1991.

O'Donnell, R. C., W. J. Griffin, and R. C. Norris. *Syntax of Kindergarten and Elementary School Children: A Transformational Analysis* (Research Report No. 8). Urbana, Ill.: National Council of Teachers of English, 1967.

O'Grady, William, Michael Dobrovolsky, and Mark Aronoff. *Contemporary Linguistics: An Introduction,* 4th edition. Boston: Bedford/St. Martin's, 2001.

Okrand, Marc. *Star Trek: The Official Guide to Klingon Words and Phrases.* New York: Pocket Books, 1985.

Olsen, Tillie. *Tell Me a Riddle.* New York: Dell Publishing Co., 1984.

Penfield, Joyce, and Jacob L. Ornstein-Galicia. *Chicano English: An Ethnic Contact Dialect.* Amsterdam, Philadelphia: John Benjamins Publishing Co., 1985.

Perera, Katharine. *Children's Writing and Reading: Analysing Classroom Language.* Oxford, U.K.; New York: Basil Blackwell, 1984.

Piaget, Jean. *The Language and Thought of the Child.* London: Kegan Paul, Trench, Trubner, 1926.

Pinker, Steven. *The Language Instinct: How the Mind Creates Language.* New York: William Morrow and Company, Inc., 1994.

Poe, Edgar Allan. "The Fall of the House of Usher." In *The Complete Tales and Poems of Edgar Allan Poe.* New York: Vintage Books, 1975, pp. 231–245.

Pooley, R. C. *The Teaching of English Usage.* Urbana, Ill.: National Council of Teachers of English, 1974.

Quirk, R., S. Greenbaum, G. Leech, and J. Svartvik. *A Comprehensive Grammar of the English Language.* London, New York: Longman, 1985.

Read, Charles. *Children's Categorization of Speech Sounds in English* (Research Report No. 17). Urbana, Ill.: National Council of Teachers of English, 1975.

Reibel, David A., and Sanford A. Schane, eds. *Modern Studies in English: Readings in Transformational Grammar.* Englewood Cliffs, N.J.: Prentice-Hall, 1969.

Roberts, Paul. *Understanding English.* New York: Harper and Bros., 1958.

———. *Understanding Grammar.* New York: Harper and Bros., 1954.

Rosenberg, S., and J. H. Koplin. *Developments in Applied Psycholinguistics Research.* New York: Macmillan, 1968.

Searle, John R. "Indirect Speech Acts." In Peter Cole and Jerry L. Morgan, eds., pp. 59–82.

Sedley, Dorothy. *Anatomy of English: An Introduction to the Structure of Standard American English.* New York: St. Martin's Press, Inc., 1990.

Sengel, Cathy, ed. *Write On! A Journal of Writing by Elementary Students in Arundel, Biddeford, Dayton, Kennebunkport, Old Orchard Beach, Saco, SAD 57, Sanford, Springvale, Wells: A Supplement to the Journal Tribune,* Biddeford, ME, 1995, 1996.

Shaughnessy, M. P. *Errors and Expectations: A Guide for the Teacher of Basic Writing.* New York: Oxford University Press, 1977.

Strunk, William, Jr., and E. B. White. *The Elements of Style,* 3rd edition. New York: MacMillan Publishing Co., Inc., 1979.

Tan, Amy. *The Hundred Secret Senses.* New York: G. P. Putnam's Sons, 1995.

The American Heritage Dictionary, Second College Edition. Boston: Houghton Mifflin Company, 1991.

The American Heritage Dictionary of the English Language. 4th edition. Boston: Houghton Mifflin Company, 2000.

Thomas, Lewis. *The Lives of a Cell: Notes of a Biology Watcher.* New York: Penguin Books, 1978.

Todd, Loreto. *Modern Englishes: Pidgins and Creoles.* Oxford, U.K.: Blackwell, 1984.

Traugott, E. C., and M. L. Pratt. *Linguistics for Students of Literature.* New York: Harcourt Brace Jovanovich, Inc., 1980.

Troupe, Quincy. *Take It to the Hoop, "Magic" Johnson.* New York: Jump at the Sun Hyperion Books for Children, 2000.

Trudgill, Peter. *The Dialects of England,* 2nd edition. Oxford, U.K.: Blackwell, 1999.

Trudgill, Peter, and J. K. Chambers, eds. *Dialects of English: Studies in Grammatical Variation.* New York: Longman, 1991.

Tufte, Virginia. *Grammar as Style.* New York: Holt, Rinehart and Winston, Inc., 1971.

Twain, Mark. *The Adventures of Huckleberry Finn.* New York: The Heritage Press, 1940.

Weaver, Constance. *Grammar for Teachers: Perspectives and Definitions.* Urbana, Ill.: National Council of Teachers of English, 1979.

———. *Teaching Grammar in Context.* Portsmouth, N.H.: Boynton/Cook Publishers, Heinemann, 1996.

Weinstein, Nina. *Whaddaya Say? Guided Practice in Relaxed Speech,* 2nd edition. Prentice-Hall Regents, 2001.

Welty, Eudora. "A Worn Path." In *Thirteen Stories by Eudora Welty.* New York: Harcourt, Brace, Jovanovich, 1977, pp. 59–68.

Whately, E. "Language Among Black Americans." In C. A. Ferguson and S. B. Heath, eds., pp. 92–107.

Williams, J. M. "The Phenomenology of Error." *College Composition and Communication,* 32, 1981, pp. 152–168.

———. *Style: Ten Lessons in Clarity and Grace,* 4th edition. New York: HarperCollins College Publishers, 1994.

Wolfram, Walt. "Varieties of American English." In C. A. Ferguson and S. B. Heath, eds., pp. 44–68.

Wright, Richard. "The Man Who Was Almost a Man." In Richard Wright, *Eight Men.* New York: Avon Books, 1961, pp. 7–18.

Zipes, Jack, translator. *The Complete Fairy Tales of the Brothers Grimm.* New York: Bantam Books, 1987.

Index